W9-DAL-420

Dictionary of Media and Communications

Dictionary of Media and Communications

Marcel Danesi

M.E.Sharpe
Armonk, New York
London, England

Library of Congress Cataloging-in-Publication Data

Danesi, Marcel, 1946–
  Dictionary of media and communications / Marcel Danesi; foreword by Arthur Asa Berger.
     p. cm.
  Includes bibliographical references.
  ISBN 978-0-7656-8098-3 (hardcover : alk. paper)
  1. Mass media—Dictionaries. 2. Communication—Dictionaries. I. Title.

P87.5.D359 2008
302.2303—dc22   2008011560

Printed in the United States of America

The paper used in this publication meets the minimum requirements of
American National Standard for Information Sciences
Permanence of Paper for Printed Library Materials,
ANSI Z 39.48-1984.

BM (c)   10   9   8   7   6   5   4   3   2   1

Images provided by Getty Images and the following: AFP: page 235; Andreas Solaro/Stringer/AFP:
82; Aubrey Beardsley/The Bridgeman Art Library: 27; Bernard Gotfryd/Hulton Archive: 190; Blank
Archives/Hulton Archive: 16; Buyenlarge/Time & Life Pictures: 5, 155; CBS Photo Archive/Hulton
Archive: 256; Dave Bradley Photography/Taxi: 127; Deshakalyan Chowdhury/Stringer/AFP: 60;
Disney/Hulton Archive: 118; Ethan Miller: 43; Evan Agostini: 55; George Pierre Seurat/The Bridge-
man Art Library: 234; Hulton Archive/Stringer: 36, 92, 129; Italian School/The Bridgeman Art Library:
153; Mario Tama: 67; Michael Ochs Archive/Stringer: 147; Paul Nicklen/National Geographic: 223;
RDA/Hulton Archive: 53; Shelly Katz/Time & Life Pictures: 178; Stringer/AFP: 303; Stringer: 137;
Susanna Price/Dorling Kindersley: 134; Time & Life Pictures/Stringer: 55, 182, 184; Transcendental
Graphics/Hulton Archive: 188; Vince Bucci/Stringer: 221; Walter Sanders/Time & Life Pictures: 219;
Yoshikazu Tsuno/AFP: 229. Image on page 116 provided by Erich Lessing/Art Resource.

CONTENTS

FOREWORD

With each year that passes, the mass media and the various means of communication available to us exert a greater and more direct impact upon our cultures, societies, economies, and everyday lives. Most of us live in a media-saturated society and spend increasing amounts of time with different kinds of media. According to a 2005 study by the Kaiser Family Foundation, young people from the ages of eight to eighteen in the United States devote approximately forty hours a week to using media of all kinds for recreational purposes.

In addition to more time, most of us also spend more money on accessing the media and on buying devices for recording information and for communicating with one another. Consider how much your family spends, for example, on all of the following:

> access to the Internet,
> cable and satellite services,
> video game players and video games, and
> cell phones and cell phone contracts,

not to mention all of the other gizmos and gadgets that come flooding onto the market in rapid succession. Think, for example, of the price tag on those large-screen high-definition digital television sets; some run into thousands of dollars.

Every day, meanwhile, we send billions of e-mail messages and receive billions of others—wanted or unwanted—from friends, family members, fellow student and colleagues, or spammers. Internet technology makes it as easy to send someone a message 10,000 miles away as it is to send a message to someone ten feet away. In barely more than a decade, cell phone use has exploded all over the world, with still new (non-talking) uses of the device—

from texting to searching the World Wide Web to accessing satellite navigation systems—constantly are being developed. Cell phones have already exerted a major impact on society and our daily lives, shaping everything from politics to the dating behavior of adolescents. At the same time, video games and video game players now constitute a multibillion-dollar industry, even larger than the film industry. Apple's iPods, other portable media players, and all the devices created for them have radically altered the way many of us, especially young people, access and listen to music.

Powerful tools for using the Internet likewise have had a transformative effect, enabling millions of people to spend time blogging, buying and selling products on eBay, looking up information on Google and other search engines, ordering books and other products on Amazon.com and similar sites, compiling their pages on Facebook and MySpace, watching videos on You Tube, and guiding their avatars on Second Life. We use the Internet now to do everything from finding dates and marriage partners to looking up travel information, obtaining medical data, paying bills, and buying stocks.

As the media and the means of communication have grown in importance and influence, studying them has become ever more widespread in high schools and universities. Courses on subjects that involve media literacy—such as advertising, marketing, linguistics, anthropology, and sociology—have become common. These courses are designed to teach students about the impact of the media and communications on our institutions and way of life, as well as on those in other countries—also part of the "global village."

Given the ubiquitous nature of old and new media and the new technologies that are constantly being developed, it is invaluable to have a single, handy reference book that covers all of them and related cognate fields (disciplines) in an informed and insightful manner. The *Dictionary of Media and Communications* enables students from high school to graduate school to find accessible, authoritative explanations of essential theories and concepts in all relevant subject areas. Also included are portraits of leading figures in media scholarship and clear, straightforward explanations of practical methods and constructs used in media studies, communications, and related fields, such as semiotics and psychoanalytic theory.

With more than 2,000 entries of varying lengths, the *Dictionary of Media and Communications* is an authoritative and reader-friendly reference that enables anyone interested in the media and communications to find clearly written definitions and explanations. In addition to defining terms, individual entries may also include examples of how the terms are used and background history on the origins and development of related concepts. For visual appeal and to illustrate diverse subjects in terms that are meaningful to readers, the volume also includes dozens of photographs, line drawings, and diagrams.

In addition to the alphabetical listing of definitions, the *Dictionary of Media and Communications* contains several information-packed appendices. The Chronology is a detailed list of historic events for various media types, industries, means of communication, and cognate fields. To help readers pursue further research, the Bibliography suggests recommended books in the field, also organized by media and communications categories. Finally, Resources on the World Wide Web offers similar assistance with an extensive list.

The *Dictionary of Media and Communications* is an invaluable resource that is readable, comprehensive, and authoritative. It is more than a reference book. Because of the centrality of media and communications in modern life, it is, in effect, an introduction to contemporary culture and to the wide-ranging theories and concepts that scholars have developed to better understand the world—some would say the "brave new world"—in which we now live.

Arthur Asa Berger
Professor Emeritus
Broadcast and Electronic Communication Arts
San Francisco State University

INTRODUCTION

In 1938, a truly significant event took place that epitomized the power of the emerging role of the media in the modern world. That event was the radio adaptation of H.G. Wells's novel about interplanetary invasion, *The War of the Worlds.* It was created by the famous actor and director, Orson Welles, as a radio drama simulating the style of a news broadcast. Welles pulled off his "reality-inducing effect" by using a series of fake "on-the-spot" news reports describing the landing of Martian spaceships in New Jersey. An announcer would remind the radio audience, from time to time, that the show was fictional. But many listeners believed that what they were hearing was factual. In New Jersey, many people went into a state of panic, believing that Martians had actually invaded the Earth. Concerned citizens notified the police and the army; some ran onto the streets shouting hysterically; and a few even contemplated escaping somewhere—anywhere. The event was a watershed one in the history of the modern world, becoming itself a topic of media attention and, a year later, leading to the first psychological study of the effects of the media on common people, called the *Cantril Study,* after Hadley Cantril who headed a team of researchers at Princeton University. Cantril wanted to find out why some believed the fake reports and others not. After interviewing 135 subjects, the research team came to the conclusion that the key was critical thinking—better-educated listeners were more capable of recognizing the broadcast as a fake than less-educated ones.

The Cantril report also laid the foundation for a systematic study of the media in universities and colleges, leading eventually to the establishment of departments, institutes, journals, book series, and the like for the study of modern media. Since the 1940s, such study has skyrocketed, becoming an area of intense interest, not only on the part of academics and researchers, but also on the part of virtually everyone.

A seemingly different path of study was opened up in the late 1940s by the late engineer Claude Shannon (1916–2001). Shannon was the one who laid the foundations for investigating the relation between communication (in all its forms) and technology. He did this by devising a theoretical framework intended originally to improve the efficiency of telecommunication systems. Known as the "bull's-eye model," the framework was intended originally to identify the main components of such systems and describe in precise mathematical terms how they functioned in the transmission and reception of information. In bare outline form, Shannon's model consisted of a *sender* aiming a *message* at a *receiver* as if in a target range—hence the designation bull's-eye model. Shannon also introduced terms such as *feedback* and *noise* into the lexicon of communications study. However, few at the time saw a connection between the study of media and communications until a Canadian professor at the University of Toronto started to amalgamate the two domains in the 1950s. That professor was the late Marshall McLuhan (1911–1980), whose work on the relation between media and communications technologies brought to common awareness the fact that culture, social evolution, and technology are intrinsically intertwined. Ever since, the study of media and communication as an integrated phenomenon has been the rule in academia.

McLuhan's basic approach was to show that there exists a built-in synergy between media, mass communications technologies, and culture. He claimed that each major historical era took its character from the medium used most widely at the time. For example, he called the period from 1700 to the mid-1900s the "Age of Print," because in that period printed books were the chief media through which mass communications took place. But that is not all that occurred. The Age of Print changed the state of the world permanently, he suggested, because print literacy encouraged a radical new form of individualism and the subsequent growth of nationalism. The "Electronic Age" displaced the Age of Print in the twentieth century. The consequences of that displacement also have been colossal. Because electronic technology has increased both the breadth and rapidity of communication, it has radically changed how people interact and behave socially. Phones, radios, computers, and instant messaging devices have influenced the lives of everyone, even those who use them sporadically or who do not use them at all. The Electronic Age may in fact be leading, as McLuhan suspected, to the end of individualism and literacy-inspired notions of nationalism generated by the previous Age of Print.

In a fundamental way, the study of the media-communication nexus is an exercise in unraveling the psychological reasons why we evolve through communication devices and why modern economies and political systems depend so much on these devices. Without the media and its supporting mass communications technologies to "spread the message," so to speak, fads and crazes such as sports spectacles, Hula Hoops, recipes, posters, songs, dance crazes, sitcoms, and clothing fashions, would hardly gain popularity. The world we live in is largely fabricated by a media-communications interconnection. No wonder, then, that studying this interconnection has become so critical. Mass communications technologies have literally brought about Huxley's "brave new world"—a world described rather accurately by the prophetic 1999 movie, *The Matrix.* Like the main character of that movie, Neo, we all live our daily lives "on the screen" and our engagement with reality is more often than not through the "matrix"—which means both the network of circuits that defines computer technology and "womb." With the advent of the Internet, new generations are now born within two kinds of wombs—the biological one and a technological one, as the movie so brilliantly brings out.

The study of the media-communications nexus now has its own set of theories and analytical frameworks. These provide concepts and discourses that can be applied in part or in whole to a study of all modern-day cultural trends or processes. The appeal of such study is that it leaves the interpretation of these processes open to variation. This is the reason why there is no one theory of the media, but many. Media analysts today use a blend of concepts and techniques at various stages of analysis and for diverse purposes.

PURPOSE OF THIS DICTIONARY

As McLuhan anticipated, the media and mass communications devices are at the center of our world, shaping lifestyle and worldview. Relatively young by academic standards, media and communication studies started growing in the late 1950s, after McLuhan's influential writings started receiving international attention. The field has since produced a vast repertory of notions, ideas, techniques, theories, and methods of analysis. Many of these were originally borrowed and adapted from cognate disciplines such as psychology, linguistics, semiotics, philosophy, anthropology, and sociology; but many others have been self-generated, and are thus new, interesting, and often controversial. Newcomers to this area may thus experience unease or consternation with the vast repertory of terms that populate the field. This dictionary is an attempt to provide a comprehensible map through that field.

Thus it contains entries dealing with the basic ideas, concepts, personages, schools of thought, theories, and technical trends that come up recurrently in the literature on media and communication. Since the literature also makes frequent references to cognate fields such as semiotics, psychology, linguistics, mythology, literary studies, cultural anthropology, and a few others, some of the most frequently used terms and ideas within these are also included. I must warn the user, however, that to keep the proportions of this dictionary within the limits of a compact practical reference work, I have had to limit my choices to the main items that recur in the relevant literature. Inevitably, there will be some omissions and gaps. Nevertheless, I have tried to cast as broad a net as possible, so as to gather within two covers the bulk of the ideas and technical terms that the beginning student or interested general reader will need to know in order to decipher the relevant literature.

Cross-references to other terms contained in this dictionary are indicated with small capitals. The commentary provided for each of the personages consists of a brief statement about his or her relevance and/or contribution to the field. Only those personages to whom the technical literature regularly alludes have been included in this dictionary. A bibliography of relevant works is included at the back. Also listed are timelines for specific media or media genres, as well as a list of useful Web sites.

Hopefully, the user will find in it all the relevant information she or he might need for conducting a personal analysis of the media-communications nexus that now "rules the universe," so to speak. I also hope to have provided a framework for understanding the world we live in and probably will live in for the foreseeable future.

ACKNOWLEDGMENTS

I wish to thank the editorial staff at M.E. Sharpe for all their advice, support, and expert help in the making of this dictionary. I am especially grateful to Peter Mavrikis, without whom this volume would never have come to fruition. Needless to say, I alone am responsible for any infelicities that remain in the volume.

I also wish to thank Victoria College of the University of Toronto for having allowed me the privilege of teaching and coordinating its Program in Semiotics and Communication Theory over many years. Another debt of gratitude goes to the many students I have taught. Their insights and enthusiasm have made my job simply wonderful! They are the impetus for this dictionary.

Dictionary of
Media and
Communications

A roll footage used in an edited film sequence, consisting mainly of interviews or images that relate to the theme or topic being showcased

A&E Network [abbreviation of **Arts and Entertainment Network**] cable and satellite television channel launched in 1984 that produces and broadcasts programs dealing with the arts and educational topics, as well as documentaries, biographies, and popular entertainment formats. Web site: www.aetv.com

A&R executive [abbreviation of **Artists and Repertoire executive**] an executive of a record company who oversees artists and the recording process

AAA [*see* **American Academy of Advertising**]

AAAA [*see* **American Association of Advertising Agencies**]

AAI [*see* **audience appreciation index**]

AB roll sequence of two segments (video, musical), composed so that as one fades away the other one blends in

abbreviation shortening of words, phrases, or sentences: for example, *hi (hello)*; *bye (good-bye)*. Abbreviation is a major feature of communication in online chat rooms, text messages, and other types of digital communi-

cations: for example, *bf = boyfriend*; *gf = girlfriend.*

ABC [*see* **American Broadcasting Company**]

abduction in contrast to, but also in complement with, INDUCTION (generalizing on the basis of observations of particular patterns inherent in something) and DEDUCTION (forming a conclusion on the basis of given premises); this term was proposed by American philosopher CHARLES PEIRCE to characterize a method of reasoning carried out by informed hunches or "best guesses" on the basis of previous experience, knowledge, or understanding. In classic mystery stories, the detective-protagonist solves a crime by using abduction—that is, crime scene clues are interpreted in terms of skilled inference and previous experience.

aberrant decoding interpretation of a media product or text that is not the one intended by the creator of the product or text. The term was coined by UMBERTO ECO in 1965 to describe what happens when a message that is put together according to a specific code (a set of meanings) is interpreted according to another code. For example, specific groups who are exposed to a particular media message (such as an ad for beer) will decode it differently—an abstinent group might see it as an immoral message, while another group might view it as a lifestyle message that promotes beer as a component of that lifestyle.

aberrant reading interpretation of a text in a way that was not intended or expected by its author

aberration distortion of a video image, caused by a corrupt signal or improper adjustment

Aboriginal People's Television Network [abbreviated as **APTN**] television network launched in 1999 with headquarters in Winnipeg (Canada) devoted to broadcasting the stories and cultural interests of Canada's First Nations. It is available nationally on basic cable and via satellite. Web site: www.aptn.ca

above-the-fold 1. top part of the front page of a newspaper (story and/or photo) that is visible when the newspaper is folded; 2. the most valuable part of a Web page, placed at the top part of the screen so that the user does not have to scroll down to see it; 3. any prominent story (in any medium)

above-the-line advertising promotional message for which a commission is paid, such as commission for an ad in a magazine or a stand at a trade fair

above-the-title the location of credits that appear before the title of a movie (for example, the names of the starring actors, the name of the director, and the name of the producer)

absence the exclusion of a SIGN (a word, a symbol) from a specific loca-

tion to show that the same position can be filled by other signs, but with different meanings. For example, in the sentence *The . . . ate the cake*, the empty slot can be filled by nouns such as *boy*, *girl*, *woman*, or *man*. Absence is a technique for showing ways in which meaning is determined.

absence-of-language technique advertising strategy employing the omission of taglines, slogans, or any other kind of verbal commentary, suggesting implicitly that a product "speaks for itself." Print ads without captions and TV commercial scenes without dialogue or explanation are common absence-of-language techniques. Sometimes, the technique is intended to provoke the viewer through the image.

absolute cost actual cost of placing an ad in some medium (magazine, newspaper, radio, television, Internet)

absolute time length of time that an audio disc has been playing

abstract data type in computer programming, a data set defined by the programmer in terms of the information it can contain and the operations that can be performed with it

abstract expressionism a movement in twentieth-century art that broke away from the concept of art as representation, promoting instead a mode of painting that expresses the

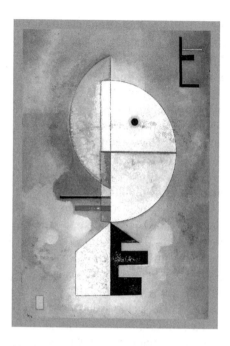

Upward (1929) by Wassily Kandinsky

emotions spontaneously through the act of transferring paint onto a canvas. The term was used originally to describe Russian-born artist Wassily Kandinsky's painting style between 1910 and 1914. Influenced by European avant-garde artists, the abstract expressionist movement found its main home in New York City in the 1950s. Abstract expressionist paintings consist mainly of shapes resulting from the gestures made by the artist's hand, called *action paintings*; or compositions of colors and shapes for their own sake, called *color field paintings*. Jackson Pollock, Willem de Kooning, Mark Rothko, Helen Frankenthaler, and Robert Motherwell are some well-known abstract expressionists.

absurdist theater [also called **theater of the absurd**] popular and influential nonrealistic drama genre of the 1950s and 1960s. Influenced by existential philosophy, and especially by Albert Camus's essay "Le Mythe de Sisyphe" (1942; "The Myth of Sisyphus"), absurdist dramas are characterized by such features as the elimination of traditional plot lines, the reduction of language to a game, the downgrading of characters to archetypes, the allusion to settings and locations as nonspecific, and portrayals of the world as alienating and incomprehensible. Key works in the genre include Samuel Beckett's *Waiting for Godot* (1952) and Eugène Ionesco's *Le Rhinocéros* (1959).

AC Nielsen leading global market research firm, founded in 1923, best known for its NIELSEN'S RATINGS, which measure audience size and reaction to media programs and events. Web site: www.acnielsen.com

Academy Award [also called the **Oscar**] prestigious honor conferred annually by the ACADEMY OF MOTION PICTURE ARTS AND SCIENCES in the United States to outstanding actors, directors, composers, and others involved in motion pictures

Academy of Motion Picture Arts and Sciences professional organization founded in 1927 to promote the advancement of the motion picture industry; composed of over 6,000 motion picture professionals, including actors, directors, writers, producers, and technical artists. Web site: www.oscars.org

Academy ratio the ratio (1.33 to 1) of the width of a film frame to the height of the frame, as standardized by the Academy of Motion Picture Arts and Sciences before the development of widescreen format

acceleration factor increased efficiency in communications technologies, which causes a more immediate impact of events upon the media

accent distinctive manner in which a language is pronounced, characteristic either of individuals, a region, a social group, or some other community

access ability of people to view, investigate, or question the products, activities, or motives of major media outlets and companies

access channel in cable television, a nonbroadcast channel dedicated to local issues (for example, educational, governmental, among others)

access controller 1. device that moves image data to a video controller; 2. hardware that provides data link connectivity for area network providers such as Ethernet

access head disk drive component of a computer that moves to a specific part of the disk's surface to read the information stored there

access number telephone number dialed by a computer to link it to an Internet service provider or other type of network provider

access panel group monitored for research purposes so as to document their television viewing habits

access provider [*see* **Internet service provider**]

access television television that broadcasts independently of state controls, usually with a small budget and reaching a limited area

accessed voices individuals who are given exposure by the media (celebrities, politicians, experts) because their views are considered to be distinctive or, at least, not necessarily representative of those of the general public

accessing practice of including verbal quotations and taped interviews from various media originating from people not employed by the media organizations

accessory shoe camera bracket to which an accessory such as a flash unit may be attached

accordion insert advertisement inserted in a magazine, folded in an accordion style

acculturation adaptive process by which change in culture occurs when two or more societies (with their own cultural traditions) come into contact for an extended period of time. Often the result is a bidirectional adaptation, whereby the beliefs, conventions, customs, and art forms of each society in contact become fused or mixed (to varying degrees); or one society may undergo partial or total adaptation to the culture of the other society (or societies).

accumulation audience-counting method by which people exposed to a specific media product are counted once within a specified time period

acid house electronic disco music popular in the 1980s, associated with the use of the drug Ecstasy

acid jazz musical genre consisting of a blend of funk, jazz, and soul music that emerged in the 1980s

acid rock type of rock music popular in the 1960s that used peculiar instrumental effects suggestive of psychedelic (hallucinatory) experiences

ACORN [acronym for **a classification of residential neighborhoods**] consumer research method of classifying residential areas according to the type of people who live in them, the type of homes in which they live, and other such categories

acoustic rock style of rock music played mainly on acoustic instruments (instruments without amplification)

acoustics study of the wave patterns produced by language sounds (consonants, vowels, tones, etc.). Now classified as a branch of PHONETICS, the physical analysis of linguistic sound waves is traced to *Tonempfindungen als physiologische Grundlage für die Theorie der Musik* (1863; *On the Sensation of Tone as a Physiological Basis for the Theory of Music*) by the German physicist HERMANN VON HELMHOLTZ. Acoustic phoneticians record and analyze speech waves with devices and instruments designed to identify recurrent patterns.

acquiescent audience people who are receptive to advertising and are more likely to be impressed by humorous, clever, or eye-catching ads

acquisitions editor editor of a book publishing house who seeks new works or evaluates submissions

acronym word, form, or abbreviation constructed with the initial letters of a phrase, expression, or group of words (or parts of words): for example, *CD = compact disc, DNA = deoxyribonucleic acid, laser = light amplification by stimulated emission of radiation, IQ = intelligence quotient*. Acronymy is a major feature of the language used in online social sites such as chat rooms, text messages, and other types of digital communication venues: for example, *cm = call me; ruok? = are you OK?; g2g = got to go.*

Acta diurna (*Acta publica* or *Acta populi*) the first known newspaper, written on a tablet, which reported on matters of public interest in ancient Rome, after 27 B.C.E.

actant in narrative theories, a recurrent role that manifests itself in stories across the world and across time: for example, a *hero*, an *opponent*, a *helper*, etc. The notion was developed primarily by the twentieth-century French semiotician ALGIRDAS JULIEN GREIMAS, who claimed that actants relate to each other in a binary fashion, giving the narrative its trajectory and plot form: *subject* vs. *object*, *sender* vs. *receiver*, *helper* vs. *opponent*, and so on.

actantial theory model of narrative analysis based on the concept of ACTANT

action code 1. CODE used to describe events in a narrative; 2. commands used in computer programming

action code script (abbreviated as **ACS**) scripting language used in some modem Doom source ports

action genre story that revolves around pugilistic action, martial arts action, or some other form of violent combat featuring a large number of action sequences

action replay repeat of a brief filmed segment, often in slow motion

action shot scene involving movement in a film or television program

action theory in some philosophical systems, the idea that actions are different from behaviors. The term comes up occasionally in media studies in discussions of the relation between media and its effects on human behavior.

ActionMedia trade name of a digital video system developed by Intel that allows a computer to record, play back, and manipulate video

active audience in USES AND GRATIFICATIONS THEORY, the people who do not accept a media representation or text as it is presented to them, but interpret it, or interact with it, for their own purposes and in their own way, regardless of the intention of the creator of the representation or text

active listening manner of listening to a speaker, group, or media product (such as a documentary, feature film, or television program) so as to take into serious consideration the point of view being put forward

active participation way in which media intrude upon and influence the stories they are supposed to be reporting impartially

active pixel region area of a computer screen that displays graphic information

active reader in USES AND GRATIFICATIONS THEORY, the individual who does not read a media representation or text as it is presented to him or her, using it instead for his or her own purposes and in his or her own way, regardless of the intentions of the maker of the representation or text

active video part of a video signal that contains picture information

activism theory, doctrine, or practice of assertive, often militant, action, such as mass demonstrations or strikes, used as a means of opposing or supporting a controversial issue, entity, or person

actual malice reckless disregard of the truth or falsity of some published or broadcast story

actuality the live recording of an event on location as it actually unfolds

ad [*see* **advertisement**]

ad agency [*see* **advertising agency**]

ad campaign [*see* **advertising campaign**]

ad copy printed text or spoken words in an advertisement

Ad Council [*see* **Advertising Council**]

ad hoc balancing of interests in First Amendment cases, factors that should be taken into consideration in determining how much freedom the press is granted

ad impression opportunity to see an advertisement; in online advertising, ad impressions are the number of times an ad is downloaded from a Web page

ad panel [*see* **advertisement panel**]

adage [also called **aphorism**] formulaic statement designed to bring out some generally accepted intuition, experience, or truth, gaining currency over time: for example, *haste makes waste*; *necessity is the mother of invention.*

adaptive control expenditure model used by advertisers that takes into account consumer responses to advertising campaigns. It does so typically by using statistical methods that indicate the success of a campaign and, thus, how much money can be poured into it.

Adbusters Canadian group of social activists with a popular Web site and magazine who are critical of the advertising process itself. The Web site and magazine of the same name were founded in 1989 by Kalle Lasn and Bill Schmalz in Vancouver. The organization offers not only serious critiques of advertising and consumerism, but also many clever parodies of advertising campaigns, articles, and forums on how one can recognize media manipulation, information on lawsuits and legislation on consumer issues, and links for sending e-mails to big businesses to contest their marketing strategies. Web site: www.adbusters.org

added value extra or additional promotion service or benefit that a publication can offer its advertisers, such as supplements or special sections

addendum section of a book, magazine, or Web site that is tacked on, usually at the end, such as an appendix or a further reading section

addressable technology equipment enabling a program provider (such as a cable television provider) to switch to pay services

addressee in ROMAN JAKOBSON's model of communication, the receiver(s) of a message; the person(s) to whom a message is addressed

addresser in ROMAN JAKOBSON's model of communication, term referring to the sender(s) of a message; that is, the person(s) who addresses a message to someone

adjacency commercial break between television programs

Adler, Alfred (1870–1937) Austrian psychiatrist who coined the term *inferiority complex*, which he saw as the primary source of characteristic behaviors and of most neuroses—in contrast to FREUD's emphasis on sexual drives as the primary psychic forces. Adler's most influential works are *Über den nervösen Charakter* (1912; *The Nervous Constitution*) and *Menschenkenntnis* (1927; *Understanding Human Nature*). His works are often cited in psychological stud-

ies of media reception and communication problems.

admass segment of society at which an ADVERTISING CAMPAIGN is aimed

administrative research term first used by PAUL LAZARSFELD in 1941 to describe the type of research carried out by teams of researchers or institutions, using empirical methods (such as opinion polling) and seeking to answer clearly defined problems (who watches TV, why they watch it, how effective are advertising messages, and so on)

adnorm measure of readership averages for print publications over a two-year period, used as a baseline for comparing specific ads on average terms

Adobe Acrobat trade name for software developed by Adobe Systems that converts documents and formatted pages in such a way that they can be viewed on a computer

Adobe Photoshop graphics editing software developed by Adobe Systems

Adorno, Theodor (1903–1969) influential German Marxist thinker who was a leading figure in the so-called FRANKFURT SCHOOL. Adorno berated pop culture as an aberration of true culture. He and MAX HORKHEIMER (another Frankfurt School founder) coined the term CULTURE INDUSTRY to describe the process by which mass forms of culture were produced—in analogy with the industrial manufacturing of commercial products. Adorno did not see pop culture as a threat to social authority, but rather as a way to homogenize cultural products so that they can be consumed easily and without thought. His ideas are often cited in media studies. His work *The Culture Industry: Selected Essays on Mass Culture* (English translation published posthumously in 1991) is considered significant.

adperson [previously **adman**] person whose job is in the field of advertising

ADR [*see* **automatic dialogue replacement**]

ADSL [*see* **Asymmetrical Digital Subscriber Line**]

adspeak kind of jargon used in the advertising field

adspend amount of money spent on advertising a particular product

adult contemporary music genre popular music that appeals mainly to an older audience; this genre can include music that was once aimed primarily at teenagers, such as the music of Frank Sinatra, the Beatles, the Rolling Stones, or Madonna

adult movie [also called **porn movie**] sexually explicit movie that is primarily of prurient interest

advance statement given to the media in advance of an event's occurrence so as to optimize coverage

adventure spy genre narrative that involves espionage, mystery, crime, and/or adventure

adventure story action tale revolving around daring heroes and sly villains in fantastic situations. Robert Louis Stevenson's novel *Treasure Island* (1883) is an example of this popular form of children's literature.

advergame term that appeared in *Wired* magazine's "Jargon Watch" column in 2001, now applied to free online games commissioned by major companies to promote their products. Advergaming is the practice of using games to advertise a product, organization, or viewpoint. Typically, companies provide interactive games on their Web sites in order to draw potential customers to them so that users will spend more time on the Web sites, becoming more aware of their products.

advertisement [abbreviated as **ad**] public promotion of a product or service by means of a notice, such as a poster, newspaper display, or paid announcement in some electronic or digital medium, designed to attract public attention or patronage

advertisement panel [abbreviated as **ad panel**] specially designed advertising space in a newspaper or magazine

advertiser manufacturer, service company, retailer, or supplier that advertises its product(s) or service(s)

advertising public announcement, promotion, support, or endorsement of a product, a service, a business, a person, an event, etc., in order to attract or increase interest. A poster found in Thebes, dated to 1000 B.C.E., which offered gold for the capture of a runaway slave, reveals that advertising has been practiced since antiquity. In both the ancient and medieval worlds, advertising was also carried out by town criers—people who read advertising materials to the public—since many people were illiterate. In the seventeenth century, the *London Gazette* became the first newspaper to set aside a section for purposes of advertising. Book publishers, seed companies, railroads, and steamship lines were among the early users of nationwide advertising. Today, advertising has morphed into a dominant form of social discourse influencing lifestyle, worldview, economic systems, politics, and even traditional values, since it is designed to suggest how people can best satisfy their needs and reach their goals.

advertising agency [abbreviated as **ad agency**] company that creates AD-VERTISING CAMPAIGNS for products. The first modern agency was founded in 1841 by Philadelphia entrepreneur Volney B. Palmer. A few years later, Palmer opened offices in major East Coast cities (New York, Boston,

and Baltimore). In the first decade of the twentieth century advertising agencies began to hire psychologists to help create campaigns designed to increase the desire to buy goods through persuasion techniques. American psychologist John B. Watson, for instance, was hired by the J. Walter Thompson Agency. Today the ad agency business has developed into an enterprise so huge that, for some critics, it has come to symbolize the style of American capitalism—a style based on hype and evangelical fervor.

advertising boycott boycott organized against companies so as to persuade them to abandon an advertising campaign for a specific social or political reason

advertising brief list of objectives and instructions issued by a company to an advertising agency for the design of an ADVERTISING CAMPAIGN

advertising campaign [abbreviated as **ad campaign**] series of advertisements constructed around the same theme or using the same style, which together attempt to make the identical pitch for a product in a specific way. For example, the McDonald's "I'm lovin' it!" campaign directed its message to a young audience; the DeBeer's "Diamonds are Forever" campaign used images of elegance, romanticism, and the like to pitch its message about the beauty and classic elegance of the company's diamonds.

Advertising Council [abbreviated as **Ad Council**] private nonprofit organization founded in 1942 that produces and disseminates public service announcements on behalf of various sponsors. Web site: www. adcouncil.org

advertising impressions number of times that an advertisement actually reaches an intended audience, that is, the total number of views by all audience members

advertising media communication channels that carry advertising messages to consumers. These include print media (newspapers, magazines, pamphlets), electronic media (radio, television), outdoor signs and posters, phone directories, direct mailings, novelties, and the Internet.

advertising page exposure measure of the opportunity for readers to see a particular print advertisement, whether or not they actually look at the ad

advertising plan explicit outline of what goals an advertising campaign should achieve, how to accomplish those goals, and how to determine whether or not the campaign was successful in achieving those goals

advertising rate amount of money charged for advertising space or time

advertising space any space available for advertising in a media product (for example, newspaper,

magazine, radio program, television slot)

advertising specialties special items, such as T-shirts, mugs, pens, or cards, given away as part of an advertising campaign

advertising techniques procedures designed to inform or persuade people. Among the most common techniques are the ATTENTION-GETTING HEADLINE, the basic appeal, the comparison of products, the PRODUCT CHARACTER, REPETITION IN ADVERTISING, the SLOGAN, and the TESTIMONIAL.

advertising time amount of time on radio or television set aside for advertising

advertorial advertisement that has the appearance of a news article or editorial, in a print publication

advice column section of a newspaper, magazine, or Web page that is intended to give advice to readers who have sent in questions or queries

advocacy advertising type of advertising used to promote a particular position on a controversial political or social issue

advocacy journalism type of journalism intended to promote a position on a political, controversial, or social issue

aerial [also called **antenna**] metallic apparatus used for sending and/or receiving electromagnetic waves or signals

aerial advertising ads of products or services displayed in the air from balloons or planes

aerial perspective technique of making objects appear more distant by portraying them less sharply; based on the phenomenon of atmospheric distortion

aerial shot camera shot taken from a high position above the action

aesthesia in both art criticism and psychology, a subject's sensory and emotional reaction to a stimulus (a melody, painting, etc.), inducing a heightened sensitivity to its beauty

aesthetics the perception and experience of beauty and meaning in art; aesthetics deals in particular with the question of whether such perception exists in the mind of the interpreter or whether it is an intrinsic part of a work of art (independent of an interpreter). The term was introduced in 1753 by the German philosopher Alexander Gottlieb Baumgarten. Media scholarship has shown that aesthetic value is often determined by tradition, trends, and other social pressures on tastes, regardless of the intrinsic value of a work. For example, in the early eighteenth century the plays of William Shakespeare were viewed as barbaric and obscene. Today, they are considered to be among the greatest works of theater ever written.

affective behavior category of human behavior based on feelings, sentiments, and emotions

affiliate local radio or television station that is part of a national network

affiliate fee monthly fee that cable programming services charge local cable operators for the right to carry their programs

affiliate marketing practice of promoting companies that pay to have their products or services advertised on a centralized Web site

affiliate partner company that puts advertising for other companies on its own Web site

affiliate program form of advertising on the Internet in which businesses use banners or buttons on their Web sites to advertise the products or services of another business

affirmative disclosure identifying the source of information contained in an advertisement, required by the Federal Trade Commission or other authority, which may not be desired by the advertiser. This consists generally in some statement that admits to some limitation in the product or the offer made.

Afrocentric talk term coined by American researcher Jennifer Wood to refer to the use of oral storytelling traditions and themes by African Americans to make sense of their world and thus to build self-identity and a sense of dignity

Afropop contemporary music from Africa and African communities

Afropop Worldwide public radio international that features AFROPOP music. Web site: www.afropop.org

afterimage visual sensation in which an image persists after the visual stimulus has been removed; for example, the spot of light one sees following a burst of light, such as that from the flash of a camera

afterpiece short comedic entertainment that follows the performance of a play

agate line standard measure of newspaper advertising space, used especially for classified advertisements (1 column wide by 1/14 inch deep)

age profile audience for a particular media event, ad, or product, classified according to age group

agency 1. means or mode of acting or behaving in a socially meaningful way; 2. ability of individuals to act self-consciously and to exert their will through involvement in social practices; 3. an establishment that conducts business for another party (e.g., an ADVERTISING AGENCY)

agency commission agency's fee for designing and placing advertisements

agency roster list of different advertising agencies that work for the same company

agenda list of items or issues to be covered (e.g., by the media) in order of their purported importance

agenda setting according to one theory, influential role played by the media in their determination of which issues are covered and their relative order of importance

agent person who is authorized to act as the representative of another party (for example, a literary agent who represents a writer)

aggregator Web site that collects syndicated news from other Web sites

aggressive cues theoretical model that identifies certain classes of people as acceptable media targets for real-world aggression

agit-prop practice of using the media to spread propaganda

agora 1. a gathering place; in particular, the marketplace in ancient Greece; 2. a marketplace on the Internet

AI [*see* **artificial intelligence**]

AIDA [acronym for **Attention, Interest, Desire, and Action**] model of how to use advertising to get the consumers' attention, then develop their interest in a product, followed by consumers' desire to purchase the product, and finally resulting in consumers' action to actually go out and purchase it

aided recall research method frequently used to determine what consumers remember about an advertisement they have seen or heard

AIR [*see* **average issue readership**]

airbrush technique for covering imperfections or removing flaws from photographic images

airdate date of a radio or television broadcast

airplay occasion when a recording is broadcast on the radio, or the number of times a record is actually played

airtime amount of time given to a program in radio and television broadcasting

airwaves radio waves making broadcasting possible

album recording of music that is issued and marketed as a single product, e.g., a record album or a CD album

album cover jacket of a record album (originally for a 33 1/3 rpm record album), often of interest either because of its relation to the musical

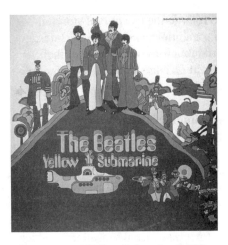

Album cover of *Yellow Submarine* (1969)

text or its representation of a theme. Famous album covers include those created for the Velvet Underground by ANDY WARHOL, featuring the image of a banana, and several created for the Beatles, especially the *Sgt. Pepper's Lonely Hearts Club Band* (1967) cover.

alienation term coined by KARL MARX to describe a sensed estrangement from other people, society, or work. Today, psychiatrists define alienation as a blocking or dissociation of a person's feelings. Some philosophers believe that alienation is produced by a shallow and depersonalized society. Fourth-century theologian Saint Augustine wrote that. due to its sinful nature, humanity was alienated from God. To Austrian psychoanalyst SIGMUND FREUD, alienation resulted from the split between the conscious and unconscious parts of the mind. French social theorist Émile Durkheim suggested that alienation stemmed from a loss of societal and religious tradition. Existentialists saw some measure of alienation as an inevitable part of the human condition.

alienation effect in Marxist theory, the result of using alienating techniques, such as unsettling lighting effects or bizarre soundtracks, that force an audience to develop a critical attitude toward a performance or message to which they are exposed

Al Jazeera influential satellite television channel, based in Qatar and launched in 1996, that broadcasts in Arabic. Al Jazeera came to international notice after the terrorist attacks of September 11, 2001, because of its contrasting coverage of world issues compared with that of Western media. Web site: www.aljazeera.net/English

all-channel legislation U.S. federal law, passed in 1962, requiring all television sets to be equipped with both VHF and UHF receivers

allegory literary work with a purely symbolic meaning; that is, a work in which the characters and events symbolize spiritual, moral, or political meanings or ideas. Some historically important allegorical works are *Le roman de la rose* (thirteenth century) by Guillaume de Lorris and Jean de Meung; *The Divine Comedy* (1321) by Dante Alighieri; and *Pilgrim's Progress* (1678) by John Bunyan.

alliteration rhetorical (poetic technique) consisting of the repetition of the initial consonant sound(s) in several words in a phrase, expression, etc.: *The sun always shines in summer*; *Peter plays the piano perfectly*

alliteration technique advertising method based on ALLITERATION, usually involving the name of the brand being advertised, purportedly enhancing the probability that a product's name will be remembered: *Marlboro man*; *Guinness is good*; *Frosted Flakes*; *Tony the Tiger*

allness attitude the outlook of people who think that they know everything there is to know about someone or something. In the field of semantics, this attitude is thought to make communication more difficult.

allofmp3.com one of numerous Russian Web sites that offer popular music (for downloading to a computer or mp3 player) for a fraction of what iTunes charges

allusion indirect reference (to person, character, idea, etc.) in common discourse or narrative art

Alpha international code word for the letter A, used in radio communications

alphabet system of symbols, commonly called *letters* or *characters*, used for representing speech sounds. Alphabets are distinguished from other systems by the fact that, ideally, each letter in the system stands for a particular sound in a word. A syllabary, on the other hand, consists of symbols representing syllables; a pictographic system consists of picture symbols for representing things and ideas (rather than sounds in words); and an ideographic system consists of picturelike symbols that stand for complex ideas (such as motion, states, etc.).

alphanumeric letters, numerical symbols, and punctuation marks, mathematical symbols, and other conventional symbols, used in some combination to create words, phrases, or entire sentences. This is a major feature of language used in chat rooms, text messages, and other types of digital communications: *g2g = Got to go; 2dA = today; gr8 = great.*

alt Internet Web site that posts discussions about alternative subjects of all kinds

alterity [also called **otherness**] view that emphasizes diversity in philosophy, the arts and sciences, and media representations. This concept gained prominence after MICHEL FOUCAULT's allegation in the 1980s that the Other—anyone who was different in sexual orientation, ethnicity, etc., from those with social power—had been excluded from or marginalized by Western systems of representation.

alternate media any media of advertising other than direct mail

alternative comedy style of comedy and/or humorous material that is deliberately different from mainstream comedy

alternative media nonmainstream media forms (such as pamphlets or graffiti) that arise to complement and sometimes challenge traditional media forms

alternative newspapers [*see* **alternative press**]

alternative press nonmainstream press with a small circulation, which espouses radical viewpoints, especially in the area of politics

alternative rock rock music that is performed by relatively unknown musicians and/or is promoted by small record companies

Althusser, Louis (1918–1990) French Marxist scholar whose ideas are often cited in the literature on media and pop culture, especially his view that media are part of ideological systems. Among his important works are *Pour Marx* (1965; *For Marx*) and *Lénine et la philosophie* (1969; *Lenin and Philosophy*).

AM radio [abbreviation of **amplitude modulation radio**] radio broadcasting system based on a carrier wave of constant frequency but of varying amplitude

Amazon.com Web-based bookstore that has become one of the largest bookstores in the world

ambient advertising [also called **ambient media**] advertising intended for the outdoors (posters, ads on subway platforms, ads on buses) so that people can be exposed to an ad during their everyday activities

ambisonics [also called **surround sound**] technique of using several separate audio channels to record and produce sounds so that they completely surround listeners

ambivalence category used by advertisers to describe consumers who are neither interested in, nor opposed to, advertising

ambush interview line of questioning that is intended to catch an interviewee off guard

America Online [abbreviated as **AOL**] online service provider created by Steve Case in 1985 as Quantum Computer Services. It changed its name to America Online and its corporate structure in 1991. In January 2000, AOL announced its plans to merge with Time-Warner; the merger was approved by the Federal Trade Commission in January 2001, and the new corporate entity became one of the world's largest media conglomerates. Web site: www.corp.aol.com

American Academy of Advertising [abbreviated as **AAA**] association of advertising educators, students, and professionals, dedicated to the evaluation and improvement of advertising education. The association publishes the well-known *Journal of Advertising*. Web site: www.aaasite.org

American Association of Advertising Agencies [abbreviated as **AAAA**] U.S. national trade association founded in 1917 whose members are ad agencies. Web site: www.aaaa.org

American Broadcasting Company [abbreviated as **ABC**] broadcasting network created in 1943 that, along with CBS and NBC, was one of the BIG THREE in the golden era of television from the 1950s to the 1970s. ABC is now a New York City-based American communications corporation, whose holdings include television and radio stations, Internet services, and print publications. The company was acquired by Walt Disney Company Media Networks in 1996. Web site: www.abc.org

American dream belief that anybody can succeed in America, regardless of background, race, gender, and so on

American Society for Composers, Authors and Publishers [abbreviated as **ASCAP**] major U.S. performing rights organization founded in New York City in 1914 to protect authors, composers, and publishers by licensing and distributing royalties. ASCAP's earliest members included Irving Berlin and John Philip Sousa. Web site: www.ascap.org

American Standard Code for Information Interchange [abbreviated as **ASCII**] standardized way of converting text into a format that can be interpreted by any computer

American Telephone and Telegraph Company [abbreviated as **AT&T**] one of the largest communications companies, providing voice, data, video, and online communications services to residential, business, and government customers throughout the world. AT&T also operates a cable television system and offers local telephone service through its cable lines in some parts of the United States. Its headquarters are in New York City. Web site: www.att.com

Americanization purported influence that the United States has on the culture of other nations. The term has a negative connotation if the influence is imposed unwillingly; it has a positive connotation if the influence is sought voluntarily.

A-movie in contrast to a B-MOVIE, a film that is considered to be of the best quality aesthetically and technically

amplification technological enhancement of sound transmission to increase volume

amplification of deviance process whereby some activity, labeled as deviant, is exaggerated as a result of social reaction to it, which is largely shaped and influenced by the mass media

amplifier device or equipment that makes sound louder

anachronism something that is, or seems to be, out of its proper time; for example, using the word *thou* rather than *you* would be considered an anachronism in modern English

anaglyph photograph or painting showing different perspectives or aspects of something with two contrasting colors that are superimposed on each other. The image is perceived as a three-dimensional object when viewed with "3-D glasses" (two correspondingly colored lenses).

anagram a word or phrase produced by rearranging the letters of another word or phrase: for example, *Elvis = lives*; *Presbyterian = best in prayer*; *deliver = live red*

analog 1. mechanism in which data are represented by continuously variable quantities; 2. transmission of a continuous electrical or radio frequency wave; opposite of DIGITAL; 3. recording that uses magnetic tape

analog channel communications line (such as a telephone line) that carries ANALOG signals

analogy 1. comparison between two things that are similar in some respects, so as to explain one of the things or make it easier to comprehend: *the atom can be understood as a miniature solar system*;

2. process by which language forms are created on the model of already existing forms: the suffix *-ize* (used for example in *apologize, realize, categorize, symbolize*, etc.) has been extended to create new words such as *energize* or *digitize*

analytic editing type of video or film editing in which a sequence of images is constructed to follow a plot, rather than to explain it

analytical engine calculating machine invented by British mathematician CHARLES BABBAGE in the 1830s, of which only a part was ever built. Babbage's engine was, in effect, the first general-purpose digital computer, although it was conceived long before electronics technology appeared. It had the capacity to perform various mathematical operations, using punched cards as a form of permanent memory.

anamorphic lens a lens that "squeezes" or distorts a filmed image for widescreen projection

anarchist cinema genre that revolves around the theme that life is meaningless or unfair and that includes an anti-authoritarian element.

anchor main presenter of the news in a televised newscast

anchorage in advertising, the ability of captions to influence the meaning gleaned from images (photos, print ads, etc.). The term was coined by the twentieth-century semiotician ROLAND BARTHES.

ancillary market movie revenue source other than the domestic box office one (foreign box office, video rights, television rights)

ancillary-to-trade any product or service, such as advertising, that supports trade

Andersch, Staats and Bostrom's model of communication model proposed in 1969 stressing the transactional nature of communication, in which meanings are created and interpreted by both the sender and the receiver in tandem, and are partially shaped by outside influences

androcentric revolving around or emphasizing a male perspective

anecdote short account that helps to illustrate or stimulate interest in a more general issue

Ang, Ien (1960–) international media scholar known for her work on audiences, identity politics, and media representation. Some of her important works include *Desperately Seeking the Audience* (1991) and *Living Room Wars: Rethinking Media Audiences for a Postmodern World* (1996).

angle main point or focus of a story, in journalism usually emphasized as a headline

animal communication [also called **zoosemiotics**] discipline that studies ways in which animals communicate, focusing on innate signaling systems

animated motion picture movie based either entirely or in part on ANIMATION

animation moviemaking technique of showing slightly different drawings in rapid succession, creating the illusion of continuous motion (this visual illusion is also illustrated by "flip books")

animatronics technique of using electronic and/or mechanical devices to animate puppets, models, or any relevant object

anime [also called **manga**] Japanese comic-book drawing technique characterized by very large eyes and a layout in which the panels run from right to left

annals records of published events or information within a particular field

annotation act or process of providing critical commentary or explanatory notes to a text or performance

announcement formal or public notice uttered or communicated in some medium (oral, written, or recorded)

announcer person who introduces radio or television programs or shows; in sports, person who provides continuous commentary during the broadcast of a sports event

anomie term coined by sociologist Emile Durkheim to refer to the sense of alienation and purposelessness experienced by a person or a class as a result of a breakdown or lack of standards and values. The term is often used in the literature by those who believe that anomie makes some people more susceptible to the effects of mass media.

anonymous written, created, or produced by an unknown person or persons

anonymous audience listeners or recipients who have no connection to any single group and who are unknown to the creator of a media product

anonymous FTP method of connecting to a remote computer without requiring special permission or a password to download files

anonymous remail service for forwarding e-mails or newsgroup postings so that personal details are excluded

answerprint final edited version of a filmed piece to be checked for final corrections or modifications

antenna [see **aerial**]

anthology collection of various works taken from a specific genre within a medium (for example, essays, poems, sitcoms, or documentaries)

anthology drama popular form of early television programming that brought live theater to television audiences

anthropology study of humankind from all points of view (evolution, culture, etc.). Lewis Henry Morgan, who conducted research on the cultures of the Iroquois in the nineteenth century, is considered the North American founder of the discipline; in Europe, British scholar Edward B. Tylor is credited with its foundation. In the 1970s, anthropological methods such as ethnography (studying some cultural phenomenon through systematic observation) were adopted by media researchers to gain insights into the ways in which traditional forms of culture have been changed by the mass media and mass communications technologies.

anthropomorphism in literature and the arts, the attribution of human qualities to objects, animals, plants, or gods

anthroposemiotics branch of SEMIOTICS studying sign use in the human species (as opposed to sign use across species). *Biosemiotics* is the more generic term, used to refer to the study of sign use across species.

anti-aliasing technique that minimizes the distortion of a digital image or sound signal, accomplished by "smoothing," or removing components that have too high a frequency to be resolved by the recording device

anticlimax rhetorical technique of sequencing ideas in a phrase or sentence in diminishing importance, usually for some humorous or satirical effect: *He is intelligent, handsome, but short. Thousands died in that horrific war; a great deal of time was also lost.* The term *anticlimactic* is often used to describe a sudden change from something serious to something trivial or from something compelling to something dull.

antics ludicrous or extravagant actions performed by an actor playing an exaggerated comic role

antihero character in a story who lacks the traditional qualities associated with heroes, such as bravery, strength, idealism, or courage

antilanguage 1. language created by a specific group in order to exclude outsiders from the group; 2. language created and sustained by a specific group to express opposition to a dominant linguistic order. An example of anti-language is that found in some rap lyrics, characterized by intentional misspellings and other devices that are in breach of standard English.

antimonopoly controls regulatory legislative measures designed to inhibit the control of business or supply by a single entity (for example, to prevent media conglomerates from monopolizing the delivery of mass communications)

antinarrative [*see* **antinovel**]

antinomy putting together two reasonable but opposite premises in a seemingly contradictory fashion so as to achieve some rhetorical effect: for example, *what is bad is really good for you*; *inelegance is in fashion*

antinovel [also called **antinarrative**] novel lacking the traditional elements of the narrative, such as plot structure, realistic characters, etc. *Molloy* (1951) by Samuel Beckett is an antinovel.

antirealism storytelling technique in which no attempt is made to represent a situation realistically

antithesis use of words, phrases, clauses, or expressions of opposing meaning to emphasize contrasting concepts: for example, *He is laughing*; *I am crying. They are growing*; *I am shrinking.*

antitrust laws legislative measures designed to protect trade and commerce from unlawful control by large corporations or single entities

antiwar genre narrative that revolves around a plot or a situation that brings out the absurdity or depravity of war

antonomasia 1. use of a title or honorific (*Your Honor, Your Majesty*, etc.) in place of the person's name; 2. using the name of a well-known personage to describe someone who has

similar characteristics (for example, calling a philanderer a *Don Juan*)

antonym word that means the opposite of another word: *light* is the antonym of *dark*; *hot* is the antonym of *cold*

AOL [*see* **America Online**]

AP [*see* **Associated Press**]

Apache silence in sociolinguistic analysis, the use of silence as a form of communication in situations where words are difficult to find

aphorism [*see* **adage**]

apocalyptic thriller genre in which the story revolves around a cataclysmic event or disastrous end to life on earth

apocryphal of questionable authorship or authenticity

apologue fable intended to impart a moral lesson, in which animals or inanimate objects represent human characters: for example, the stories in Aesop's *Fables* (sixth century B.C.E.) and in the late nineteenth-century Uncle Remus tales by American writer Joel Chandler Harris

aporia in discourse theory, the state or expression of doubt or uncertainty about how to proceed in a conversation or in a communicative exchange

apostrophe rhetorical strategy whereby an actor (or writer) turns from the other characters, the audience, or the reader to address a person, a god, etc., who is either absent or deceased: for example, *What is life, my long-departed uncle?*; *Oh Death, who are you?*

apothegm [also called **maxim**] terse statement designed to embody a self-evident truth: for example, *Beauty is skin deep*; *Night follows day*

appeal 1. degree of likability of an advertisement; 2. program or ad campaign asking for donations for a particular cause

appendix material added to the end of a text (book, Web page, video)

apperception process of understanding by which new observations are related to past experience. This term is used in the psychological literature on media processing.

Apple Computer Corporation trade name for a computer technology company founded in 1976 by Steve Jobs and Steve Wozniak that has developed, among its many products, the Apple Macintosh personal computer and the iPod. Web site: www .Apple.com

application service provider [abbreviated as **ASP**] 1. technology for delivering software applications and data via the Internet; 2. a business that sells ASPs on a subscription or rental basis

application software computer software designed for a specific task, such as word processing, accounting, or inventory management

appreciation index measure of how much someone has enjoyed a television or radio program that he or she has viewed or listened to. The subject is asked to record his or her degree of enjoyment as a score from 1 to 10.

appropriation process by which innovative or resistant cultural forms are taken up and commodified by media or culture industries; for example, rap music and lifestyle have been appropriated by various brands to advertise their products via images and personalities associated with rap culture

APTN [*see* **Aboriginal People's Television Network**]

arbitrariness in Saussurean SEMIOTICS, the theory that a SIGN stands for something in an arbitrary way and not in a way motivated by the nature of its referent. There is no evident reason for using, for example, *cat* to designate "a small feline considered to be a domestic animal." Indeed, any well-formed word could have been coined for this naming purpose—as long as it was consistent with the word-formation patterns of English.

arbitrary code system of signals or symbols that bears no direct relation to the ideas it portrays or reflects

Arbitron provider of radio and television rating and marketing services, founded in 1949, that publishes regular reports for selected markets. Web site: www.arbitron.com

archetype an inherited memory represented in the brain by a recurring image, form, or pattern. This meaning of the term was introduced by psychologist CARL GUSTAV JUNG to refer to symbolic and ritualistic forms that manifest themselves universally across cultures. A humorous clownish or jester figure, known as the *trickster*, for instance, is an archetype. This archetype surfaces as a buffoon or fool at various rituals (as in carnivals), in narratives (for example, *Rumpelstiltskin*), and in the assumed character of modern-day comedians. Jung suggested that archetypes are the building blocks of culture, enabling people to react to various life situations in ways similar to their ancestors.

archie early search system (considered the first Internet search engine) for locating publicly accessible files or software

architecture-opera exhibition consisting of a walk-through installation and a live opera, presented on a set with video sculptures

archive public records or historical documents that have been preserved for future access; material (such as newspaper articles and film segments) that can be used again if needed

archive site on the Internet, a site that provides a large collection of downloadable public-domain files and programs

Areopagitica pamphlet (1644) written and distributed by John Milton, which defended freedom of the press and the inviolability of books

argot jargon used by a particular group for in-group communication (although it can spread to the society at large). The term is generally used to refer to the language used by criminals or those belonging to delinquent organizations.

argument summary of the plot or theme of a literary work

Aristotle (384–322 B.C.E.) Greek philosopher, a student of PLATO, whose ideas on logical thinking and on the nature of reality have influenced (and continue to influence) modern-day Western philosophy and scientific method. Aristotle's notion of CATHARSIS has become widespread in the study of media audiences.

Arnold, Matthew (1822–1888) nineteenth-century British poet and social critic whose ideas against the banality of popular forms of culture are still cited today. His classic study *Culture and Anarchy* (1869) is a polemic against Victorian materialism.

Arpanet [abbreviation for **Advanced Research Projects Agency Network**]

wide-area network created in the 1960s by the U.S. Department of Defense for the free exchange of information between universities and research organizations, also used by the military for its own communications. Arpanet was the network from which the Internet evolved.

art any work or text (a painting, a sculpture, a musical composition, etc.) that evokes an AESTHETIC reaction, impelling people to contemplate its meaning and its qualities. The drawings found during the Paleolithic period, some 20,000 to 35,000 years ago, are likely to be the first works of art. Twenty-first-century art includes a wide range of media, such as film, video, sound recordings, and digital images.

art deco design style of the 1910s, 1920s, and 1930s, which emphasized sleek elegance in form, reflective of "modern" technology. The style became popular in 1925 at the Paris exhibition called *Exposition Internationale des Arts Décoratifs et Industriels Modernes.* Prominent examples of art deco style include the interior of the Chrysler Building (1930) and Radio City Music Hall (1931), both located in New York.

art director individual who coordinates creative artwork in advertising, or the individual who oversees the design of a television or movie set

art film experimental film created as an artwork, not aimed at mass audiences, but at cinema connoisseurs

Isolde (1895) by Aubrey Beardsley

art nouveau style of painting of the late nineteenth and early twentieth centuries, characterized primarily by the depiction of leaves and flowers in flowing, sinuous lines. The earliest examples of art nouveau are usually considered to be a chair designed in 1882 and an engraved frontispiece for an 1883 book (*Wren's Early Churches*) by English architect Arthur Mackmurdo. The illustrations of Aubrey Beardsley are considered the most prominent examples of this style. In the twentieth century, the art nouveau style became fashionable in interior decor as well as magazine illustrations.

article 1. text on a particular subject in a newspaper and magazine; 2. online message or posting

articulation 1. process of expressing something; 2. in Marxist theory, a term referring to the joining together of social forces in a hierarchical way (with one being dominant over the other); for example, in many present-day societies, capitalism is the dominant force even in political systems that include different modes of production

artificial intelligence [abbreviated as **AI**] branch of computer science devoted to the development of programs that will allow computers to simulate or even replicate patterns of human intelligence (problem solving, speaking, etc.)

artificial language linguistic system invented for a particular purpose. The best-known artificial language devised to facilitate communication among people of different languages and cultural backgrounds is Esperanto.

ASCAP [*see* **American Society for Composers, Authors and Publishers**]

ascription in media studies, adjustment of statistical information to reflect unexpected circumstances; for example, the reduced circulation of a magazine due to a printing delay

A-side the more important side of a music single (recording) that usually contains the title track

ASCII [*see* **American Standard Code for Information Interchange**]

ASP [*see* **application service provider**]

aspirer in advertising research, the type of individual who wants products that improve his or her lifestyle image

assets data components (audio, video) that are used in multimedia applications

assignment desk [also called **news desk**] in print and televised media, staff responsible for dispatching reporters and/or camera crews to cover news events

assimilation [*see* **acculturation**]

assistive technology [abbreviated as **AT**] technology designed to assist disabled individuals

Associated Press [abbreviated as **AP**] major international news agency founded in 1949 in New York City. Serves as a source of news information and visual images for print media, radio, and television. Web site: www.ap.org

association psychological notion which contends that concepts are formed on the basis of one thought leading to another that is connected with it in some way (through experience, analogy, comparison, etc.). Starting in the 1920s, psychologists of the behaviorist school used the theory of association to explain the development of mental skills and the acquisition of language. The theory has been used to explain how certain media products are received and linked both to each other and to social life.

association principle in advertising, persuasive technique that aims to associate a product with a cultural value or theme, even though the cultural value may have no actual connection to the product

assonance poetic effect achieved by using words containing the same or similar vowel sounds: for example, *I hate to be late for my date*

asterisk a symbol (*) used to indicate an omission or a reference to a note. Asterisks are sometimes used to replace letters of words, or entire words, that are considered obscene.

Asymmetrical Digital Subscriber Line [abbreviated as **ADSL**] high-speed technology providing high-speed Internet access to local telephone service customers over conventional phone lines

Asynchronous Transfer Mode [abbreviated as **ATM**] high-speed communications network technology that allows multiple types of traffic (voice, video) to be transmitted over a network in bundles called cells

AT [*see* **assistive technology**]

AT&T [*see* **American Telephone and Telegraph Company**]

ATM [*see* **Asynchronous Transfer Mode**]

atmosphere 1. dominant mood or tone elicited by a work; 2. ambient noise added to a recording in order to make the sound track more realistic

atmospherics 1. noises that interfere with radio reception, caused by natural disturbances in the atmosphere; 2. in advertising, tools for the creation of an "atmosphere" or identity for a brand, such as its name, logo, and so on

ATR [acronym for **awareness, trial, repeat**] advertising model which claims that a consumer first becomes aware of a product through advertising, then buys it once to try it, and will buy it again if it is acceptable or suitable

attack ad political advertisement that employs repeated negative assaults on another candidate's character

attention economy theory that links the present-day wealth of information to an economy, or scarcity, of attention by individuals, particularly as consumers; the proliferation of available information on the Internet is viewed as a significant factor in attention economy

attention-getting headline style of headline used in printed advertisements, designed to immediately attract the attention of the consumer. Some headlines attract attention by promising that some benefit will ensue from buying a product (such as a savings in money, improvement in physical appearance). Other headlines are worded to arouse curiosity, or to attract the attention of a specific group (e.g., "For those who are young at heart").

attention model of mass communication paradigm that presents the design of mass communication in terms of attracting and maintaining the attention of consumers, viewers, or listeners

attention value likelihood that an advertisement or media product will attract and maintain attention and/or interest

attitude in media studies, the disposition of an individual toward a media product, especially as acquired through cultural conditioning

attitude change theory in media studies, a principle that aims to explain how people's attitudes are formed and/or changed through media exposure

audience any group of people exposed to media. Some audiences (such as those for sports events or concerts) are physically present at the media event. Other audiences (such as those for novels, television, or radio) are not. Additionally, audience members need not undergo the experience at the same time (for example, not everyone reads the

book or sees the movie at the same time). The idea of *audience* entered media studies through psychological research on people's responses to certain media messages according to age, social class, gender, and so on. It is now believed that there is a constant dynamic interplay between audiences and producers of media products. Audience research aims to identify the views, habits, and opinions of media audiences of all kinds.

audience appreciation index [abbreviated as **AAI**] measure of audience reaction to a certain media product. The measure is used as a factor in ratings research.

audience competence knowledge that audience members build up regarding their interests, which may create an increase in audience satisfaction

audience differentiation classifying audiences into categories, such as age, social status, gender, and education, so as to determine the needs of each group

audience duplication percentage of people reached by an advertisement (or other media event) more than once

audience ethnography research method in which the researcher joins a specific audience group in order to observe their reactions to media from within the group

audience factor average number of audience members for a specific type of program or event

audience flow particular pattern shown by audiences who change radio or television channels throughout a given period of time

audience measurement research technique that identifies what kinds of audiences receive a particular kind of media product and how they react to it. The audience is determined according to some variable or set of variables (age, class, gender, ethnicity).

audience positioning advertising, designing, and showcasing a product in such a way as to appeal to an audience characterized as having certain demographic or psychographic features

audience segment specific group of individuals exposed to a media product. The group is determined according to some variable or set of variables (age, class, gender, ethnicity, specialized tastes, media habits).

audilog diary kept by selected audience members to record which television programs they watched over a given period of time. It was introduced by AC NIELSEN as a means of rating television shows.

audimeter electronic recording device that keeps track of when a television set is in use and to what station it is set. It was introduced

by AC NIELSEN to monitor viewing habits.

audio related to sound or its reproduction; recorded sound material of any kind, including the sound component of a video or film recording

audio branding building a brand identity through auditory association techniques, such as jingles and songs

audio console unit consisting of electronic and/or digital components such as a radio tuner or a disc player

audio description oral description of what is happening on screen for the visually impaired

audio feed sound recording sent from one place to another

audio insert device on video equipment that allows dubbing (the addition of new sound effects or dialogue to previously recorded material)

audio recording sound reproduction of any kind. The first device that allowed for sound reproduction was Thomas Edison's phonograph, invented in 1877.

audiocassette an AUDIOTAPE in a small plastic box for use in a tape recorder. Audiocassettes have virtually disappeared, having been replaced by other kinds of audio recording and playback devices.

audiology science devoted to the diagnosis and treatment of hearing problems. Audiologists also study the effect of partial or total hearing loss on a person's ability to communicate.

audiophile individual who has an avid interest in stereo or high-fidelity sound recordings

audiotape narrow magnetic tape used to record sound for subsequent playback

audiovisual [abbreviated as **AV**] materials, such as films and DVDs, that present information in audible and pictorial form

Audit Bureau of Circulation independent body consisting of members from the media and the advertising field, which provides circulation figures for print media. It also audits the circulation of print publications to insure that reported circulation figures are accurate. Web site: www .accessabc.com

Austin, John L. (1911–1960) British philosopher who developed a logical theory of speech acts, describing utterances in terms of the functions they have and the actions they are designed to bring about. His ideas are often cited in media and communication studies.

auteur filmmaker or director who is perceived as having a unique personal style or approach to filmmaking and who takes complete control over all aspects of film production

auteur theory view that a director may be regarded as a film's author, whether or not he or she wrote the script

author creator of a media product (book, poem, play, program, etc.). In traditional literary theory, the author is seen, implicitly, as the one who injects a personal viewpoint into a work; the role of the reader is to discern and comprehend the author's viewpoint. Recent theories, however, view the meaning of a work as resulting from a negotiation of meaning between the author and the reader.

authoring systems and software computer systems and/or software that allow for the creation of multimedia texts (texts that incorporate print, video clips, images, and sound)

authoritarian theory hypothesis which claims that the role of the press is to serve the interests of government, not of the citizenry, and should submit to governmental control

autobiography BIOGRAPHY of a person written by himself or herself. The term probably was coined by the British Romantic poet Robert Southey in 1809.

autofunction device used for video editing and playback that performs functions such as focusing or tracking

automatic dialogue replacement [abbreviated as **ADR**] process that allows actors to re-record dialogue while watching themselves on screen (during feature film production)

autonomy in aesthetic theory, the act of creating a work without any reliance on some other idea, cultural product, or value

autoscript type of prompting device or system used by television announcers or presenters

AV [*see* **audiovisual**]

availability time and number of slots in a medium available for advertising purposes

avant-garde experimental work whose style or content falls outside the mainstream

avatar 1. in VIRTUAL REALITY environments (such as certain types of Internet chat rooms), a picture, photograph, or animation of a human user, chosen by the user to depict his or her virtual-reality identity; 2. in advertising, a brand icon designed to move or morph freely across media

average audience 1. average number of homes or persons tuned into a radio or television program during a minute of broadcasting time; 2. average number of persons who viewed an issue of a print publication

average frequency 1. average number of times that the same individual is reached by the same advertising

campaign; 2. average number of opportunities that individuals have to view an advertisement

average hours per head average number of television viewing hours that an entire population spent, or could have spent, watching a particular program or series

average issue readership [abbreviated as **AIR**] estimated number of people who have read an issue of a publication during the period that it has been in print

average quarter-hour average number of people listening to a radio program, or watching a television program, during a 15-minute period

avi extension for a multimedia video format file

awareness test advertising research technique that measures the cumulative effect of an AD CAMPAIGN in terms of a product's ability to enter into consumer consciousness

axiom notion universally believed to be true and therefore accepted without proof. Mathematics, for instance, is constructed on the basis of axioms, which are consistent with one another and few in number.

Ayer Agency one of the first documented AD AGENCIES in the United States, founded by advertising pioneer Francis W. Ayer in 1869 in Philadelphia

B movie [also called **B picture**] 1. motion picture produced on a low budget; 2. low-budget motion picture produced to accompany the main feature of a double billing during the 1930s and 1940s

b2b advertising [*see* **business-to-business advertising**]

Babbage, Charles (1792–1871) English mathematician who designed a machine (called the analytical engine) that he claimed would be capable of carrying out complex operations. Although he never built even a working model of the machine, lacking appropriate technology and funding, its principles of design foreshadowed the modern computer. His book *Economy of Machines and Manufactures* (1832) became the basis of the field of study known today as *operational research.*

baby boomer individual belonging to an age category of people born during the period after the end of World War II (1945) through 1961. This category is quoted often in the media literature. Baby boomers constitute a market segment in advertising.

back catalog all the publications, recordings, videos, etc., that a particular artist or company has ever produced

back cover back of a book or magazine on which text is normally added

for various purposes (for advertising, to explain the contents of the book, etc.)

back issue previous issue or edition of a periodical

back projection cinematic technique in which the background for a scene is created by projecting images onto a screen that is behind the action being filmed; also called background projection or rear-screen projection

background 1. setting or part of scene (in a movie, photograph, etc.) that appears to be located at the back of the scene; 2. information that provides details or resources for a news story; a *background story* provides information on events that preceded the current news story

background music music that accompanies action or dialogue in a film or television program, usually added at the postproduction stage

backing 1. accompaniment provided for a solo musician or singer, usually recorded on a separate track; 2. in the theater, a flat piece of scenery placed behind an opening such as a window or door

backlist list of books that are not currently promoted by a publisher but that are still in print

backup 1. accompaniment to the main performer of a piece of popular music; 2. a reserve or replacement, as in backup computer files or a backup schedule for filming

badge distinctive branding that is given to a product in order to increase its appeal

Baird, John Logie (1888–1946) Scottish electrical engineer who was a pioneer in the televising of moving objects

Bakhtin, Mikhail (1895–1975) Russian literary theorist who claimed that communication, including both literature and dialogue among people, is not merely an exchange of information, but rather, a negotiation of meanings. Bakhtin also introduced the idea that pop culture serves the same kind of social functions as medieval carnivals. Among his most important works are *Problemy tvorchestva Dostoevskogo* (1929; revised in 1963 as *Problemy poetiki Dostoevskogo*; translated in 1973 as *Problems of Dostoyevsky's Poetics*) and *Voprosy literatury i estetiki* (1975; *The Dialogic Imagination*, 1981).

balance leveling of a signal coming from each channel in a stereo audio recording, so that the sound can be blended for various acoustic and aesthetic purposes

balanced programming the practice of giving fair and/or impartial coverage to a topic or issue

ballad 1. song or poem, in folk or traditional style, dealing with ro-

mance and love; 2. popular romantic song with a slow tempo

balloon in comics and cartoons, figure resembling a balloon, which contains words that represent either the speech or thoughts of a character

bandwagon effect advertising strategy that focuses on the pressure to conform to a commonly held view; it incorporates exaggerated claims that everyone is using a particular product

bandwidth 1. range of frequencies involved in radio and telecommunications transmission; 2. amount of data that a communication channel, such as an Internet connection, is capable of transmitting

bank 1. place of storage, such as a data bank; 2. secondary part of a headline, running just below it (normally in smaller type)

banned books books that have been banned from public libraries or schools for social, political, moral, or other reasons. Among the most famous banned books in the United States are *The Adventures of Huckleberry Finn* (Mark Twain), *Of Mice and Men* (John Steinbeck), and *The Catcher in the Rye* (J.D. Salinger).

banner 1. print media term for the headline of a story of unusual importance, stretching over the entire width of the page; 2. slogan used by a newspaper immediately below its

P.T. Barnum

in Europe in the late 1500s, lasting until the mid-1700s, characterized by ornamentation. In music the style is emblemized by the composers Johann Sebastian Bach (1685–1750) and Antonio Vivaldi (1678–1741).

barrier signal a defensive nonverbal signal, such as crossing the arms or holding a hand in front of the face

barter deal in television syndication, an arrangement whereby no money is exchanged between the local station and the syndicator. The syndicator offers a new program in exchange for a portion of advertising revenue.

title; 3. online advertising message that runs across the top of a Web page

banner exchange agreement between two businesses allowing banner advertisements to be displayed on each other's Web site

Barnum, P.T. (1810–1891) famous U.S. showman who presented such popular and sensationalized attractions as General Tom Thumb, a midget, and Chang and Eng, conjoined twins. With James Bailey, he founded the Barnum & Bailey Circus, which merged with the Ringling Brothers Circus in 1919 to become the Ringling Brothers and Barnum & Bailey Circus. To promote his attractions, Barnum relied on colorful advertising and publicity stunts.

Baroque style in painting, literature, and music that first appeared

Barthes, Roland (1915–1980) French semiotician who has become widely cited in media and pop culture studies, particularly concerning his view that modern systems of representation, as well as performances and spectacles, are recreations of ancient myths. Popular wrestling, for instance, is a complex performance in which bodies, facial expressions, gestures, and speech evoke ancient forms of theater and spectacle. Barthes was also a founder of the "New Criticism," a literary movement prominent after World War II, which emphasized the interpretation of a text itself, independent of authorial intentions or historical factors. His most quoted work in media studies is *Mythologies* (1957).

base and superstructure in Marxist theory, an economical system is called the "base" of society, around which a "superstructure" (consisting of laws, religion, culture, etc.) is constructed

base band 1. in telecommunications, the narrow range of frequencies required for transmitting a single message; 2. form of a satellite signal as it is being transmitted, before it is converted into sound and/or pictures

BASIC [abbreviation of **beginner's all-purpose symbolic instruction code**] a simplified high-level programming language developed in the mid-1960s by John Kemeny and Thomas Kurtz at Dartmouth College. It is widely considered to be one of the easiest programming languages to learn.

basic cable service package of television channels that a cable company makes available to subscribers, usually at a lower cost than packages that include premium channels

Basic Telecommunications Agreement of 1997 accord drawn up by the World Trade Organization to allow free trade for telecommunications services. The agreement was signed by 69 countries.

Bass's double action model of internal news flow (1969) model that describes news as being processed in two stages before release: first, by those who gathered the information (reporters, researchers, etc.), and second, by those who process the information to make it consistent with the values and norms of the news organization (editors, writers, etc.)

bathos sudden stylistic descent from the lofty to the trivial, producing a comical effect: or example, *What shall I do? I lost my best friend and my scarf!*

baud rate speed of data transfer within a network in bits per second

Baudrillard, Jean (1929–2007) French sociologist often quoted in media studies. Among Baudrillard's ideas, perhaps the one most discussed is that of the simulacrum, which claims that people have become so accustomed to viewing reality through the media that they are no longer capable of distinguishing practically between fact and fiction. The gap between the two is filled by a simulacrum, or a mode of seeing one in terms of the other. Among his most quoted works in the media literature are *La société de consommation* (1970; *The Consumer Society*, 1998) and *Simulacres et simulation* (1981; *Simulacra and Simulations*, 1994).

Bay Psalm Book the first book published in the American colonies in 1644; originally titled *The Whole Booke of Psalms*

BBC [*see* **British Broadcasting Corporation**]

beach box device that connects an external microphone to a digital video camera, designed to provide better sound recording quality

beam (n) 1. shaft of light; 2. directional radio signal; (v) 3. to broadcast radio or television signals

beat generation 1950s generation of American writers, including Jack Kerouac, Allen Ginsberg, William S. Burroughs, and Lawrence Ferlinghetti. Beat writers became famous for their eccentric lifestyle and literature, which was intended to denounce the American dream of wealth and prosperity. Their style was typically improvisational and dealt with the role of drugs, sex, and mysticism in modern human life. The beat writers are often considered to have set the stage for the hippie and counterculture movements of the 1960s.

bebop style of jazz music that originated in the 1940s, when a number of young American musicians began experimenting with more complicated chord patterns and melodic ideas in a combo (small group) setting

beginner's all-purpose symbolic instruction code [abbreviated as BASIC] programming language developed in the mid-1960s by John Kemeny and Thomas Kurtz at Dartmouth College. It is widely considered to be one of the easiest programming languages to learn.

behaviorism the study of observable and quantifiable behavior as the only legitimate form of psychological

inquiry (term coined in 1913 by John B. Watson). Behaviorism traces its roots to the ideas and methods of the Russian psychologist Ivan Pavlov. In 1904, Pavlov introduced the idea of *conditioned response*, on which behaviorism is based. He demonstrated the notion with an experiment that has become a classic in the annals of psychology. He started by presenting a piece of meat to a dog, noting that the animal would salivate instinctively, as anticipated. Pavlov called this the dog's *unconditioned response*. He then began to ring a bell while presenting the meat; after a number of repetitions, the dog began to salivate in response to the ringing bell, even if no meat were presented. The ringing, Pavlov noted, would not have made the dog salivate initially, but associating it with the meat eventually brought about a *conditioned response* in the dog. Starting in the 1960s, behaviorism became marginalized within psychology. Today it has been revived somewhat to explain certain types of behaviors and is thus viewed as part of a more comprehensive theory of human behavior. It is used as well in media studies to explain responses to mediated stimuli.

Bell, Alexander Graham (1847–1922) Scottish-born American inventor of an apparatus for the telephonic transmission of voice, first demonstrated in 1875, patented as the telephone in 1876.

Bell, Daniel (1919–) American sociologist whose work concerns the effects of political and economic structures, including mass media, on the individual. Among his frequently cited works are *The End of Ideology* (1960) and *The Cultural Contradictions of Capitalism* (1976).

below-the-fold 1. the lower half of the front page of a newspaper, generally considered to have less importance than the upper half; 2. the parts of a Web page that can be seen only by scrolling down the page

benchmark 1. point of reference; 2. in advertising, a measure of a target audience's response to the early stages of an advertising campaign, which is later compared to the response at the end, so as to test the efficacy of the campaign

Benedict, Ruth (1887–1948) American anthropologist who conducted important research on Native American cultures in the 1920s and 1930s. Benedict claimed that culture largely determined the choices that individuals made throughout their lives. Among her most influential works are *Patterns of Culture* (1934); *Zuñi Mythology* (1935); *Race: Science and Politics* (1940); and *The Chrysanthemum and the Sword: Patterns of Japanese Culture* (1946).

Benjamin, Walter (1892–1940) philosopher and aesthetician associated with the FRANKFURT SCHOOL, often cited in media literature with regard to his view that pop culture provides a channel for the release of pent-up emotions

Berne Convention [full form: **International Convention for the Protection of Literary and Artistic Works**] international copyright agreement, originally adopted in 1886. The agreement provides a framework for the protection of intellectual property, copyright, patents, and trademarks.

Berners Lee, Tim (1955–) inventor of the World Wide Web and director of the World Wide Web Consortium, which seeks to create protocols and standards for the sharing of information

Bernstein, Basil (1924–2000) British sociologist who developed the concept of social code as a means of understanding social beliefs and behaviors. Among his works are *Class, Codes, and Control* (1971) and *Pedagogy, Symbolic Control and Identity* (1996).

best seller product such as a book, compact disc, etc., that sells very well, often shortly after it is published or issued

BET [*see* **Black Entertainment Television**]

Beta trade name for a video format, known for the fact that it was overtaken in the consumer marketplace by VHS

Bettelheim, Bruno (1903–1990) American psychologist (born in

Austria) who is well-known in media studies for his penetrating analyses of fairy tales. Bettelheim claimed that the fairy tale represents a universal need to engage with the workings of the imagination and an innate sense of fantasy. Its elements (from the characters to its settings) are essentially ARCHETYPES, in the Jungian sense of the term. His major work is *The Uses of Enchantment: The Meaning and Importance of Fairy Tales* (1976).

Bezos, Jeffrey Preston (1964–) founder and CEO of Amazon.com (in 1994)

bias 1. failure to cover the news in an impartial manner (intentionally or not); 2. a high-frequency voltage combined with an audio signal during recording in order to reduce distortion

bibliography list of books, articles, etc., consulted and thus considered to be pertinent to a given subject. The *General Catalogue of Printed Books* maintained by the British Library, the catalogs of the Bibliothèque Nationale in Paris, and the Library of Congress in Washington, D.C., are widely used bibliographical collections. Publishers also issue bibliographies for informational (and publicity) purposes. In the United States, *Publishers Weekly* first appeared in 1872, and *Books in Print* in 1948. The International Federation for Documentation and the American Documentation Institute are institu-

tions that promote the standardization of bibliographical methods and research.

Big Band music music popular in the 1930s and 1940s, performed by large dance or jazz bands, usually featuring improvised solos by lead players

big beat [also called **electronica**] type of electronic music that blends elements of rock with other styles, distinguished by its constant rock-style drum beats

Big Brother concept introduced by George Orwell in his 1949 novel *1984*, describing a totalitarian society in which the government, like a "big brother," constantly watches and monitors its citizens in order to detect any signs of unrest or nonconformity

big city dailies newspapers published in cities such as New York, Los Angeles, Chicago, and Boston

Big Five studios the five major motion picture studios—Paramount, MGM, Warner Brothers, Twentieth Century Fox, and RKO—during the 1930s and 1940s

Big Four networks CBS, NBC, ABC, and Fox, the leading television networks (before the advent of cable and satellite television)

big idea an innovative new idea behind an ADVERTISING CAMPAIGN intended to attract potential consumers

big screen movies made to be seen in a movie theater rather than on television or on a Web site

Big Three networks the original networks—CBS, NBC, ABC—considered the leading television networks before the advent of Fox and of cable and satellite television

Bildungsroman literary genre that emerged in the early part of the Romantic period; a novel revolving around the development of a young protagonist in psychological and social terms. Perhaps the most famous *Bildungsroman* is Goethe's *The Sorrows of Young Werther* (1774). J.D. Salinger's *The Catcher in the Rye* (1951) is a well-known American example of the *Bildungsroman*.

billboard 1. outdoor advertising sign; 2. poster advertising a newspaper by showing the main headline of the day (usually found outside newspaper stands); 3. advertising message shown before, after, and during the breaks of a television program

billing 1. listing of performers, with prominence given to the leading performers; 2. way in which a performance, product, or spectacle is publicized

Biltereyst, Daniel (1962–) well-known scholar who has written on film censorship and reality television; his articles have been published in journals such as *European Journal of Communication* and *Journal of International Communication*.

binarism a STRUCTURALISM theory that we extract meaning from two forms (words, symbols, etc.) simultaneously by detecting a minimal difference between them. The words *cat* and *rat* differ minimally in terms of the initial sounds with which they are constructed. This *binary* difference keeps the two words distinct. Binarism can be applied to a vast array of forms; for example, in music the difference between a major and minor chord is signaled in a binary fashion by a semitone difference in the middle tone of the chord.

binary feature element that is either present [+] or absent [–] in the constitution of form, thereby keeping it distinct. The word *cat* is marked as [+singular] and *cats* as [–singular]. The [±singular] is a binary feature.

binary opposition refers to the fact that many aspects of meaning are perceived in terms of opposites, such as *good vs. evil, night vs. day*, etc. An opposition often leads to a connected set of derived oppositions. So, for example, in a narrative the *good* characters are opposed to the *evil* ones in terms of derived oppositions such as *us vs. them, right vs. wrong, truth vs. falsity*, and so on, which manifest themselves in actions, statements, plot twists, etc. In social theory, some binary oppositions, such as *self vs. other, us vs. them, man vs. woman, young vs. old*, are seen as potentially dangerous because of the tendency of people to identify with the positive element in the opposition, seeing the other as negative.

biodata biographical details about an individual

biography 1. account of a person's life in the form of a book, movie, television program, etc.; 2. literary genre dealing with people's lives as metaphors of life in general. In the ancient and medieval worlds, biographies were written primarily about the most prominent individuals— heroes, rulers, saints, etc. Giorgio Vasari's *Vite de' più eccellenti architetti, pittori e scultori italiani* (1550; *Lives of the Most Eminent Architects, Painters, and Sculptors*) marked a humanistic interest in the lives of other types of individuals. As a literary genre, the biography traces its roots to *The Life of Samuel Johnson, LL.D.* (1791) by James Boswell.

biopic [abbreviation of **biographical picture**] movie that presents the biography of (usually) a well-known person

biotechnology 1. use of microorganisms as agents to produce useful materials or aid in industrial processes; 2. application of technological facts and principles to biological science, as in bioengineering

bit [short for **binary digit**] the smallest unit of information handled by a computer; one character of a system that uses only two characters (0 and 1).

In groups of eight, bits become the familiar BYTES that are used to represent all types of information, including the letters of the alphabet and the digits 0 through 9.

bit caster radio station accessible only on the World Wide Web

bit map an image stored in the form of BITS. Bit maps cannot be enlarged without some distortion of quality.

BITNET [acronym for **Because It's Time Network** or **Because It's There Network**] network created in 1981 connecting computers in the educational and research domains (at universities, schools, institutes, etc.) to communicate news of developments in academic, scientific, and related matters.

biweekly newspaper or magazine that is published once every two weeks

black box technologies television systems (such as TiVo) that allow viewers to record and save programs by digital storage means rather than onto videotape, as with older VCR systems

Black Entertainment Television [abbreviated as **BET**] American cable network with programming targeted at African American audiences in the United States

black-and-white movie or photograph using only black and white

BlackBerry

BlackBerry trade name for a hand-held wireless device that provides e-mail and Internet services, along with phone, text messaging, and software applications

blacklist 1. list of people who are not approved or who are to be boycotted; 2. list of people from whom correspondence (especially e-mail correspondence) is not welcome

blackout any interruption or exclusion of a broadcast for technical reasons, on account of a labor dispute, or due to government prohibition

blanket coverage advertising to the general public (with no target group in mind)

blat slang term for tabloid newspaper

bleed 1. to print something so that the colors blend into each other; 2. to print something beyond the edge of a page

bleep out to efface an offensive word or phrase uttered on radio or television

blind booking practice of renting films to exhibitors without letting them view the films beforehand

blind certificate type of online COOKIE used to track which Web sites have been visited by an individual by identifying the computer system used

blink ad television commercial lasting just one second

blitz intensive, short-term marketing campaign

block-booking early movie studio tactic of getting theaters to accept marginal or inferior films in order to obtain access to major films with the most popular stars

block printing technique of printing from carved blocks of wood or other materials

blockbuster film or book that gains widespread popularity and achieves enormous sales

blockbuster era period from the 1970s onward, when movie studios started making relatively inexpensive movies for large audiences. These movies came packaged with cable deals, video/DVD products, etc.

blockbuster mentality movie-making philosophy characterized by the taking of reduced risks by producing movies with blockbuster potential

blog [abbreviation of **weblog**] Web site with a regularly updated list of commentary and links to information on the Internet. A blog often serves as a publicly accessible journal for an individual or community of individuals, and tends to reflect the distinct character and personality of the site's users. Blogs are set up with easy-to-use authoring tools.

blogosphere parts of the World Wide Web where bloggers communicate with each other

blogware software designed to help people set up blogging sites

blowup enlargement of a photograph, or part of a photograph, so that its details can be seen more clearly

blue-eyed soul soul music performed by white musicians, rather than African American musicians

bluegrass music type of folk music originating in the southern United States, typically played on banjos and guitars and characterized by rapid tempos and jazzlike improvisations

blues style of music that evolved from southern African American

secular songs in the early 1900s, distinguished by slow tempo and sorrowful melodies and lyrics and played on simple instruments. After 1950 some blues musicians, including B.B. King and Ray Charles, used electric guitars and louder electric basses. Record companies applied the terms *rhythm and blues* and *soul* to music in these styles.

Bluetooth trade name for a technology that enables portable electronic devices to connect with each other and the Internet

Blumler, Jay G. (1924–) one of the founders of USES AND GRATIFICATIONS THEORY. Among his key works are *Television in Politics* (with D. McQuail; 1968) and *The Uses of Mass Communication* (as editor, with E. Katz; 1974).

blurb short complimentary text, often written about a book on its cover or jacket

BMI [*see* **Broadcast Music Inc.**]

Boas, Franz (1858–1942) German-born American anthropologist who laid the foundations for modern theories about the effects of culture on human behavior and development. Boas argued that differences in human behavior are determined primarily by environment, not genetics. He was among the first to emphasize field research—studying a people by living among them. His books include *The Mind of Primitive*

Man (1911) and *Race, Language, and Culture* (1940).

body double actor whose job is to substitute for a starring actor for some reason during filming (for stunts, for specific action sequences, etc.)

body language set of mannerisms, gestures, postures, and facial expressions that represent or communicate something. The elements of body language are divided into *witting* (gestures, expressions, etc., used intentionally to communicate something) and *unwitting* (gestures, expressions, etc., used instinctively to reveal an emotional or affective state).

Bollywood name (mimicking "Hollywood") that refers to India's prolific movie industry

book collection or assemblage of pages held together in some way and containing verbal text and (sometimes) figures and illustrations. The clay tablets of ancient Mesopotamia and the scrolls of ancient Egypt, Greece, and Rome were the earliest books (or proto-books). By the fourth century C.E., a ringed assemblage, called a codex, became popular as a book form. It was made with wooden tablets covered with wax. In the early Middle Ages scribes in monasteries used quill pens to copy books. As a result of this costly process, books were rare objects, read primarily by clerics and aristocrats. The Chinese

had invented printing on paper from movable type in the eleventh century. Paper was introduced to Europe in the fifteenth century by Islamic scholars. The technology for movable metal type was perfected by the German printer Johannes Gutenberg, making the production of paper-based books rapid and much more affordable. The first book printed with such technology was the Bible in 1455. The mass-produced book encouraged literacy among all classes of people.

book club 1. organization that sells books to members, generally at reduced rates, such as *Book-of-the-Month Club* and *Literary Guild*; 2. informal group formed to read and discuss books

book superstores large book chains, such as Barnes & Noble and Borders, that sell not only books but also other products (videos, records, etc.) and usually include a coffee shop and other amenities

bookmark address of a Web site that is stored in a computer's memory so that it can be revisited easily

books on tape audiotape books that generally feature actors or authors as narrators of entire or abridged versions of popular fiction and trade books

boom long, adjustable stand or pole used to suspend a microphone or camera

boomerang response any audience response to a media text that is the opposite of the one intended

boosted sample used primarily for marketing purposes; to sample from a portion of a population, rather than the whole

bootlegging illegal pirating of CDs, DVDs, etc., that are produced and sold without permission from the original copyright holder

borderless world common reference to the global economy in the age of the Internet

Bourdieu, Pierre (1930–2002) French sociologist, well-known for his treatment of the notion of CULTURAL CAPITAL. Among his key works are *Sens pratique* (1980; *The Logic of Practice*, 1990) and *La distinction* (1979).

boutique agencies in advertising, small regional ADVERTISING AGENCIES that offer personalized services

bowdlerize to eliminate from a piece of writing whatever is construed as being obscene or offensive. The term was coined from the surname of Dr. Thomas Bowdler, the English editor who, in 1818, published Shakespeare's plays in an edition, titled *The Family Shakespeare*, from which he excised "those words and expressions which cannot with propriety be read aloud in a family."

box office 1. booth in a theater where tickets can be purchased; 2. income from ticket sales for a movie or entertainment event

brainwashing 1. severe, forcible indoctrination, usually with a political or religious intent, aimed at destroying someone's basic convictions and attitudes and replacing them with an alternative set of fixed beliefs; 2. application of a concentrated means of persuasion, such as an ADVERTISING CAMPAIGN, in order to induce a specific belief or motivation

brand 1. trademark or distinctive name identifying a product or a manufacturer; 2. product line so identified; for example, a popular brand of soap

brand awareness measure of how many people are aware of a brand and to what degree

brand development index [abbreviated as **BDI**] comparison of the percent of a brand's sales in a market to the percent of the national population in that same market

brand image imbuing a product with an identity or distinct "personality" by giving it an appealing name, designing a distinctive logo for it, devising appropriate pricing (for a specific market segment), associating it with a certain lifestyle through advertising, and so on

brand loyalty the tendency of consumers to buy the same brands they have bought in the past

brand magazine consumer magazine published by a retail company for readers with demographic characteristics that are similar to those consumers with whom the company normally does business

brand manager person who has marketing responsibilities for a specific brand

brand name product name that is designed to convey a specific IMAGE with which consumers can identify or relate to. In the last two decades of the nineteenth century many U.S. firms began to market packaged goods under brand names. Previously, such everyday household products as sugar, soap, rice, and molasses had been sold in neighborhood stores from large bulk containers. The first brand names of products date from about 1880, and include *Ivory*, *Pears*, *Sapolio*, *Colgate*, *Kirk's American Family*, and *Packer's*. Along with *Bon Ami*, *Wrigley*, and *Coca-Cola*, such products quickly became household names.

branding 1. practice of attaching distinctive meanings to a product, thus identifying it to consumers in a specific way (in terms of quality, in terms of its lifestyle connotations, etc.); 2. integration of brands with media events, programs, etc. Today, branding is used in cultural stud-

ies literature to refer to the process whereby the messages of brand advertising and those of other cultural sectors are no longer separate. Revlon, for instance, spent millions of dollars in the early 2000s for close-up shots of its products during the broadcasting of the American TV soap opera *All My Children*.

Break dancing acrobatic style of dancing to rap music, characterized by body spins on the ground

breakfast television informal, magazine-style television program broadcast early in the morning

breaking news unplanned news coverage of an event that is in the process of unfolding or has only recently happened

bricolage technique of putting together different elements from a media text to create something new. Bricolage involves the borrowing and mixture of sources to produce new forms. The notion has been used in particular to describe subcultures that appropriate elements of mainstream culture in order to transform or subvert their meanings (as in punk fashion).

Brin, Sergey (1973–) Russian-born American cofounder of Google, along with Larry Page

British Broadcasting Corporation [abbreviated as **BBC**] one of the first broadcasting systems, established in

1922 in the United Kingdom. The BBC is noncommercial and is, therefore, funded by an annual license fee paid by television owners.

British invasion a musical movement that began in 1964 when British rock bands such as the Beatles and the Rolling Stones achieved immense popularity in the United States and elsewhere

broadband high-speed connection capable of transmitting a large quantity of data. Cable TV uses broadband, and so do many computer connections.

Broadcast Music Inc. [abbreviated as **BMI**] agency that collects license fees on behalf of American music creators. It was established in 1939 by the American radio industry. Web site: www.bmi.com

broadcast radio radio programming reaching mass audiences. Experimental radio broadcasts began around 1910, when Lee De Forest produced a radio program from the Metropolitan Opera House in New York City, starring the famous opera singer Enrico Caruso. Many historians consider radio station WWJ, in Detroit, the first commercial radio station. It began regular broadcasts on August 20, 1920. Others claim the distinction for station KDKA in Pittsburgh. KDKA grew out of an experimental station that began in 1916. The station's broadcast of the 1920 U.S. presidential election results on

November 2, 1920, is generally considered to constitute the starting point of professional broadcasting.

broadcast spectrum portion of the electromagnetic spectrum on which the Federal Communications Commission allows broadcasters to transmit

broadcast television television programming reaching mass audiences. Experimental telecasts took place in the late 1920s and the 1930s. In the United States, CBS and NBC were leaders in such telecasts. In 1936 the RADIO CORPORATION OF AMERICA (later RCA Corporation), which owned NBC, installed television receivers in 150 homes in the New York City area. NBC's New York station began experimental telecasts to these homes. A cartoon of *Felix the Cat* was its first program. NBC established the first regular TV broadcasts in the United States in 1939. Television broadcasting was suspended in 1941, when the United States entered World War II, until after the war's end in 1945.

broadcasting transmission of programs (radio, television, Web-based, etc.) for public purposes and utilization. Many historians identify the Westinghouse Electric Corporation as the first commercially owned radio station to broadcast to the general public, shortly after World War I. The station was called KDKA, and it broadcast mainly variety programs. The American Telephone and

Telegraph Company was probably the first broadcaster to charge fees regularly, starting in 1922, for airing commercials. Early radio programming consisted of variety shows as well as adaptations of stage works redesigned for radio in the form of action serials, situation comedies, and so-called soap operas. The Public Broadcasting Act of 1967 led to the establishment of noncommercial broadcasting and the founding of the Public Broadcasting Service (PBS) in the United States. Public stations operate on contributions from various sources, including government, viewers, corporations, and benefactors. Broadcasting technologies continue to develop. Direct Broadcast Satellite (DBS) uses satellite signals for transmission.

broadsheet [also called (erroneously) **broadside**] 1. early colonial newspaper imported from England, consisting of a single sheet; 2. full-size newspaper; 3. a newspaper that covers the news in a serious, informative way

brochure booklet or pamphlet containing advertising material

Bronze Lion award for advertising given at the Cannes International Advertising Festival

browse to look up and view Web sites

browser software program allowing a user to browse the Internet and to download and view Web files

buddy movie film genre that focuses on the relationship between friends

buffoonery comedy characterized by ridiculous jokes, antics, and tricks

bulk mail mail (usually advertising) that is sent by regular (snail) mail at reduced rates

bulk rate reduced rate offered to advertisers who buy large amounts of advertising space

bull's-eye model of communication model that depicts communication as a mathematical process dependent on probability factors, that is, on the degree to which a message is to be expected or not in a given situation. It is called the *bull's-eye model* because it envisions the process as consisting of a *sender* aiming a *message* at a *receiver* as if in a bull's-eye target range:

bullet model [alternative name for **hypodermic needle model**] model positing that media have direct powerful effects on people

bulletin board Web site that allows members of an interest group to exchange messages, chat online, and exchange software

Bulletin Board System precursor to the Internet, using software capable of dialing up a connection and uploading and downloading information

bundling any transmission system that allows for the delivery of television, video-on-demand, audio, high-speed Internet access, phone service, and fax via cable

burden of representation 1. the difficulties that media face when they use a single personage to represent an entire group; 2. the fact that a few personages from a previously under-represented group in the media will bear the burden of promoting a positive role model for the entire group

burlesque variety show that includes comedy skits and sometimes a strip-tease act. The term was used originally to characterize the plays of the Greek dramatists Aristophanes and Euripides and the Roman playwright Plautus. The two main genres of literary burlesque are known as the mock epic (which treats a lofty subject in a ludicrous way) and the travesty (which satirizes a serious subject in a frivolous way). In the United States, the word was applied to a form of theater that became the rage in the 1920s and 1930s, characterized by comedy acts, musical acts, and the striptease.

burn to copy data onto a compact disc, DVD, or other digital format

burst campaign concentrated advertising period for a product, especially before it is launched

bus physical signal path that allows signals to travel between system components within a device such as a computer or set-top box, or between computers in a network

business-to-business advertising advertising aimed at businesses and not at consumers

button fatigue in television audience measurement research, the phenomenon of weary viewers failing to log on and report their viewing habits

buying motive explanation of consumers' desires to purchase particular products

byline identification, usually printed at the beginning of an article, of the journalist or reporter who is responsible for the story

byte basic unit of electronic data storage, equal to 8 BITS. Files and computer memory are measured in bytes, kilobytes, megabytes, or gigabytes.

cabaret 1. club or restaurant that provides entertainment consisting of singing, dancing, or comedy; 2. the show that takes place at a cabaret

cable wire or bundle of wires that carry electric current, or a bundle of glass fibers that carry pulses of light. Cables provide the most practical means of transmitting communications signals.

cable drop system system connecting individual homes to the coaxial cable that distributes cable television

cable modem modem connecting a computer to the Internet via a specified INTERNET SERVICE PROVIDER

cable network television network that consists of channels distributed by companies to paying subscribers (usually by transmitting signals via cables, rather than through the air)

Cable News Network [abbreviated as **CNN**] international news broadcasting company, based in the United States and founded in 1980, which was the first to introduce 24-hour news coverage

cable telephony telephone service offered by a cable television company

cable television television service via cable. Cable television was first used in the late 1940s in order to broadcast television signals to places that either could not receive them through the air, or who could receive them only with much interference. Some cable systems carry more than 100 channels; this large number has made NARROWCASTING possible. Unlike broadcasting, which tries to appeal to the largest possible audience, narrowcasting offers programs that appeal to a particular interest. Cable channels may specialize in news, movies, comedy, science, music, health, religion, weather, and so on. Customers pay a monthly fee for service, plus additional fees for certain channels. Most cable services also offer one or more channels that make movies or special events available on a pay-per-view basis. These can be ordered either by telephone or through a set-top box.

cablecast any broadcast that is transmitted via a cable television network

cache area in a computer's memory that stores frequently used data so that it can be retrieved more quickly than data stored the computer's internal hard disk. Caches allow a user faster access to Web pages because the cache stores these in a temporary file.

cacophony literary and rhetorical technique aimed at creating a dissonant effect through the use of words with harsh sounds: for example, *yuk* for *disgust*; *blah* for *boring*

callback 1. practice of interviewers or researchers of making a further attempt to contact a person or group for an interview; 2. a second audition for a role in theater, television, or film

calligraphy art of handwriting, usually perceived as being beautiful or artistic

call-in phone call from a radio listener or a television viewer to a talk show, a current affairs program, etc., upon invitation of the program to do so

calotype early system of photography using translucent paper from which prints could be made

calypso 1. Caribbean ballad, especially Trinidadian, consisting of syncopated rhythms and usually dealing satirically with public issues; 2. Caribbean dance music, often played by a steel band

camcorder portable video camera and recorder

cameo 1. in literature, a brief depiction of someone or something; 2. brief appearance of a well-known actor in a scene in a movie, television program, etc. (also called a *cameo role* or *appearance*)

cameo appearance single brief appearance by a well-known performer in a play, movie, or television program

camera 1. device for taking photographs or motion pictures; 2. part of a device that converts images into electronic impulses for television broadcasting

camera angle relation between the position of a camera to the action being filmed (higher, lower, closer, etc.) in order to provide a different view of the action

camera control unit console in a television production room that controls the cameras on the studio floor remotely

camera lucida instrument that projects an image onto a surface such as a piece of paper (so that the image can be traced)

camera obscura instrument that uses a dark chamber with a small aperture that brings the image of an outside object into focus on a facing surface. The camera obscura is the precursor of the modern camera.

cameraperson [previously **cameraman** or **camerawoman**] someone who operates a movie or television camera

camera-ready material that is in its finished format, ready to be photographed or scanned for publication

camera shot 1. the part of the subject that is recorded on film by a camera; 2. a particular view of a scene, a person, etc.

camera work series of camera techniques used in shooting movies or in making television programs

camp a style of performance that is affectedly feminine, exaggerated, or deliberately brash in an amusing manner

campaign journalism 1. journalism that relates to the events, issues, etc., that come up during a political campaign; 2. by extension, any type of journalism that reports a story from a particular viewpoint in order to promote a cause

Campbell, Joseph (1904–1987) American scholar famous for his ideas and writings on myth, based on the writings of Sigmund Freud and Carl Jung and the novels of James Joyce and Thomas Mann. Campbell analyzed the ARCHETYPES that surface in all myths (the hero, the mother, the father, the trickster, the journey, etc.). His book *The Hero with a Thousand Faces* (1949) has influenced many subsequent studies of myth. Campbell's four-volume *Masks of God* (1959–1967) has also become a classic in the field.

Canadian Broadcasting Corporation [abbreviated as **CBC**; also called **Société Radio-Canada**] government-owned public service Canadian radio and television network. The CBC operates two television networks; one broadcasts in English and the other in French. The CBC also operates two cable television news networks.

Cannes Film Festival Poster, September 1939 (The actual event was postponed to 1946, after World War II.)

candid camera hidden camera used to film people unawares, often in situations designed to elicit amusing responses

canned laughter prerecorded laughter used for a specific broadcast event (especially for a sitcom) in place of a real audience

Cannes Film Festival one of the oldest and most prestigious film festivals in the world, held each May in the city of Cannes in southeastern France

Cannes Lions International Advertising Festival annual festival held to recognize the best advertisements, including television commercials, print marketing, direct marketing, and online advertising. The festival awards the prestigious Palme d'Or to the best production company.

canon 1. in aesthetic theory, the standard by which a work is judged; 2. a sanctioned or authenticated group of literary works

cant 1. group-based language with its own distinctive markers (tone, grammatical features), especially jargon; 2. boring style of speech characterized by clichés and worn-out phrases.

Cantril Study famous media effects study, conducted by Hadley Cantril and his team of researchers at Princeton University following the famous "War of the Worlds" broadcast of 1939 by Orson Welles as part of *Mercury Theater of the Air Presents.* The broadcast was a radio version of H.G. Welles's 1898 novel, but it interspersed fake "news" reports of Martian landings in New Jersey, which were so realistic that near panics occurred in many areas—despite periodic announcements by CBS that the program was merely a dramatization. The Cantril researchers wanted to find out why some listeners believed the fake reports and others did not. After interviewing 135 people, the team came to the conclusion that the key was critical thinking—better-educated listeners were more capable of recognizing the broadcast as a fake than were less-educated ones. The study was origi-

nally published in 1940 by Princeton University Press.

CAP codes [full form: **Committee of Advertising Practice codes**] codes of advertising standards and practices, drawn up by the Committee of Advertising Practice (a U.K. agency), designed to protect consumers

capitalism political and economic system based on the private ownership of the means of production and distribution of goods. Capitalism is characterized by a free competitive market and by the "profit motive."

caption 1. tagline for an advertisement; 2. verbal text accompanying an illustration or photograph; 3. short on-screen text that explains or relates to the visual image (for example, the name of the person who is talking)

capture theory view that regulators are influenced by the interests of the industries they regulate

car card [also called **bus card**] poster placed on buses, subway cars, etc.

card rate advertising charge without any discounts

caret symbol written on a section of text indicating where something (a letter or a word) is to be inserted

caricature distorted or exaggerated visual portrayal of someone (usually

Caricature of Charles Dickens (1868)
by André Gill

exhibits, games, rides, and shows; 2. feasting and merrymaking just before Lent. The idea of carnival has been used to explain the appeal of pop culture spectacles, which allow people to temporarily ignore the restrictions by which they normally abide.

carrier company that delivers telecommunications messages

cartel large group of businesses that agree to operate as a monopoly, especially to regulate prices and production

cartoon drawing that caricatures an event or personage. There are three main types of cartoons: *editorial cartoons*, which caricature current events in magazines and newspapers; *gag cartoons*, which usually caricature groups rather than individuals, in magazines and on greeting cards; and *illustrative cartoons*, which are used to illuminate aspects of a new product or educational topic in a humorous way. The term is also used to refer to strips of drawings (comic strips) and to animated humorous

a well-known personage) for comical effect. By extension the term is used to refer to any representation of this kind, including verbal. The use of caricature can be traced to the ancient Egyptians and Greeks. It was also used by Italian artists of the Renaissance. In the eighteenth century it emerged as a form of satire. Spanish painter Francisco José de Goya, for instance, used caricature to satirize political and social injustices in his 80 etchings called *Caprichos* (1799). In 1841, the English weekly magazine *Punch* became the first magazine to use caricature. In the United States, *The New Yorker* magazine continues the tradition.

carnival 1. traditional form of outdoor amusement that consists of

Looney Tunes characters Sylvester and Tweety, introduced in the 1940s.

films intended primarily for children (also called *toons*).

cascading style sheet technique for storing font, spacing, and color information in a style sheet that can be applied to any text on a Web page

case study analysis based on exhaustive compilation of data regarding an individual or group

case-study method method of media research that makes use of a group of case studies from which to draw general conclusions and principles

cassette sealed plastic device containing audiotape or videotape

cassette recorder device for recording and playing audiotape or videotape

cast actors and other performers who play the parts in a play, dance, movie, etc.

Castells, Manuel (1942–) Marxist theorist known for his critical studies of media. His key works include *The Urban Question: A Marxist Approach* (1977) and *City, Class and Power* (1978).

casting agency agency that auditions and hires actors for a particular production

Casting Society of America [abbreviated as **CSA**] American association of film, television, and theater casting directors, founded in 1982

castoff estimate of how much space a piece of text will occupy when it is printed

casualization the trend in the media industry of full-time jobs becoming increasingly reorganized into part-time or project-based employment

catachresis vague, improper or ambiguous use of language for effect: for example, the misuse of the suffix *-ish* to mean "bad qualities" as *clownish*, *childish*, etc.

catalog album in record retailing, any album that is more than three years old

catalyst effect the support the media can garner for an issue simply by showcasing it, leading to an increased interest in the issue, to financial commitment to it on the part of audiences, etc.

catchline word or phrase at the top of a script that identifies an item on a program

catchword first word or phrase on a page of printed text, designed to draw attention to it

catharsis the "purification" or "emotional release" that the theatrical representation of tragic events has on an audience (as coined by ARISTOTLE). Through the tragic drama, the audience's pent-up emotions are sublimated and thus cleansed. This term is now used in media studies to refer to the purported purging effect of some media representations.

catharsis hypothesis claim that the representation of sexuality and violence in media has a preventive effect. The claim posits that engaging in fantasy sex or violence releases potentially negative impulses that otherwise might be acted out in real life.

cathode-ray tube outmoded vacuum tube used on older television sets for creating images and text on a screen

CATV [*see* **community antenna television**]

CBC [*see* **Canadian Broadcasting Corporation**]

CBS [*see* **Columbia Broadcasting System**]

CD [*see* **compact disc**]

CD-ROM [*see* **compact disc read-only memory**]

CD-RW [*see* **compact disc rewritable**]

cease-and-desist order directive issued by a regulatory agency, such as the Federal Trade Commission, requiring an advertiser to stop running a deceptive or unfair advertisement, campaign, or claim

celebrity person who is widely known primarily because of media

exposure. A celebrity is usually an actor, a television personality, a pop musician, etc.

cellular phone [also called **cell phone**] wireless telephone that transmits and receives messages via radio signals. It enables people to communicate over a wide area by using a network of radio antennas and transmitters arranged in small geographical areas called cells. The first commercial cellular system went into operation in 1983 in the United States. Cellular service is now available throughout most of the world.

cellular radio radio that receives frequencies that operate in cells according to position. This reception allows car radios to be swapped to the right frequency as the car travels from cell area to cell area.

celluloid 1. photographic film used in making movies; 2. by extension, the cinema as an art form

censorship the control of what people may say, hear, write, or read. In most cases, this kind of control comes from a government agency or from various types of private groups. Censorship can be directed at books, newspapers, magazines, motion pictures, radio and television programs, and speeches. It also may influence music, painting, sculpture, and other arts. In the United States, the Bill of Rights and the Supreme Court serve as checks on unlimited censorship.

censorware term used to describe Web content-filtering software

central processing unit [abbreviated as **CPU**] microprocessor chip that translates commands and runs programs. The CPU coordinates computer functions, retrieves instructions from memory, executes instructions, and stores results in memory locations.

centralized organizational structure a method of organizing international ADVERTISING CAMPAIGNS whereby decision making occurs through a company's central office

Certeau, Michel de (1925–1986) French scholar who wrote influential books critiquing pop culture and mass media, including *L'invention du quotidien* (1980; published in English as *The Practice of Everyday Life*, 1984) and *Heterologies: Discourse on the Other* (1986).

chain break pause for station identification and commercials during a network telecast

channel 1. physical system used in the transmission of signals (such as the air in speaking); 2. television or radio station broadcasting on a specified frequency band

channel capacity amount of information that a communications system can carry

channel of communication any system (antenna, cable, etc.) capable of transmitting information

channel of distribution route used by a company to distribute its products (through wholesalers, retailers, mail order, etc.)

channel surfing [also called **channel-hopping**] going from channel to channel (with a remote control) with no particular program in mind

chanson de geste one of more than 80 Old French epic poems of the eleventh to the fourteenth centuries celebrating the deeds of historical or legendary figures, especially the exploits of Charlemagne and his successors. The *Chanson de Roland* (circa 1100), attributed to the Norman poet Turold, is the most popular of the chansons. It recounts the Battle of Roncesvalles in 778 and the heroic feats of Roland, a knight of Charlemagne's court. Roland's death in a suicide-like defense of a mountain pass renders him a Christian martyr.

character 1. role played (by an actor) on stage, in a movie, etc.; 2. personage depicted in a text (a play, a novel, a movie, etc.); 3. famous or well-known person (also called a *personage*); 4. symbol used in a writing system or code (for example, a computer code)

character actor actor who normally plays a particular type of role (the "bad guy," the "sidekick," etc.)

charade game in which two competing groups of participants choose a team member to act out the syllables of a hidden word or an entire phrase using pantomime so that the group members can guess the word or phrase

charge artist member of a theater troupe who is responsible for overseeing the physical layout and appearance of a stage

charts list of the best-selling musical recordings over a given time period (week, month, etc.)

chat group group of computer users sharing a common interest who communicate with each other on-line

chat room Web site where computer users can exchange messages in real time

chauvinism excessive or biased allegiance to a particular gender, group, or cause

checkbook journalism practice of paying money to get an exclusive story that will purportedly sell many copies of a newspaper or magazine and/or bring prestige upon the journalist

chiaroscuro use of light and dark colors or shades together in drawing, painting, or cinematic representation to emphasize contrast. Prominent artists who used the technique include Leonardo da Vinci, Raphael, Michelangelo Merisi da Caravaggio, Georges de La Tour, and Rembrandt.

chiasmus rhetorical technique consisting of the inversion of two parallel phrases or clauses: *I went to New York*; *to Chicago went he*

Chicago School school of philosophical inquiry at the University of Chicago between 1894 and 1904. Founded by John Dewey (1859–1952), its notable members included George H. Mead, James H. Tufts, James R. Angell, Edward Scribner Ames, and Addison W. Moore. The Chicago School sought to apply the principles of pragmatism to social inquiry. As such, it rejected strictly empirical approaches and attempted to understand the ways in which human groups shaped meanings collectively and interactively. This implied a systematic questioning of received notions and standard explanations that makes the Chicago School a representative of critical inquiry. A leading contemporary exponent of Chicago School pragmatism is philosopher Richard Rorty.

chick flick film that is intended or perceived to appeal primarily to women, given its romantic or sentimental plot, or its focus on human relationships or the changing role of women in society

chief income earner in marketing, the individual in a household earning the highest income

chief shopper in marketing, the individual who does the shopping for the household

Noam Chomsky

duced the phrase "manufacturing consent" to refer to the manipulation of the media in order to gain a consensus on political ideologies and programs. Among his works are *Manufacturing Consent: The Political Economy of the Mass Media* (1988) and *Media Control* (1997).

chopsocky genre of film featuring violent martial arts action

choreography art of planning a dance and other movements or forms that accompany music

children's movies films that are intended to appeal to children. The pioneer in this area was Walt Disney (1901–1966), who first became known in the late 1920s and 1930s for creating such cartoon film characters as Mickey Mouse and Donald Duck. He later produced feature-length cartoon films as well as movies about wild animals in their natural surroundings and films starring human actors.

children's television television programming, including television channels, intended to appeal primarily to children, consisting typically of cartoons, educational stories, and the like.

Chomsky, Noam (1928–) American linguist and social critic, internationally renowned for his methods of linguistic analysis and his work on power structures in media and the dangers of globalization. He intro-

chorus 1. group of people who sing together; 2. type of song performed by many singers together; 3. repeated part of a song coming after each stanza, in which a whole group of singers often joins the soloist; 4. in ancient Greek drama, group of singers and dancers who engage in dialogue with the actors and comment on the action on stage

chroma key filming technique whereby the background of a filmed scene is altered or replaced without affecting the foreground

chromaticism 1. style or composition in music based on the chromatic scale (a scale consisting of twelve notes whereby every note is a semitone apart from the next one; 2. the science of colors

chronemics study of cultural history in terms of eras, dates, and the significant events associated with them

chronicle long historical narrative, often including legends and myths, presented in chronological order

chronology order in which events occur, and its significance to a storyline or to some other aspect of a movie, program, etc.

churn the turnover in cable subscribership, whereby the number of new subscriptions offsets the number of cancellations

cine club independent rival to conventional movie theaters, typically showing independent films

cineaste filmmaker or any film enthusiast

cinema art, industry, or business of making movies developed originally from the technology of moving pictures. According to most historians, the first true movies were the ten-part version of the trial of French army officer *Alfred Dreyfus* (1899); *Cinderella* (1900); and *A Trip to the Moon* (1902) by French magician Georges Méliès. Although shown originally in Paris, Méliès's films were an instant success and were subsequently shown in many countries. In the United States, Edwin S. Porter's 1903 film, *The Great Train Robbery*, became a sensational hit.

cinema advertising advertising shown on cinema screens before the featured film

cinéma vérité 1. cinematic style stressing the stark, realistic portrayal of life, as seen in Carl-Theodor Dreyer's *La passion de Jeanne d'Arc* (1928) and Luis Buñuel's and Salvador Dalí's *Un chien andalou* (1929); 2. alternate term for DOCUMENTARY, meaning literally the "cinema of reality"

CinemaScope brand name for an early widescreen projection system for movies, developed in 1953 by Twentieth Century Fox, intended primarily to lure the curious away from their television sets

cinematheque small movie theater with an intimate atmosphere

cinematic relating to films, filmmaking, or to the style in which films are made

cinematographer person responsible for the lighting and camerawork in the making of a movie

cinematography the art or technique of shooting movies

Cinerama trade name for a method, introduced in the 1950s, of producing early widescreen movies with enhanced three-dimensional effects; like CINEMASCOPE, Cinerama was intended to attract people to the movie theaters and away from their television sets

circular advertisement (or similar text) distributed to a large number of people

circulation average number of copies distributed of some publication (newspaper, magazine, etc.) during a given period. In advertising, this term is also used to refer to the total number of people who have an opportunity to observe a billboard or poster.

citizen journalism [also called **civic journalism**] practice centered on the participation of readers and journalists in community issues, making newspapers a forum for discussion and engagement

city desk newspaper section devoted to financial topics and/or local news

city editor newspaper editor who is responsible for financial news and/or local news

civil society a society in which institutions, social relationships, and organizations operate under the rule of the state, but are not necessarily aligned with it

clandestine stations illegal or unlicensed broadcast stations operated by clandestine groups or agencies (revolutionary subcultures, intelligence agencies, etc.)

clapper board pair of hinged boards used at the start of each take in a film, identifying the film and scene

classic rock rock music of the 1960s and early 1970s, associated especially with the hippie movement

classical music music composed by musicians considered to be the founders of high musical art (Bach, Mozart, Beethoven, Chopin, etc.). The term *classical music* is used to contrast with *popular music*, which includes country music, jazz, and rock music. *Classical* also has other meanings. If capitalized, it refers to a style of music that developed in the late 1700s.

classical narrative structure dominant mode of storytelling found in Hollywood films, consisting of three distinct stages: a state of equilibrium or order; a period of disruption to that state; and a climactic resolution that restores the equilibrium

classicism 1. a literary and artistic style associated with the ancient Greeks and Romans; 2. a style, movement, or period distinguished by qualities that suggest ancient classical art and writing: for example, the art and music of the period that spans the mid-1700s to around 1820 is called *classical*

classification system of identifying movies according to content: PG, PG-13, R, etc.

classified ad small notice, usually on a special page of a newspaper or magazine, indicating that something is wanted or offered (a job, an apartment, a pet, a car, etc.). Classified ads are usually grouped into categories, such as "real estate," "help wanted," etc.

Claymation trade name for a stop-frame animation method that uses clay figurines

clean feed 1. video recording without captions; 2. sound recording without commentary; 3. earpiece used by radio or television announcers so that they can hear all sound apart from their own statements

cliché word or phrase that has lost its original effectiveness through over-use: for example, *All's well that end's well*; *Father Time*; *Mother Nature*; *lips sweeter than wine*

click stream the series of choices (clicks) made by a user or browser on the Web

click through clicking on a banner ad or other onscreen ad that allows the user to get to the advertiser's Web site

click through rate fee applied to advertisers for the display of banner ads. Each time a visitor clicks through the ad, the advertiser is charged a fee.

cliffhanger story, play, or motion picture that depends on strong and sustained suspense for its dramatic interest

climax 1. rhetorical technique consisting of the progressive arrangement of ideas from the least to the most forceful: *First we comment on what they did, then we attack them,* *and finally we obliterate them*; 2. point at which a narrative, performance, etc., takes a decisive turn

Clio Award annual award for excellence in product package design and brand advertising

clip extract from a recording

clip art commercially produced artwork, usually copyright-free, available on-line and through many digital products (such as CD-ROMs), that can be used to enhance presentations of text

closed captioned any television broadcast that has captions that can be seen at the bottom of the television screen if the television set has the appropriate device

closed-circuit television television system in which video cameras are hooked up by cable to monitors. Surveillance systems use this type of television.

closed text a type of text (usually narrative) from which only a limited range of meanings can be extracted (term coined by UMBERTO ECO). Detective or crime scene stories are usually closed texts because the idea is to figure out the identity of the murderer or criminal. An *open text*, on the other hand, is one from which readers can extract multiple meanings.

close-up filmed shot that shows a person's face (or other part of the body), to the exclusion of other parts

cluster group group of people with similar traits (lifestyle, social background, etc.) for the purpose of audience analysis

clutter the appearance of many separate commercials during one television commercial break

CNN [*see* **Cable News Network**]

cobranding practice of displaying two or more corporate logos in certain venues (such as in bookstores where coffee brands are sold), on a product Web site, etc., to indicate joint business partnership

cobweb site Web site that has not been updated in a long time

co-culture a cultural strand that exists alongside a mainstream culture. For example, some aboriginal societies have preserved their original cultures, which exist alongside mainstream culture.

coda 1. in music, a section at the end that brings the work to a formal conclusion; 2. by extension, any concluding addition to a text (verbal, artistic, etc.)

code 1. system of signs with specific functions (alphabet code, decimal number system, etc.); 2. system of cultural meanings implicit in a media product that is built into it. Basically, a code is a system of elements (features, traits, meanings, images, etc.) that we perceive to be a part of

something. For example, the code that underlies an action adventure hero is based on the ancient view of heroes as having superhuman strength, as being moral and good-looking, as having (often) some tragic flaw or weakness, and so on. This code is implicit in how fictional heroes are portrayed. One of the first to use code theory to study media and pop culture was ROLAND BARTHES, who claimed that a print ad, for example, can be decoded (understood) as a text with two levels—the literal level, consisting of the objects and straightforward message of the ad, which is a "noncoded" level; and the symbolic level, based on ideological and cultural meanings, which is the "coded" level. STUART HALL argues that sometimes the audience does not actually receive the coded message of a media text, but rather that it can decode it in oppositional ways, that is, in ways that the maker of the text did not anticipate or desire.

codes of narrative a set of codes supposedly underlying narrative texts singularly, in part, or in combination. These include ACTION CODE, ENIGMA CODE, REFERENTIAL CODE, SEMANTIC CODE, SYMBOLIC CODE

codex 1. book formed by putting together sheets of paper; 2. collection of ancient manuscripts in book form. The codex was popularized by early Christians, who cut pieces of papyrus into sheets and sewed them together on one side. They bound the pages with thin pieces of wood. As a result, a reader could open it at any page. The codex remains the major book form today.

cognition faculty of knowing based on reasoning, intuition, or perception, or a combination of these

cognitive dissonance sense of anxiety resulting from a discrepancy between beliefs and actions, such as opposing air pollution while engaging in activities, like driving, that cause pollution (term coined by American psychologist Leon Festinger). To avoid this sense of anxiety, people will typically search for information that will confirm or reinforce their beliefs, rather than contradict them.

cognitive psychology theory theory of media claiming that exposure to media shapes cognition

cognitive style mode or way in which information is processed: for example, *auditory* cognitive style (= processing information audio-orally), *visual* cognitive style (= processing information visually), and so on

cognitivism 1. psychology movement or school, which emerged in the 1950s, emphasizing the study of mental processes by seeking parallels between brain function and computer operations; 2. general approach in psychology that focuses on how the mind handles different kinds of information and problems

cold medium [also called **cool medium**, as opposed to **hot medium**] according to MARSHALL MCLUHAN, any medium that requires a greater degree of interaction from the user in order to determine meaning

collage a work of art created by cutting, arranging, and adhering various materials, such as cloth, paper, photos, and other objects, onto a surface

collateral materials the print, visual, and other materials that go into a marketing or advertising campaign

collective identity identification with a community or the institutions by which it is represented, based on gender, class, lifestyle, and nation

collective representation creation of media texts or products by a community that reveal something crucial about it (its history, beliefs, etc.)

collective unconscious As defined by CARL GUSTAV JUNG, an inherited part of the unconscious mind that is shared by all members of a culture. It includes thought patterns called ARCHETYPES, which have developed through the centuries. According to Jung, archetypes enable people to react to situations in ways similar to their ancestors. For this reason, the collective unconscious contains wisdom that guides all humanity.

collocation the meaning that a word or phrase develops by virtue of its association with other words that are used commonly with it. For example, *pretty* is linked with *girl, boy, woman, flower, garden, color,* etc. (e.g., *pretty girl, pretty boy*); whereas *handsome* is associated with *man, vessel, overcoat, airliner,* etc. (e.g., *handsome man, handsome vessel*). The collocation may overlap, but when it does, it involves subtle nuances in meaning: for example, *pretty boy* vs. *handsome boy.*

colonialism 1. the rule of a group of people by a foreign power; 2. in Marxist theory, any form of economic, political, or social oppression (unjust treatment) of one group by a group of different cultural background

colonization in advertising, use of the symbolism of a culture in order to appeal to its members

color field painting technique established by a group of artists during the 1950s and 1960s that aimed to reduce painting to the purity of color on a flat plane

color grading process of preparing film so that color effects are uniform throughout the movie (now done digitally)

color temperature warmth of any color as measured on the Kelvin scale

colorcast television program broadcast in color

Columbia Broadcasting System [abbreviated as **CBS**] early television network that, along with ABC and NBC, was one of the BIG THREE in the golden era of television, from the 1950s to the 1970s. CBS is best known in the annals of broadcasting history for the work of broadcaster Edward R. Murrow (1908–1965), who become renowned during World War II (1939–1945) for his on-the-scene radio broadcasts describing German bombing attacks on London. His listeners in America could hear the bombs exploding in the background.

Columbia Pictures early Hollywood studio established in 1914, producing many popular family films, including *The Karate Kid* (1984) and the *Spider-Man* films (from 2002).

column article in a newspaper or magazine that appears on a regular basis, and that is usually written by the same person, usually on the same subject. For example, *Dear Abby,* one of the most famous advice columns, was written under the name of Abigail Van Buren starting in 1956. The column has been published in over 1,200 newspapers in the United States and other countries. It consists of responses to reader questions about such subjects as family life, marriage, health, death, and social issues.

comedy form of drama or entertainment that deals with humorous or ridiculous aspects of human behavior

comedy-variety hour television entertainment program that features a wide variety of acts

comic book magazine using cartoon characters. Most tell stories, though they have also been used for education, artistic expression, and other purposes. Because of their popularity, characters from comic books have been used in advertising. Many characters have also appeared on radio and television and in motion pictures, as well as in books, plays, songs, and as toys. Characters called *superheroes*, who have extraordinary powers, are especially popular. Among the first American comic books are the *Famous Funnies* (first sold in 1934). In 1938 Jerry Siegel and Joe Shuster put out the first *Superman* comic, one of the most popular characters in the history of comic books. Superman inspired the creation of other heroes, notably Captain Marvel and Batman. Starting in the 1970s, many independent or "alternative" artists experimented with new styles, more sophisticated formats, and stories suited to adults; this form is usually called a graphic novel. The most celebrated examples are *Maus: A Survivor's Tale* (1986) and *Maus II* (1991) by Art Spiegelman. They tell of the artist's relationship with his father and the experiences of his parents in the Holocaust.

comic-book movie genre of film based on a comic book, comic book character, or comic strip

First issue of *Spider-Man* (1962)

comic opera opera with a humorous plot and a happy ending

comic relief interlude inserted or introduced in a serious literary work, play, movie, etc., designed to provide relief from tension through humor

comics story consisting of CARTOONS arranged in panels (horizontal lines or strips). Dialogue and thoughts are shown in BALLOONS. Historians trace the origin of comics to the Richard Felton Outcault's series *Hogan's Alley*, first published in 1895. Two other early comic strips were *The Katzenjammer Kids* (1897) by Rudolph Dirks and *Little Bears* (1892) by James Guilford Swinnerton. Comics quickly became a popular feature of newspapers. The first successful daily strip, by Bud Fisher, came out in 1907 with the title *Mr. A. Mutt*; it was later renamed *Mutt and Jeff* and was turned into a comic book in 1911. The first mass-produced series was *Famous Funnies*, which first appeared in 1934. The 1938 publication of *Action Comics*, featuring the *Superman* comic strip, inspired countless other comic books. The adventure comic genre, however, actually began with the publication in 1929 of *Tarzan* and *Buck Rogers*. In 1934, Alex Raymond's *Flash Gordon* and Al Capp's *Li'l Abner* (a satirical comic strip) gained broad appeal. One of the most respected comic strips of all time was *Peanuts* by Charles M. Schulz, which appeared in more than 2,000 newspapers and was translated into more than 20 languages.

coming-of-age movie movie dealing with young people and the problems they face during adolescence

comix comics and comic strips designed for adults, especially those involving eroticism

commedia dell'arte comedic style that was extremely popular in Italy in the sixteenth and seventeenth centuries, in which stock characters improvised their dialogues from standard plot outlines, usually wearing traditional masks and costumes. The *commedia* style was eventually adopted by conventional theater. *Arlecchino* (Harlequin) was a lecherous and artful character. *Pantalone*

(Pantaloon) was a greedy and lustful merchant who tried to disguise his age by wearing tight-fitting Turkish clothes. The *Doctor* used senseless Latin phrases and prescribed worthless remedies. The boastful *Captain* was actually a coward and a childish lover. *Pulcinella* (Punch) was a potbellied rascal who planned outrageous plots to satisfy his desires. *Columbine*, a female character, was intelligent and charming, standing out noticeably in a world characterized by masculine idiocy.

commentary news or other report, broadcast live from an event (for example, a televised baseball game)

commercial radio, television, or Internet advertisement. Commercials were first developed for radio in the 1920s. Based on narrative, the persuasive qualities of the human voice, and often the allure of musical jingles, the radio commercial became a highly effective vehicle for promoting products. With the advent of television after World War II, the advertising industry adapted the idea of the radio commercial to the new visual medium. And, of course, today, commercials are found throughout cyberspace.

commercial art art created for commercial reasons, especially advertising

commercial break slot during a radio, television, or Web program during which commercials are broadcast

commercial laissez-faire model of media communication model claiming that there should be "free trade" in the marketplace for media products, as there is for goods

commercial radio radio run by a privately owned business. In contrast to public and nonprofit radio, commercial radio stations sell broadcasting time to advertisers who want to reach listeners. Sponsors pay the stations for time during and between the programs to advertise their products.

commercial television television run by a privately owned business, which sells broadcasting time to advertisers

commodification in Marxist theory, the idea that in capitalist societies, works of artistic or cultural value are valued in ways that parallel how commodities or articles of trade are valued

commodification of information idea that information is a commodity that can be bought and sold like goods, not something that should be freely available

commodity fetishism in Marxist theory, view that the commodities produced and sold under a capitalist system take on the characteristics of fetishes

common carrier communications company (such as a phone company) that provides telecommunications services to the general public

common culture cultural forms, rites, beliefs, symbols, etc., that all members of a community share and that define the community as such

communal sense idea that the meanings attached to things are shaped by the beliefs held by specific communities

communication exchange of messages through some CHANNEL and in some MEDIUM. Communication theorists usually classify communication into *modes*, that is, different ways of exchanging messages: for example, *gestural* (hand-based communication); *vocal* (voice-based communication); *visual* (picture-based communication); *signaling* (bodily based communication); and so on. When pluralized (*communications*), the term refers to media systems or technologies of communication.

communication network any system (such as the Internet) that connects people for communication purposes

communication science [also called **communication studies**] discipline that studies communication in all its dimensions and manifestations. The technical features of communication systems were first studied by the American electrical engineer Claude E. Shannon. In 1948 he developed a model of communication that has become the point of reference for all subsequent models. In Shannon's model, communication is said to occur between a *sender* (a speaker, a radio transmitter, etc.) who (or which) *encodes* a message—that is, uses a CODE to construct it—and a *receiver* (a listener, an audience, etc.) who (or which) has the capacity to *decode* the message—that is, to use the same code to decipher the message. The sender uses a natural MEDIUM or artificial device, or both, to convert a message into a physical signal so as to be able to transmit it across a CHANNEL. Any interference in the channel is called NOISE; the process by which the receiver regulates itself by feeding back information on the transmitted message is called FEEDBACK.

communication theory any theory aiming to explain how (and perhaps why) communication takes place. Communication theorists investigate verbal and nonverbal forms (gesture, body language, facial expression) of human communication, animal communication, and the effect of technological change on communication and culture.

communications [used in the plural] system of communicating by some technological means (telephone, radio, television, computers). In media studies, *communications* refers to the study of providing information and entertainment through media such as magazines, newspapers, radios, televisions, computers, etc.

Communications Decency Act of 1996 U.S. legislation intended to prevent the transmission of pornography on the Internet. The Act has been criticized as a breach of freedom of speech as well as for its difficulty of implementation.

communications gap misunderstanding caused by a failure in communication between different individuals or cultural groups who do not share a common reference system (language, set of values, etc.)

communications satellite satellite used to relay radio, telephone, television, and other signals around the world. Communications satellites play a major role in modern forms of broadcasting, delivering programs to local cable companies or directly to homes through direct broadcast satellite (DBS) systems. The International Telecommunications Satellite Organization (INTELSAT) owns the largest system of communications satellites.

communications spectrum range of electromagnetic frequencies used in wireless communication systems

communicative competence capacity to use and adapt speech to match social contexts or to carry out social functions

communicology term sometimes used for COMMUNICATION SCIENCE

communiqué official announcement given by an agency or person to the press or the public

communisuasion communication that is intended to be persuasive or suggestive

community antenna television [abbreviated as **CATV**] outmoded term for CABLE TELEVISION

community publishing construction of Web pages by local schools, clubs, and nonprofit groups, carried on-line by newspaper Web sites

commutation test procedure for fleshing out meaningful differences in forms and media texts, consisting of substituting (commuting) elements in forms and texts in specific ways or locations. For example, in the word pair *cat* and *rat*, one element of sound—the initial consonant in each word—produces a difference in meaning. In advertising studies, the test consists of removing an image or a word from an ad and replacing it with another, in order to see what kind of subject or audience reaction it produces.

compact disc [abbreviated as **CD**] disc without grooves whose data is stored digitally and is readable only by laser

compact disc read-only memory [abbreviated as **CD-ROM**] compact disc containing digital information (such as data and instructions) that cannot be manipulated or altered

compact disc rewritable [abbreviated as **CD-RW**] compact disc that offers full recordability and re-recordability

comparative analysis 1. comparative study of the mass media systems in different areas of the world; 2. in advertising, analysis of different media available for producing an ADVERTISING CAMPAIGN

compassion fatigue diminution or loss of sympathy on the part of an audience for a group or cause because of overexposure by the media

compensation payments made by networks to affiliates for clearing content

competence in linguistics, the ability to use language and understand its rules, structures, etc.

competitive check analysis of rival advertising trends conducted on the basis of data supplied by monitoring agencies

compilation film film put together from previous footage

compiler computer program that converts another program from a high-level language to an intermediate one

complicity of users idea that an audience does not want the full truth in news reports about difficult situations, reinforcing a reporter's tendency to censor coverage

composer creator of music for a film score, a television program, etc.

compositing merging of different levels of film or digital images

composition 1. way in which the parts of a media text are put together; 2. the social characteristics of a target audience

compulsory heterosexuality in feminist theory, the idea that homosexuality is repressed in media representations and heterosexuality emphasized or portrayed as the norm

computer electronic device capable of performing a vast array of tasks (calculating, word processing, etc.) on the basis of the instructions (called a program). *Digital computers* operate using numerical digits to represent something; *analog computers* operate using numerical values to represent a continuous range; *mainframe computers* are computers housed in specific locations (early mainframe computers had more memory, speed, and capabilities than *personal computers*); *personal computers* are smaller computers designed for individual use, which now have many of the same capacities as mainframe computers; *supercomputers* are powerful mainframe computers with a vast computation capacity.

computer animation use of computers to create film animation, rather than the traditional (now largely abandoned) hand-drawing techniques

computer art graphic element or other artwork created on a computer; or art generated by a computer itself, given appropriate instructions

computer-assisted personal interview face-to-face interview during which the interviewer inputs the responses directly into a computer for immediate analysis

computer conferencing a meeting of two or more people at distant sites, each at a computer exchanging messages

computer games games found online or available in some format such as CD-ROM

computer graphics pictures (charts, drawings, figures, icons, etc.) on a computer screen, as opposed to alphabetic and numerical symbols and characters

computer literacy understanding of the basic principles of computers and their uses, including computer terms

computer memory capacity of a computer to store data, measured in BYTES. *Random Access Memory* (RAM) can be read or changed by the user; *Read-Only Memory* (ROM) can only be read, not altered.

computer network combination of hardware, software, and connections that allows individual computers to communicate with each other and share common resources such as files, software, hardware peripherals, and electronic mail. Networks may also protect shared data from mistakes made by any one individual and assure that data is transmitted correctly. Since the first computer networks debuted in the late 1960s, they have had an enormous impact on the way information is stored, distributed, and processed.

computer science systematic study of all aspects of computers—design, operation, etc.

computer-telephone integration integration of computer and telephone systems so that the same networks can be shared by both

conative function the way in which a message influences a receiver or the response of the receiver (the term is associated with ROMAN JAKOBSON's model of communication)

conceit amusing or imaginative expression that connects things that are perceived to be dissimilar: for example, *my life is a barnyard*

concentrated marketing promotion of a product in one market area

concentration of ownership ownership of numerous media companies by a few individuals or companies

concept album musical album centered on a story line or theme. The British rock group The Who was

among the first rock groups to record such albums, starting with *The Who Sell Out* (1967). Probably the most popular of these albums is the rock opera *Tommy* (1969).

conceptual art art movement that views the representation of traditional objects as irrelevant and that focuses instead on ideas and information as the essential elements of a work. Conceptual artists use various media, such as written documents, photographs, video, film, charts, and maps, in nontraditional ways.

concrete music type of electronic music created by combining recordings of live sounds (natural, mechanical, etc.) with previously composed musical tracks

concurrence-seeking tendency the inclination of people in audiences to agree with each other or to respond to a media event in similar ways

condensation in the field of psychoanalysis, one of the mechanisms by which dreams express subconscious feelings, condensing the emotions into symbolic forms

conference 1. meeting of two or more persons to discuss common concerns; 2. meeting to discuss the previous edition of a newspaper, magazine, etc., in order to plan for the forthcoming one

confidence limits range within which the statistical findings of a survey can be said to be trustworthy or useful for inferential purposes

confidentiality the practice of media professionals to keep secret the names of those who provide them with information

conglomerate large business organization consisting of a number of media companies

conglomeration process by which one individual, group, or organization buys up media systems or outlets. For example, when one newspaper or newspaper chain buys other newspapers, the press industry is said to be undergoing conglomeration. Supporters of conglomeration claim that it is a desirable business practice that protects jobs and brings stability to the marketplace. Opponents claim that it confers too much power on dominant owners who can shape knowledge of events to suit their interests.

congruence theory premise that people prefer balance and consistency among their beliefs and that changes in attitude occur largely in order to create agreement with existing beliefs

conjuncture in Marxist theory, the interrelation of all social factors that bring about social change. The factors include political climate, technology, and economics.

connectionism in computer science, the execution of multiple operations in tandem, rather than in sequence.

The power of connectionism in computer design entered popular culture in 1996 when chess master Garry Kasparov played against a supercomputer called Deep Blue, which operated on the basis of 256 microprocessors connected to each other. Deep Blue had the capacity to compute more than 100 million chess positions per second. Although Kasparov won the match (with three wins, two draws, and one loss), Deep Blue was the first computer to win a game against a chess master.

connectivity ability to communicate with another piece of software, hardware, or entire communication system

connotation added or associated senses of something (a word, symbol, figure, story, etc.). The word *square* means, at a primary literal level, "plane figure with four equal sides and four right angles." However, it is also used with a large number of added meanings, all of which nevertheless imply the square figure or its uses: *he's a square* (a person who is too conventional or old-fashioned; *a square meal* (an adequate meal); *lay it out squarely on the table* (say something honestly). Creative texts (poems, novels, etc.) are interpreted primarily in connotative ways.

consensus shared acceptance of norms, values, beliefs, worldview, etc.

consistency practice of ensuring that media coverage is uniform and does not contradict itself, so that audiences will be more likely to accept the coverage as believable

consolidation reduction of media outlets and concentration of ownership in a few large companies

conspiracy of silence agreement not to broadcast a certain piece of sensitive information among those who have it

conspiracy theory belief that there is a conspiracy among those in control of the media to cover up or suppress sensitive information

constituency specific readership of a newspaper or magazine. The implication is that the political views of the readership are shaped by the newspaper or magazine.

construct the specific concept or hypothesis underpinning any media product (e.g., political or social theories)

constructivism [also called **constructionism**] 1. art movement originating in Moscow around 1920, emphasizing abstract geometric figures constructed with industrial materials; 2. philosophical view that reality does not exist outside the artifacts, representations, and theories constructed by human beings to interpret that reality; 3. theory that the language(s) spoken by someone filters (constructs) that person's perception of reality

consumer activism direct action by consumers to protest some aspect of advertising, production, or sales, particularly concerning their influence on social values

consumer advertising advertising of products and services for the general public (as opposed to specialized, trade, or professional advertising)

consumer behavior ways in which people behave when obtaining, using, and disposing of products (and services)

consumer culture 1. a lifestyle or value system in which worth does not reside in people themselves but in the products with which they surround themselves; 2. view of society as being dominated by consumerism

consumer jury test method of testing advertisements that involves asking consumers to compare, rank, and otherwise evaluate an advertisement or an ad campaign

consumer panel group of consumers who report on products they have used so that manufacturers can improve them on the basis of what they report

consumer research studies conducted by advertising and marketing firms regarding consumers, including determining their needs, lifestyle choices, etc.

consumer sovereignty 1. the view

that a consumer should have the power to influence what is produced; 2. the view that the consumers of media products should dictate what is broadcast

consumer survey collection of data regarding the lifestyle, habits, etc., of a specific group of potential consumers

consumerism 1. concern or preoccupation with material goods; 2. advocating the rights of consumers, as against the efforts of advertisers

consumerization process by which a society evolves into a predominantly consumerist one, as a result of forces such as globalization

contact 1. ROMAN JAKOBSON's term for the physical context in which a message is transmitted and the connections that exist or are established between the participants; 2. person who provides information to a journalist

contagion effect theory that the media have the emotional power to bring about a craze. A classic example is the "Cabbage Patch doll craze" of 1983, when hordes of parents were prepared to pay anything to get the dolls for their daughters at Christmas. Another example is the hysteria generated by the arrival of the new video game system by PlayStation in 2007. Such examples of mass hysteria are attributed to the contagion effect and are thus explained as having been

created by effective media marketing campaigns.

contemporary hits radio radio station broadcasting the latest trends in popular music

content 1. meaning of a message, a program, a movie, etc.; 2. in multimedia, information sources and programs that can be digitized for a communications network. The *content* is what the work means, and the *form* how it has been created.

content analysis 1. study of how the mass media create their CONTENT and why they do so; 2. any statistical description of media content, as for example, how many times a certain theme, word, etc., appears in a text, a program, and so on; 3. technique of counting the number of times that an item appears in a media text

content management management of the material contained on a Web site

content providers media companies or individuals that produce material to be broadcast on a particular network or Web site

context situation, background, environment (physical, social, psychological), function, utilization, etc., that determines the meaning of something. A discarded cigarette butt is seen as rubbish if it is found on a city street. But if the butt is inserted in a picture frame, displayed in an art gallery, and given a title such as *A Final Smoke*, then its meaning would be vastly different. The cigarette butt's context of occurrence and social frame of reference will determine its meaning.

contextual advertising online advertising technique by which ads automatically intrude into a Web session, whether wanted or not

continuity scheduling advertisements to appear at regular intervals over a period of time

continuity editing editing a film to make sure that time sequences, along with costumes, references in the action, etc., are consistent throughout the film

contracting company independent broadcasting company that sells advertising time and space

contrast technique of opposing two elements in some way (two words, two symbols, two forms) so as to signal a difference. The words *night* and *day* contrast with each other in meaning, whereas *cat* and *rat* contrast with each other both in meaning and in the initial sound with which they are constructed.

contributed content Web site Web site that allows visitors to add contributions to its content. Two well-known contributed content Web sites are www.wikipedia.com and www.urbandictionary.com; the former is an online encyclopedia that encourages users to add to an entry or to correct it; the latter is a dictionary containing pop culture terms as contributed by users.

control group in a media-based experiment, the group that is not exposed to something for purposes of investigation (in contrast to an experimental group, which is)

controlled circulation circulation of a magazine free of charge to readers who meet a specific set of advertising criteria

conundrum type of riddle based on punning: for example, *When is a window not a window? When it's ajar.*

convention in media content, certain standardized elements of style that distinguish specific genres

convergence 1. erosion of traditional distinctions among media due to concentration of ownership, globalization, and audience fragmentation; 2. process by which formerly separate technologies such as television and the telephone are brought together by a common technological base (digitization) or a common industrial strategy. The Internet is a perfect example of technological convergence; it can deliver digitized print, images, sound, voice, data, etc., equally well. Large corporations such as AOL are examples of industrial convergence; they bring together various media systems (television broadcasting, newspapers, etc.) under a single corporate umbrella.

convergence theory view that all media are constantly undergoing CONVERGENCE

conversation communication by means of language

conversation analysis identification and study of the patterns that undergird conversations, from turn-taking to topic switching, and the reasons why these take place

conversion rate proportion of people contacted through some marketing scheme who actually end up purchasing a particular product

converter [also called **set-top box**] device in a radio or television receiver for changing from one range of frequency to another, allowing users to get different channels

cookie 1. file that a Web site creates to identify visitors and potentially track their activities on the site and on the Web; 2. information profile about a user that is automatically accepted by the Web browser and stored on the user's hard drive

co-op placement placement of ads on the Web pages of on-line booksellers

cooperative advertising practice by which two companies share advertising costs

cooperative news gathering practice whereby member newspapers share the expenses of acquiring news and returning profits to the members

cooption the appropriation by advertisers of trends in youth culture, making them appear to be their own, and subsequently promoting their products through the template of these trends

copy 1. spoken words or written text in an advertisement; 2. text designed to be read out loud on radio or television

copy editor person whose job it is to check and correct written texts for publication

copyright exclusive right held by the creators of original works to reproduce, distribute copies of, perform publicly, or display their original work, or to create derivative works based on the original. The duration of copyright is the author's life plus 50 years (in Canada), plus 70 years (in the European Union), or plus 75 years (in the United States).

copy testing technique of measuring the effectiveness of advertising messages by showing them to specific types of consumers

corantos early seventh-century one-page newssheets, published in Holland and imported to England by British booksellers

core audience percentage of people who watch or listen to an entire program from beginning to end

corollary something that follows logically from something else, requiring little or no additional proof

corporate advertising advertising of an entire corporation rather than of its products

corporate media mass media controlled by large corporations

corporate portal Web site that allows access and provides links to all the information and software applications held by a corporation

corporate video video produced by a company to inform or educate its employees

Corporation for Public Broadcasting U.S. nonprofit agency that funds local noncommercial broadcasters for cultural or educational programming

corporatization process of making a government agency behave like a private company under marketplace rules

corrective advertisement advertisement that a regulatory body requires of an advertiser that will correct misleading information contained in a previous advertisement

correlation analysis statistical study of any potential relation between

media and audience reactions or behaviors

correspondence column section of a newspaper or magazine where readers' letters are contained

correspondent journalist or reporter who regularly reports on a particular area of information, usually from the same geographical area

cost-per-thousand [abbreviated as **CPM**] cost of reaching 1,000 consumers, calculated by the cost of placing an advertisement divided by the number of thousands of consumers it reaches

costume drama drama set in a particular historical period, requiring costumes and sets that are authentic to the period

cottage industry industry characterized by relatively smaller operations and closely identified with its personnel

couch potato person who watches a lot of television

counteradvertising advertising that is designed to respond to a competitor's advertising

counterculture a subculture whose values contradict those of the dominant culture. The term crystallized in the 1960s to refer to young people who rejected the worldview and the lifestyles of the middle class. They used music and other forms of protest to argue against gender and race discrimination, the Vietnam War, and other causes that were prominent during the era.

counterleak revealing to a reporter that somebody else has leaked information, so as to induce the reporter to believe that there is a conspiracy

counterprogramming scheduling of television programs in order to attract audiences that have been watching similar programs aired at the same time on other channels

coupon ad print advertisement with a discount coupon attached, which the consumer can cut out and use at a retail store or can return to the advertiser

coups and earthquakes syndrome supposed practice of Western societies to ignore news events related to other societies unless they involve political turmoil or natural disasters

courtroom TV television channel that presents information, stories, and documentaries dealing with criminal cases, as well as broadcasting actual trials

cover story most important story in a magazine, featured on its front cover

coverage attention the media give to a certain person, event, etc.

coverlines suggestive headlines on magazine covers designed to shock or intrigue potential consumers

cowboy genre narrative that revolves around the time frame of the 1800s in the American West, featuring a heroic cowboy and his horse, often fighting Native Americans or outlaws

CPM [*see* **cost-per-thousand**]

CPU [*see* **central processing unit**]

crane shot film shot taken from a crane (a large movable arm for a camera), creating a higher angle from which to view the scene

crawl scrolling text across a television or movie screen to convey information such as programming credits or news updates

creative director person in an advertising agency who coordinates the creation of advertisements for a product or service

credits the names of photographers, camerapersons, costume designers, etc., who were part of the production team; often broadcast at the end of a film or program

creole language that evolves from contact with another language, becoming the native language of a community (Haitian Creole, Guyanese Creole, etc.)

crew persons who carry out technical work for a television program or film

(camerapersons, lighting managers, etc.)

crisis definition theory that a crisis is defined as such only when it is covered by media, forcing those in authority to act accordingly

critic person who expresses opinions about a work (a book, a film, etc.)

critical media theory theory that the media operate primarily to justify and support the status quo at the expense of ordinary people

critical news analysis news coverage that is perceived as being neutral and highly reliable

critical research term first used by PAUL LAZARSFELD in 1941 to describe research that takes as its object the impact of media on people by examining how certain media products influence audience behaviors, as well as the relation of media to culture and history

critical studies examination of the overall impact of the media on society

criticism examination of literary, artistic, or media texts (novels, poetry, films, television programs, etc.) in terms of their aesthetic worth, their social import, their style, their genre characteristics, and so on. Traditionally, criticism revolved around issues such as the author's intent, the structure used to make the work, etc. In the early twentieth century, the New Criticism movement, influenced by T.S. Eliot, proposed the study of works aside from historical context or authorship. By mid-century, several other trends emerged: *psychoanalytic* criticism focuses on the unconscious aspects of the work (archetypes, dreams, myths, etc.); *semiotic* (or *structuralist*) criticism focuses on the meanings of texts in sign-based terms; *hermeneutic* criticism looks at the language with which, and cultural context in which, a work is created; *Marxist* criticism interprets works in terms of ideological factors and forces at work in its production; *feminist* criticism investigates the role and representation of women in works; and *deconstructivist* criticism looks at a work in terms of the meanings it creates by itself, rather than through some external channel.

Croce, Benedetto (1866–1952) Italian philosopher and critic who argued that art allows human beings to give expression to their instinctive sense of beauty and ugliness

crosscutting repeated alternation between filmed sequences to give the impression that the sequences are simultaneous

cross-media advertising advertising the same product in several media forms and outlets (radio, television, print, etc.)

cross-media ownership ownership of several media outlets (press, radio, television, etc.) by one company

crossover 1. media product that was made for one medium, but that gains popularity in another (for example, a novel such as *The Godfather* that is known more in its movie form than in its book form); 2. any popular work that crosses over to another genre where it may become even more popular (for example, from rock to country). The music of Elvis Presley was considered to be pure rock music in the 1950s and 1960s. It started to cross over to the country field in the late 1970s and is still classified as both "early rock" and "country."

cross promotion technique by which two or more advertisers associate with each other to reach more people

cross-reference reference from one part of a book, index, or table to another

crossword puzzle with sets of numbered squares to be filled in with words, according to given clues, one letter to each square, so that the words may be read both across and down

cryptogram something constructed in code or cipher: for example, 1–14–4 = *and* (each number stands for a letter in the English alphabet, in order)

cryptography making or deciphering messages in a secret code that has a *key*, or method, for identifying the hidden message

Woman in a Hat (1934) by Pablo Picasso

CSA [*see* **Casting Society of America**]

C-SPAN U.S. cable television channel that covers politics and current affairs

cubism twentieth-century art movement based on the use of cubes and other geometric forms, rather than a naturalistic representation. The movement started in Paris around 1908, becoming popular in the 1920s, marking the beginning of abstract art. Cubist painters include Pablo Picasso, Georges Braque, and Marcel Duchamp. Cubist sculptors include Picasso, Raymond Duchamp-Villon, and Aleksandr Archipenko.

cue 1. written text to a piece of audio; 2. sign given for some action, event, or broadcast to begin

cue card card placed near a television camera that a presenter reads, while appearing to look straight at the viewers

cult film film that gathers a devoted group of followers

cultivation differential degree to which persons have been undergoing the CULTIVATION EFFECT and the degree of influence this has had on their views and beliefs

cultivation effect process by which audiences are purportedly inclined to accept values, beliefs, etc., that are presented to them by media coverage over an extended period of time

cultural capital particular knowledge and background possessed by audiences, which shape their interpretation of media texts

cultural imperialism belief that the cultural artifacts of a politically and economically dominant power enter into another country and eventually dominate it, thereby spreading the cultural, political, and specific values of the dominant power to the exclusion of indigenous values and voices

cultural memory complex of symbols, rituals, etc., that are acquired from being immersed in a culture, which, over time, becomes part of memory

cultural proximity desire of people to see or hear media products from the comfort of their own cultural backgrounds

cultural relativism view that different cultures predispose their members to view the world in different ways. Essentially, relativists maintain that what is right or wrong depends on the

particular culture concerned. What is right in one society may be wrong in another, and thus no basic standards exist by which a culture may be judged right or wrong.

cultural studies tradition of research that contends that the examination of cultural context is essential for an accurate understanding of media

cultural theory the idea that cultural meanings are negotiated by media and audiences as they interact

culture the arts, beliefs, language(s), institutions, rituals, etc., practiced by a specific group of people

culture industries in the FRANKFURT SCHOOL specifically, and in early culture theory generally, profit-making enterprises that have debased culture by turning it into a commodity. In this view, the function of culture is not to enrich or enlighten but to manipulate and indoctrinate.

culture jammers a group social activists with a popular Web site and magazine that are critical of the advertising process itself. The Web site and magazine offer not only serious critiques of advertising and consumerism, but also many clever parodies of advertising campaigns, articles and forums on how one can recognize media manipulation, information on lawsuits and legislation on consumer issues, and links for sending e-mails to big businesses to contest their marketing strategies. Culture jammers see themselves as a loose global network of media activists aiming to change the way in which information flows. They claim that brands, fashions, celebrities, spectacles, and entertainments are all that consumer culture has to offer. It is only by "deconstructing" the symbols of branded culture that true culture can reassert itself.

culture of deference the tendency of news reporters to censor themselves so that the organization for which they work will not find their coverage objectionable

culture wars any clash of tastes and ideologies with regard to cultural products. For example, in the United States there is currently a "culture war" between right-wing ideologues, who consider pop culture products portraying sex and violence generally to be improper and even destructive of "traditional values," and civil libertarians who see such popular expressions as necessary to keep a political system based on freedom of speech intact and functional.

cumulative audience [abbreviated as **cume**] 1. number of people who listen to a radio station for at least five minutes a day; 2. proportion of a target audience who have had the opportunity to hear or see an advertisement during some broadcast

Curran, James (1973–) scholar whose work on globalization comes up frequently in the media literature.

Among his works are *Mass Media and Society* (as editor, with Michael Gurevitch, 1991) and *Culture Wars: The Media and the British Left* (with Ivor Gaber and Julian Petley, 2005).

current events news or a discussion of news of the present time

curtain raiser story that precedes the main story, so as to provide background information

custom publishing creation of customized versions of print newspapers, magazines, or books for particular audiences

cutaway short scene inserted between two scenes in order to avoid clumsy editing

cut-in scene that is inserted into another scene in a film

cutting room room in which film editing is carried out

cyberadvertising placement of commercials on on-line sites

cybercafé café that provides computers where people can pay to browse the Internet

cybercommunications communications that take place over the Internet

cyberculture culture that is evolving over the Internet, including chatrooms, profile sites, etc.

cyberfeminism study of the effects of new technologies on women's issues

cyberjunkies persons who spend too much time on the Internet, becoming "addicted" to it

cybermall on-line shopping site linking a home page with a large number of online businesses, allowing customers to make purchases

cybermarketing any kind of Internet-based marketing strategy or promotion (targeted e-mails, bulletin boards, etc.)

cybernetics science that studies communication in living organisms, computers, and organizations. The science was founded in 1948 by Norbert Wiener, who claimed that the control systems in machines process information in ways that are analogous to the ways in which the nervous system processes stimuli, that is, primarily on the basis of the nature of the stimuli. Known as *feedback*, this concept is the founding notion of cybernetics.

cyberporn pornographic material available on the Internet

cyberpunk movement associated with the technological breakthroughs of the early 1980s and their effect on the popular culture of the era

cybersex sexual activity involving virtual reality on the Internet

cybershopping buying goods and services over the Internet

cybersleuthing in popular culture, crime solving that uses advanced cyber technologies

cyberspace the realm in which electronic information exists (term coined by American writer William Gibson in his 1984 science fiction novel *Neuromancer*). The term has given rise to a host of derived terms, such as cybercafes, cybermalls, etc.

cybersurfer person who spends a lot of time on the Internet

cyberterrorism terrorism that employs the Internet to communicate with fellow terrorists and to enter the communication systems of targets in order to destroy them

cyberwar use of electronic communications and the Internet to damage an adversary's computer systems and files

cyborg human body or other organism whose functions are taken over in part by various electronic or electromechanical devices

D3 digital tape format that is capable of recording composite video signals

DAB [*see* **digital audio broadcasting**]

dactylology communication by signs made with the fingers, especially as practiced by people who are speech-impaired

Dadaism (also called **Dada**) art and literary movement, starting around 1916 and fading by 1922, that rejected traditional forms of art through incongruity and nonsensicality. The term *dada*, a French baby-talk word for "hobbyhorse," was chosen arbitrarily by Romanian-born writer Tristan Tzara because it was nonsensical. Revoking all accepted values in traditional art making, Dadaists used art techniques that were deliberately unintelligible and outrageous.

DAGMAR [full form: **defining advertising goals for measured advertising results**] model intended to identify the effects that advertising has on consumers, measured in stages, from awareness of the product to action (purchasing)

daguerrotype (early forerunner of the photograph) process of recording images on polished metal plates

daily 1. newspaper published every day; 2. in film, an unedited print of a day's filming, usually created for review by the director

Daily Me news Web site that lets users tailor contents to their liking. Some media analysts argue that this type of site empowers common people to become more sophisticated information consumers, drawing those who might otherwise be disinclined to reflect critically on information into the world of news and public affairs. Others argue that it cuts users off from the full richness of news and information, confining them to their preexisting preferences. Web site: www.DailyMe.com

dance music style of popular electronic music with a disc jockey talking or rapping as people dance (usually in a club setting)

dance program reality television program featuring dancers, usually in competition

darkroom room isolated from all outside light that is set up and equipped for developing photographs

DARS [*see* **digital audio radio service**]

DAT [*see* **digital audiotape**]

data [singular, **datum**] 1. information of any type (usually in the form of facts and figures and obtained through surveys, experiments, etc.); 2. information available on computer (text, images, numbers, etc.) that can be stored or processed

data analysis compilation and interpretation of DATA so as to ascertain patterns implicit in it, often by employing a statistical method

data compression [*see* **digital compression**]

data entry putting information in a computer by keyboarding, scanning, or some other way

data mining compiling and sifting through large quantities of DATA so as to extract from it any usable patterns; for example, using demographic data to analyze the shopping habits of a targeted advertising population

data protection any strategy, such as legislation or software applications, used to prevent DATA from being used in an unauthorized fashion

data sheet online document that provides a detailed description of a product, service, etc.

database organized compilation of DATA structured logically (alphabetically, topically, etc.) for quick access and utilization. A few computer databases became commercially available in the 1960s; online databases (usually available to anyone) started in the 1970s.

database management system computer program that allows a user to organize and manipulate the information in a DATABASE

database marketing strategy whereby advertisers store information about consumers so that they can use it to personalize or target messages according to consumer characteristics such as age, gender, social class, lifestyle, etc.

database modeling technique of using the information in a DATABASE to create a Web site or to simulate or predict something, such as trends in a market

datacasting 1. distribution of digital data, usually online; 2. transmitting data on demand (such as weather reports)

dataveillance (imitating **surveillance**) any massive electronic compilation and distillation of consumer DATA

dateline line at the beginning of a printed news story or news release giving the place and date of the story's origin

DATV [*see* **digitally assisted television**]

Davis, Angela (1944–) prominent feminist social critic whose analyses of the representations of race, gender, hegemony, homophobia, and sexuality in representational practices are widely cited. Her works include *Women, Culture, and Politics* (1989) and *Blues Legacies and Black Feminism* (1998).

day-after recall test advertising research method designed to ascertain how much someone can remember about an advertisement or commercial the day after it was broadcast

day player actor or technician who is hired on a daily basis for a film production

daypart partition of a day into blocks for programming and advertising purposes (for example, 6 A.M. to 10 A.M., 10 A.M. to 3 P.M., 3 P.M. to 7 P.M., 7 P.M. to 12 midnight)

d-book book that can be downloaded in electronic form from the Internet

DBS [*see* **direct broadcast by satellite**]

deadline time by which COPY must be submitted for publication or broadcast

dead spot geographic area where radio or television reception is poor, even though it falls within the usual range of the transmitter

dead zone area where mobile phone networks do not operate

dealer aids advertising materials and devices used by stores to stimulate sales (posters, in-store television sets showcasing a product, and the like)

dealer tie-in advertising that publicizes the names of local dealers who stock a product

death metal music type of heavy metal music characterized by hard-edged loud instrumentation, brutality in lyrical material, growling vocals, and horror symbolism

Debord, Guy (1931–1994) French social critic who described the purportedly destructive effects of modern-day circus-like spectacles on human cultures. Among his best known works are *La société du spectacle* (1967; published in English as *Society of the Spectacle*, 1973) and *Commentaires sur la société du spectacle* (1988; published in English as *Comments on the Society of the Spectacle*, 1990).

decentralized system in advertising, mode of operation in which a manager, rather than a centralized department, is responsible for marketing and advertising a product

deceptive advertising advertising that is purported to make misleading or untruthful claims

decipher in literary and media studies, to determine the meaning of a complex or ambiguous text (to *decipher* a novel, to *decipher* a movie, etc.)

deck secondary part of a newspaper headline that summarizes a story

decode [synonym for **decipher**] to determine the meaning of a complex or ambiguous text. The term implies that there is a hidden CODE in the text that guides its reception and understanding at an unconscious level.

decoder 1. person who decodes media texts; 2. device designed to unscramble mixed signals or to select signals so that a program can be received on a television set

deconstruction approach to literary and media texts instigated by JACQUES DERRIDA in the 1960s and 1970s. Because of the relative nature of language, Derrida claimed, no text can have an unchanging or central meaning. Deconstruction is also called POSTSTRUCTURALISM. It challenges traditional assumptions about texts as mirrors of reality because words, being what they are, refer to other words. Since texts are structured on BINARY OPPOSITIONS (e.g., man vs. woman, good vs. evil), they tend to produce biased interpretations, wherein one of the two concepts in the binary opposition is given prominence, and this has vast cultural consequences. Deconstructionist readings of media texts thus involve an examination of the unarticulated oppositions that underpin their seemingly straightforward surface meanings.

decor scenery used on a stage or a movie set

dedication 1. inscription in a literary or musical work, intended as a tribute to an individual or cause; 2. musical piece played or requested as a greeting or tribute, especially on the radio

deduction [in contrast to **abduction** and **induction**] process in which a conclusion about a particular follows from a general premise: for example, *All cats are mammals*; *Pumpkin is a cat*; *therefore we can deduce that Pumpkin is a mammal.*

deep focus cinematic technique of bringing the components of a scene into focus by using a camera shot that shows a large depth of field

defamation statement about a person that is untrue and impugns his or her reputation in some way

default option or mode (a font style, a letter case, etc.) that will automatically be selected by a computer when the user does not specify an alternative

defensive communication message that recipients will intentionally misinterpret or reject because it jars with their own values, beliefs, or worldview

deficit financing in television parlance, strategy used by a TV production company of leasing programs to a network for a fee that is less than the cost of production in the hope of recovering the loss later through rerun syndication

definition degree of clarity that an image or sound has (in a photo, on a television screen, on a monitor, in a recording)

defocusing filmic technique of blurring an image deliberately for a psychological effect

delay line device that delays the transmission of an electronic signal according to a pre-arranged or preset interval

delay system mode of operation employed to delay the transmission of a live broadcast by a few seconds so that infelicities such as profanities can be removed

deleted scene any scene deleted from a film or program either for artistic, political, or legal reasons

deliberative listening interpreting a media text with the sole intention of deciphering the message built into it (rather than simply taking it in for enjoyment or some other such reason)

delivery system computer system combining the hardware and software required to play a certain multimedia product

demand programming radio format based on requests by listeners

demo sample or entire version of a recording, produced for promotional purposes

demodulation process of translating an ANALOG signal into DIGITAL form

demographic editions national magazines that tailor their advertising according to the demographics of their subscribers (age, gender, occupation, education, income, ethnicity, education)

demographic segmentation classification of media audiences or consumers according to demographic characteristics (age, gender, class, economic level, education)

demographics classification of audiences and consumers according to their age, sex, income, education, and other variables. It does not include classification by their subjective attitudes or opinions.

demonization undermining of a person (or group) by the media, usually by means of an attack on personal characteristics of an individual (or the leader or members of a group)

demonstration effect claim that some people buy products to impress or keep up with their neighbors

denotation initial, specific, or literal meaning of a word, text, etc., as opposed to its connotative meaning. The denotative meaning of *square* is a "plane figure made up of four equal lines meeting at right angles." On the other hand, in the expression *a square person*, it has a nondenotative meaning (unfashionable, old-fashioned). In advertising analysis the term is often used to refer to the surface meaning of an ad, that is, what the ad is designed to highlight about the product. However, the actual meaning of an ad depends on some encoded message that is beyond its denotative meaning (usually involving lifestyle, instinctive needs and fears, etc.).

denouement final part of a plot in a drama or narrative in which the outcome is clarified

dependency theory hypothesis that people who are exposed habitually to a medium tend to become psychologically dependent on the medium, much as a drug user becomes dependent on a drug

depth interview method of advertising research, whereby a trained interviewer meets with consumers, asking each of them a series of unprepared questions that aim to identify attitudes and values that might have been missed with other methods. The interviewer does not use predetermined questions because the purpose of the interview is to give respondents the opportunity to express their personal views and tastes openly and spontaneously.

depth of field distance in front of a camera within which actors and an entire scene can be shown in focus. This technique guides the viewer's eye to particular characters or areas on the screen.

deregulation loosening or elimination by the government of ownership and other rules for media systems

Derrida, Jacques (1930–2004) French philosopher who founded the DECONSTRUCTION movement that has been applied broadly to media studies. Derrida's main contention is that the meaning of a text cannot be determined with any degree of certainty because it shifts according to who analyzes it, when it is analyzed, how it is analyzed, and so on.

desensitization process through which audiences, as a result of viewing portrayals of violence or degradation in the media, are thought to become insensitive to violence and suffering in real life

desexualize 1. to remove sexual features or ideas from a media text, so as to make it acceptable to a wider audience; 2. to deemphasize sexuality or the role of sex and gender in media portrayals

design audit process of checking and evaluating the design of a brand product, an ad, a Web site, etc.

design grid basic form or grid used as a template for designing a magazine's page layout

designated market area [abbreviated as **DMA**] geographic designation, used by AC NIELSEN, that specifies which population areas fall into a specific television market segment

desk in newspaper parlance, a department concerned with a certain topic or area of coverage (e.g., sports desk, city desk)

desk editor in newspaper parlance, person who prepares texts in a final version for publication

desktop publishing [abbreviated as DTP] publication by means of computers equipped with specialized software, rather than by means of traditional typographical practices

detective story work of fiction that centers on a crime, featuring a detective who will solve the crime by questioning suspects, putting together clues, and eventually hunting down the perpetrator. The detective generally withholds the significance of the clues until the end. Edgar Allan Poe's C. Auguste Dupin, who appeared in an 1841 story titled "Murders in the Rue Morgue," is considered the first fictional detective. Charles Dickens followed Poe's lead with *Bleak House* (1852–1853) and his unfinished novel, *The Mystery of Edwin Drood*. Shortly thereafter, *The Moonstone* (1868), by Wilkie Collins, became the first popular detective novel. Sir Arthur Conan Doyle's *A Study in Scarlet* (1887) introduced Sherlock Holmes, perhaps the most famous of all fictional detectives. Today, the detective story has become one of the most popular forms of fiction in movies and television.

Cover of *The Union Jack* (1900) featuring Detective Sexton Blake

determination in Marxist theory, claim that the economic system used in a society determines its "superstructure" (culture, beliefs)

determinism doctrine or view that every human act is caused by something or is subject to universal laws of causation, thus denying any free will (the ability to make choices freely)

development theory idea that media systems and governments should work together to ensure that a country will be better served, or to promote partnerships with other countries

deviance behavior that departs from or challenges social norms. Deviance is a major theme in crime narratives, for example, and in MORAL PANIC theory.

deviancy amplification spiral social phenomenon whereby media coverage of a deviant event makes it appear to be more common than it is and causes people to pay more attention to it than they otherwise would

diachrony [in contrast to SYNCHRONY] change in language over time; by extension, any kind of change in any representational system. Diachrony refers to evolutionary tendencies within systems to produce change in those systems.

dial radio or television plate or disk, with numbers or letters on it for tuning into a station. Dials are now largely obsolete, having been replaced by devices such as remote controls. The term has remained, however, in expressions such as: "Turn the dial" and "You can always dial that program out."

dialect variant of a language used by a particular group of speakers. Dialects may arise from geographic or social factors. For example, American and British dialects of English differ due to geographic distance; dialects within British English reflect differences in the level of education, economic status, and the like.

dialectic philosophical term describing the process of examining ideas logically, through discussions based on questions and answers. PLATO's *Dialogues* used the dialectic method, which he based on observations of his teacher Socrates, who used it to reveal truth through disputation. Plato's student ARISTOTLE used the term as a synonym for *logic*. Hegel used the term dialectic with a different meaning, namely as one phase of any historical development that tends to be confronted and replaced by its opposite which, in turn, tends to be replaced by a phase that is somehow a resolution of the two opposed phases. This meaning was adopted by Marx and elaborated to encompass the tension that exists in capitalist societies between the proletariat and the ruling classes

dialogics as defined by MIKHAIL BAKHTIN, the construction of verbal utterances in a dialogue on the basis of opinions and ideologies, which reflects a web of ongoing power struggles between people

dialogue 1. conversation of any kind; 2. literary genre modeled on everyday conversation; 3. words spoken by characters in a text (book, radio, movie, program, etc.)

dial-up access nonpermanent connection to the Internet requiring a modem or other device that allows a user to dial a telephone access number in order to make such a connection. This method of connection is now largely obsolete.

diary column column written by journalists or bloggers about their lives

diary method market research technique whereby respondents keep a regular written account of the advertising materials (ads, commercials, posters, etc.) they have noticed, the purchases they have made, and the products they have actually used

diaspora scattering of any community that once lived together in a single location because of some event (war, persecution); the term has been applied traditionally to the Jewish diaspora

dictionary reference book or listing containing words, phrases, and expressions with their definitions and other information

dictum authoritative saying or pronouncement: *Those who ignore history are condemned to repeat it*

didactic containing a moral, social, or ethical message; of an instructional nature

diegesis the fictional world created by narratives

diegetic elements originating in a narrative (including dialogue and sound effects) that appear to be arising out of the plot. In film, nondiegetic elements are those that do not

originate in the narrative, such as soundtrack music and credits.

différence FERDINAND DE SAUSSURE'S term for CONTRAST, which claims that two forms are kept distinct in meaning through some minimal difference such as a sound: for example, *pin* versus *bin*. By extension, the term is now used to refer to any difference, including social differences, such as *young* versus *old*. The term is used in current media analysis to support the view that meanings are constantly shifting and thus reconstructing each other through minimal differences.

diffusion spread of media content either generally throughout society or specifically within a target audience

digerati [in imitation of **literati**] people with expertise in, or professional involvement with, computers, the Internet, or the World Wide Web

digest compilation of articles, stories, reviews from different sources, brought together in a magazine, book, or broadcast, often in summarized or condensed form

digicam [*see* **digital camera**]

digital 1. any medium that operates by means of a digital system; 2. any form of transmission in which a signal is sent in small, separate packages (in contrast to ANALOG)

digital audio broadcasting [abbreviated as **DAB**] audio broadcasting using digital recordings, which give clearer sound than analog recordings

digital audio radio service [abbreviated as **DARS**] delivery of digital audio signals by satellite directly to homes or automobiles

digital audiotape [abbreviated as **DAT**] audiotape cassette or other magnetic tape that offers high-quality digital sound

digital cable television digital television delivered to homes via cable

digital camera [abbreviated as **digicam**] camera that takes and stores pictures in digital form. Like previous cameras, digital cameras have lenses, apertures, and shutters, but they do not use film. Instead, they use devices that transform images into digital information. Digital photos can then be manipulated and printed using a computer.

digital compression [also called **data compression**] 1. method of representing data in an abbreviated form by removing redundant data, by replacing repeated data with a shortening code, or some other such technique; 2. digitizing signals so that they can be carried over one channel

digital delivery daily online distribution of daily newspapers

digital divide view that digital technology and its attendant culture contribute to the exacerbation of

social inequalities, because not everyone has equal access to such technology and, even among those who do, not everyone is equally competent in using it. Unequal access or unequal competence is thus said to create classes of "information haves" and "information have-nots."

digital film production production of films using primarily digital technology, rather than previous technologies

digital galaxy [in imitation of **Gutenberg galaxy**] notion that digital technologies have changed the ways in which people communicate and interact

digital imaging any form of photography that is based on digital technology. It has been suggested that this term should replace *photography* altogether.

digital media media based on digital technologies

digital media players computer programs or systems that allow individual users to display video or audio data on home computers. RealPlayer, Windows Media Player, and QuickTime are examples of such systems.

digital music distribution platforms online sites like PressPlay, Rhapsody, MusicNet, iTunes, and others that allow for downloading of music files

digital photography [also called **digital imaging**] photography using digital cameras and equipment

digital radio radio broadcasting that is transmitted digitally, with the capacity to provide a greater choice of channels and a superior sound quality than all previous nondigital systems

digital recording audio recording made with digital equipment, producing a high-quality clear sound

digital retouching use of digital technology to alter a photograph, either to remove imperfections or to change something in the photo without revealing that it was altered

digital rights management protection of digitally distributed intellectual property

digital service line [abbreviated as **DSL**] line providing access to the Internet that is faster than the previous dial-up modem devices

digital television [abbreviated as **DTV**] television set and television broadcasting system using digital technology

digital terrestrial broadcasting course of action aiming to make all forms of broadcasting digital

digital versatile/video disc [abbreviated as **DVD**] round flat platter on which motion pictures, computer programs, and other types of infor-

mation are stored digitally. A DVD is the same size as a standard compact disc (about 4 3/4 inches or 12 centimeters) in diameter, but it can store much more information. Each side of a DVD can contain two data layers, one beneath the other. A single DVD currently has the capacity to store up to 17 gigabytes (billion bytes) of information. DVD technology was one of the first types of digital technology that made it possible to integrate computer, audio, and video material.

digital video editing editing video materials using digital technology

digital video recorder [abbreviated as **DVR**] video recording and playback device attached to a television set that allows users significant control over the content they record or see

digitally assisted television [abbreviated as **DATV**] television signals transmitted partly through digital means

digitally originated graphic [abbreviated as **DOG**] small logo used to identify a television channel, shown typically in one corner of the screen

digitization [also called **digitalization**] conversion of any kind of data (text, images, sound, graphics) into an electronic language that can be used by computers or other digital systems. Because it offers unprecedented opportunities for manipulation of data, digitization raises crucial questions about authorship, intellectual property, and selectivity of information. This term is now used to characterize the evolutionary characteristics of all media—which are becoming digitized throughout the world.

digizine [abbreviation of **digital magazine**] magazine that can be accessed by computer from a Web site

diglossia use of different forms of the same language or, sometimes, of different languages in the same speech area, one of which is sometimes considered more important or functional than the other

Dijk, Jan A.G.M. van (1952–) scholar whose work on the effects of new media technologies on cultures and societies is often cited in the media literature. Among his most influential works are *The Network Society* (1999) and *Digital Democracy* (2000).

dime novels [also called **pulp fiction**] inexpensive nineteenth and early twentieth century novels that deal mainly with sensationalized adventure, crime, horror, or romance. The term *dime* comes from the fact that they were originally sold for a dime.

dionysian as defined by Friedrich Nietzsche, the creative and intuitive aspects of the human psyche, as opposed to the mind's rational mode of thinking

dipstick survey survey intended to identify only one aspect of some audience behavior, such as the number of viewing hours independently of the TV programs watched

direct action advertising advertising intended to elicit a quick response in consumers, appealing directly to emotional needs

direct broadcast by satellite [abbreviated as **DBS**] generic term for the broadcasting of radio and television signals over a wide area by satellite technology. DBS began in 1994.

direct cinema a type of CINÉMA VÉRITÉ developed in the 1960s in the United States, in which the setting is not a studio or designated area but the real world (the ghetto of a real city, the backstreets of a town, etc.)

direct mail advertising practice of sending people leaflets or brochures through the mail. Today, such advertising also takes place in online versions, where it is called *spam.*

direct marketing marketing practices that are aimed directly at (and are accessible to) consumers, bypassing retailers (for example, through mail order and the Internet)

direct response television [abbreviated as **DRTV**] advertising strategy seeking immediate response to a television commercial by providing an on-screen phone number, e-mail address, or Web site

direct sponsorship radio and television programming bearing the name of the advertiser who has sponsored a program or series (appearing in the program's title)

directional medium advertising medium that gives potential consumers information on where to find products; for example, a directory, a catalog

directness of address the way in which television addresses people. Since television is essentially a domestic medium, its style is typically conversational (rather than formal), engaging audiences directly and emotionally, rather than logically and rationally.

director person who plans and controls the performance of a play, a motion picture, or a show on television, radio, or the Internet. In traditional film theory, the director is considered more important than the scriptwriter; often the two are one and the same person.

direct-to-home multichannel broadcast service for television and radio transmitted via communication satellite that subscribers receive directly on their own receivers

director's cut version of a movie over which the director has complete control; often, this version is not released to theaters

disaster movie film genre in which the plot revolves around a natural disaster (such as an asteroid hitting earth) or a human-related disaster (such as a ship sinking in the ocean)

disc a storage device, built into a computer or removable as a separate device (such as a flat plastic object)

disc jockey [abbreviated as **DJ**] announcer for a radio program that consists chiefly of recorded popular music; by extension, anyone who plays recorded music for a specific function (such as at a wedding, a dance, etc.)

disclosure of information act of passing on information that was intended to be kept secret. This term is used especially in journalism jargon.

disco music flamboyant, dance-oriented popular music genre that emerged in the 1970s. Disco music was emblemized by the 1977 movie *Saturday Night Fever.* The punk rock and new wave movements that surfaced in the mid- and late 1970s began partly as a backlash against the perceived superficiality and glitziness of disco.

discography list or catalog of recordings (by a performer, a group, etc.) or of writings or annotations about them

discourse 1. use of language in communication; 2. serious discussion about a subject; 3. particular style of talking and writing (as in the "discourse of science"). This term was used by MICHEL FOUCAULT to describe how language is used by people and institutions to shape social reality. In this sense, discourse is seen as a form of power because it articulates and ensconces (through language) the ideas that are accepted as truth. The term is now extended to include nonverbal and other kinds of "languages" (visual discourse, narrative discourse, and other discourses).

discursive contestation ability of the audience of a news broadcast to challenge its content and slant (as opposed to passive reception of the broadcast)

discursive form as defined by philosopher SUSANNE LANGER, anything constructed in linguistic form and thus governed by the properties of that form. One of these is *detachment*, since one can focus on a word in a sentence or a phrase without impairing the overall understanding of the sentence or phrase. Presentational forms, on the other hand, cannot be detached without impairing the overall meaning; for example, one cannot focus on a note or phrase in a symphony without destroying the sense of the work.

discursive gap breach in language that can exist between senders (such as television newscasters) and receivers (such as audiences). The popular press has attempted to close this gap by using primarily colloquial or slang language.

discussion group on the Internet, a Web site that lets any visitor write

a message on a particular subject, which is then displayed on the site

dish antenna television antenna in the form of a dish that can receive many channels and services from a satellite

Disneyification the spread of American representations of childhood culture, as symbolized by the Walt Disney Company, which are seen to be intrusive into other cultural views of childhood

disparaging copy advertising copy that is critical of another company's products or campaigns

dispatch news item sent by a news correspondent or agency to a network, station, or Web site

displacement capacity of words (and symbols generally) to displace referents (the things to which they refer), evoking them mentally (not physically). A word such as *cat* is a sequence of sounds (or letters) that evokes a particular mental image of an animal, even if the animal is not physically present. The animal is thus said to have been "displaced" from the physical world to the mental world. In MARXIST THEORIES OF MEDIA, the term is sometimes used to refer to the process by which the meaning of something is transferred to something else; for example, portraying punk musicians as having the same characteristics as criminals, thus implying that they are socially deviant.

display advertising 1. advertising that includes product or company features and symbols (such as a logo) in addition to the ad text itself; 2. advertising taking up a substantial area of a newspaper page

dissemination distribution of an idea, statement, or information through a medium

dissident press press that publishes articles, reviews, etc., that are perceived as opposing the mainstream press, usually challenging the social and political status quo

dissonance conflict between the ideas, values, or views that a person holds and those directed at him or her through some form of communication (especially the media)

dissonance theory view that people will experience a kind of discomfort when confronted with new information and thus will attempt to limit the discomfort through manipulation of the information (selection of some aspects and rejection of others, adapting it to previous information, etc.)

distantiation idea that media products "keep a distance" from the ideological systems within which they were created. The term was used in the past to refer, for example, to classical musicians in Soviet Russia (Shostakovich, Prokofiev, etc.) whose compositions, though created in Soviet Russia, "kept their distance" from Communist ideology.

distinctive feature aspect of language or some other code that keeps forms within the code discernibly distinct. For example, the difference between the s sound in *sip* and the z sound in *zip* exists as the absence or presence, respectively, of the vibration of the vocal cords during pronunciation. Such vibration is a distinctive feature.

distribution system electronic system that moves signals over a cable television network from the headend, where signals are received and processed, to the geographical areas that receive cable service

diurnals daily accounts of local news printed in England in the 1600s. Diurnals are the forerunners of the modern dailies.

diversification a company's venture into ownership of other related or unrelated enterprises, thus "diversifying" its business

DJ [*see* **disc jockey**]

docudrama dramatization of real-life events (such as the sinking of the Titanic) through film, radio, or television

docufiction 1. any fictional narrative using documentary techniques; 2. work in which actual recorded events are combined with recreations or imaginary scenes

documentary nonfictional movie or program dealing with events or issues in a factual manner, including interviews, film footage, and other types of information

docusoap documentary that follows the lives of real people at home, work, play, and other locales, resembling the style of a fictional SOAP OPERA

DOG [*see* **digitally originated graphic**]

dog-eat-dog marketing and advertising strategy of attacking the competition mercilessly through disparaging ads and other promotional strategies

Dolby trademarked electronic circuit that improves the quality of recorded sound by reducing noise

dolly shot filmic tracking shot using a moving platform (dolly) rather than some other platform (for example, a guiding rail)

domain name 1. on the World Wide Web, a name that identifies the owner of a site in some way (with a sequence of words, phrases, abbreviations, symbols, etc.); 2. more generally, the Internet address of a computer or network (for example, .edu, .org, etc.)

domestic comedy a television hybrid of the SITCOM in which characters and settings are usually more important than the complicated situations that characterize sitcoms. The basic structure of the text revolves around a

domestic problem that the characters have to solve.

dominant culture culture that is accepted as the norm, or the mainstream, by most people living in a specific society

dominant discourse form of DISCOURSE that is given the highest social authority or precedence over other discourses. For example, in a religious society, the discourse of clerics and theologians is dominant, whereas in secular societies it is not.

dominant ideology system of beliefs and values that a culture accepts as the norm

dominant reading one of three supposed readings or interpretations that can be gleaned from a media text (the other two being SUBORDINATE and RADICAL) whereby the audience accepts the meanings, values, and viewpoints built into the text by its makers

doorstepping practice of journalists to pressure an individual who is an unwilling source of information by standing outside the person's residence or place of work, or by asking questions as the person walks by

doo-wop style of singing and songwriting, starting in the 1950s, characterized by catchy melodies, simple rhythms, beautiful vocal harmonies, and often featuring a choral accompaniment with the expression "doo-wop" (hence the name of the genre)

dot-com any company that conducts its business primarily through the Internet. The term refers to the fact that the Internet address of such companies ends in ".com."

dot-com crash the burst of the "dot-com bubble" (the increase in dot-com businesses that gained rapid success in the late 1990s) in which many dot-com businesses went bankrupt in the early 2000s

dot-comer person who owns or works for a dot-com enterprise

double substitute who resembles an actor and who stands in for him or her, especially in scenes that are dangerous or that require some special skill

double exposure exposure of two images on the same piece of film, making it seem that they have been shot at the same time

double feature [also called **twin bill**] two films shown on the same bill (for a single price of admission)

double opt-in method by which users who want to receive information from a Web site can register themselves as subscribers

double-spotting technique of running a commercial twice in a row

downlinking transmission of data from a satellite downward to receivers within its range (called a *footprint*)

downloading transferring data from the Internet to a computer, or from one computer to another

downtime period of time in which a communication network is inoperative, because of maintenance or mechanical breakdown

drabble short fictional work, usually around 100 words in length

drama [also called **theater**] 1. play (usually serious in tone) written to be performed on a stage or platform with appropriate props; 2. by extension, any play in any media (e.g., radio, television). It is not known how or when drama began, but nearly every culture has had some form of it. Some archaeologists claim that it may have developed from religious rituals and ceremonies in which people impersonated gods or animals. Others suggest that drama may have originated in rituals of praise performed for a dead hero, when the deeds of the hero's life were acted out. Eventually, the stories of the lives were performed apart from the rituals, leading to the birth of drama. A third theory claims that drama evolved from mythic storytelling, which developed into dramatic retellings of events. There are four main forms of Western drama. First, the *tragedy*, which revolves around some tragic event or life story, usually of a hero who dies at the end because of a flaw in his or her character or on account of a devious act perpetrated by an evil personage. Second, the *serious drama*, which emerged in the 1800s and which shares many of the features of tragedy, but in which the hero is more ordinary than the traditional tragic hero and which does not necessarily have to end in his or her death. Third, the *melodrama*, which revolves around the actions of a villain who threatens the "good characters" in the play, and which usually has a happy ending. Fourth, the *comedy*, which aims to evoke laughter, but which can raise serious questions.

drama documentary [also called **docudrama**] television or radio program that dramatizes real events, fictionalizing them somewhat for effect

drama series television or radio drama broadcast in episodes

dramatic irony stage technique of telling an audience about an incongruity on the stage, of which the characters in the play or movie are unaware

dramatis personae list of the names of the characters in a play or story (Latin for the "characters of the drama"), often printed at the beginning or end

dramatist someone who writes dramas for the stage, radio, television, or some other medium

dramatization adaptation of a work of fiction, or the presentation of a real-life event, in dramatic form (for the stage, radio, etc.)

dramaturgy art of DRAMA, referring to both the actual dramas and how they are staged and the analysis of drama in all its dimensions (from the script to the performance)

dramedy [blend of **drama** and **comedy**] television program that blurs serious and comic themes

dress program television program in which a real person (rather than an actor) is transformed socially by dress experts who change his or appearance by suggesting what clothes to wear, what cosmetics are appropriate, etc.

dress rehearsal final rehearsal of a play or musical performance, usually in costume

drip campaign low-profile ad campaign for a product, intended to maintain brand awareness in a subtle way, rather than through an intensive campaign

driver brand product brand that influences (that is, "drives") a purchase decision (e.g., Classic Coca-Cola versus a sub-brand of soft drink manufactured by the same company)

drive-time audiences radio audiences who listen to the radio in their cars in the morning on their way to work or school (usually 6 A.M.–9 A.M.) and in the late afternoon on their way home (usually 4 P.M.–7 P.M.)

dropped call a call on a mobile phone that is terminated because of loss of signal

DRTV [*see* **direct response television**]

dry run rehearsal that does not use any recording equipment

DSL [*see* **digital service line**]

DTV [*see* **digital television**]

dualism philosophical view that the mind and body are separate entities, and that human beings have a dual nature—the corporeal and the psychic

dubbing 1. adding music, voices, or sound effects to a film, a broadcast, or a recording by making a new sound track; 2. recording a sound track in a different language

dumbing-down making popular media texts (such as news reports) less intellectually challenging so that a larger audience can be gained

dummy layout of a newspaper page, showing where advertising materials are to be placed

duopoly single ownership of a media outlet by two organizations (as opposed to *monopoly*, in which several media outlets are owned by the same organization). Duopoly was sanctioned by the FCC in 1992.

Durkheim, Émile (1858–1917) French sociologist who saw similarities among the world's myths as evidence for a "collective consciousness" in the human species. Durkheim saw the spread of materialism as a destructive spiritual force in modern-day societies, leading to alienation and other psychic disorders. One of his most influential books is *De la division du travail social* (1893; *The Division of Labor*).

DVD [*see* **digital versatile/video disc**]

DVR [*see* **digital video recorder**]

dystopia [opposite of **utopia**] 1. place or condition that is bad or imperfect; 2. literary genre in which everything is flawed, condemning modern forms of social life. The classic example of dystopian literature is *Brave New World* (1932) by Aldous Huxley. The novel reflects Huxley's concern over the impact of science and technology on society.

ear box in the top corner of the front page of a newspaper, used for advertising or weather information

early window theory notion that media provide children with a "window on the world" before they have developed the critical ability to judge what they are exposed to, thus influencing their worldview as they grow up

earned rate discounted rate for print advertising space, reserved for frequent advertisers

easy listening style of popular music with simple melodies, lyrics, and harmonies, aimed mainly at adult audiences

eBay one of the largest online commerce companies

e-book [*see* **electronic book**]

e-business [*see* **electronic business**]

Echelon global computer surveillance system that has the capacity to intercept communications

echo plate device used in broadcasting or recording that creates reverberations or echo effects

Eco, Umberto (1932–) Italian semiotician and novelist who claims that, while the interpretation of a text may indeed be influenced by tradition and reader whims, there is nevertheless a meaning in the text that transcends these factors and cannot be simply discarded (as deconstructionsists claim). Perhaps his most influential works in the area of text interpretation are *The Role of the Reader* (1979) and *The Limits of Interpretation* (1990).

e-commerce [*see* **electronic commerce**]

economic determinism view of some social theorists that economic conditions, structures, or systems determine social and cultural conditions

economies of scale 1. view that the relative cost of some media ventures tend to decline as the size of the ventures grow; 2. more generally, the savings that can be gained by producing larger quantities of something

e-consulting [*see* **electronic consulting**]

écriture in semiotic theory, writing as a critical tool or as a means of challenging certain values, norms, social practices, ideologies, or views (originally proposed by JACQUES DERRIDA)

e-democracy [*see* **electronic democracy**]

Edison, Thomas Alva (1847–1931) American inventor of the phonograph (early record player), and contributor to the development of the telegraph, telephone, and motion pictures

editing altering texts of any kind to make them clearer, more appropriate, or more effective

editing decision list in film parlance, list of all the shots, audio tracks, and images available for editing

editing system computer system (such as software) that allows users to create, modify, add, and/or delete any type of information found on a Web site or file

edition 1. copies of a publication that have been printed on a specific date; 2. particular version of a regular broadcast

editor 1. person in charge of EDITING any text; 2. person in charge of the direction and content of a newspaper or magazine

editorial 1. article or column in a newspaper or magazine written by the editor or under his or her direction, giving opinions about a subject or event; 2. broadcast expressing the opinion of the announcer, program, station, or network

editorial policy the stance or position taken by a media outlet on a specific issue or set of issues

EDTV [*see* **extended-definition television**] .

educational advertising advertising designed to simulate education, informing ("educating") consumers about a product, especially if it has recently been introduced into the market

edutainment [blend of **education** and **entertainment**] any media product or text that both educates and entertains

effective frequency exposure to an advertisement that brings about consumer awareness with little expenditure of time, money, and effort

effective reach percentage of an audience that has had an effective exposure to an ad or commercial

effects coordinator member of a film or television production crew responsible for planning and directing special effects

effects models in media studies, models that explain any effects (psychological, social, cultural) that media may have on people, societies, and cultures, such as HYPODERMIC NEEDLE THEORY, MORAL PANIC THEORY, and USES AND GRATIFICATIONS THEORY

effigy dummy made to represent a hated person or group, used to critique, affront, or insult the person or group

e-fraud [*see* **electronic fraud**]

ego in psychoanalysis, the part of the psyche containing consciousness and personal memories. The ego is one of the three basic constituents of human character, the others being the ID and the SUPEREGO. In classical psychoanalytic theory, the ego is said to resolve conflicts among a person's instinctive impulses, his or her sense of guilt, and the demands of social reality. In popular usage, the word has come to mean selfishness, losing its psychoanalytic sense.

eighty-twenty rule in marketing, rule-of-thumb which assumes that 80 percent of the products marketed will be consumed by 20 percent of the customers

e-journalism [*see* **electronic journalism**]

elaborated codes [in contrast to **restricted codes**] DISCOURSE patterns that are thought to be characteristic of the middle classes and educated individuals, involving the use of a large vocabulary, full grammar, and other formal speech devices

e-learning [*see* **electronic learning**]

electronic book [abbreviated as **e-book**] digital book having the appearance of a traditional paper book but with its content stored digitally. E-books can be updated from a bookstore or a Web site that sells them.

electronic bookmark function on an Internet browser that allows a user to return to a Web page easily

electronic bulletin board systems computerized systems, e-mail or Web-based, that allow users to post and share messages, computer programs, and other digital information

electronic business [abbreviated as **e-business**] 1. Internet company; 2. practice of conducting business through the Internet

electronic cartoon [abbreviated as **e-toon**] a humorous drawing that is produced online

electronic church use of electronic media to broadcast religious subject matter

electronic commerce [abbreviated as **e-commerce**] business transactions carried out over the Internet

electronic consulting [abbreviated as **e-consulting**] consulting services on such matters as Web page design, offered to companies that do business on the Internet

electronic democracy [abbreviated as **e-democracy**] use of the Internet to distribute information freely on matters of a political, social, and/or ideological nature

electronic fraud [abbreviated as **e-fraud**] criminal fraud that takes place on the Internet

Electronic Frontier Foundation nonprofit agency that supports the protection of individual civil liberties in the world of advanced communications technology

electronic game [*see* **computer game**]

electronic journalism [abbreviated as **e-journalism**] publication of news that occurs on the Internet or in some other electronic broadcast medium

electronic learning [abbreviated as **e-learning**] learning involving the utilization of electronic technology, such as computer networks and Internet-based coursework

electronic magazine [abbreviated as **e-zine**] magazine that is accessed online

electronic mail [abbreviated as **e-mail**] mail sent from one computer to another. To send and receive e-mail messages, an individual must have an e-mail address, which serves the same function that a street address does for traditional mail delivery, now called "snail mail." Such addresses are obtained from commercial businesses known as Internet service providers (ISPs) or online services. These also supply the computer software needed to compose, send, receive, and read e-mail.

electronic media media such as radio and television (in contrast to PRINT media)

electronic money [abbreviated as **e-money**] currency in digital form that can be transmitted through computer networks and systems such as the World Wide Web

electronic music [also called **electronica** or **techno**] style of music that became popular in the 1980s, using equipment such as synthesizers and computers to produce its characteristic "electronic sound"

electronic news gathering recording of news events using small video cameras and a minimal crew

electronic news production system software that allows newsroom production on a desktop computer

Electronic Numerical Integrator and Computer [abbreviated as **ENIAC**] world's first all-electronic general-purpose computer; designed and built in 1946 by American engineers John W. Mauchly and J. Presper Eckert, Jr., at the University of Pennsylvania. ENIAC was 1800 square feet in size, weighed 30 tons, contained 17,468 vacuum tubes, and had 6,000 manual switches.

electronic program guide on-screen television guide providing information about programs and channels

electronic publishing [abbreviated as **e-publishing**] publication and distribution of books online or in some electronic format (such as CD-ROM)

electronic shopping [abbreviated as **e-shopping**] buying products and services online

electronic smog electronic fields produced in the atmosphere because of overflow radiation from radar, broadcasting transmissions, electrical appliances, or mobile phones; considered by some to constitute a serious health risk

electronic town hall use of electronic media (television, Internet) for political purposes on the part of both politicians and the public

electronica [*see* **electronic music**]

electrotactile illusion semblance of touch produced by VIRTUAL REALITY technology

elegy poem or song lamenting a deceased person. The elegy became popular in the ancient world through the writings of Callimachus (third century B.C.E.) and Catullus (first century B.C.E.). Among the best-known English-language elegies are *Lycidas* (1638) by John Milton and *Elegy Written in a Country Churchyard* (1751) by Thomas Gray.

ellipsis 1. omission of a word or words necessary for making a complete grammatical construction, because the construction can be understood in the context in which it occurs: for example, *Sarah is as smart as her brother* instead of *Sarah is as smart as her brother is smart*; 2. series of dots used in writing or printing to indicate an omission: *The colors are red, blue, orange . . . and yellow*

Ellul's theory of technique [after philosopher Jacques Elull] idea that technological advances make communication and social interaction increasingly efficient

e-mail [*see* **electronic mail**]

e-mail campaign advertising campaign that uses e-mails to deliver pitches for a product, service, or political purpose

embedded journalism news coverage in which correspondents actually take part in some aspect of a war (such as accompanying a specific battalion) in order to report on it "as it happens"

emblem visual symbol designed to ennoble something or someone or to represent it as distinctive in some way: for example, the emblem used by the Girl Scouts

emergent attribute benefit, quality, concept, or experience that is associated with a brand: for example, the "friendliness" of Google

emergent culture 1. idea that radical cultural forms tend to emerge spontaneously from the general population to challenge the status quo; 2. notion developed by British social critic RAYMOND WILLIAMS that at any point in its history, a new form of culture emerges to prominence

Emmy Award honor conferred annually by the American Academy of Television Arts and Sciences for outstanding achievement in television. Emmys are given to performers, directors, writers, art directors, costume designers, editors, sound mixers, and performers. The first Emmys were awarded in 1949. Web site: www.emmys.org

e-money [*see* **electronic money**]

emoticon string of keyboard characters that, when viewed sideways (or in some other orientation), can be seen to suggest a face expressing a particular emotion. An emoticon is often used in an e-mail message or newsgroup posting as a comment on the text that accompanies it. Common emoticons include the *smiley* :-) or :) and the *winkey* ;-) and the *yawn* :-O, among others.

emotional appeal advertising technique designed to appeal to the emotions rather than to the rational intellect of the consumer

emotive function as defined by ROMAN JAKOBSON, the role played by the addresser's (sender's) emotions in the construction and delivery of messages in communication

empathy feeling of identification with the experience or emotions of another person

empirical data data that comes from actual observations

empiricism view in philosophy and psychology that we learn through experience and thus that we are born with an "empty slate" (tabula rasa), as opposed to *innatism*, which asserts that we are born with all knowledge structures already intact and that the environment simply triggers them

empowerment process (political, social) that gives people the ability to make their own choices and control their lives

encoder person, group, or institution that creates a message on the basis of a specific CODE or codes

encoding [opposite of **decoding**] process of making or saying something with the resources of a specific CODE. The quantity "'four" can represented with the digit "4" or "100"—the former is encoded from the decimal code and the latter from the binary code of numbers. Analogously, a media text, such as a sitcom, is put together with a specific social code (father as head of the family, mother as wise leader of the family, etc.), which shapes how it is perceived, which audiences it is meant to attract, and so on.

encryption electronic masking of information on the Web that can be deciphered only by a recipient who has the unmasking code, known as the *decryption key*

enculturation process whereby someone acquires the values, beliefs, and worldview of the culture in which he or she is reared or to which he or she is exposed

encyclopedia reference work (paper, electronic) giving information on all or specific types of knowledge. In ancient times, scholars presented information in any order they chose, and they had few ways to check its accuracy. They also scattered these in various forms (in scrolls, on papyri, etc.). The word *encyclopedia* did not come into common use until the 1700s, when the modern concept of this work surfaced as a result of the ideas of Enlightenment scholars who started listing items of knowledge in alphabetical order and according to field (science, music, art, language, etc.). The first popular encyclopedia of this kind was constructed by Denis Diderot as a 28-volume work titled *Encyclopédie ou dictionnaire raisonée des sciences, des arts et des métiers* (1751–1772)—*Encyclopedia of Sciences, Arts, and Trades*—that set the standard for all subsequent encyclopedias. Until the mid-1980s, most encyclopedias were only available in book form. The first compact disc encyclopedia was produced by Grolier in 1985. *Compton's Multimedia Encyclopedia* was released in this format in 1989, integrating various media (sound, pictures, etc.) and text in what came to be called a CD-ROM. There are now online encyclopedias, the most widely used being WIKIPEDIA (Web site: www.wikipedia.org). Since these can be updated, many predict the end of the paper encyclopedia.

endnote reference that appears at the end of a chapter or book, rather than at the bottom of a page

endorsement public support given to a product for advertising purposes

engraving art of carving images on a hard surface

enhanced television services optional or additional services, such as subtitles and closed captioning, provided by some channels or cable companies

ENIAC [*see* **Electronic Numerical Integrator and Computer**]

enigma baffling puzzle or riddle. The Riddle of the Sphinx, solved by Oedipus, is probably the first enigma ever composed: *What is it that walks on four at sunrise, on two at noon, and on three at dusk?* The answer is *human beings* who crawl (on all fours) at birth (the sunrise of life), stand up as they grow (the noon hour of life), and need a cane to make it through old age (the dusk of life).

enigma code one of the five CODES used in the construction of media texts, based on secrets and how they work emotionally and intellectually in texts. The other codes are called ACTION, REFERENTIAL, SEMANTIC, and SYMBOLIC.

enlargement copy of a photographic image that is larger than the original

Enlightenment [also called the **Age of Reason**] eighteenth-century philosophical movement that emphasized reason and science (rather than faith and religion). The Enlightenment lasted until the late 1700s; its leaders included several French philosophers—the Marquis de Condorcet, Denis Diderot, Jean-Jacques Rousseau, and Voltaire—and the English philosopher John Locke. Philosophers of the Enlightenment started the tradition of organizing knowledge in ENCYCLOPEDIAS and of creating institutes for the preservation of knowledge and the conduct of scientific inquiry and debate.

énoncé in cultural theory, the way in which a content of a text is presented since, as its French name implies, the text has to be enunciated or expressed in a specific way

entailment 1. process of coming to a logical conclusion on the basis of the given premises or facts; 2. in linguistics, any sentence that is inferred from another: for example, *Bill is a bachelor* entails *Bill is not married.*

enterprise fiction literary genre of fictional works, written primarily by women, revolving around the theme of female triumph (enterprise) in a male-dominated world through hard work and determination

entertainment mode of contact with an audience that aims to provide an experience that is pleasurable. Entertainment is characterized by a constant search for novelty and the avoidance of offending or alienating important audience segments. In Marxist theory, entertainment is seen as part of capitalist IDEOLOGY, since it is claimed that entertainment is used to justify discursive and social practices, especially discriminatory ones, such as sexism.

entertainment reporter journalist or broadcast announcer who reports on entertainment news, especially concerning celebrities

entertainment television television channel that deals with entertainment news, issues, announcements, celebrities

enthusiast in advertising jargon, any individual who loves ads and commercials for their own sake

entropy measure of information and of the efficiency of information systems based on probability factors. When an alarm system is "off" it has virtually no entropy, whereas when it is "on" it has maximum entropy. The term is also used to indicate the amount of "disorder" that exists in a system, as measured by randomness factors present in it.

epic lengthy narrative poem or song telling about the deeds of heroes and the gods. Some epics recount how a culture or people began. The earliest epics were probably sung and had no established text, just the outline of a well-known tale. In Western culture, the epic began with the *Iliad* and the *Odyssey* by Homer, who may have lived during the eighth or ninth century B.C.E. Both form a cycle based on the partly historical and partly mythical Trojan War. Homer was followed in Roman culture by the poet Virgil. Epics start *in medias res* (in the middle of things), that is, after a significant portion of the action has already taken place and with an "invocation" in which the poet asks a Muse for divine inspiration. Epic poetry declined during the 1700s with the rise of prose fiction. Its appeal was revived in the Romantic period by English poet William Wordsworth with his epic poem *The Prelude* (1805, published 1850) and by American poet Walt Whitman with his *Song of Myself* (1855); and in the twentieth century by British poet T.S. Eliot with his *Four Quartets* (1943). The popular series of *Star Wars* movies (starting 1977) have epic structure, starting *in medias res* and having the same type of thematic content of ancient epics, especially the Homeric epics.

epigram short, usually witty poem or saying. In ancient Greece, epigrams were inscribed often on statues, buildings, coins, and the like. Popular sayings are really epigrams: *When it rains it pours*; *The only way to get rid of a temptation is to yield to it* (Oscar Wilde).

epilogue 1. short section added to the end of a work, providing further information, insight, etc.; 2. speech given by an actor to address an audience directly at the end of a play

episode 1. part of a serial (novel, movie, television, etc.) that is published or broadcast separately; 2. incident in a plot that has significance for the overall story

epistemic as defined by MICHEL FOUCAULT, the ways of thinking and knowing that are characteristic of a specific intellectual era: for example, "medieval thought," "Enlightenment philosophy." For Foucault, an episteme is a form of knowledge grounded in discourse derived from a specific era and mode of thought. For instance, the gender of an individual (the role he or she is expected to play according to his or her biological sex) is an episteme that can only be interpreted in specific discourse and cultural terms, not to mention historical traditions.

epistemology in Western philosophy, the study of knowledge in all its dimensions, from what it is to how it is acquired and encoded by language. It also includes the study of the relation between knowledge, belief systems, truth, and reality.

epithet descriptive word or phrase (usually with satirical or critical intent) used in place of the actual name of someone, highlighting an attribute or feature of his or her personality: for example, *egghead* for "a smart person"

eponym person for whom a place or thing is named

e-publishing [*see* **electronic publishing**]

equal time Federal Communications Commission requirement that when a political candidate is allowed to broadcast a message by commercial media, opposing candidates must be offered equal time

equilibrium in a narrative, the state of stability present at the start and the state to which it returns after the resolution of tensions. A narrative starts off typically with a situation in which things are as they are (hence in equilibrium). Then something happens to upset the equilibrium (a crisis, a challenge). This state of imbalance is eventually resolved and the initial stable state is put back, regained, or re-evoked in some way.

escapism use of media (such as going to the movies) to escape from daily routine or pressing personal problems

escapist genre any text (novel, television program, film, piece of music) that provides pure entertainment, rather than engagement, allowing people to "escape from reality" temporarily

e-shopping [*see* **electronic shopping**]

essentialism view that a text always contains an "essence" that defines it as an exemplar of a genre

esthetics [*see* **aesthetics**]

e-system [*see* **electronic system**]

etching the art of engraving a figure, symbol, or word on a hard surface

ethics rules or principles of behavior that are purported to guide actions

ethnocentrism tendency of seeing things in terms of the values, beliefs, and worldview associated with one's ethnic heritage

ethnographic research [also called **participant observation**] anthropological method of describing peoples or groups by becoming involved with them in some way (such as living among them for a period of time). The term also refers to a written, photographic, or filmed report that provides such a description.

e-toon [*see* **electronic cartoon**]

euphemism word or phrase used in place of another because it is considered less offensive or discordant: for example, *pass away* for *die*; *vomit* for *throw up*

Euro English an official language of the European Union

eurocentricism tendency of Europeans, or those of European heritage, to evaluate things in terms of their European cultural heritage

evaluation research advertising method of analyzing how well an ad campaign has met its original aims

event television television programming that involves reporting an event live, such as a baseball game or a concert

evergreens in television syndication, popular and enduring network reruns such as *I Love Lucy* and *Seinfeld*

exclamation abruptly uttered word or phrase expressing a strong emotion, such as fright, grief, imploration, hatred, and so on; for example, *Yikes! Help!*

exclusive story that has only been covered in one media outlet in advance of other outlets

exegesis critical explanation or analysis of a text

existentialism twentieth-century movement in philosophy, writing, and the arts which denied that life has any intrinsic meaning or purpose and thus that individuals must assume responsibility for their actions. Existentialism crystallized from the ideas of Danish philosopher and theologian Søren Kierkegaard and German philosopher Friedrich Nietzsche. Existentialist writers emphasize the isolation that an individual experiences in a cold and barren universe. The most prominent existentialists include writers Albert Camus, Jean-Paul Sartre, and Gabriel Marcel; and philosophers Karl Jaspers and Martin Heidegger.

exnomination view claiming that widely held values are rarely challenged because they are not articulated as such. The term was introduced by ROLAND BARTHES to explain why the dominance of those in power goes unexamined—because it is not named as such (exnominated). This ensures that people will see the values of dominant groups not as tied to any special interests, but rather as implicit human values. The term has been used, by extension, to explain why stereotyping persists in the media.

exogenous stations clandestine broadcasting operations situated outside the regions to which they transmit programs

experiential advertising advertising method based on getting the consumer to experience the product directly (for example, by trying it)

experimental group group that is being experimented upon (as opposed to the control group, which is not) in order to see if it reacts, behaves, or does something differently

experimental research research using actual subjects to discover if a media text or an advertising campaign produces observable (and sometimes measurable) results

exposé newspaper report, television documentary, or Web site designed to reveal a scandal, crime, etc.

expression 1. look on someone's face that communicates some thought or

The Scream (1893) by Edvard Munch

emotion; 2. word or phrase communicating a specific concept: *in the mood*, *night and day*, etc.; 3. interpretation of a musical text that draws out its emotional qualities

expressionism early twentieth-century art movement emphasizing the inner experiences of humans (such as fear, love, etc.). Edvard Munch's expressionist painting *The Scream*, for example, conveys a feeling of anguish and inner torment in a very dramatic way.

extended-definition television [abbreviated as **EDTV**] enhanced television transmission system that offers a very high definition and wider aspect ratio

external search method of finding information from external sources or from the World Wide Web

external service in international broadcasting, service used by a country to counter enemy propaganda and spread information about itself

extra actor employed temporarily in a minor role in a film production

extramercial in cyberadvertising (advertising online), an ad that slides down a Web page

eye candy nonessential features on a Web page

eye tracking 1. advertising research method whereby the eye movement of subjects is recorded in order to determine which parts of the brain are activated while viewing an ad or commercial; 2. technique of following the eye movements of Internet users in order to determine what they look at and for how long, so that Web page designers can improve the effectiveness of their sites

eyeballs Internet users who visit a particular Web site frequently

eyewitness account report of an event by someone who was there to observe it

e-zine [*see* **electronic magazine**]

fable story designed to impart a moral lesson or a verity about human life; the characters are often animals or mythical creatures who are given human traits, and the moral is often stated explicitly at the end. The animal stories of Aesop (sixth century B.C.E.) are among the best-known and oldest fables in history. Another collection of beast fables is the Sanskrit *Panchatantra* (ca. third century C.E.). A popular collection of fables, entitled *Le roman de Renart*, emerged in France between the late twelfth and fourteenth centuries. The fables of Jean de la Fontaine, published between 1668 and 1694, became internationally renowned. Other fabulists include the nineteenth-century Danish writer Hans Christian Andersen and the twentieth-century Italian novelist Italo Calvino.

fabliau generally satirical, often bawdy tale composed and recited by wandering minstrels; the genre emerged in France in the twelfth century and was popular through the mid-fourteenth century. Around 150 fabliaux have survived. The form was emulated by medieval writers, including Geoffrey Chaucer, whose *Canterbury Tales* contains six fabliaux. The fabliau is considered a precursor to the modern short story.

fabula in narrative theory, any story with FABLE-like qualities and structure

Facebook online social networking site, founded in 2004, where personal profiles can be posted. It was originally developed for university students, faculty, and staff, but has since expanded to include anyone. Web site: www.facebook.com

facial expression appearance assumed by the face, unconsciously or wittingly, to communicate something (usually an emotional state). Facial expressions include winking, smiling, grimacing, and the like. In 1963 psychologist Paul Ekman established the Human Interaction Laboratory in the Department of Psychiatry at the University of California at San Francisco for the purpose of studying facial expressions. Ekman and his research team have established some facial expressions as universal signs of particular emotions.

facsimile [*see* **fax**]

fact sheet 1. information sheet or booklet that provides details about a subject covered by a broadcast or news story; 2. sheet containing data about a product, used by advertisers to help them create ads and campaigns

factory studios the first film production studios

fad a craze or fashion trend that is taken up with great enthusiasm for a brief period of time: for example, the hula hoop fad, the sudoku fad, and so on

fadeaway filming technique of gradually decreasing light or sound until it disappears completely

fade-in technique of gradually introducing images or sounds until they become visible or audible

fade-out 1. technique of gradually removing images or sounds until they become invisible or inaudible; 2. gradual loss of a broadcast signal

Still from *Snow White and the Seven Dwarfs* (1937)

fair use legal principle stating that under certain limited conditions (e.g., for educational purposes) individuals may make copies of copyrighted material without seeking the permission of the copyright holder

Fairness Doctrine U.S. broadcasting regulation (abolished in 1987) that required broadcasters to cover issues of public importance fairly and to provide equal air time to representatives of opposing viewpoints

fairy tale story revolving around fairies or other imaginary supernatural beings who become involved in human affairs using magic. *Tales of Mother Goose* (1697) by French writer Charles Perrault and *Fairy Tales* (2 volumes, 1812–1815) by the Grimm brothers, Jacob and Wilhelm Karl, are among the best-known fairy tales in Western literature.

false claim untrue or exaggerated claim made in the advertising of a product or service

false consciousness in Marxist theory, the claim that common people develop a false sense of their social identity, which helps maintain the status quo and is thus of great advantage to the ruling class, which wants to avoid change in social structure. Essentially, false consciousness occurs when people are conditioned not to see any need to take political action in their own best interests.

family movies movies designed for viewing by families together; the story line often revolves around relations between children and parents

family viewing television programming that is deemed suitable for children

famous-person testimonial in advertising, the endorsement of a product by a well-known person (a movie star, an athlete, etc.)

fan (derived from "fanatic") a person with a strong liking for or interest in a performer, program, event, or sport

fan fiction fictional story written by the fan of a celebrity, in which the celebrity is the main character (posted typically on Web sites)

fantasy literary genre that features imaginary or magical worlds, characters, and events, usually intended for children. The most famous fantasy in children's literature is, arguably, Lewis Carroll's *Alice's Adventures in Wonderland* (1865), revolving around the adventures of a girl named Alice, who reaches a magic land after she follows a white rabbit down a hole in the ground. Perhaps the most popular fantasy novel by an American author is L. Frank Baum's *Wonderful Wizard of Oz* (1900), which follows the adventures of a girl who has been carried by a cyclone from Kansas to a magic land. E.B. White's *Charlotte's Web* (1952), about friendship among animals on a farm, is another classic example of a fantasy story.

fanzine magazine produced by fans for other fans of a celebrity or a hobby (such as a particular video game). The early fanzines were created around punk bands in the mid-1970s and then spread to other domains of popular culture, such as sports (teams, for example, published fanzines). Today, Internet discussion sites and blogs have taken on the functions of fanzines, rendering them virtually obsolete.

FAQ [full form: **frequently asked questions**] section on Web sites that provides answers to questions that visitors often have about the site or the information it contains

farce comedy genre intended to evoke laughter through caricature by placing characters in improbable or ludicrous situations. In the medieval period, farces were often based on folk tales. Today, farce, slapstick, and buffoonery are used interchangeably to designate any comedy involving pranks (e.g., throwing a pie in someone's face, pushing unsuspecting people into swimming pools, etc.).

Farnsworth, Philo T. (1906–1971) American pioneer in television technology, who built an electronic television camera tube known as an *image dissector* in 1927; it produced an electronic signal that corresponded to the brightness of the objects being televised

fashion shoot session for photographing models wearing clothing fashions, usually for publication in a magazine

fashion show exhibition of clothing in the latest styles, worn and displayed by models on a runway, usually accompanied by music. Many media critics now identify fashion shows as a specific genre of variety show.

fast-forward function on a tape recorder that causes the tape to wind forward rapidly

fast motion film action that appears faster than is naturally possible because it was shot at a slower speed than the speed at which it is projected

FastTrack network application that permits users to interconnect, search file directories, and share music, video, and other files

fax [abbreviation of **facsimile**] device allowing the electronic transmission of printed or pictorial documents across telephone lines or through wireless technology from one location to another

FCC [*see* **Federal Communications Commission**]

fear appeal advertising message that makes the audience anxious or fearful, emphasizing ways in which the product can help people overcome their anxiety or fear

feature 1. longer, more probing article or story in a print medium (newspaper or magazine) covering human interest topics as opposed to hard news; 2. item for a radio or television program, usually consisting of interviews

feature film main film shown at a motion picture theater (or on television), usually the longest of two or more films shown in one program

feature syndicates clearinghouses (such as United Features and King Features) that provide the work of journalists, feature writers, and cartoonists to newspapers and other media outlets

Federal Communications Act of 1934 U.S. legislative act that established the Federal Communications Commission

Federal Communications Commission [abbreviated as **FCC**] federal agency, founded in 1934, responsible for regulating broadcast and electronic communications in the United States. Web site: www.fcc.gov

Federal Trade Commission [abbreviated as **FTC**] federal agency, established in 1914, that is responsible for regulating national advertising and for ensuring consumer protection. Web site: www.ftc.gov

feedback 1. response pattern to a given communication; 2. information that is fed directly back to the sender in a communication system, enabling the system to adjust its operation as needed; in linguistic communication, the process by which people adjust their messages as they are delivering them, in response to the reactions (facial expressions, bodily movements) of their interlocutors.

feeder cables television cables that run from trunk cables to individual neighborhoods

feeding sending a program or signal from one station to other stations

Fellinesque a film or media text that blends reality and fantasy, reminiscent of the methods of Federico Fellini, the renowned Italian motion picture director. Fellini often developed the script as the film was being made. Many of his films rely heavily on the use of symbolism and imagery, creating obscure dreamlike sequences.

feminism movement advocating equal rights and opportunities for women. Feminist beliefs have existed throughout history, but feminism did not become widespread in the Western world until the mid-1800s, when women began to protest against social and political injustices, such as the barring of women from voting in elections and serving on juries, and from admission to most institutions of higher education and most professional careers. Many historians regard the feminist movement as a turning point in the history of modern societies. There have been several waves of feminism, starting in the 1960s, influencing theories of culture, gender, and the like. The first one, called strictly "feminism," took the general slant on sexual culture as serving male-oriented interests and, thus, catering to male voyeurism; the second main wave, called "postfeminism," starting in the 1980s, took the view that females have actually always been in charge of the gaze themselves, that is, that while the voyeurs may be men, what they look at is under the control of women.

feminist theory [also called **feminist criticism**] important theory emerging in the late 1960s devoted to deconstructing gender biases in media and society. Early feminist criticism viewed media representations of women as constructs that were subservient to the male psyche, arguing that these were degrading to women, as well as a source of influence in promoting violence against women. Some of these critiques were well founded, given the spread of images of women as either "sexual cheerleaders" or "motherly homemakers" in many media programs (such as TV sitcoms). However, already in the 1950s, there were sitcoms such as *The Honeymooners* and *I Love Lucy* that featured strong-willed, independent females as protagonists. Moreover, having interpreted the display of women's bodies in media and advertising as serving male voyeurism, the early feminists are now critiqued as having ignored the fact that open sexuality played a critical role in liberating women. With the entrance of Madonna onto the pop culture stage in the mid-1980s, the tide in feminist theory changed radically, leading to what is now called *postfeminism*. Postfeminists interpret the representation of female sexuality in public places and in media not as exploitation, but rather as a transgressive form of social discourse, even viewing strip-teasing and pornography as crucial players in the ongoing sexual revolution in women's liberation. The postfeminist perspective has thus come forward to provide a vastly different view of media representations of womanhood than traditional feminist and religious views.

femme fatale female character in movies and other media of great seductive charm who leads men into compromising or dangerous situations or who destroys those who succumb to her charms

Ferguson, Marjorie (1929–1999) feminist scholar whose work on the representation of women in media is widely respected. Among her most influential works are *Forever Feminine: Women's Magazines and the Cult of Femininity* (1983) and *Cultural Studies in Question* (with P. Golding, 1997).

fetish 1. object perceived as having magical powers; 2. object or body part that causes sexual arousal, often becoming an object of fixation

feuilleton section of a European newspaper containing fiction, reviews, and cultural articles

fiber-optic cable cable that carries signals rapidly over very thin glass fibers for long-distance transmissions

fiction any work whose content is imaginary rather than purely factual. The fabliaux, romances, and novellas of the Middle Ages were the forerunners of the novel, the first true fiction genre.

field of view extent of a scene that can be captured by a camera

fieldwork in marketing, research method consisting of gathering information by conducting surveys

figure a representation of someone or something (a diagram, picture, drawing, etc.)

figure of speech word, phrase, or expression that has a nonliteral sense, adding color, evaluation, or insight to a text: *He was born with a silver spoon in his mouth* = *He was born into a privileged situation*

file sharing activity of exchanging information electronically, especially through the Internet

File Transfer Protocol [abbreviated as **FTP**] common way of transferring files across the Internet, usually with a browser

film 1. thin sheet or strip of developed photographic negatives or transparencies; 2. sequence of images projected onto a screen with sufficient rapidity as to create the illusion of motion and continuity; 3. by extension, a work (narrative, documentary, etc.) realized in this form [*see also* **cinema**]

film music music composed to accompany a film

film noir moody, pessimistic filmmaking style that was very popular in the United States during the 1940s and 1950s (in French, the term *noir* means "black"). A typical film noir showed a world of corruption and crime, with cynical characters trapped in dismal situations that led invariably to their destruction. The plot generally took place in large American cities, generally at night and in dingy surroundings. The movie's gloomy tone was accentuated by edgy music and shadowy backgrounds. Some famous examples of film noir include *The Maltese Falcon* (1941), *Double Indemnity* (1944), and *The Big Heat* (1953). Starting in the 1970s some American directors attempted to recapture the film noir style with movies such as *Chinatown* (1974), *Taxi Driver* (1976), *The Grifters* (1990), and *L.A. Confidential* (1997).

film theory area of film studies that deals with film genres, rather than any specific analysis or critique of films. Film theorists look at movies as TEXTS and how they deliver meanings (aesthetic or otherwise).

filmography 1. writing about movies; 2. list of movies, usually of a given director, actor, or a specific genre

filtering software software that automatically blocks access to Web sites containing offensive material

final cut final edited version of a film released publicly

Financial Interest and Syndication rules [abbreviated as **fin-syn**] FCC rules outlining the amount of program ownership that television networks are allowed. Rescinded in the mid-1990s, the rules were intended to prohibit the major networks from running their own syndication companies.

fine arts arts (such as sculpture, painting, and music) that are perceived to have aesthetic qualities rather than simple decorative or utilitarian functions (crafts)

fin-syn [*see* **Financial Interest and Syndication Rules**]

fireside chat broadcast in which the president of the United States talks in an informal manner to the people. This type of program was initiated on radio by Franklin D. Roosevelt during the Great Depression as a way of reassuring people about his policies.

firewall software preventing unauthorized access to a computer, Web site, etc.

First Amendment amendment to the U.S. Constitution that guarantees freedom of speech and is thus continually cited in media debates: "Congress shall make no law respecting an establishment of religion, or prohibiting the free exercise thereof; or abridging the freedom of speech, or of the press; or the right of the people peacefully to assemble, and to petition the Government for a redress of grievances."

first edition 1. first print run of a daily newspaper; 2. first published version of a book

first-run syndication programming produced specifically for the syndicated television market

Fiske, John (1939–) scholar whose insights on the meanings built into media products and events (intentionally or unconsciously) have become widely cited. Among his most influential works are *Television Culture* (1987) and *Understanding Popular Culture* (1989).

fixed break practice of placing commercials in a specific place within a radio or television programming format

fixed spot item that is broadcast at a specific time; for example, news on the hour

flack derogatory epithet describing a public relations professional

flaming act of sending an offensive e-mail or of posting an offensive newsgroup item

flappers stylish and fun-loving young women of the 1920s, who showed disdain for the previous Victorian social conventions through changes in clothing and lifestyle

flash 1. brief news story that is broadcast immediately, often interrupting an ongoing program; 2. device used to produce a short bright light in photography

flash forward to jump forward to a later point in a narrative for a dramatic effect

flash prank Web site designed to shock visitors with sudden scary images and loud noises

flashback literary or cinematic technique of inserting an earlier event into the normal chronological order of a narrative, showing what happened or providing further information

flick colloquial term for MOVIE or FILM

flier leaflet used for advertising purposes

floodlight lamp with a wide angle, used to provide light broadly for filming purposes

floor manager person who is responsible for the technical aspects of filming during a film shoot or in a television studio

floppy disk small plastic disk coated on both sides with magnetic material that can record and store computer data. Floppy disks are being used less and less as new technology is making available more convenient and powerful devices such as USB ports that have rendered the floppy disk's storage capacity inadequate for many types of files.

flow 1. movement of something such as information; 2. an evening's scheduled programming; 3. view put forward by RAYMOND WILLIAMS that audiences experience television programs not as autonomous entities but as elements in a flow of similar entities

flow chart diagram used in computer science and other sciences and disciplines, which is designed to show how the procedures used in performing a task are connected to each other

fly-on-the-wall documentary documentary style, similar to CINÉMA-VÉRITÉ, in which small cameras are used to film subjects as they go about their routine business

FM radio [full form: **frequency modulation radio**] system of radio transmission in which wave frequencies are modulated in tandem with the audio signal being transmitted. The first FM system was established in 1936, but became popular only in the late 1960s. Frequency modulation has several advantages over the alternate radio broadcasting system of amplitude modulation (AM): greater freedom from interference and static; a higher signal-to-noise ratio; and operation in the high-frequency bands.

focal points five main areas of interest in the study of media and communication: the media text, the maker of the text, the audience, American society (or its equivalent in other parts of the world), and the media

focus group interview research method that brings together audiences or consumer groups to discuss a media text or an ad, under the guidance of a trained interviewer. The responses are recorded and are later analyzed.

folk music music style consisting of a people's traditional songs and melodies

folk rock style of music developed by Bob Dylan (1941–) in the 1960s with poetic lyrics set to a rock beat, but evoking traditional folk music melodies, rhythms, and themes. Folk rock was the first major challenge to rock's domination by the British in the 1960s.

folklore set of traditional beliefs, stories, sayings, and art forms. Folklore includes cures, superstitions, festival customs, games, dances, proverbs, nursery rhymes, charms, and riddles.

folktale narrative tale, usually created in early oral traditions; examples include myths, legends, fables, and fairy tales

follow shot camera shot in which a moving subject is filmed as the camera follows the subject

follow-up news report that further investigates an earlier news story

font character or set of characters of the same style of typeface (such as Times)

footage selection of film sections that have been already shot

footer 1. text that appears at the bottom of a page; 2. section at the bottom of a Web page containing links and information on how to contact the owners of the Web page and on the copyright policy in place

footnote 1. note at the bottom of a page containing information, such as a reference citation or further explanation, about the preceding text; 2. something appended to a text as an explanation, reference, or comment

footprint area supplied by a signal from a satellite

forced exposure advertising research technique whereby consumers are brought to a facility to view and provide commentary on a commercial or ad campaign

Fordism view that a product should be accessible and affordable to the workers who produce it and that they should be paid a fair wage based on the value of what they are producing. The term makes reference to automaker Henry Ford's highly mechanized and standardized mode of automobile production in the 1920s. This term is now used, by extension, to describe a type of situation that stresses conformity and uniformity. The term *post-Fordism* has recently emerged to describe a world in which new technologies and economic markets have made it possible to break away from the mechanized form of production and, by extension, from social conformity.

forecast prediction of what the weather will be like in the near future, broadcast or printed regularly (on radio, on television, in newspapers, on Web sites)

foreground in painting and filmic technique, part of a scene that is

perceived by a viewer to be nearest to him or her

foreign correspondent journalist who lives or visits another country to report news about it for broadcast or publication

form theory art and philosophical theory claiming that the physical structure of a work is separable from its content. In a work of art, the *content* is defined as the meaning of the work, and the *form* is the way in which the work has been put together. Recent form theories stress that form and content are interconnected, rather than separable.

formalism emphasis on form rather than content in a work of art

format 1. in computer science, the way data is structured so that it can be used, stored, and retrieved; 2. presentation and style that distinguishes a radio or television program from others; 3. difference in size, shape, and appearance of media products (for example, tabloid vs. newspaper format)

format clock hourly radio programming schedule

format radio radio station that plays only one type of music (for example, country) or broadcasts one type of programming (for example, news radio)

formula technique advertising technique that uses formulaic speech

Vinyl 45 record

to describe a product, imitating proverbs, sayings, etc.: for example, *A Volkswagen is a Volkswagen! Coke is it!*

forty-fives [45 rpm records] discontinued type of record disc that could be played on phonograph turntables operating at 45 rpm. It was developed by RCA in the late 1940s. It had high quality but had limited storage space.

Foucault, Michel (1926–1984) French philosopher who became widely known in the 1970s for his writings on the role of history and culture in determining how people develop beliefs and how everyday practices guide people in defining their identities. In *Madness and Civilization* (1960), for instance, he showed how definitions and perceptions of madness have changed over time to reflect changes in cultural worldviews. His most quoted work is the *History of Sexuality* (1984).

Fourth Estate a synonym for the PRESS

Fox Broadcasting Company known as the "fourth network" (after NBC, CBS, and ABC), launched in 1986 by RUPERT MURDOCH. This broadcasting company introduced many new types of programs, including reality-based shows such as *Cops.* Web site: www.fox.com

fragmentation process by which a formerly unified or mass audience fragments into segments. For example, the availability of specialty television channels has resulted in the fragmentation of the television audience. Radio underwent a process of fragmentation in the 1950s with the introduction of television. Fragmentation makes it difficult to reach mass audiences and may threaten the economic survival of media that depend on them.

frame 1. a phrase or sentence with a blank in it for assaying which kinds of words or forms are permissible there (structurally or semantically); 2. a rectangular image on a screen; 3. on a Web page, a part that allows for modification of other parts of the same page

framing 1. adjusting the position of a film in a projector so that the image can be seen correctly on the screen; 2. the way in which a film is put together by specific camera techniques; 3. the way in which people organize and interpret events (such as spectacles and programs)

franchise 1. right to sell certain products or services for a particular period; 2. conversion of a media product (such as a film) into a series of sequels and spin-offs; 3. license to use a brand name; 4. license to broadcast within a specific area and/ or for a specific time period

franchise films movies produced with the intention of making sequels

Frankfurt School [full form: **Frankfurt Institute for Social Research**] school of critical inquiry founded at the University of Frankfurt in 1923; the world's first Marxist institute of social research. Its leading members included Theodor Adorno, Max Horkheimer, Herbert Marcuse, Erich Fromm, and Leo Lowenthal. Its aim was to understand the way in which human groups create meaning collectively under the impact of modern technology and how modern societies have come under the domain of CULTURE INDUSTRIES. The Frankfurt School was highly pessimistic about the possibility of genuine individuality under modern capitalism and condemned most forms of popular or mass culture as channels of consumerist propaganda that indoctrinated the masses and disguised genuine social inequalities. The School's main contention was that typical media fare was vulgar, functioning primarily to pacify ordinary people. Though not affiliated with the School, some contemporary critics of contemporary pop culture and media, such as Thomas Frank, Todd Gitlin, and Mark Crispin Miller, draw heavily upon the general arguments made by the Frankfurt School.

free market model economic system in which nongovernmental decision makers determine how resources will be used, what goods and services will be produced, and how these will be distributed among members of society; free competition in the market helps to guide these decisions

freedom of expression basic right of any free society, without which, it is claimed, journalists, academics, and others cannot perform their vital role of seeking and spreading new knowledge

freedom of information basic right to have access to information of all kinds, from the type held by governments to that held by media organizations

freedom of speech right to speak out publicly or privately, through any medium of expression, including books, newspapers, magazines, radio, television, motion pictures, and electronic documents on computer networks

freedom of the press freedom to publish anything without censorship before or after. Freedom of the press has been debated since modern printing began in the 1400s. Some governments place limits on this freedom, fearing the power of words to spur people to act against them.

freelance writer, journalist, or artist who works independently and is paid by assignment

freenet online information network run by volunteers, charging no access fees

freeware software available primarily through electronic bulletin boards and user groups that can be downloaded free of charge

freeze frame single image held still in the middle part of a motion picture sequence

frequency measurement of radio waves, indicating where a station is found on the radio dial

frequency modulation [*see* **FM radio**]

Freud, Sigmund (1856–1939) Austrian neurologist and founder of psychoanalysis. Freud claimed that human behavior was guided by the *unconscious*—the part of the psyche that contains wishes, memories, fears, etc., which manifest themselves in dreams, symbols, syndromes, and the like. Freud introduced such terms as *ego*, *id*, *superego*, and *Oedipus complex*, among others, which have become widely used in media studies.

friends on social networking Web sites, people who have access to other people's profiles and who post their own profiles

Sigmund Freud

Friendster online social networking site launched in 2002 where personal profiles can be posted. Web site: www.friendster.com

fringe time television time slot just before or after prime time, when there is more program availability

Frith, Simon (1946–) musicologist best known for his work on the sociology of popular music. In *Sound Effects* (1983), Frith examined how popular music relates to audience expectations of a social and political nature.

Froogle Google's shopping engine

FTC [*see* **Federal Trade Commission**]

FTP [*see* **File Transfer Protocol**]

full duplex network connection that makes it possible to send signals in opposite directions at the same time

full nester in marketing jargon, an older consumer who owns his or her home and is interested in living the "good life"

fully connected world concept in which most people and organizations can be linked via the Internet

functionalism 1. twentieth-century architectural movement stressing functional rather than decorative design; 2. twentieth-century psychological school founded by William James and John Dewey; 3. in media theory, the claim that the consumption of media products is due to the individual's active view of these products as functional. In effect, media and psychological functionalism is based on the view that individuals can make their own choices. Media are not seen as manipulation systems but rather as tools that are used by people for recreation or even to gain knowledge of the world. Functionalism holds that if there were no need for the media, the media would not exist. The media, therefore, are adaptations to our needs. Functionalists ask, therefore, how the media contribute to social equilibrium, how the media system constitutes an integrated whole, and what needs the media answer or fulfill.

funk music style of popular music derived from jazz, blues, and soul, characterized by a heavy bass line and syncopated rhythms

funnies part of a newspaper where cartoons and comic strips are published

futurism Italian art movement that lasted from 1909 to about 1916. Futurist artists glorified the power, speed, and excitement of the machine age.

gag joke or comic skit told or acted out by a comedian or by comedians together

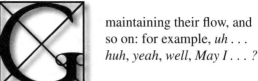

gag order restriction of the publication, discussion, or broadcasting of specific information

gallery television studio production room where the director and the members of the production crew sit during filming or taping

Gallup Poll public opinion poll on a political or social topic or issue, as developed by George H. Gallup, an American statistician who specialized in public opinion surveys. The poll became well-known after it predicted correctly the outcome of the 1936 presidential election. Gallup also developed a method of measuring audience interest in news features and advertising. Web site: www .galluppoll.com

Galtung, Johan (1930–) Norwegian analyst of news media and a leader of the global peace movement. Galtung has studied the socio-psychological reasons why certain items receive media attention, while others (just as socially important) do not.

Galvanometer test research method that measures physiological changes in consumers when they are asked a question or are shown some stimulus material (such as a print ad)

gambit speech strategy used for opening and closing conversations,

maintaining their flow, and so on: for example, *uh . . . huh, yeah, well, May I . . . ?*

game console computer console for game playing, usually operated with a game controlling device, such as a joystick or game pad

game show television program in which a game is played by contestants, offering prizes to the winner

gangsta rap style of rap music in which the lyrics deal with themes involving gangs, gangsters, and/or criminal lifestyles

gangster film film genre dealing with gangsters or with plots revolving around criminal activity with gangsters as primary role players

garage music style of electronic dance music inspired by disco and associated primarily with urban styles of rap and hip-hop

gatekeepers in media studies, those who make the decisions regarding what will appear in media and especially which items are newsworthy and which are not

gateway page opening page of a Web site containing the key words that enable a search engine to locate it

Gauntlett, David (1971–) major researcher on media effects, whose work is quoted often in the relevant media literature. Among his most influential works are *Moving Experiences: Understanding Television's Influence and Effects* (1995) and *Media, Gender, and Identity* (2002).

gaze in feminist theory, the act of looking at representations of women, which reveals information about the power relations that exist between men and women. In Western society, the gazers have typically been the males; the ones gazed at, the females. This pattern is apparent in the artistic and erotic portrayals that have characterized the history of Western visual representation. Following the rise of feminism and GENDER THEORY, gazing patterns have started to change radically.

gazette local newspaper or one that is associated with an organization

gender sexual identity constructed in cultural context. For example, in Western society, men are often portrayed as "sex-seekers," showing an aggressive interest in sex as part of their gender identity, and women as the targets of their interest; in other cultures, such as several Native American traditions, that interest is seen as part of female gender identity.

gender theory in feminism, theoretical framework that evaluates representations, genres, etc., in terms of how they represent gender and how they reflect ideologies (for example, patriarchy)

gendered genre movie genre, television program, or television channel directed at a specific gender by providing themes, characters, and situations that are purported to appeal to a specific gender exclusively; for example, *WE: Women's Entertainment* is a network designed to appeal primarily to women, while *Spike TV* is designed to appeal primarily to men.

genderlect [blend of **gender** and **dialect**] language choices that are characteristic of males or females in speech situations

general audience made up of people from all walks of life, and with "generic" or "random" properties, rather than segmented into demographic categories (age, class, etc.). This category is used in rating systems as a comparison base to the demographically segmented ones.

Generation X the children of "BABY BOOMERS," born in the 1970s and purported to lead a lifestyle that is vastly different from that of their parents, based on a rejection of their parents' values. They are more inclined than their parents to use new media technologies as sources of information and entertainment.

generational marketing marketing and advertising tailored to specific generations of consumers (BABY BOOMERS, GENERATION X, teenagers, older people)

genre category or classification of works of art based on subject matter, themes, and/or style. Examples of literary genres are poetry, prose, drama, fiction, science fiction, and mystery novel. Examples of television genres are sitcom, soap opera, quiz show, and talk show.

geodemographic clustering technique of classifying consumers on the basis of the DEMOGRAPHIC characteristics common to the area in which they live

geographics measurement of where audiences and consumers live

Gerbner, George (1919–2005) widely quoted media theorist whose concept of the CULTIVATION EFFECT has become a target of major discussion and debate. His model of communication, developed in 1956, emphasizes the interactive role of the sender and the receiver, the context, and the medium used during the different stages of communication. His major work is *The Global Media Debate* (1993).

Gestalt psychology school of psychology, founded around 1912 by Max Wertheimer, that stresses the study of patterns, or forms, as the important part of perception and experience, since form in its totality is seen as being more important than the sum of its parts. Gestaltists rejected STRUCTURALISM, the most common psychological theory in the early 1900s, based on studying the separate elements of experience and

perception such as feelings, images, and sensations, and BEHAVIORISM, which called for the study of observable aspects of behavior.

gestural dance dance deliberately structured by gesture patterns, including body language, eye contact, and posture

gesture movement of the body, especially the hands, to communicate something, unconsciously or wittingly. The former are called, more precisely, natural gestures and the latter conventional gestures. Several main types of gesture have been identified. *Illustrators* are gestures that literally illustrate vocal utterances: for example, the circular hand movements typically employed when talking of a circle; or moving the hands far apart when talking of something large. *Emblems* are gestures that directly translate words or phrases: for example, the "OK" sign, the "Come here" sign, the hitchhiking sign, waving, obscene gestures, etc. *Affect displays* communicate emotional meaning: for example, the typical hand movements that accompany states and expressions of happiness, surprise, fear, anger, sadness, contempt, disgust, etc. *Regulators* are gestures that are used to monitor, maintain, or control the speech of someone else. Examples include the hand movements for "Keep going," "Slow down," "What else happened?" *Adaptors* are the gestures used to satisfy some need: for example, scratching one's head when puzzled, rubbing one's forehead when worried, and so on.

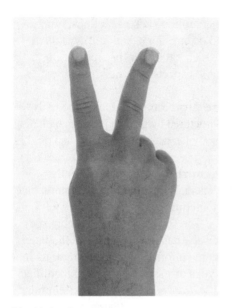

The V-sign for peace

computer memory required to store a single character

girl groups musical ensembles made up exclusively of female performers and, usually, portraying a gendered view of topics

Gitlin, Todd (1941–) radical American critic of the mainstream media and popular culture. His most influential works are *Inside Prime Time* (1983) and *Watching Television* (1986).

glam rock popular rock music style of the 1970s, characterized by performers who wore glamorous clothing and jewelry

ghetto cool the adoption of a "ghetto" lifestyle (in a real or simulative way), generally in imitation of GANGSTA RAP and other hard forms of hip-hop culture

ghost site Web site that is no longer being updated but is still available for viewing

ghostwriter person who writes something for another person, usually a celebrity, pretending to be the author

GIF [full form: **graphic interchange format**] computer image format used commonly for nonphotographic images on Web sites

gigabyte unit equivalent to 1,024 megabytes, a byte being a unit of

global advertising advertising directed at global audiences and thus adapted to the global context. For example, the use of sexual themes in the promotion of an automobile would be attenuated or removed in a global advertising campaign so as to avoid offending societies where sexuality is not expressed openly.

global branding inserting brand products into world markets, adapting their promotion to the legal, social, and cultural exigencies of each market

global marketing use of a common marketing plan to sell a product everywhere in the world

global media media systems, such as AOL or Disney, that possess communication and media networks (and distribution capacities) that embrace most of the world

Global Positioning System [abbreviated as **GPS**] system comprised of 24 satellites (21 active and three spares) that allows users to precisely identify their location anywhere on the globe

Glyph indicating "No Smoking!"

global village term coined by MAR-SHALL MCLUHAN to characterize a world that is united electronically, in a virtual (or cybernetic) village. McLuhan argued that the medium in which information is recorded and transmitted is decisive in shaping trends and in charting future progress. So, by simply switching on their television sets to satellite-transmitted programs, or visiting Web sites, people tend to feel connected to others in an abstract, rather than real, fashion.

globalization process by which formerly separate, discrete, or local cultures, businesses, or institutions are brought into contact with one another and with new groups of people in an interactive fashion, generally through the Internet. This gives the sense that the world is a single place. Supporters of globalization claim that it liberates populations from local and often restrictive lifestyles, generates wealth, makes possible the movement of people and ideas, and contributes to the development of human rights. Critics claim that it eliminates crucial social and cultural differences.

glocal genre any media text produced by local groups but incorporating global forms and ideas

glocalization process whereby local or regional cultures are becoming increasingly similar to each other as a result of aspects of globalization (economic, technological, etc.)

gloss short definition, translation, or explanation of a technical term, usually inserted in a footnote or in parentheses

glossary alphabetical list of GLOSSES, often placed at the end of a work or a section of the work (such as at the end of a chapter)

glyph public sign that provides information visually

Goffman, Erving (1922–1982) sociologist who examined the self-image or *persona* that people present in social situations, arguing that social life was very much like the theater, as people perceived themselves as playing specific roles, adapting to the situation linguistically, behaviorally, and in other ways. His most important work is *The Presentation of Self in Everyday Life* (1959).

go-go popular style of music originating in Washington, D.C., in the 1970s, which featured a strong beat and "go-go dancers," scantily clad women dancing alone to the music on special raised platforms during a band performance or during a floor dance

Gold Lion award given at the Cannes International Advertising Festival for achievement in various categories, including print marketing, outdoor advertising, and television commercials

gold record a golden replica of a record that has achieved at least one million in sales

golden age of cinema period of movie production during the 1920s and 1930s when cinema was in its infancy and when Hollywood movies enjoyed an unprecedented, and since unparalleled, popularity

golden age of radio period from the late 1920s to the late 1940s when radio was the dominant medium for home entertainment

golden age of television period from the early 1950s to the late 1980s when television was the dominant medium for home entertainment, before the rise of the Internet

golden oldie piece of music that was popular in a previous era

gonzo journalism style of journalism that is more concerned with such things as the reporter's relation to the story or the emotional effects on the people involved in the story, rather than the actual facts of the story

Google largest Internet search engine, founded in 1998, which has an index of over 10 billion Web pages. The name originated from a play on the word *googol*, which refers to 10^{100} (the number represented by a 1 followed by one-hundred zeros). The word has found its way into everyday language as a verb, meaning, "to use the Google search engine to obtain information on the Internet." Internet address: www.google.com

gopher computer program that searches file names and resources on the Internet, organizing them into menus that contain links to other files or databases

gospel music evangelical music derived from African American spiritual and blues vocal music. Gospel music's first influential composers and performers included Thomas A. Dorsey, who coined the term; C.A. Tindley; Gary Davis; Sister Rosetta Tharpe, who first brought gospel into nightclubs and theaters in the 1930s; and Mahalia Jackson. Gospel music has had a significant influence on rhythm and blues, soul music, and other pop music styles.

gossip column regular newspaper or magazine column dealing with

A Goth at the Wave Gothic Festival, Leipzig, Germany, May 25, 2007

rumors and gossip about celebrities and well-known public figures

gotcha journalism news reporting in which journalists nab evildoers or interview people caught in some illegal act

goth form of punk music and lifestyle, especially among youths, characterized by the wearing of dark clothes, the use of dark cosmetics, and other gothic forms of symbolism, intended to challenge mainstream society

Gothic 1. architectural style prevalent in Europe from the twelfth through the fifteenth centuries, emphasizing light and verticality, typified by the Cathedral of Notre-Dame de Paris; the style was revived in the nineteenth century; 2. literary style generally characterized by darkness and gloom. The term was used during the late 1700s and early 1800s to describe a type of popular fiction that revolved around mysterious and supernatural events; the novels were called Gothic because they took place in gloomy castles built in the Gothic style of architecture. The first such novel was *The Castle of Otranto* (1764) by Horace Walpole. Other early gothic novels include *The Mysteries of Udolpho* (1794) and *The Italian* (1797) by Ann Radcliffe; *The Monk* (1796) by Matthew G. Lewis; *Melmoth the Wanderer* (1820) by Charles Maturin; *Frankenstein* (1818) by Mary Shelley; and *Wuthering Heights* (1847) by Emily Bronte.

governmentality concept developed by MICHEL FOUCAULT meaning, essentially, the art of government; intended to imply that governing is not limited to the political sphere, but reaches out to all spheres, from the cultural to the artistic

GPS [*see* **Global Positioning System**]

graffiti inscriptions of various kinds scratched, carved, or drawn on a wall, pole, or other public surface. Graffiti have allowed linguists to reconstruct earlier stages of a language, and social scientists to examine the ideologies or lifestyle of certain groups (as has been done to study the graffiti of gangs, teen cliques, etc.).

grammatology term coined by JACQUES DERRIDA, term referring to the priority of writing over vocal speech in the development and use of language, contrary to what linguists have traditionally maintained. Derrida claimed that pictographic language preceded vocalized language and that, to this day, writing has a much more crucial function in human affairs than do other forms of language.

Grammy Awards honors given annually for outstanding achievement in music. The first Grammies (the name is an abbreviation of *gramophone*) were given in 1958. They are now awarded in dozens of categories, from best composition to the best musical arrangement. Web site: www.grammy.com

gramophone machine used formerly for playing records, invented in 1887 by Emile Berliner, a German immigrant to the United States

Gramsci, Antonio (1891–1937) Italian Marxist intellectual and politician who is often quoted in media studies because of his notion of HEGEMONY, or domination of the media by those in power in order to subtly influence public opinion in their favor. His influential *Lettere dal carcere* (published posthumously in 1947; published in English as *Letters from Prison* in 1973) actually outlines a less dogmatic version of communism than that of most Marxists.

grandiloquence form of speech and discourse characterized by pompous or bombastic diction and mode of delivery

graph 1. in mathematics, diagram representing changes in a variable; 2. unit in writing representing a sound, a syllable, or entire concept

graphic art form of visual art relating to methods of reproduction such as printing, engraving, or etching. The term is used generally in reference to the illustrations found in advertisements, book designs, posters, and the like.

graphic design craft of combining text and illustrations in design (for example, in ad texts, book covers). Writers produce words while photographers and illustrators create images; the graphic designer incorporates these elements into a complete layout.

graphic display computer screen with the capacity to display graphics

graphic equalizer device on an electronic playback machine that allows separate adjustments to be made to the sound quality

graphic novel novel developed from COMIC BOOKS, in which cartoon images are interspersed in the written text. An example of a graphic novel is Frank Miller's *Batman: The Dark Knight Returns* (1986).

graphical user interface [abbreviated as **GUI**] display format that allows a computer user to select commands, call up files, start programs, and do other tasks by using a mouse to point to icons or lists of menu choices on the screen as opposed to having to type in text commands. The first GUI to be used in a personal computer appeared in Apple Computer's Lisa, introduced in 1983; its GUI became the basis of Apple's extremely successful Macintosh (1984).

graphics 1. pictorial manipulation of data, used in computers, the graphic arts, and so on; 2. pictorial display of information on a computer

Graphics Interchange Format [*see* **GIF**]

G-rating movie and television classification indicating that the movie or program is suitable for general audiences

grazing act of watching several television programs simultaneously

green light process procedure leading to the decision to make a movie

green room small room near a broadcast studio in which program guests wait before they are interviewed or where actors can go to rest

greenwashing public relations strategy of companies to counter the advertising tactics of environmentalists

Greimas, Algirdas Julien (1917–1992) French semiotician who

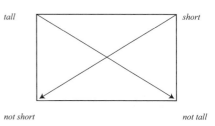

amplified the field NARRATOLOGY, the study of narratives of all kinds. Greimas's most significant contribution in the field is the "semiotic square," which posits that OPPOSITIONS hold in a square-like fashion rather than in a binary manner. For example, the word *tall* takes on meaning in contrast to *not tall*, *short*, and *not short*. Thus, the meaning of *tall* is gleaned from a semiotic square of oppositions.

gripe site Web site providing an opportunity for users to counter or challenge another person or an institution

gross audience compilation of all the audiences studied for an advertising campaign or media experiment. The gross audience may actually include duplicated audience members.

gross cover number of times a radio or television commercial has been seen or heard

gross rating point method of determining the effectiveness of outdoor advertising, with 1 percent of a sample group represented by a point in a statistical method of analysis

Grossberg, Lawrence (1947–) American cultural theorist who has sought to show how audiences become attached to certain performers, texts, or programs. His most influential book is *We Gotta Get Out of This Place* (1992), in which he contends that rock culture, once considered deviant and aberrant, has become part of conservative culture.

ground entire or connecting surface of a scene in a movie shoot

group in Web talk, network of online individuals who share a common interest

group system method of organizing an advertising agency into groups, each with its own area of specialized expertise (marketing, ad creation)

grunge style of rock music made famous by the late musician Kurt Cobain, derived from punk rock, and characterized especially by anguished lyrics; also used to describe the style of clothing worn by followers of grunge, consisting of torn jeans and flannel shirts

guerrilla marketing marketing that uses nontraditional media and strategies to promote products or services

GUI [*see* **graphical user interface**]

guide publication that lists programming (radio or television) times and typically describes the content of each program listed

Gutenberg Galaxy [after Johannes Gutenberg (c. 1390–1468), a German printer] term coined by MARSHALL McLUHAN to refer to the world that resulted from the availability of cheap books and the spread of literacy as a consequence of the invention of print technology.

gutter press generic term to describe tabloid newspapers

gynocriticism in FEMINIST THEORY, study of the writings produced by women and how they convey the "female experience"

Habermas, Jürgen (1929–) German philosopher who sees art as the force of change in cultural systems. Habermas is widely known for his critiques of the tendency of Western capitalist democracies to evaluate social progress in terms of economic efficiency. His major works include *Theorie und Praxis* (1963; *Theory and Practice*, 1973), *Erkenntis und Interesse* (1968; *Knowledge and Human Interests*, 1971), *Theorie des kommunikativen Handelns* (1981; *A Theory of Communicative Action*, 1984), and *Der philosophische Diskurs der Moderne* (1985; *The Philosophical Discourse of Modernity*, 1987).

habitus [term coined by Marcel Mauss and later used by PIERRE BOURDIEU] the ways in which society's dominant classes talk, act, and behave. Noting that success in society depends largely on the individual's ability to absorb the habitus of the dominant class, Bourdieu suggested that it is similar to, but more fundamental than, knowing a language.

hacker 1. individual who uses his or her computer expertise to gain unauthorized access to a computer system or a site either to learn about the system or to examine and/or manipulate its data; 2. more generally, an aficionado of information technology

hacker ethic view that users should have absolute free access to information posted on the World Wide Web

hacktivism the use of hacking for political or social purposes [blend of **hacking** and **activism**]

halftone image produced by breaking down photographs into a series of dots that appear as shades of gray on a page

Hall, Stuart (1932–) influential media scholar who has become well-known as a major proponent of RECEPTION THEORY, or the view that audiences are not passive consumers of media texts but, rather, selectors of them according to their particular preferences. Among his best-known works are *Encoding and Decoding in Television Discourse* (1973) and *Representation: Cultural Representations and Signifying Practices* (as editor, 1997).

halo brand product brand that lends value to a company's subbrands by association. The halo brand is also called the master brand.

halo effect theory that the way someone looks and acts can lead observers to make unwarranted assumptions about the person. For example, someone who is unkempt and appears scruffily dressed might be judged (perhaps mistakenly) to be someone who would not be suitable for a white-collar job. In media studies, it is used to refer to the phenomenon of viewers reporting not what they actually watched but what they believe they should have watched.

hammocking technique of inserting a television program between two highly popular programs to boost its ratings

hang time amount of time someone spends visiting a Web site

Haraway, Donna (1944–) important feminist critic whose analyses of the *cyborg* have ignited a wide-ranging debate on the amalgamation of humans with technology and especially of the effects of this amalgamation on women. Her most cited book is *Simians, Cyborgs, and Women: The Reinvention of Nature* (1991).

hard copy printed copy of a text, as opposed to electronic copy (contained in a computer file or document)

hard disc permanent storage disc in a computer. The term is also used to refer to the entire hard drive.

hard news news stories that are designed to help audiences make intelligent decisions about an issue or event, with little accompanying commentary

hard rock type of rock music that is characterized by loud guitar accompaniment and a strong insistent beat, with singing that often simulates a form of shouting

hard sell aggressive methods of advertising

hardback book published with a rigid cover, usually more expensive and in a larger format than paperback

hardcore 1. extreme form of a pop music style such as punk or hip-hop; 2. sexual portrayal in movies that is completely explicit

hardware [in contrast to **software**] the computer's actual machinery and equipment, including memory, cabling, power supply, peripheral devices, and circuit boards. Hardware specifies a computer's capability; software instructs the computer what to do.

Harlequin traditional COMMEDIA DELL'ARTE character; a wily, unscrupulous comic servant. By the early seventeenth century Harlequin had been transformed into a faithful valet involved in amorous exploits. He wore tight-fitting peasant clothes with colored patches decorated with bright triangles and diamond shapes. He carried a slapstick and wore a black half-mask.

harmony 1. in music, two or more tones used together and perceived as pleasant-sounding; 2. chord structure and movement in a piece of music (as distinguished from melody and rhythm)

Hartley, John (1948–) influential culture theorist, whose analyses of television have become widely quoted, particularly *Reading Television* (written with John Fiske, 1978)

Hawthorne effect tendency of research subjects to give the type of information that they believe is required by the researchers. More generally, it refers to how people react to different situations and are influenced by factors in those situations (such as the type of interview used by researchers, the personality of the researchers, etc.). The term comes from the name of a factory called the Hawthorne Works, where a series of experiments were carried out between 1924 and 1932.

Hays Code set of censorship guidelines for movies in the United States issued in 1934. Under severe criticism, the Code was abandoned in 1967 and replaced by a rating system.

HDTV [*see* **high definition television**]

headend equipment that allows cable subscribers to receive transmission signals. The headend receives signals from an antenna or antennas, processes the signals, sending them through the distribution system to customers.

headline 1. short title printed in heavier type at the top of a newspaper article telling what it is about; 2. line printed at the top of a page giving the running title, page number, and possibly other information related to content

headline news newscast or channel that deals only with topical news and/or events that are currently taking place

headphones pair of earphones joined across the top of a listener's head

headset headphones that have a small microphone for two-way communication, used by television producers, camerapersons, and others during filming, taping, or broadcasting

Hearst, Randolph (1863–1951) one of the most prominent figures in the history of newspaper publishing in the United States. Hearst helped bring about the era of YELLOW JOURNALISM, employing circulation-boosting tactics. In 1935 he owned 28 major newspapers, 18 magazines, radio stations, movie companies, and news services.

heavy metal rock music style marked by amplified and sometimes distorted guitar "power chords," a hard beat, a thumping bass, and an aggressive style of singing. Heavy metal emerged in the late 1960s from the heavy, blues-oriented music of Steppenwolf and Jimi Hendrix. In the 1970s and 1980s bands such as Led Zeppelin, Black Sabbath, Kiss, AC/DC, Aerosmith, Def Leppard, Iron Maiden, Mötley Crüe, and Van Halen developed the style further.

heavy viewer person who watches television frequently and, for that reason, is often included in target study audiences

Hebdige, Dick (1951–) media analyst renowned for his studies of youth subcultures. His best-known book is *Subculture: The Meaning of Style* (1979).

hedge redundant phrase used in conversation, such as "I mean" and "you know," which nevertheless has a communicative function, such as making a statement less blunt or conveying personal assurance

hedonism ancient Greek philosophy that pleasure is the only true goal of life and that its pursuit is what motivates humans. British philosophers Jeremy Bentham and James Mill and his son, John Stuart Mill, renamed the philosophy *utilitarianism*, expanding it to encompass the well-being of the greatest number of people, not just individuals.

Hegel, Georg Wilhelm Friedrich (1770–1831) German philosopher who defined a process of human progress (which became known as the Hegelian dialectic) that involved the generation and interaction of opposing concepts. To understand any aspect of culture or the human condition, one must retrace its origin and development through this process. His works include *Phänomenologie des Geistes* (1807; *The Phenomenology of Mind*), *Wissenschaft der Logik* (1812–1816; *Science of Logic*), and *Grundlinien der Philosophie des Rechts* (1821; *Philosophy of Right*).

hegemony [as defined by Italian Marxist **Antonio Gramsci**] the efforts on the part of the dominant class in a society to gain the consent of those who are dominated. The instruments of hegemony range from outright coercion (incarceration, secret police, threats, physical elimination) to gentler and more "managerial" tactics (education, religion, control of the mass media). The concept of hegemony has found widespread use in media studies, where it is used to refer more to the cultural production of consent, rather than overt forms of coercion.

Heidegger, Martin (1889–1976) German philosopher who posited that the individual living in a consumerist mass culture is always in danger of being deprived of a sense of self-worth. He called the resulting mental state *nihilism*. His most influential work, *Sein und Zeit* (1927; *Being and Time*), dealt with the fundamental philosophical question of "being-in-the-world," or "What is the meaning of being?" His work had a significant influence on French philosophers MICHEL FOUCAULT and JACQUES DERRIDA.

Helmholtz, Hermann von (1821–1894) German physicist whose research on the physics of sound ranked as the outstanding work of his time in acoustics

herd journalism practice of reporters staking out a house or following a story in large groups

Herder, Johann Gottfried von (1744–1803) German philosopher who claimed that national character is encoded in a people's language and literature. His *Ideen zur Philosophie der Geschichte der Menschheit* (1784–1791; *Outlines of a Philosophy of the History of Mankind*) opened the way to the modern-day systematic comparative study of civilizations.

Herman and Chomsky's propaganda model [as articulated by Edward Herman and NOAM CHOMSKY in *Manufacturing Consent: The Political Economy of the Mass Media* (1988)] a model of news reporting that claims that the overriding consideration of news agencies is supporting the views of those in power, thus essentially producing a form of propaganda rather than impartial news commentary

hermeneutics 1. systematic study of texts on the basis of their language and their history; 2. study of how people interpret texts. The essence of hermeneutic method is to locate a text in the context of the times in which it was produced, not in terms of current ideas and theories.

hero/heroine 1. personage, often supernatural or mythical, endowed with bravery and strength (in myth, the hero is remarkable for his or her bold exploits and is favored by the gods); 2. principal character in a work of fiction

herstory 1. the biography or study of a particular woman or group of women;

2. a view of history from the female perspective, as opposed to *history = his story*, or the conventional view of history from the standpoint of men

heterogeneous audience audience consisting of demographically diverse members, that is, members who differ in age, gender, education, class, ethnicity, religion, or another variable

heteroglossia exposure to, or construction of, an unfamiliar language or languages, implying new perspectives or new meanings

heterophily differences of opinion, values, or viewpoints that arise between two people conversing with each other

heterotopia the different "social spaces" (features of language, delivery, turn-taking sequences, etc.) that arise surreptitiously and unconsciously between two people conversing with each other

heuristic 1. designed to facilitate learning (for example, a pedagogical method); 2. in computer science, a program that can adapt to user instructions, activities, or responses (for example, checking spelling and grammar)

hidden-fear appeal [also called **scare copy**] advertising technique designed to promote such goods and services as insurance, fire alarms, cosmetics, and vitamin capsules by evoking the fear of poverty, sickness, loss of social standing, and/or impending disaster

hierarchy of effects series of steps by which consumers receive and use information in reaching decisions about whether or not to buy a product. The steps include: awareness of the product, knowledge about it (and the company that makes it), tastes connected with it, preference, conviction, and purchase.

hieratic flowing script (executed with reed pens on papyrus) developed by the Egyptians around 2700 B.C.E. in place of HIEROGLYPHIC writing

hieroglyphic ancient Egyptian writing system, originating around 3000 B.C.E., based on stylized pictorial symbols. These represented not only people, things, and ideas, but also a few consonant sounds. The latest hieroglyphic writing dates from 394 C.E. Hieroglyphic writing was deciphered after the discovery in 1799 of the Rosetta Stone, a slab that had the same text in Greek and hieroglyphic writing. Jean François Champollion compared the two, thus deciphering the hieroglyphs.

high-concept movie movie produced with a large budget on the belief that it can be easily marketed and turned into a commercial success

high culture vs. low culture distinction made between forms of culture considered to be of greater or lesser worth. High culture is often associated with FINE ARTS such as classical music, the ballet, opera, and painting, and low culture with popular spectacles such as wrestling and erotic movies. This distinction raises the question of what cultural content is better or worse and, more importantly, who has the right (if any) of deciding so. In actual fact, most people can easily distinguish between the two levels of culture. Great works of art foster engagement; many popular media artifacts, on the other hand, are designed solely to provide distraction and entertainment, even though the dividing line between the two is often blurry indeed. Many of the forms intended originally for entertainment have themselves evolved into works of art. Some pieces of jazz and rock music, for example, are now listed alongside the works of the great classical composers. Some types of advertising, too, may be considered artistically interesting.

high definition television [abbreviated as **HDTV**] television system that presents a picture that is wider than conventional television screens and has twice as many lines of scanning for increased clarity and detail. HDTV uses digital technology to process the original signal, transmit it, and reproduce it in the television set. In addition to providing digital high-resolution video, HDTV transmits a digital audio signal that results in CD-quality sound. Essentially, the technology used to create HDTV produces picture and sound that rival those found in movie theaters.

hi-fi [abbreviation of **high fidelity**] reproduction of sound by a radio, CD player, or other device with as little distortion of the original sound as possible

high-speed photography filmic technique in which consecutive multiple shots are taken quickly to capture an action that is too fast to be seen with the naked eye

hip-hop youth-based music and lifestyle that emerged in African American neighborhoods of New York in the 1970s, characterized originally by rap music and breakdancing. Rap came to national prominence with Sugar Hill Gang's *Rapper's Delight* (1979). In its original form, hip-hop combined spoken street language with cuts, called samples, from older records. The themes of hip-hop lyrics originally revolved around political issues, racial discrimination, masculinity, and an implicit mockery of the existing social order. Over time, hip-hop has become more melodic and eclectic, incorporating elements from the blues, rhythm and blues, jazz, and soul.

hippies counterculture youth of the 1960s and 1970s. The hippies rejected the traditions and lifestyles of bourgeois (capitalist) society. They proclaimed a world based on love and peace, strongly opposing the Vietnam War. Many lived together on communes, refusing to be tied down to a fixed job. They were sometimes called "flower children" because they gave people flowers to symbolize

Hippies (also called "freaks") in Los Angeles in the summer of 1967

their worldview. They let their hair grow long and walked barefoot or wore sandals. Many used marijuana, LSD, and other drugs. The Beatles helped spread the hippie movement with their songs, as did the Grateful Dead, Jefferson Airplane, Joan Baez, and Bob Dylan, among other such musicians of the era.

historicism 1. theory that forces beyond human control influence the course of human history; 2. theory that each historical era develops its own unique forms of culture that can only be understood in context

historiography study of history in general, or of the history of a movement, era, trend, etc.

history technique in advertising technique whereby a significant historical event is incorporated into the ad, either by allusion or by direct reference

hit a record, play, movie, or other creative product that has become a success with both audiences and critics

hit rate number of occasions that a Web site has been viewed by Internet users

Hoggart, Richard (1918–) MARXIST cultural theorist and founder of the Centre for Contemporary Cultural Studies at the University of Birmingham. In *The Uses of Literacy* (1957), Hoggart laments the passing of true culture under the forces of capitalist-based consumerist economics.

Hollywood city originally founded by Horace Wilcox in 1887, a prohibitionist who envisioned a community based on religious principles. It was consolidated with Los Angeles in 1910 and became the center of the movie industry by 1915. By the 1960s, it also was the source of much American network television programming. Web site: www .hollywoodchamber.net

holography photography without lenses, whereby a three-dimensional image is recorded on a plate or film by laser, which splits into two beams, forming a pattern reflecting the shape of the photographed object. When the pattern is exposed to light, a three-dimensional image (a hologram) is formed.

home page 1. the page that is loaded when someone opens up their brows-

er to use the Internet; 2. the first page of a Web site that welcomes a user

home video theater system composed of audio and video equipment that recreates the movie theater experience in the home. The system includes a large-screen television and a multi-speaker sound system.

homology in Marxist theory, view that a media text is designed to deliver meaning in politically controlled ways (either explicitly or implicitly)

homophily situation in which interlocutors share the same values, ideas, beliefs, and worldview during dialogue, conversation, or other form of verbal communication

hooks, bell (1952–) [written in lower-case style] prominent African American feminist critic (born Gloria Watkins) whose work on race and gender representations in the media have become topical and widely quoted. Among her works are *Black Looks* (1992) and *Reel to Real: Race, Sex, and Class at the Movies* (1996).

horizontal integration acquisition of a smaller company by a larger one, such as, for example, a large newspaper taking over a smaller rival newspaper

Horkheimer, Max (1895–1973) a founding member of the FRANK-FURT SCHOOL. His *Dialektik der Aufklärung* (1947; *Dialectic of Enlightenment*), written with THEODOR

ADORNO, is a widely quoted work that traces the origins of modern-day totalitarianism to the Enlightenment concept of instrumental reason.

horror genre literary genre intended to provoke feelings of fear or shock. Horror stories are of ancient origin and form a substantial part of folk literature. They may feature supernatural beings such as ghosts, witches, or vampires, or may address more realistic psychological fears. In Western literature, the horror genre emerged in the eighteenth century with the GOTHIC novel. The horror genre was also one of the first to become popular in movies, remaining so to this day.

host 1. person who welcomes and speaks to invited guests on radio and television programs; 2. in a computer network, the main computer controlling functions and files; 3. computer linking individual personal computers to the Internet

hosting business of putting Web sites onto the Internet

hot in reference to a microphone, *hot* means that the microphone is "on"

hot medium [in contrast to **cold medium**] MARSHALL MCLUHAN's term referring to any medium, such as film and radio, that requires little interaction and interpretation on the part of an audience

hot spot building or area where wireless Internet users can access an Internet connection

house music style of dance music, derived from DISCO MUSIC, using electronic or synthesized sound effects

house organ magazine published by a company for its employees and clients, containing information about the company, its products, and its employees

houses using television [abbreviated as **HUTs**] percentage of homes watching television during a specific time period and within a specific region

html [abbreviation of **hypertext markup language**] computer language that is used to prepare HYPERTEXT documents on the World Wide Web. The text coding consists of commands in angle brackets < > that affect the display of elements such as titles, headings, text, font style, color, and references to other documents.

http [abbreviation of **hypertext transfer protocol**] protocol used for exchanging files on the World Wide Web. Web browsers are http clients that send file requests to Web servers, which in turn handle the requests via an http service.

huckster a publicity agent or writer of advertising copy (usually used as a pejorative)

human interest reporting style that is designed to touch audiences emotionally on issues that are important to most people. Often a human-interest story focuses on the trials and tribulations of ordinary humans caught in extraordinary predicaments

humanism a cultural movement in Renaissance Europe, characterized by a revival of classical letters, an individualistic and critical spirit, and a shift of emphasis from religious to secular concerns

humor state of producing or perceiving something as funny, generally accompanied by laughter. Humor takes many literary and media forms: *wit* is humor based on cleverness; *satire* deals with human weaknesses, making fun of them; *sarcasm* is more nasty, often taking the form of indirect stinging commentary (*That's a lovely suit—too bad they didn't have your size*); *irony* implies the opposite of what is being said or done through understatement; *farce*, *slapstick*, and *buffoonery* involve pranks and practical jokes; *parody* and *burlesque* alter a story comically; and *mimicry* involves imitating someone else for comic effect.

humor in advertising use of humor to make a product appealing, which allows a brand to keep in step with changing times and with changing humor trends

HUTs [*see* **houses using television**]

hybrid combination of art forms, styles, or genres resulting in a new form, style, or genre

hybridity in cultural theory, the crossbreeding and intertwining of different identities (in contrast to the construction of self on the basis of a single cultural model)

hype exaggerated publicity strategy for a movie, a program, a product, or a spectacle, designed to create excitement

hyperbole exaggerated statement used for effect and not meant to be taken literally: for example, *Waves as high as mountains hit the beach*

hypercard software designed by Apple that provides users with a processing tool consisting of "cards" collected together in a "stack," with each card containing text, graphics, and sound.

hypercommercialism increasing the amount of advertising and blending it into actual media content

hyperlink word, symbol, image, or other form in a HYPERTEXT document that "links," or directly transfers the user, to another element in the document or to another site. The hyperlink is activated with a mouse click.

hypermedia information retrieval system used for accessing texts, audio, video, etc., on the World Wide Web. A hypermedia navigation might include links to *music*, *opera*, *harmony*, *composers*, and *musicology*.

hyperreality the simulation of reality in media, perceived by some commentators as more authentic than actual reality. The term is used often in semiotics and psychology to portray the inability of people to distinguish reality from fantasy, especially in technologically advanced societies. Some well-known theorists of hyper-reality include semioticians Jean Baudrillard and Umberto Eco. The main thrust of hyperreality theory is that the real world has been replaced by a copy world, where we seek simulation for its own sake. For example, life within a theme park such as Disneyland allows people to engage in the fantasy worlds such a park creates and live through them temporarily. The problem, argue Baudrillard and Eco, is that such hyperreal experiences start to dominate consciousness, making it difficult for many humans to distinguish between the simulation and its object of representation. This theme is, incidentally, intrinsic in the 1999 movie *The Matrix.*

hypertext system of storing text, images, and other files that allows for links to related text, images, etc. The term surfaced in 1965. Hypertext makes it easy for users to browse through related topics, regardless of their presented order. In Internet browsers, hypertext links (hotlinks, or HYPERLINKS) are usually indicated by a word or phrase with a different font or color. These create a branching structure that permits direct, unmediated jumps to related information.

hypertext markup language [*see* **html**]

hypertext transfer protocol [*see* **http**]

hypodermic needle theory in media studies, a theory that the mass media can directly influence behavior. The theory claims that media are capable of directly swaying minds with the same kind of impact that a hypodermic needle has on the body. This theory is now largely discredited. It has been found, for example, that media impacts are indirect and are often mediated by group leaders. People of different social classes come up with different interpretations of media products, tending to perceive them as interpretive communities. However, this theory is still used by some to claim that people are influenced by what they watch on TV, to variable degrees.

hypothesis an assertion that is assumed to be valid or true because it seems likely to be so; a hypothesis is usually set forth as an assumption that must be tested and proved. The term is used in social scientific research on media primarily in the expression *hypothesis testing*, a method of assuming an hypothesis (for example, television induces violence) and then conducting a study or experiment to ascertain if the hypothesis is true or false (and to what degree it is so).

IBM [*see* **International Business Machines**]

IBOC [*see* **in-band-on-channel**]

iceberg principle in advertising, a principle claiming that advertising should aim its messages at the strong needs and desires that lie hidden deep within the psyche, in analogy to an iceberg that is only 10 percent visible, with the remainder hidden below the water

icon 1. sign or symbol resembling its referent (e.g., a star figure standing for a star); 2. a visual image; 3. picture of a sacred personage; 4. a person in pop culture who is revered (e.g., a celebrity); 5. picture on a computer screen standing for a specific command, function, etc. (e.g., icon of a file folder)

iconography 1. the imagery used in a work of art or a body of works; 2. study of art that focuses on ICONS or symbols in painting and sculpture. Icons of pagan gods have been found as far back as 3000 B.C.E. in the Middle East. Iconography became a main aspect of the Eastern Orthodox Churches, where icons are painted according to rules established by ecclesiastical authorities.

iconoscope tube first television camera tube, developed in 1923

id in psychoanalytic theory, the instincts, in contrast to the EGO and the SUPEREGO. The id is defined as part of the unconscious, where instinctual drives and accumulated memories exist, influencing behavior reflexively.

idealism philosophical theory that physical reality does not exist independently of human minds, which filter it accordingly. Idealism is the opposite of both *materialism*, which claims that mental consciousness is a purely physical phenomenon, and *realism*, which claims that physical reality is independent of human minds and can be understood objectively through the senses. Idealism starts with Plato, who maintained that the ideas produced by the mind imperfectly mirror physical reality. In the eighteenth century Irish philosopher George Berkeley extended Plato's concept by claiming, essentially, that nothing exists outside the mind, since it is the mind that classifies matter and not matter itself. German philosopher Immanuel Kant also claimed that the properties of human perception shape how reality is understood. In contrast, G.W.F. Hegel believed that the human mind was capable of truly understanding reality as it is, not as it is perceived.

ideational function of language use of language to express or construct ideas

ident visual image identifying a channel that is inserted briefly between television programs

identification 1. form of unconscious imitation on the part of people of what they have seen or heard in the media; 2. ability of audiences to identify emotionally with fictional characters

ideogram 1. picture sign representing an object or idea, rather than a word: $ = *dollars*; & = *and*

ideological criticism critical reading of a text from a specific ideological perspective, that is, from the standpoint of a specific set of assumptions, beliefs, or viewpoints

ideological state apparatus in Marxist theory, ways in which a society imposes an IDEOLOGY on its members, either by coercion or persuasion

ideology system of thought based on a specific set of assumptions, beliefs, or viewpoints that appears to be a product of common sense, but which is actually socially constructed. Those strongly committed to a particular ideology have difficulty understanding and communicating with supporters of a conflicting ideology. For KARL MARX, ideology referred to the ideas and values of the ruling classes, which are reproduced by the dominant social institutions (the law, family, religion, education). The term was coined in 1796 by the French writer Antoine-Louis-Claude, Comte Destutt de Tracy to describe his "science of ideas."

idiolect an individual's manner of speaking, including pronunciation

Illuminated manuscript

patterns, tone of voice, and typical choice of words

idiom expression that cannot be understood from the individual meanings of its words, but in its totality: *to be born with a silver spoon in one's mouth*; *to go on a wild goose chase*

idol 1. image or statue of a deity used as an object of worship; 2. by extension, any celebrity who is worshipped by certain types of fans: *a teen idol, a matinee idol*, etc.

illuminated manuscripts books written and illustrated by hand, with bright colors and precious metals.

An illusion form

Illuminated manuscripts were created as objects of luxury during the medieval and Renaissance eras.

illusion form (drawing, figure, photo) that produces an erroneous perception. People are typically fooled into seeing AB as longer than CD, even though it is not. Called the Müller-Lyer illusion, it is caused in all likelihood by the fact that people are accustomed to interpreting outward-extending arrowheads as increasing the length of lines and, vice versa, to interpreting inward-extending arrowheads as decreasing the length of lines. In cultures where such drawing techniques do not exist, it has been found that the illusion does not occur.

illusionism 1. techniques designed to make representations resemble reality; 2. techniques that produce illusions; 3. stage magic

illustration picture, figure, or diagram used to explain or decorate something, especially written text

IM [*see* **instant messaging**]

image 1. mental picture; 2. public view of something or someone, often intentionally instigated by advertising or propaganda

image advertising advertising aiming to make a brand or company name easily remembered, that is, to transform it into an IMAGE

image map graphic image on a Web site that has HYPERLINKS in it that link to another Web page

image processing computer analysis of an image, identifying its components

image schema [introduced by American linguist George Lakoff and American philosopher Mark Johnson] in linguistics and media studies, recurring abstract images that guide language and perception. These function to compress sensory information into general patterns. For example, image schemas derived from the experience of orientation—up vs. down, back vs. front, near vs. far—can be detected in such expressions as: *I'm feeling up today*; *We are getting closer to each other every day*; *He's at the top of his class*; and *She's near her goal.*

imagery 1. picture formed in the mind; 2. comparisons, descriptions, and figures of speech that help the mind form images; 3. expressive images used in art and media

imagined community idea that media audiences form abstract communities in the "mediasphere" according to shared beliefs and ideas that influence how they interpret the media. The term was coined by the American scholar Benedict Anderson.

Impression, Sunrise (1872) by Claude Monet

imaging system software capable of digitizing images

IMAX trade name for a large-format movie projection system with three-dimensional technology

IMC [*see* **integrated marketing communications**]

immediacy view that a news story will have greater impact if it refers to a recent or ongoing event

impact scheduling practice of running advertisements for a product close together (on radio or television) so as to make a strong impact on audiences

impartiality being completely objective and uninvolved in reporting the news

imperative form in advertising technique consisting in the use of the imperative form of verbs, creating the sense that an authoritative source is giving advice: for example, *Just do it!* (Nike); *Have a Bud!* (Budweiser)

imperialism 1. extending power and dominion, either by invasion or by gaining political and economic control; 2. by extension, the spread of a particular type of media fare (such as American media) to other areas of the world

impressionism art style emerging in France in the 1870s, characterized by rich hues that allow the painter to convey an "impression," rather than a realistic or exact representation, of light and form. The subject matter of impressionists consisted of the objects of everyday life (landscapes, street scenes, etc.). The principal artists of the movement were Claude Monet, Pierre Auguste Renoir, Alfred Sisley, Berthe Morisot, Édouard Manet, and Camille Pissarro.

impulse pay-per-view pay-per-view television service that makes it possible to order programs on the spot, without advance reservation

in-band-on-channel [abbreviated as **IBOC**] digital radio technology that allows for the integrated use of digital and analog signal transmissions

incentive marketing strategy, such as the giving away of free gifts, designed to provide a favorable image of the product or company

incidental music music composed to be played at the same time as some action in a film, play, or television program

indecency in broadcasting, any material that depicts sexual or other biological activities in ways deemed unacceptable by community standards

independent film [abbreviated as **indie**] any film that is not produced by a major studio, but by an "independent" producer, company, etc.

independent media media outlets not tied to a major network or large media system

independent phone companies local service telephone companies that are not affiliated with a major phone company

in-depth reporting news reporting that goes into detail and is well researched

index 1. list of the contents of a print publication; 2. in semiotics, sign whose function is pointing out something real or imaginary in temporal, spatial, or relational terms; for example, the index finger; words such as *this* or *that* and *here* or *there*.

indicator any nonverbal cue used during conversation, such as a frown, scratching the head, folding the arms, nodding, etc.

indie [abbreviation of **independent**] any production or broadcast company, group, or individual not tied to a mainstream studio, network, or media organization

individualism belief or social theory maintaining that a single individual's freedom is as important as the welfare of entire groups, communities, societies, and the like

indoctrination any forcible imposition (overt or covert) of a particular system of values and beliefs

induction [in contrast to **abduction** and **deduction**] logical process of reaching a general conclusion on the basis of particular facts; for example, if one measures the number of degrees in a large number of triangles (in the plane), one comes to the induction that there must be 180° in all triangles—a conclusion that remains valid unless or until proved differently

industrial advertising advertising to businesses, rather than to individuals

infoholic individual who has become obsessed with information, seeking it out constantly, especially on the Internet

infomediary Web site where specialized information is available

infomercial [blend of **information** and **commercial**] extended television commercial that mimics a television program. Often infomercials feature celebrities who advertise a product in talk show style.

infonesia [blend of **information** and **amnesia**] inability to remember a piece of information or its location on the Internet

information 1. anything that can be perceived, accessed, stored, and retrieved; 2. measure of the probability that a message will occur. If a message is expected with 100 percent certainty, its information value is 0. For example, in a house alarm system, the "no ringing" state is the expected one and, thus, the one that carries this value; the "ringing" state, on the other hand, carries the high-

est amount of information because it has a lower probability of (expected) occurrence.

information architecture methods used in designing a Web site

information blizzards information overload to which people are exposed by media, which is difficult to digest and reflect upon

information gap disparity in access to information among individuals and groups

information highway 1. computer network, such as the Internet, linking many users, making it possible to transfer information quickly and broadly; 2. circulation of both personal communication and mass media through new technologies

information line line of text running across a computer screen providing information about the program being executed or the file being used

information management task of controlling information and its flow within an organization or system

information overload according to one view, the excess information that INFORMATION TECHNOLOGY has produced, which is too much for people to use intelligently or even practically, and which may have deleterious effects on social systems

information processing model advertising model evaluating the effects of an advertising strategy directed at audiences who are identified as being effective in processing information

information retrieval process of using or manipulating a database in order to extract some specific information from it

information science science that concerns the production, compilation, structuring, storage, retrieval, and propagation of INFORMATION. The field is interdisciplinary, utilizing ideas and techniques from other cognate disciplines (computer science, linguistics, etc.). Today, most of the research within the field revolves around how to use computer-based methods in the organization of information. It also includes the study of *bibliometrics*, the discipline that measures such things as the growth or decline in the number of books on a specific topic.

information society world order in which the exchange of information (more than goods) shapes social and economic systems

information superhighway [variant of **information highway**]

information technology range of computer-based media systems and telecommunication, including radio, television, print, and the Internet

information theory any theory attempting to explain what information is, how it is processed, what its

uses are, etc. Perhaps the first true theory of information was the one put forward by CLAUDE SHANNON in the late 1940s, known as the BULL'S-EYE MODEL, because it depicts information transfer as a closed system between a sender directing a message at a receiver as if he or she were a bull's-eye target. Although many have since been critical of the uses of this model to explain how human communication works, its general outline and corollary notions, especially that of FEEDBACK, have proved to be useful in all areas of communication science.

information worker individual who works with information in some way, such as creating Web pages or constructing computer databases

informational appeal advertising technique describing the demonstrable characteristics of a product (how it works, how it is made, and so on)

infotainment [blend of **information** and **entertainment**] television or other media form of entertainment based on presenting factual information in an engaging way

inherent drama advertising utilizing a mini-drama style that emphasizes the benefits that accrue from purchasing a product, such as the nutritional value of a food or the gas-saving quality of a car

inheritance factor tendency for ratings of a program to rise if it is aired after a popular program; the rise is said to be "inherited" from the preceding program

in-house agency advertising agency that is owned and operated by a company to manage its advertising program

in-line graphic image that is part of a Web page

Innis, Harold (1894–1952) Canadian historian famous for his studies of the interrelation between culture, media, and technology. Innis divided media into *time-biased* and *space-biased* media. The former include handwritten and oral media that are intended to last for many generations, but are used in relatively small communities; the latter include most of the modern electronic and print media, which are designed to reach as many people as possible, but will typically not last long in time. While time-biased media favor a sense of community, space-biased media favor commercialism and imperialism. Among his most important works are *Empire and Communications* (1950); *The Bias of Communication* (1951); and *The Strategy of Culture* (1952).

inoculation effect ability of audiences to resist being persuaded by a commercial, a news program, etc., if they are warned beforehand that an attempt to persuade them is about to occur

input information introduced into a computer system that allows a user to achieve an output, that is, a desired result

input hardware computer devices or systems that allow for information to be introduced into a computer, including a mouse, a keyboard, an optical scanner, a voice recognition module, and the like.

inquiry test in advertising, a test measuring the effectiveness of an ad or ad campaign based on responses to it

insert shot close-up shot of a headline or some other item that is inserted into a filmed scene in order to show the viewer what a character in the scene can see

inside back cover page on the inside of the back cover of a publication that can be used for advertising and various information-providing purposes

inside story reportage based on the firsthand experiences of those who are inside a company or organization in the news

instant book in the book industry, strategy of publishing a topical book as quickly as possible after a major news story

instant messaging [abbreviated as **IM**] real-time communication between two or more people based on typed text, which is transmitted via the Internet. An early form of IM was used on private computer networks such as the Plato system of the early 1970s. IM systems were used by engineers and academics in the 1980s and 1990s to communicate across the Internet. IM became a popular form of communication after mobile IM devices, such as palm pilots, came onto the market en masse.

instant replay playback of a video, often in slow motion, to show a particular moment in a sports event on television

institution in media studies, the social, cultural, and political systems within which a media system operates

institutional advertising the promotion of an organization rather than a product

integrated information response model claim that product acceptance is not necessarily a result of advertising's effect on the way the product is perceived, but rather that product acceptance will tend to increase after the product has been tried

integrated marketing communications [abbreviated as **IMC**] marketing campaign that integrates public relations strategies, advertising, and other aspects together for greater effectiveness in product promotion

intellectual property original work that was created, and thus belongs to, an individual, institution, or company. The main methods used to protect intellectual property are trademarks, patents, and copyright.

Intelsat [*see* **International Telecommunications Satellite Organization**]

interactive any piece of software or computer system that allows easy communication between the user and computer

interactive advertising advertising that is sensitive and thus adaptive to input from the audience through the Internet

interactive media media that allow for two-way communication between the media and users (such as viewers), enabling users to obtain responses in real time

interactive multimedia multimedia system that allows users to control a program, or else to control the way a program works

interactive television [abbreviated as **ITV**] system integrating television, telephone, and Internet systems to deliver a wide range of choices to a viewing audience

interactivity ability to participate in, or control, media products, rather than passively receive them

intercultural communication communication between people from different social, linguistic, and cultural backgrounds

intercutting going back and forth between filmed scenes or shots of actions occurring at different time periods to give the impression that they are simultaneous

interdiction technology technology that descrambles pay channel cable television signals

interface software that allows communication between a computer and a user, including commands, prompts, and other such devices. The term is also used to refer to hardware (cards, plugs, and other devices) that allows the computer to move information.

interference unwanted signals from other sources, disrupting radio or television reception

interjection sound or expression conveying a strong emotion: *Yikes! Wow!*

intermercials commercials that run while users are waiting for a Web page to download

International Business Machines [abbreviated as **IBM**] computer manufacturer, headquartered in Armonk, New York, incorporated in 1911 as the Computing-Tabulating-Recording Co. It chose its present name in 1924. Web site: www.ibm.com

International Phonetic Alphabet [abbreviated as **IPA**] list of more than 80 phonetic symbols, first devised in the late nineteenth century by the International Phonetic Association, to make it possible to represent sounds as accurately and consistently as possible. For example, [k] stands for the same sound represented alternatively by the alphabet characters *k*, *ch*, and *q* in English: *keen, school, quiet.*

International Telecommunications Satellite Organization [abbreviated as **Intelsat**] world's first commercial satellite operator, established in 1965. Web site: www.intelsat.com

internaut an Internet user, especially a regular one

Internet the "network of networks" that connects millions (perhaps billions) of computers around the world. Networks connected to the Internet use a common protocol, TCP/IP (Transmission Control Protocol/Internet Protocol), which allows them to have unique addresses and to communicate easily with one another. The Internet grew out of a Defense Department program called ARPANET (Advanced Research Projects Agency Network), established in 1969 with connections between computers at the University of California at Los Angeles, Stanford Research Institute, the University of California–Santa Barbara, and the University of Utah. ARPANET was used by researchers and especially to provide a secure communications system in case of war. As the network expanded, academics and researchers in other fields began to use it as well.

In 1971 the first program for sending e-mail over a distributed network was developed. By 1973, the year international connections to ARPANET were made, e-mail represented most of the traffic on ARPANET. The 1970s also saw the development of the TCP/IP communications protocols, which were adopted as standard protocols, leading to the widespread use of the term *Internet*. In 1984 the domain name addressing system (.com, .net, and the like) was introduced. In 1988 real-time communication over the Internet became possible with the development of Internet Relay Chat protocols. In 1989 the WORLD WIDE WEB was created, leading to the proliferation of Web sites and users by the mid-1990s. By 1997 there were more than 10 million hosts on the Internet and more than one million registered domain names. Internet access can now be gained via radio signals, cable-television lines, satellites, and fiber-optic connections, in addition to the public telecommunications network.

Internet protocol standard that allows digital computers to communicate over long distances. On the Internet, information is broken down into small packets, sent individually over different routes at the same time, and then reassembled at the receiving end. Protocols collect and reassemble the packets and then send them to the desired destination.

Internet radio online radio station that either simulcasts versions of on-air radio broadcasts over the World Wide Web, or else creates its own programming

Internet relay chat software that allows Internet users to join conversations or chats organized in an informal way around particular subjects at specific Web sites

Internet service provider [abbreviated as **ISP**] company that provides Internet connections and services. ISPs provide computer users with a connection to their site, as well as a log-in name and password. They may also provide software packages, e-mail accounts, and a personal Web site. ISPs are all connected to each other through network access points (public network facilities on the Internet backbone).

Internet telephony system that allows users to make phone calls using the Internet. To make calls, users need to install a sound card, microphone, and loudspeaker in their computers, along with special software that manages the system

Internet television online television station that either simulcasts versions of on-air television broadcasts over the World Wide Web, or else creates its own programming

interpellation [term coined by LOUIS ALTHUSSER] in Marxist theory, style or register in which people are addressed in conversation, which relates to their position in society.

interpersonal communication exchange of information between individuals, using not only language, but also other modes, such as gesture, body posture, and so on

interpersonal framing signals that inform people who are talking to each other whether or not the conversation is serious and what purpose it has

interpersonal function of language use of language to bond with others, as opposed to its use for exchanging information

interpretant [term coined by **Charles Peirce**] the meaning that someone perceives from a sign

interpretation 1. deciphering what something means; 2. an individual's understanding and/or execution of a work (of art, music, or theater) through acting, performing, etc. (for example, a pianist's interpretation of Bach's preludes and fugues)

interpretive community group of people who interpret a text or media product homogeneously

interpretive journalism news reporting that explains events in the light of broader social or philosophical issues

interstitial advertisement in cyberadvertising (advertising online), use of images that seem to appear and disappear mysteriously on the screen as users click from one Web page to the next

intertextuality interrelation of a text (such as a novel) with other texts external to it (such as a religious text, a scientific text, etc.). An external text can be cited directly (as in a bibliographic reference in a scholarly paper) or indirectly, as for example, Homer's *Odyssey* in James Joyce's *Ulysses.* In advertising, intertextuality involves allusions to pop culture, other ads, and the like.

intervention video fictional or documentary video produced to raise awareness about a specific social or political issue

interview encounter during which a journalist or a radio or television announcer asks someone relevant questions about a topic

intimization technique of making a news story more appealing by adapting it to reflect widely held views or beliefs on the part of audiences

intonation melodic patterns built into utterances for specific effects or communicative purposes (to express surprise, doubtfulness, etc.). In many languages, intonation also serves a grammatical function, distinguishing one type of phrase or sentence from another. Thus, *You like it* is an assertion when spoken with a drop in pitch at the end, but a question when spoken with a rise in pitch at the end.

intranet private computer network, providing members with Internet and World Wide Web features, such as e-mail and Web pages. By sealing the intranet off from the larger Internet, people can protect information from unwanted and possibly criminal sources. As security issues have arisen around the Internet, intranets have gained in popularity, particularly among businesses.

intransient advertisement advertisement that the target audience can keep; for example, the ads in newspapers and magazines

intrapersonal communication internal dialogue (talking to oneself)

inverted-pyramid style reporting style in which news stories are structured and presented, starting with the most important items and ending with a short background piece

investigative reporting type of reporting in which a journalist does research to expose someone or something for engaging in incorrect behavior and to reveal who is trying to cover it up

invisibility underrepresentation of certain minority groups by the mainstream media, thus making them "invisible" to the majority of audiences

IP terminal special unit that allows users to create and edit video before transmitting it to the main page

IPA [*see* **International Phonetic Alphabet**]

iPod trade name for a portable device designed and marketed by Apple Computer onto which users can download music or programs; by extension, any such device

irony amusing or subtly mocking phrase or statement in which the literal meaning stands in opposition to the intended meaning. For example, if an opera singer goes off key a few times, someone in the audience might shout out ironically "You sure know the song well!" By extension, the term is used to refer to any mocking or incongruous text or performance. For example, when a character knows something that the other characters do not know, a sense of irony is evoked. In *Oedipus Rex* by Sophocles, Oedipus kills a man, not knowing that the man is his father Laius. Oedipus puts a curse on Laius's killer. The irony is that he has unsuspectingly cursed himself.

ISP [*see* **Internet service provider**]

ITV [*see* **interactive television**]

Jakobson, Roman (1896–1982) Moscow-born American linguist well-known for  his work on communication theory, often quoted in media studies. Jakobson saw language as an adaptive communicative instrument serving human needs and whims, and influenced by the structure of cultural codes. A comprehensive collection of his writings can be found in *Selected Writings* (1971–1982).

Jameson, Frederic (1934–) prominent Marxist theorist well-known for his works on POSTMODERNISM. Among his most influential books are *Marxism and Form: Twentieth Century Dialectical Theories of Literature* (1971) and *Postmodernism, or the Cultural Logic of Late Capitalism* (1991).

jargon specialized vocabulary used typically by members of a profession or line of work (doctors, musicians, psychologists, etc.): for example, *perorbital hematoma = black eye*, in medicine; *licorice stick = clarinet*, among jazz musicians. By extension, any form of pretentious or hollow language.

Java programming language used to create tiny programs that give additional versatility to Web page design

jazz musical form, often improvisational, developed by African Americans. The specific origins of jazz are not known. It emerged as an amalgam of several styles in New Orleans at the start of the 1900s, including West African music, black folk music, and light classical music popular in the late nineteenth century. Most early jazz was played by small marching bands or by solo pianists. In 1917 a group of white New Orleans musicians called the Original Dixieland Jazz Band recorded a jazz phonograph record, creating a sensation; the term "Dixieland jazz" was immediately attached to it. In 1922 the New Orleans Rhythm Kings, and in 1923 the Creole Jazz Band, led by cornetist King Oliver, became popular throughout the United States. The term "cool jazz" surfaced 1948, when tenor saxophonist Stan Getz recorded a slow, romantic solo of Ralph Burns's composition *Early Autumn* with the Woody Herman band. This style was adopted by a group of young musicians that included Miles Davis, Lee Konitz, Gerry Mulligan, and arranger Gil Evans. Their recordings emphasized a lagging beat, soft instrumental sounds, and unusual orchestrations that included the French horn and the tuba. The recordings, with Davis as leader, were later released as *Birth of the Cool.*

jazz journalism lively form of popular tabloid journalism of the 1920s

Jensen, Klaus Bruhn (1956–) expert on the research methodologies used in communication theory, often quoted on matters regarding the use of such methodologies in the field. His most cited book is *Handbook of Qualitative Methodologies for Mass Communication Research* (1991; coauthored with Nicholas W. Jankowski).

jingle brief and catchy piece of music, composed to advertise a product or to identify a station or a presenter

jive jazz-based swing dance popular in the 1930s and 1940s

JOA [*see* **joint operating agreement**]

joint operating agreement [abbreviated as **JOA**] agreement that allows a failing newspaper to merge aspects of its operations with a successful competitor, as long as its editorial and journalistic operations and perspectives remain unaltered

Joint Photographic Experts Group [abbreviated as **jpeg**] computer format for images that allows users to compress data, albeit with some loss of quality

journal magazine or periodical that deals with an area of special or specialized interest, generally published by a professional body for its members

journalese type of communication style characteristic of journalists

journalism writing, collection, preparation, and distribution of news

and related commentary through media. The term was originally applied to the reportage of current events in printed form, specifically newspapers, but it now includes electronic forms as well (radio journalism, television journalism, online journalism).

journalist person whose job it is to write for a newspaper or magazine, or to prepare news for radio, television, or Web broadcasting

joystick handheld control lever having an upright stick on a pivot, used to play computer games

jpeg [*see* **Joint Photographic Experts Group**]

jukebox machine that plays records when a coin is inserted, invented in 1906. The term *jukebox* referred to the original kinds of places that maintained such machines, called "juke joints." By 1941 there were nearly 400,000 jukeboxes in the United States. The jukebox became an icon of the early rock culture of the 1950s, soon after the Seeburg Company produced the first jukeboxes in 1950 to play 45 rpm singles.

jump cut cut from one shot in a film to another similar shot within the same footage, giving the impression that something has jumped, thus forcing the audience to reflect on what had occurred just before.

jumpstation Web site that provides links to other Web sites

Jung, Carl Gustav (1875–1961)
Swiss psychiatrist whose concept of
the ARCHETYPE has become widely
used in media and advertising studies. Jung saw archetypes as unconscious thought patterns shared by
all humanity, which gain expression
in the various symbols and forms
(myths, tales, fantasies, rituals, etc.)
that embody them across cultures:
for instance, the phallus figure
is an archetype found in rituals,
sculptures, and other representational forms throughout time
and across cultures, normally as
a symbol of reproduction or of
masculinity.

junk mail unsolicited advertising
and promotional material that arrives
through the mail and through the
Internet

**Kant, Immanuel
(1724–1804)** German
philosopher, famous for his
theory of knowledge. In his
Kritik der reinen Vernunft
(1781; *Critique of Pure
Reason*), for example, Kant discusses
the nature of knowledge in mathematics and physics, arguing that the
propositions of mathematics encode
real experience, reflecting the mind's
unique ability to grasp reality and then
formalize this grasp through formal
categories (such as propositions).

karaoke form of entertainment in
which people sing popular songs
accompanied by pre-recorded music,
played by a machine that may also
display the words on a screen

Katz, Elihu (1926–) eminent media
scholar who co-created the TWO-
STEP FLOW THEORY model of media
processing. Among his most influential works are *The Export of Meaning*
(1990) and *Media Events: The Live
Broadcasting of History* (1992).

Kennedy-Nixon TV debate famous
television debate between Richard
M. Nixon and John F. Kennedy that
turned the 1960 U.S. presidential
election in favor of Kennedy. People
who heard the debate on radio maintained that Nixon had won it, coming
across as the better candidate; those
who saw it on television claimed the
opposite. Nixon looked disheveled
and worried; Kennedy looked confi-
dent and came across as a young and
handsome "president of the future."

Kennedy went on to win the
election; a debate emerged
in media studies shortly
thereafter on the effects of
television on viewers.

keyboarder person whose job it is to
input data in a computer

keyed advertisement advertisement
that asks its viewers to write down a
specially coded address that will indicate where they saw it, thus helping
advertisers glean the effectiveness of
advertising in a particular newspaper
or magazine

kidvid video aimed at children

kilobyte unit of computer memory
equivalent to 1,024 BYTES

kinescope early television picture tube developed by VLADIMIR
ZWORKYN for RCA

kinesics study of body language,
that is, postures, gestures, touch
patterns, and the like and the messages that they convey during human
interaction. Kinesic communication
is partly based on innate signaling
systems, but in larger part on cultural
traditions (handshaking, touching,
etc.).

kinetoscope parlors early movie
parlors that used a motion picture
device called a kinetoscope, which
was encased in a wooden cabinet
and which could be viewed through
a slit

KISS [full form: **keep it short and simple**] advertising philosophy that the best type of advertising message is one that is concise and clear

kitsch a form of entertainment or art that is considered to be in poor taste or lacking aesthetic quality

knowledge gap view that those who already are knowledgeable (educated, well-informed) receive more benefit from the media and new information technologies than those who are not—hence the formation of a "knowledge gap" between the two

Kristeva, Julia (1941–) Bulgarian-born French feminist scholar whose work on INTERTEXTUALITY is widely quoted. Using psychoanalytic theory, Kristeva has also been concerned with the representation of otherness, especially in horror films. One of her most quoted books is *Language: The Unknown* (1989).

Kuleshov effect theory, proposed by Russian film theorist Lev Kuleshov, that a single shot or piece of film can be given a different interpretation when shown next to another one

label 1. the identifying element of a product, package, or other item; 2. trademark used by a record company: for example, the RCA label, the Naxos label

Lacan, Jacques (1901–1981) French psychoanalyst who claimed that the unconscious part of an individual's mind reflects the structure of the language he or she speaks. Lacan also divided the psyche into three levels—the imaginary, the symbolic, and the real. His ideas have recently been applied to the study of pop culture, which is portrayed as a symbolic bridge between the imaginary and the real world. His major concepts are found in *Écrits: The First Complete Edition in English* (2006).

lampoon satirical work designed to ridicule something or someone. One of the best-known U.S. publications written in the style of a lampoon is *Mad Magazine.*

LAN [*see* **local area network**]

landing page Web page where a user arrives, normally via a HYPERLINK

Langer, Susanne (1895–1985) American philosopher often quoted in media studies because of the important distinction she made between the *discursive* symbols used in language and the *nondiscursive* or *presentational* ones used in various forms of art. The former possess the property of detachment, allowing communicators or readers to focus on specific items in utterances without impairing overall understanding; the latter, on the other hand, cannot be broken down and detached without impairing the meaning—one cannot focus on a note in a piece of music without destroying its sense.

language [from Latin *lingua*, meaning "tongue"] as its etymology suggests, language can be defined as the "use of the tongue" to create meaning-bearing forms called words, phrases, and sentences. Wherever there are humans, there is language. And all languages serve humans in similar ways, such as naming (and thus classifying) the things of reality that are relevant and meaningful to them. There are about 6,000 languages spoken in the world today, not including dialects (local forms of a language); of these, only around 200 languages have a million or more speakers. All languages share five basic characteristics: (1) distinctive sounds, known as *phonemes*, which are used to signal differences in meaning; (2) meaning-bearing units known as *morphemes*; (3) grammatical structure (rules for combining morphemes into larger forms called *sentences* and *utterances*); (4) strategies for using language in various personal and social ways; and (5) resources for making new words and, thus, new meanings. Most languages use from 20 to 60 vocal sounds to make their words, indicating that vocal sounds are not meaningful elements in themselves, but rather that they are building blocks in the constitution of larger structures (such as words). Words are units of sounds that have meaning, standing for objects, actions, or ideas. Grammatical structure is the manner in which words are related to each other to form larger units of meaning such as sentences. The strategies for using a language for various purposes, such as communication and representation, are the result of traditions that are deemed important by a speech community. Finally, language provides the means through which people can adapt creatively to new situations and experiences. Every time we come up with a new word, we are acknowledging that a small part of the world has changed.

language pollution use of language to confuse or mislead

langue [term coined by **Ferdinand de Saussure**] native speakers' unconscious knowledge of the structure of the language they speak. Saussure compared *langue* to the rules of chess. No matter how well or poorly someone plays, his or her ability to play chess in the first place is dependent on an unconscious knowledge of the chess game itself. Now, the actual moves he or she makes during a specific chess game depend on factors that are external to this knowledge, involving how best to respond to an opponent's moves, relying on past experience to come up

with an appropriate move, and so on. Analogously, the ability to speak and understand a language is dependent upon knowing the language game itself (*langue*); whereas the actual use of *langue* in specific social situations depends upon psychological, social, and communicative factors. He called the latter *parole*.

LAPS test [full form: **literary, artistic, political, scientific value test**] a standard of obscenity established in *Miller v. California* (1973), whereby a work is considered to be obscene if it lacks serious literary, artistic, political, or scientific value. In the late 1960s a California court found Marvin Miller guilty of sending obscene unsolicited advertising material through the mail. In 1973 the case reached the Supreme Court; the Court ruled that states may censor material if they apply the LAPS test. As a result, standards for obscenity differ widely in different parts of the country.

Lasswell's model of communication a model of communication theory formulated in 1948 by Harold Lasswell, which stipulates that the roles played by the communicants, the nature of the channels they are using, what they are saying, to whom they are saying it, and the effect it is supposed to make are pivotal factors in shaping the message that is communicated

late night time period in radio and television scheduling after PRIME

TIME, and thus late at night, characterized by programming with controversial and/or bawdy content

latency period of dormancy in which a complex of thoughts, feelings, or mental images remain undeveloped or unexpressed; 2. amount of time it takes data to move across an Internet connection

Latin American music popular music genres created by Latin American artists, such as the tango, the rumba, the samba, the salsa, and others. Latin American music has always had an important influence on the popular music of the United States. Since the 1950s, a number of Latin American rock music performers have injected a Latin American style into rock music generally, gaining widespread popularity. These include Ritchie Valens, Carlos Santana, Gloria Estefan, and the group Los Lobos.

laugh track pre-recorded laughter that is added to a sitcom or comedy program in appropriate spots

law of primacy theory that the initial argument that is presented to audiences will stand a better chance of convincing them than will subsequent ones

layout design of a printed page or a Web page, showing the position of text and graphics

Lazarsfeld, Paul (1901–1976) widely quoted media scholar who pioneered the study of the effects of media on audiences. With ELIHU KATZ, he created the TWO-STEP FLOW model. His most important work is *The People's Choice: How the Voter Makes Up His Mind in a Presidential Campaign* (1944).

lead 1. main story on the front page of a newspaper; 2. main role in a play, movie, or program

lead-in introductory piece before a program or segment on radio or television

leak disclosure of confidential information to the media

leased channels in cable television, channels that allow customers to buy time for producing their own programs or for presenting their viewpoints

leased line line hired from a telecommunications company providing a permanent link to an Internet service provider

legend [*see also* **urban legend**] 1. story (often about a heroic figure) popularly believed to have a historical basis, but which is not always verifiable (for example, the legend of King Arthur and the Knights of the Round Table); 2. by extension, any personage or celebrity whose fame has become enduring through media exposure

legitimation process by which certain values, ideas, beliefs, or opinions pass into the mainstream of public opinion

leitmotif 1. melody associated with a character, situation, or element in a musical drama or opera; 2. any recurring theme in a poem, a novel, a TV sitcom, a movie, etc. Even though the German composer Richard Wagner did not use this term, it is often applied to the study of his operas, in which specific melodic phrases are used to identify characters or themes.

lemma heading or entry that indicates the topic of a work or passage (for example, a heading title on a book page indicating the title of the book)

letterhead 1. stationery with a printed heading that a company, individual, or institution uses for official letters and documents; 2. the printed heading that appears at the top of a letterhead

Lévi-Strauss, Claude (1908–) Belgian-born French anthropologist whose notion of mythic opposition is often quoted in the media literature. Lévi-Strauss saw innate oppositions in human consciousness—such as good vs. evil, mother vs. father—as the motivating forces in the creation of early myths and thus of the foundations of early cultures and languages. Such oppositions continue to surface in modern-day representational, linguistic, symbolic, and ritualistic activities. Among his most

influential works are *Anthropologie structurale* (1958; *Structural Anthropology*, 1963) and *Le cru et le cuit* (1964; *The Raw and the Cooked*, 1969).

lexicography study and craft of dictionaries and dictionary making. Dictionaries are generally subdivided into general, specialized, and thesauruses. A general dictionary contains definitions and information on everyday language and selected technical terms; a specialized dictionary provides technical information on terms used in a particular field (mathematics, physics, medicine, law, etc.); a thesaurus contains, essentially, lists of synonyms and antonyms. The information provided by a dictionary may include the history of words (known as etymologies), associated idioms and expressions, dialectal variants, slang, and the like. Bilingual dictionaries translate the words, expressions, and phrases of one language into another. Today, there are various online dictionaries that have the advantage (over print ones) of providing updated information daily. For this reason, many lexicographers are predicting the demise of both the print dictionary and the print ENCYLOPEDIA, which can only be updated by revisions and subsequent republication.

lexicon 1. list of special terms used in a particular field (lexicon of mathematics, lexicon of literary terms, etc.); 2. total stock of words, phrases, and expressions in a language

libel 1. false and malicious statement that damages a person's reputation; 2. published or broadcast statement that unjustifiably exposes someone to ridicule or derision

libertarianism philosophy asserting that good and rational people can tell right from wrong if presented with all the facts. For this reason any form of censorship is seen to be unnecessary. Libertarians maintain that control of the media does not belong to the government but to the people whom the media serve.

libido in psychoanalysis, the energy associated with the instincts that motivate a large part of behavior. The term was coined by SIGMUND FREUD, who posited that the libido develops in stages: in the oral stage, the infant gets pleasure from activities such as breast suckling; in the anal phase, the child gets pleasure from being able to control bowel movements; in the genital phase, which starts at around puberty, sexual urges dominate the libido. This notion has been used occasionally in advertising studies to explain how some kinds of ads are designed to stimulate the libido.

library music music for films or television shows that is available for a fee from a specialized library

license 1. permission to engage in a business or other regulated activity; 2. permission to operate a specific radio frequency

Liebes, Tamar (1943–) often-quoted scholar on the effects of media on audiences and on the processes involved in the decoding of media texts. Among her most influential works are *Media, Ritual, and Identity* (as editor, with James Curran, 1998) and *The Export of Meaning* (with Elihu Katz, 1990).

lifestyle segmentation way of grouping audiences according to their habits, the kinds of music they like, etc.

light viewer in media research parlance, a person who watches very little television

lighting equipment and techniques used for lighting a play, a movie set, or a television set. As such, it is part of the overall film text, being used to bring out various meanings, emphases, nuances, etc., that the text is designed to produce.

limited effects theory view that the effects of media on people are limited by variables such as class, education, cultural background, and age. Essentially, the theory argues that the mass media have relatively few effects on people.

line producer member of a film production team responsible for the daily operations, such as procuring technical help and ensuring that maintenance is carried out

linear perspective art technique by which the perception of depth and

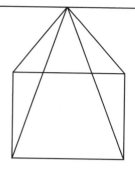

Box in linear perspective

distance on a surface is produced by parallel lines that converge on the horizon. The technique simulates visual perception by showing images in the same perspective as we see them in the real world—in visual perception, distant objects appear smaller and less distinct than near objects.

lines speech or dialogue that an actor has to deliver

linguistic competence abstract knowledge of language. This term was coined by the American linguist NOAM CHOMSKY, who defined it as the innate knowledge that people employ unconsciously to generate and comprehend sentences, most of which they have never heard previously. Chomsky proposed a system of analysis, which he called *transformational-generative grammar*, that would allow the linguist to identify and describe the general properties of linguistic competence, sifting them out from those that apply only to particular languages. The former, called *universal principles*, are purported to be part of a species-specific language faculty that has genetic information built into it about what languages in general must be like; the latter, known as *parameters*, are said to constrain the universal principles to produce the specific language grammar to which the child is exposed. Although Chomsky assigns some role to cultural and experiential factors, he maintains that the primary role of linguistics must be to understand the universal principles that make up the speech faculty.

linguistic relativity hypothesis a claim that language shapes worldview. The hypothesis has a long history, going back to the ancient world. It was in the eighteenth century, however, that it came to be discussed and debated formally by language scientists and philosophers, such as Johann von Herder, who claimed that there was an intrinsic link between language and ethnic character, and Wilhelm von Humboldt, who argued that the grammar and vocabulary of a specific language shaped the thought and behavior of the people born into it. In the first part of the twentieth century, anthropologist Edward Sapir and his student Benjamin Lee Whorf researched native American languages to test the validity of the hypothesis, coming to the conclusion that languages do indeed seem to guide how people think and act. Given the importance of their work, the hypothesis is now also known as Sapir-Whorf hypothesis. The Sapir-Whorf version of linguistic relativity claims that the grammar and vocabulary of a particular language provide the cognitive strategies for interpreting reality, since they make available words and structures for certain specific events, while ignoring others. This does not block understanding among speakers of different languages, as translation and paraphrases demonstrate. But it does show that there is diversity in human language that reflects diversity in cultural and psychological experiences.

linguistics the science of language. Linguists study the formal aspects of language (sound systems, grammar, vocabulary, and so on), its uses in communication, its relation to cognition, and its interrelation with culture and society.

links speech excerpts that introduce the next item in radio and television programming

linotype older technology that was used to carry out the mechanical setting of print type (rather than manual)

lip-sync [full form: **lip synchronization**] technique of mouthing a recorded statement or a song without actually speaking or singing, giving the illusion that one is performing it live

listenership number and type of people who listen to a radio broadcast or station

listening share share of total radio audience that is faithful to a specific radio station

listings information on what a spectacle or event will contain (venue of performance, times, admission prices, contact details)

listserv Internet discussion group whose members use e-mail or instant messaging to exchange messages among themselves and/or with other groups

literacy 1. ability to read and write a language proficiently; 2. by extension, any ability to decipher texts (media literacy, visual literacy). Those who cannot read and write are called *illiterate*. It is believed broadly that without literacy, people's ability to function in society diminishes considerably. The worldwide literacy rate has risen since 1900. By the mid-1990s, 73 percent of the world's population was thought to be literate. With the advent of the Internet, more and more people are becoming literate than ever before in the history of humanity. Models and perception of literacy are shaped by the medium in which the written word is expressed. The Internet and the many devices that it has permitted for recording and sending messages is reshaping how the written word is being used and thus how literacy will eventually be redefined in the near future. In effect, the World Wide Web is fast becoming the new platform upon which linguistic and stylistic trends will emerge.

literal 1. following the exact words of the original (for example, a literal translation); 2. interpreting words concretely, without exaggeration or imagination. A word such as *square* has the literal meaning "plane figure constructed with four equal lines meeting at right angles." But it can also be used with other meanings, as in *He's a real square* and *We finally squared our differences.*

literary criticism discipline concerned with the study of literature. Western literary criticism began with PLATO. Subsequently, ARISTOTLE developed a set of principles of literary analysis that is still used today, including the distinction between the literal and the metaphorical. Since the Renaissance, literary criticism has primarily focused on the value of literature as an imaginary frame for viewing reality. In the twentieth century, a radical reappraisal of traditional critical techniques crystallized, leading to the development of DECONSTRUCTION and POSTSTRUCTURALISM, among other approaches.

literary journalism style of journalism that presents stories by adapting fictional storytelling techniques to nonfictional materials

literature 1. in its broadest sense, everything that has ever been written, including comic books and pamphlets, as well as the novels of Fyodor Dostoyevsky and the plays of William Shakespeare; 2. in a narrower sense, writing considered to have worth and aesthetic qualities. Literature has two main forms: fiction and nonfiction. The former is imaginary writing, even though authors may include facts about real persons or events; the latter is factual writing about real-life situations, including such genres as history, biography, autobiography, and the diary.

litotes rhetorical technique of understatement, especially by employing a negation of the contrary: for example, *I received not a few e-mails on that issue*; *This is no insignificant problem*

Little Three studios [in contrast to the **Big Five**] Columbia, United Artists, and Universal motion picture production studios, which had smaller production operations than the Big Five

live broadcasting of an event as it unfolds

live shot filmed event that is broadcast live without a presenter at the scene

live voiceover commentary for a pre-recorded video, often used in news reporting

LiveJournal Web site that allows users to create and modify their social network sites and Web pages

lobbying action taken by a group of supporters and representatives of a particular cause or organization to gain the support of a political party, a media organization, or an individual

local access programming television programming selected and/or produced within communities and aired on channels provided to the community by the cable television operator

local area network [abbreviated as LAN] network connecting two or more computers, usually within the same building. Local area networks now exist for the home, monitoring control of heat, water, and various appliances, as well as security systems.

local media media outlets and organizations serving a small area of a country (for example, neighborhood newspapers, local radio stations)

localization method of making national or international media products more suitable or appropriate for a smaller local media market

localized advertising strategy ad campaign aimed specifically at a particular region (country, state, province, or city)

location filming filming that takes place in specific real-life locations, away from the studio or set

log file record of how many users have visited a Web site and how they navigated through it

logging (on and off) to register or terminate an action or activity with a computer as an authorized operator

McDonald's Golden Arches logo

logo [abbreviation of **logotype**] distinctive design or trademark used by an organization or a company for itself or for its products so that they can be easily recognized. Logos are the pictorial counterparts of brand names. Well-known logos in the United States include Ralph Lauren's polo horseman, Lacoste's alligator, the "good hands" of the Allstate Insurance Company, the "rock" of the Prudential Insurance Company, the McDonald's "golden arches," the Macintosh "apple," and the "stagecoach" of the Wells Fargo Company. Logos are often designed to evoke historical or cultural themes or symbolism. For instance, the logo of the apple suggests the biblical story of Adam and Eve, even though the original fruit was named simply a "forbidden fruit"— it was depicted as an apple by the early religious painters. Its biblical symbolism is encoded into the Macintosh logo.

logocentrism belief that language shapes worldview

logograph symbol for a word without any cues as to its pronunciation: 1 = *one* in English, *uno* in Italian; & = *and* in English, *e* in Italian.

lógos [in contrast to **mythos**] 1. in philosophy, reasoning about reality or the power of reasoning itself; 2. in Christianity, the word of God, made incarnate in Jesus Christ

longitudinal studies in marketing research, studies that are conducted over long periods of time

long-playing record record format introduced by Columbia Records in 1948 that could reproduce over 20 minutes of high-fidelity sound on each of two sides of the record

look and feel the appeal of a Web site's design, layout, and user-friendliness

lookism the claim that good-looking people achieve greater success in life because others are influenced positively by their looks

Lotman, Jurij M. (1922–1993) Estonian semiotician well-known for his study of the relation between biology and culture. His major contribution to culture study is the idea that culture is a system of signs, called the *semiosphere*, that provides the resources for cognitive survival, in the same way that the *biosphere* provides the resources for physical survival. His most important work in English is *Universe of the Mind: A Semiotic Theory of Culture* (1990).

loudspeaker device for making sounds louder, especially in a radio, record player, or public-address system

low culture [*see* **high culture vs. low culture**]

low-budget films films that are produced very cheaply, with minor actors and simple production techniques, usually dealing with horror, crime, or prurient themes

low-involvement hierarchy the idea that indifferent customers respond to an ad's appeal only through repeated exposure

Lull, James (1950–) American communications scholar whose work on audiences is widely quoted (his work is found mainly in journals and periodicals). His method of audience analysis stresses ethnographic analysis, rather than statistical analysis of audience behaviors and reactions to media stimuli.

Lumière brothers two French brothers, Auguste (1862–1954) and Louis Jean (1864–1948), who are identified as having invented the technology behind motion pictures. The brothers held a public screening of projected motion pictures on December 28, 1895, in a Paris café. Thomas Edison, adapting a projector developed previously, presented the first public exhibition of projected motion pictures in the United States on April 23, 1896, in a New York City music hall.

lurking act of reading newsgroup postings or chatroom conversations without participating

Lyotard, Jean-François (1924–1998) well-known and often-cited theorist of postmodernism. His most important work is *La condition postmoderne:*

Rapport sur le savoir (1979; *The Postmodern Condition: A Report on Knowledge*, 1984).

lyric 1. type of song-like poetry that communicates subjective feelings; 2. [plural, **lyrics**] the verbal text of a popular song

macaronic any statement or text characterized by a mixture of Latin words or words from another language, usually for comic effect

MacBride Commission commission set up by UNESCO in 1978 to assess the impact of Western technology and media on developing countries

MacGuffin in a book, play, or movie, an event that seemingly drives the plot but which later turns out to be unimportant. The term was popularized by director Alfred Hitchcock, who explained it in a 1939 lecture at Columbia University: "In crook stories it is most always the necklace and in spy stories it is most always the papers."

machinery of representation claim that the mass media is a "machine" that produces representations of reality that audiences perceive as authentic

macro-level effects purported large-scale effects of the media on cultures and societies

macrophotography close-up photography producing images that are life-size or larger than life

magalogue a designer catalogue made up to look like a magazine

magazine newspaper-like publication, but smaller in size, issued at regular intervals, and containing a collection of articles or stories (or both). Most popular magazines also include illustrations and photographs. The magazine concept traces its roots to early printed pamphlets and almanacs. One of the first was the German *Erbauliche Monaths-Unterredungen* (Edifying Monthly Discussions), published from 1663 to 1668. Pamphlets appeared in England and America in the 1700s, primarily as literary publications. One of the first true magazines, called *The Gentleman's Magazine*, published from 1731 to 1914, started out as a collection of excerpts from various books and pamphlets. The first magazine published in America, called the *American Magazine*, came out in 1741 in Philadelphia and lasted only three months. (Benjamin Franklin's *Poor Richard's Almanack*—though not considered a true magazine—was first published in 1732.) Two other magazines, *The Columbian* (1786) and *The American Museum* (1787) quickly followed. In 1830, *Godey's Lady's Book*, the first American magazine for women, started publication. During the American Civil War (1861–1865), *Harper's Weekly* became popular for its drawings of the battlefront. The late 1800s and early 1900s saw a boom in the magazine industry, with *Life, Time, Sports Illustrated, Vanity Fair,* and *The New Yorker* coming onto the scene. Magazines have had considerable impact on modern society. During the 1960s, for example, magazines such as *Cosmopolitan* and

Time magazine

Ms. conveyed new visions of women outside their traditional portrayals as homemakers. Today, many magazines cater primarily to specialized interests. Called *niche publications*, they are designed to attract target audiences and advertisers who want to reach them. In the late 1980s, British-born editor Tina Brown brought back the more general magazine by reviving *Vanity Fair*. With the computer age, magazines called ELECTRONIC MAGAZINES (e-zines) are now available over the Internet.

magazine program television program organized in a "magazine style" with features such as reports or close-up interviews of celebrities. An example of such a program is *Entertainment Tonight* on American television.

magic bullet theory view that the media are powerful shapers of individuals. Like a "magic bullet," media products are said to be a "killing force" to people's minds.

magic realism style in art, literature, or media that presents magical, occult, or mythic themes in a realistic manner

magnetic tape thin plastic strip coated with iron oxide on which sounds, video, or other kinds of data can be recorded

magnification process of enlarging a photograph or other image

mail form Web page designed to be used as an online order page

mail server computer whose only function is to distribute e-mails through the Internet

mainframe computer large central computer to which users are connected by terminals

mainstream media [synonym of **mass media**] dominant, powerful media organizations, such as the major newspapers and television networks

mainstreaming 1. in cultivation theory, the ability of television to move people toward a common view of how things are by the way they represent or depict them; 2. efforts by media outlets to include nonwhite and nonmale personnel among their employees

makeup cosmetics, preparations, and the like applied to the face or body to modify one's looks, and used for particular effects in theater, the movies, and television. Makeup is especially important in establishing character onstage, and is thus used to suggest age, occupation, personality, and so on.

makeup artist member of a film, television, or theater production team who is responsible for makeup and hairstyling

male gaze in FEMINIST THEORY, the idea that men have traditionally exercised psychological power over women by being the lookers, with women functioning as those who were looked at. Although this power relation has been changing radically, its remnants are still found somewhat in media and advertising

male-as-norm in FEMINIST THEORY, idea that language referring to females, such as the suffix *-ess* (as in *actress*), the use of *man* to mean "human," and other such devices, strengthens the perception that the male category is the norm and that the corresponding female category is a derivation and thus less important. Sexist terms such as *chairman, anchorman*, etc., are cited as examples of how the English language mirrors social gender biases.

Maletzke's model of communication often-cited model created by theorist Gerhard Maletzke in 1963 of the contextual and psychosocial factors that influence communication activities and patterns, such as the self-image of the interlocutors and the type of social environment in which the communication takes place

Malvern screen thin, flexible LCD television screen that can be rolled up

managing editor editor of books or newspapers who is responsible for the overall editorial process, including budgeting and scheduling matters

manga [also called **anime**] Japanese comic-book drawing technique distinguished by characters drawn with very large eyes and (sometimes) a layout in which the panels run from right to left

manifest meaning the meaning in a media text that is obvious, as opposed to a latent or subtextual meaning. For example, the manifest meaning of some television sitcoms (such as *Married with Children*, which was popular in the 1980s and 1990s) may be entertainment, but its latent meaning might be a critique of the traditional family.

manufacturing consent [term coined by NOAM CHOMSKY] the camouflaged practice by governments or institutions of gaining the consent of common people by controlling or manipulating what the media show and how they do so

manuscript any document written by an author before it is edited and published. Before the computer age, the term referred to any handwritten document. Now, it refers to any computer-generated document (in a specific kind of file). In antiquity, people living around the Mediterranean Sea wrote manuscripts on papyrus, leather, and wax tablets. During the Middle Ages, manuscripts were written on parchment and on vellum (a refined form of parchment). Since the 1400s, paper has been used to prepare manuscripts. Scholars known as philologists study ancient (and medieval) manuscripts in order to reconstruct the cultures and social systems of the era from which they emanate.

Marconi, Guglielmo (1874–1937) Italian inventor who popularized wireless telegraphy, known shortly thereafter as radio. Marconi shared the 1909 Nobel Prize in Physics with Karl Ferdinand Braun of Germany, who had developed ways of increasing the range of radio transmissions. In 1900 Marconi established the American Marconi Company, which made it easy and practical to send signals across the Atlantic for the first time.

Marcuse, Herbert (1898–1979) FRANKFURT SCHOOL philosopher and a leading figure in the New Left movement that emerged in the 1960s.

Guglielmo Marconi

Marcuse argued that the media help indoctrinate and manipulate common people, promoting a false consciousness that plays into the hands of the system of power that oversees the social order. His most quoted book is *An Essay on Liberation* (1969).

marginality pushing minority groups to the periphery in media coverage

markedness way of classifying words or grammatical categories as being general, or *unmarked*, or specific and thus *marked*. In English, the word *man* is unmarked for gender because it is the general form standing for males and females together: *Man does not live by bread alone.* On the other hand, *woman* is the marked form because it is constrained to signifying females alone. This creates the impression, by extension, that masculinity is the norm, and that femininity is a special case in point.

market area geographical area that represents a particular market of buyers for a specific product

market forces mathematical relationship that exists between the supply and demand for a product or service, which ultimately dictates what it will cost

market liberalism ideology claiming that market forces should be allowed to develop on their own momentum without any outside interferences or impositions (by governments, controlling agencies, interest groups, etc.)

market power influence that results when a large share of sales is controlled by a major company. Market power enables large companies to limit competition and to raise prices above competitive levels. Such companies often put up obstacles called *entry barriers* that are designed to thwart new firms from getting started in an industry. The most extreme form of market power is called a *monopoly*. In a monopoly, a single firm or a group of firms controls the supply of a product or service for which no substitute exists.

market research 1. information-gathering activities carried out in order to improve marketing and advertising strategies for a product;

2. study of the probable users of a product. Many marketing firms use surveys to determine what kinds of people make up a market; others observe what customers actually buy to learn about their habits; others analyze the effect that the public image of a company or its products has on consumers.

market segmentation process of dividing a market strategically, so as to be able to develop advertising materials for the segment or segments that are believed to be favorably responsive to them

market share that part of an audience that can be linked to a particular medium or program

market test any technique evaluating reactions to promotional and advertising campaigns. Marketing agencies determine potential markets for a product or service before it is advertised. A research team then tests draft advertisements in the potential markets. On the basis of this market test, the manufacturer will decide whether an ad campaign is worthwhile.

marketing process of promoting products and services through techniques such as segmentation, testing, etc. Since the early 1990s, businesses have used the Internet to carry out many of their marketing activities. Marketing over the Internet generates more detailed information about customer interests and buying behavior than was ever possible before.

marketing communications skillful deployment of media outlets (radio, television, online communications, print advertising) to promote a product or service

marketing firm business that provides advice on the distribution and sales of goods and services, including recommendations on pricing, packaging, advertising, merchandising, and distribution

marketing intelligence information collected about a market that can be used to shape a marketing or advertising campaign

marketing model model of the marketing process, usually generated by specially designed computer software, that allows marketers to assess how to best utilize advertising resources

marquee 1. sign over the entrance of a theater or other venue that displays the name of the featured event and/or performers; 2. piece of text that scrolls across a screen in a highlighted band

martial arts movie film genre in which the martial arts play a dominant role, especially in the action sequences

Marx, Karl (1818–1883) German social theorist who predicted that capitalism would eventually collapse under pressure from working people. For Marx, the prevailing economic system determines the intellectual and cultural history of a society. He proposed a system, called communism, in which all citizens give according to their means and take according to their needs. His theories have influenced the policies of governments in many countries, as well as numerous academics, even in capitalist nations.

Marxism socioeconomic theory developed by KARL MARX and Friedrich Engels. It constitutes the blueprint behind communism, holding that all people are entitled to enjoy the fruits of their labor, but are prevented from doing so in capitalist systems, which divide society into two classes—nonowning workers and nonworking owners. Marx called the resulting situation "alienation," and he theorized that when the workers repossessed the fruits of their labor, alienation would be overcome and class divisions would cease to exist. The collapse of the Soviet Union and China's adoption of elements of a free-market economy in the 1990s marked the end of Marxism as a practicable theory of society, though it retains interest as a critique of market capitalism and a theory of media effects.

Marxist theories of the media theories that espouse Marxist philosophy in explaining the modern mass media. Essentially, Marxist critics maintain that the media reinforce the values of those in power by representing them as the norm. The best-known Marxist theories of the media come under the rubric of the FRANKFURT SCHOOL.

masala style of Hindi filmmaking that combines various genres (action, romance, comedy, adventure)

mask 1. covering of the eyes, the mouth, or the entire face, sometimes used by fictional heroes (for example, Zorro and the Lone Ranger wore eye masks, while early Hollywood bandits wore a mouth mask to cover their identities); 2. covering of the entire face worn by a Greek or Roman actor in ancient drama to portray a character and magnify the voice; 3. any ritualistic covering over the face. Masks are divided into four types. First, ceremonial masks were used in many tribal societies to influence or appeal to the gods. These masks represented the gods and were worn during ceremonies, suggesting that the gods were present in spirit. Second, theatrical masks, such as those used by the ancient Greeks in their dramas, allowed the audience to follow the play and to grasp the characters portrayed by the actors. The Chinese and Japanese also used masks in this manner. Third, burial and death masks have been used since antiquity in ceremonies relating to death. Typically, in many tribes the masks represent dead persons, and it is thought that their spirits return during the ceremony. In Western countries, death masks are sometimes used to preserve the memory of an important personage. Famous death masks include those of Ludwig van Beethoven and Napoleon. Finally, festival masks are used in such festivals as Carnival and Mardi Gras.

mass a large group, the collective aggregate (one of the most frequently used words in media and communications). Its meaning is most often pejorative. It is claimed that the people living in a mass culture, for instance, tend to lose their individual identity and assume a group or collective identity. As such, they are likely to do things as a group that they would never do alone (for example, engage in riots or illegal activity).

mass communication 1. communication system that reaches massive numbers of people; 2. actual process of designing and delivering media texts to mass audiences

mass communication theory any theory that aims to explain or predict cultural and social phenomena as interrelated with mass communication and mass media systems

mass culture type of culture found in urban societies, where various cultures, subcultures, countercultures, and parallel cultures exist in constant competition with each other. The mass culture dominates the other cultures at the same time that it is composed of them. So, for instance, American pop culture is a mass culture. But within it there are subcultures and parallel cultures (goth culture, Hispanic culture, etc.)

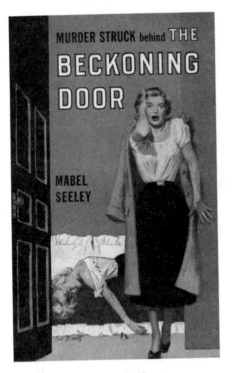

English mass market paperback novel (1952)

popular in Europe and the United States in the 1800s. Many were cheaply made, inexpensive editions of novels.

mass marketing marketing that is directed at large numbers of people

mass media media (radio, television, newspapers, periodicals, Web sites) that reach large audiences. Attached to the meaning of this term, however, is the erroneous view that large agglomerations of people are one-dimensional or homogeneous. As research on media audiences has shown, this is hardly the case. DENIS MCQUAIL's characterization of the mass media, in his 1969 book *Towards a Sociology of Mass Communications*, is used commonly today as a general framework for the study of mass media. He identifies the main features of the mass media as follows:

that nevertheless are part of its social fabric.

mass manipulation model of media communication model claiming that consumers and audiences take in media texts and advertising campaigns passively and that they are being constantly influenced surreptitiously by them

mass market paperback paperback book intended for a mass market, typically found on racks in drugstores, in supermarkets, at airports, and in bookstores. Mass market paperbacks first became

- They usually require complex formal organization.
- They are directed toward large audiences.
- They are public and their content is open to everyone.
- Audiences are heterogeneous.
- The mass media establish simultaneous contact with a large number of people who live at a distance from each other.
- The relationship between media personalities and audience members is mediated (nondirect).
- The audience is part of a mass culture.

mass society in culture theory, a society consisting of very large numbers of people, who (it is believed) are easily manipulated by the mass media and government bureaucracies. One of the most frightening and evocative images of mass society can be found in George Orwell's novel *1984* (1949).

master antenna television [abbreviated as **MATV**] television transmission whereby a single (master) antenna delivers television signals to hotels, apartment buildings, mobile home parks, and other locations where it is impractical for individual viewers to have a separate antenna

master brand [also called **parent brand**] dominant brand in a business, such as Sony audio video equipment, to which SUBBRANDS can be added (Sony movies)

master shot wide camera shot that allows viewers to see all the ongoing action in a scene

materialism 1. philosophical theory claiming that consciousness is a purely physical phenomenon; 2. in culture theory, idea that culture is expressed through material products and that this is ultimately destructive of true culture

matinée theater performance or movie showing that is held in the afternoon, often with cheaper seats than evening performances or showings

MATV [*see* **master antenna television**]

maxim concise statement or saying, perceived as expressing some inherent truth: for example, *Look before you leap*; *Two heads are better than one*

maximal awareness point at which an advertising campaign convinces consumers to buy an advertised product

McCombs and Shaw's agenda-setting model of media effects model created by Maxwell E. McCombs and Donald L. Shaw in 1976, which claims that the way in which the media present events determines how they will be perceived and thus how important they will become in public awareness

McDonaldization [term coined by George Ritzer in *The McDonaldization of Society* (1993) and later expanded upon by the American sociologist Alan Bryman in *The Disneyization of Society* (2004)]. As Bryman states, McDonaldization as the process "by which the principles of the fast-food restaurant are coming to dominate more and more sectors of American society as well as the rest of the world." Bryman compares this process to "Disneyization," which he defines as the correlative process "by which the principles of the Disney theme parks are coming to dominate more and more sectors of American society as well as the rest of the world." The term is now used to characterize the process by which large corporations are taking over more and more sections of society.

McLuhan, Marshall (1911–1980)

Canadian communications theorist whose ideas on technology, culture, and the media have been the source of considerable debates in media studies. McLuhan argued that technological changes in the ways in which we encode information lead to radical changes in society. Thus, each major historical epoch is shaped by the communication medium that it uses most widely. For example, he called the epoch spanning the early 1700s to the mid-1900s the age of print, because print was the chief medium by which people gained and exchanged knowledge. The age of print encouraged the growth of individualism, democracy, and the separation of work and leisure, among many other things. The electronic age replaced the age of print in the early twentieth century. Because it can reach so many people in many parts of the world, electronic media have since "shrunk" the world into a "global village" where everyone (no matter where they live in the world) can become involved in the lives of everyone else, leading to the growth of international virtual communities. McLuhan's fascinating works include *The Mechanical Bride: Folklore of Industrial Man* (1951), *The Gutenberg Galaxy: The Making of Typographic Man* (1962), *Understanding Media: The Extensions of*

Marshall McLuhan

Man (1964), *The Medium Is the Massage: An Inventory of Effects* (1967), and *War and Peace in the Global Village* (1968).

McLurg's Law claim that news about events farther away have less value than news about similar events from the place where they are being reported. For example, the law predicts that news about a single casualty in one's local area will have much higher newsworthiness than news about hundreds or thousands of similar casualties in some remote area of the world (with respect to where one lives). The term refers to the name of a British news editor who claimed that news events diminish in importance relative to their distance from London. Today, it has a more generic meaning.

McNelly's model of news flow model defined by J.T. NcNelly in 1959, showing how the stages through which a news event passes, before it is published or broadcast, influence the way in which it is ultimately perceived

McQuail, Denis (1938–) well-known media analyst who has written extensively on theories of mass media and on USES AND GRATIFICATIONS models. Among his books are *Communication Models for the Study of Mass Communications* (1981) and *Mass Communication Theory* (1983). He proposed several theoretical models, including the accountability of media model (concerning the responsibilities of the media) and the model of audience fragmentation (which results from wider choice among television audiences).

Mead, George Herbert (1863–1931) American philosopher often cited in media studies because of his analysis of how social structures influence individual experiences. He is probably the source of the concept of "construction of the Self," which claims that selfhood is not inherited, but constructed by the individual through contact with others.

Mead, Margaret (1901–1978) American anthropologist, known especially for her studies of adolescence as a construction of modern societies. Mead maintained that the child-rearing practices of a culture influence how someone matures.

Among her best-known works are *Coming of Age in Samoa* (1928), *Growing Up in New Guinea* (1930), *Sex and Temperament in Three Primitive Societies* (1935), *Male and Female* (1949), and *Culture and Commitment* (1970).

mean world syndrome view holding that audiences get the impression from the media that violent crimes occur more frequently than they actually do. From this impression, audiences develop the view that it is a "mean world" out there.

meaning what is understood when something is presented or communicated. The technique of OPPOSITION is often used in media studies to flesh out what something means. This approach assumes that the meaning is something that cannot be determined in the absolute, but only in relation to other forms and meanings; for example, *good* vs. *evil*, *hero* vs. *villain*, etc. In media representations the poles of an opposition take on specific form. Thus, for example, the evil villain in a movie might wear black and the hero a lighter color of clothing, or vice versa (as was the case with Zorro).

meaning theories theories about meaning and how it unfolds. The mainstream view of meaning is that there are two levels, a literal and a figurative level, with the former consisting of the basic meaning of something and the other a derivative form of meaning. The terms *refer-*

ence, *sense*, and *definition* are often used in discussions of meaning. Reference is the process of identifying something; sense is what the identification elicits psychologically, historically, and socially; and definition is a statement about what that identification means by convention. The terms *denotation* and *connotation* are preferred to reference and sense in contemporary theories of meaning. Consider the word *cat*. The word identifies a "creature with four legs, whiskers, retractile claws." This is its denotative meaning, which allows us to determine if something real or imaginary is a "cat." All other senses of the word are connotative; for example, *He let the cat out of the bag*; *My friend is a real cool cat.* Such senses are historically acquired meanings and can only be understood in reference to particular cultural uses of that word.

media [plural of **medium**] 1. any means of transmitting information; 2. the various forms, devices, and systems that make up mass communications considered as a whole, including newspapers, magazines, radio stations, television channels, and Web sites. Before alphabetic writing, the media for communicating information were oral-auditory and pictographic. Writing facilitated the creation and storage of printed texts. Later print technology made such texts available to masses of people. MARSHALL MCLUHAN called the social world in which the use of printed texts became widespread

the GUTENBERG GALAXY, after the German printer Johannes Gutenberg, who is traditionally considered the inventor of movable type in the West.

media analysis analysis of all aspects of the media; for example, how they evolved and how they affect individuals and society

media broker business that offers organizations media-buying, media-planning, and other such services

media buyer individual working for an ad agency who has the responsibility of buying space or time in a media outlet (a slot in a magazine, radio time) for an advertisement or ad campaign

media center 1. department of an organization responsible for releasing information to the media; 2. a computer that, in addition to its usual computing functions, also provides access to digital media such as digital radio and digital television

media circus profuse media coverage that a particular event attracts, distorting the significance of the event in the process

media concentration 1. process of buying space in only one medium for advertising or publicity, rather than in various media, thus developing strength through concentration; 2. domination of media markets by a small number (or even just one) large media corporations

media control any mechanism set up by governments to regulate the media

media convergence [also called **convergence**] process whereby old and new media technologies are available either separately or together through digitization

media councils groups of people from the media and the public who investigate complaints against the media

media dependency theory [*see also* **dependency theory**] claim that people can easily become dependent upon mass media in ways that parallel substance dependency. Supporters of this theory claim that people can easily become habituated to television or online navigation, but might be unaware of their dependency, or may not care that they have become dependent.

media dominance technique of buying a large amount of space or time in one medium for an advertisement or program, and then shifting to another medium after achieving optimum coverage and frequency. The strategy is to "dominate" media space and time as much as possible.

media effects model any model that sees media as influencing individuals and/or societies in a negative way. The best-known models of this type are the MAGIC BULLET THEORY and the HYPODERMIC NEEDLE THEORY.

media event an event that attracts a great deal of attention from the media, often organized or manufactured deliberately to gain such attention

media images impressions and views of people or events generated by the media

media institution organization involved in producing media forms (cinema, television)

media literacy [also called **mediacy**] in-depth knowledge of how the media work and how they might influence audiences—similar to literacy and the ways in which literacy permits people to better understand written texts in all their dimensions (psychological, social, etc.)

media messaging sending text, images, and sound from one mobile phone or device to another

media objectives overall aims that a company has in placing advertisements or ad campaigns in specific media outlets

media organizations organizations providing information to their customers, either directly with their own media communications or else by offering marketers a way of reaching audiences through advertising

media plan plan designed to place strategically an ad campaign in various media outlets so as to reach as many potential customers as possible with the least amount of expenditure

media reception [also called **reception**] act of reading, interpreting, etc., media texts within specific locations and cultural contexts. Reception theory generally claims that interpretation is not homogeneous or passive, but involves background assumptions, audience dynamics, and other factors.

media research studies that investigate the media, including how they influence people, how they shape social processes, how they present news, and how they structure events

media selection process of choosing the appropriate media for an advertising campaign so as to make it as effective as possible

media strategy plan of action by an advertiser for bringing advertising messages to the attention of consumers through the use of appropriate media

media text any media product or creation, such as a television program, a radio show, a newspaper column, or an advertisement. Like any written text (a novel, a poem), a media text has the property of cohesion and predictability that allows interpreters to identify it as such and experience it as a whole.

mediacy [*see* **media literacy**]

mediasphere [term coined in analogy with **biosphere** and **semiosphere**] world in which the media interrelate with social processes, influencing these processes directly, including dialogue, rituals, and the like

mediation view that media literally *mediate* reality, rather than present it in a straightforward manner. For example, the 1950s American TV sitcom called *I Love Lucy* portrayed the female gender through the character of Lucy as a strong-willed, independent female, in charge of her own life. On the other hand, the 1980s–1990s sitcom *Married with Children* depicted the same gender mockingly through the character of Betty as a boorish, sex-starved female who lived out her existence mindlessly day after dreary day. The two programs thus mediated the meaning of "female gender" through differences in character portrayal.

medium [*see* **media**]

medium is the message MARSHALL MCLUHAN's famous maxim referring to his belief that each medium shapes the nature of the message it is designed to deliver. In *Understanding Media* (1964), McLuhan stated: "The medium is the message. This is merely to say that the personal and social consequences of any medium—that is, of any extension of ourselves—result from the new scale that is introduced into our affairs by each extension of ourselves, or by any new technology."

mega-agencies in the advertising business, large ad companies that are formed through the merger of smaller ad agencies

megabyte unit of computer memory equal to one million BYTES

megaplex large movie theater complex, often with the same movie playing on several screens in the complex

Méliès, Georges (1861–1938) one of the first filmmakers who introduced the basic camera techniques of slow motion, dissolve, and fade-out. He was also the first to create film fiction narratives, from 1899 to 1912, producing more than 400 films, which combined pantomime and fantasy, including *Le voyage dans la lune* (1902; *A Trip to the Moon*).

melodrama narrative work (often in serial form) characterized by emotional conflicts among the characters. The melodrama traces its origins to Greek theater, becoming popular in the West only in the eighteenth century. Also known as "tearjerkers," melodramas today include romantic comedies and television soap operas.

meme [term coined by Richard Dawkins (1941–)] any idea, fashion, musical tune, etc., that spreads through society, which inherits it unwittingly in the same way that individuals get their personality automatically through genetic inheritance

memoir biographical genre composed from personal observation and experience. A memoir differs from autobiography chiefly in the degree of interpretation of the events in one's life. Memoirs tend to be more interpretive than factual. A diary is an example of a memoir.

memory stick small flash drive device that can store data for use in electronic devices such as computers, digital cameras, and mobile phones

merchandising creation of brand nonmedia products, such as food and toys, which are designed to take advantage of the success of a media event or product, such as a blockbuster movie

mesmerism [term coined after Franz Mesmer (1734–1815), Austrian physician] power to captivate and enthrall someone. Mesmer thought that he could cure patients by having them put their feet in magnetized water while holding cables. Mesmer believed that people possessed a mysterious quality that allowed them to have a powerful, "magnetic" influence over others. Mesmer created a sensation in his day, but the medical profession saw him as a fraud. The term *mesmerism* is sometimes used in reference to the ways in which media influence people.

message 1. any form of communication (information, feelings, ideas) passed on or transmitted in some way; 2. meaning or lesson built into a text, spectacle, or performance

messageboard Web page or group of Web pages on the Internet that allows visitors to read and respond to messages posted there

messaging sending short instant messages by mobile phone or some instant messaging device

metacommunication 1. abstract principles of communication in all its forms; 2. level of analysis designed to examine the nature of communication

metadata information contained on a Web page (publication date, author, keywords, title) that can be used by search engines to find relevant Web sites through hyperlinks

metafiction fiction that explores the nature of fiction itself, especially its traditional forms, genres, and styles

metal music [synonym for **heavy metal**] type of rock music characterized by highly amplified electric guitars, a hard beat, a thumping bass, and often dark lyrics. It came onto the scene in the late 1960s and 1970s with bands such as Steppenwolf, Led Zeppelin, Black Sabbath, Kiss, AC/DC, and Aerosmith. In the 1980s, metal was revived by bands such as Def Leppard, Iron Maiden, Mötley Crüe, Black Sabbath, and Van Halen.

metalanguage theory or statement about language, concerning the nature of language itself or of some aspect of language; grammatical statements and categories (nouns, verbs, etc.) are part of the grammarian's metalanguage

metalingual function in ROMAN JAKOBSON's communication model, any language about language: for example, *A verb is a word expressing some action*; *Is green a descriptive or demonstrative adjective?*

metamessage the "real" message implicit (or hidden) in a communication, often delivered through the tone of voice or something similar, that might be different from the apparent content of the message

metanarrative [often used as a synonym for **metafiction**] narrative that examines or explores the narrative form itself, or else includes other narratives within it

metaphor word or phrase used to designate something by association or implication. In *the professor is a snake*, the word *snake* is used metaphorically to imply, not the reptile known as a snake, but the qualities of "danger," "slipperiness," etc., that it represents. These qualities are then projected onto the professor by association. Metaphor was first identified by ARISTOTLE, who saw it as a way for people to understand abstract concepts (such as human personality). However, Aristotle later claimed that the primary function of metaphor was figurative or symbolic, rather than cognitive. Today, Aristotle's original conception of metaphor as a cognitive strategy is the definition accepted by most linguists.

metatext theory or statement about texts, whose purpose it is to examine the nature, function, and overall structure of texts themselves

metatheory theory or statement about theories, whose purpose it is to examine the nature, form, and function of theories themselves

methodology system of procedures used in any field, such as media analysis, for conducting research, or for gathering data

metonymy figure of speech standing for something of which it is a part: for example, *the press* for *journalists* and *newspapers*; *wheels* for *automobile*. In the world of shopping and commerce, certain brands become metonyms: for example, the Scotch brand of adhesive tape is used commonly to name all brands of adhesive tape; the Kleenex brand of facial tissue is commonly used to refer to all brands of facial tissue; and so on. Generally, this happens when a brand name is either the first to reach the marketplace or else is a dominant brand within it.

Metro-Goldwyn-Meyer [abbreviated as **MGM**] major Hollywood studio founded in 1924, which became a leading film production enterprise in the 1930s and 1940s and thus a symbol of Hollywood's golden age. Web site: www.mgm.com

Metz, Christian (1931–1993) French cinema analyst who argued essentially that a movie can be studied in the ways that a linguist studies language, hence introducing the concept of "film language" into the field. His best-known work is *Essais sur la signification au cinema* (1968; *Film Language: A Semiotics of the Cinema*, 1974).

microcassette small audiotape cassette that fits into a pocket-sized tape recorder or dictation machine

microcomputer [also called **personal computer**] small computer that uses a MICROPROCESSOR to process information

microfiche tiny sheet of MICROFILM, on which images are arranged in a grid pattern. A single microfiche may contain images of up to 400 regular paper pages.

microfilm photographic film on which reduced images are recorded. Microfilm can store large amounts of information in a small space. People read microfilm with a reader that enlarges the images and projects them onto a built-in screen.

micropayment small charge to Internet users for downloading something, usually on Web sites that have no sponsors

microphone device that changes sound into electrical current, which instantly travels over wires or through the air to a loudspeaker or some other device that changes it back into sound. The first microphone was the telephone transmitter, invented by ALEXANDER GRAHAM BELL in 1876. Today, microphones are used in public-address systems and in radio and television broadcasting. They are also used in recording the sound for motion pictures, in making compact discs, and in webcasting.

microphotography process of making MICROFILM

microprocessor device that does the actual work in a computer. A microprocessor consists of transistors and other parts built into a chip (usually made of silicon).

Microsoft large software corporation, based in Washington State, founded in 1975 by Bill Gates and Paul G. Allen, by simply adapting BASIC for use on personal computers. Microsoft became a publicly owned corporation in 1986, after having issued the first version of Microsoft Word, a popular word-processing program, in 1983, and Microsoft Windows, a GRAPHICAL USER INTERFACE, in 1985.

Mill's principle of utility often-cited principle enunciated by nineteenth-century British philosopher and economist John Stuart Mill, who claimed that there exists a universal tendency in human beings to assess everything, including pleasure and gratification, in terms of their utility value

Milton's paradox often-cited paradox, which states that theory and practice may not correspond, as exemplified by seventeenth-century English poet John Milton's own work as a censor during Oliver Cromwell's reign, despite the fact that he paradoxically supported freedom of the press

mime 1. play (usually comical in nature) in which people are impersonated and events mimicked (originating in Greek and Roman comedy); 2. acronym for **multipurpose Internet mail extension**, a system used to handle attachments in e-mails and newsgroup postings

mimesis imitation or simulation of sensible reality in art and literature

mimetic theory of art theory elaborated by ARISTOTLE, which claims that art is basically an imitation of the real world

mimicry art of imitating other people's voices, gestures, and appearance, often for comical effect

minimal effects model any model claiming that the media have limited effects on audiences, reinforcing existing attitudes, values, and worldview rather than influencing or changing them

minimalism arts movement originating in the 1960s, in which only the simplest forms are used, often over and over again. The musical works of American composer Philip Glass are examples of minimalist style, emphasizing simple classic melodic and harmonic forms that are repeated over and over in a specific piece: for example, *Einstein on the Beach* (1976), *Satyagraha* (1980), *Akhnaten* (1984), *The Voyage* (1992), and *La Belle et la Bête* (1994). The term also applies to the field of art. For example, American painter Ellsworth Kelly typically uses a single color and very linear drawing techniques to emphasize simplicity and its beauty.

miniseries serialized television drama, usually broadcast on consecutive nights or weeks. One of the most popular miniseries in the history of American television was *Roots*, an eight-part 1970s drama tracing the history of an African American family from slavery to freedom in early America.

Miramax major Hollywood studio founded by brothers Bob and Harvey Weinstein in 1979, producing such highly touted and popular films as *Pulp Fiction* (1994), *The Talented Mr. Ripley* (1999), and *Sin City* (2005). Web site: www.miramax.com

mirror site copy of a Web site maintained on a different file server in order to spread the distribution load or to provide data backup

misappropriation invasion of privacy by appropriating someone's name or image for commercial purposes, without the person's permission

mise-en-abyme technique consisting of bottomless reduplication, as when an image contains a smaller version of itself, which in turn contains an even smaller version within itself, and so on ad infinitum

mise-en-scène 1. actual positioning of scenery, actors, etc., on a stage or movie set for a particular scene or sequence; 2. overall look of a filmed scene

misinformed society view that society is not better informed, despite globally accessible systems of information, because these often disseminate false or inaccurate information

misprint error in the printed or published version of a text

mixdown process of putting together various audio feeds that have been recorded previously to create a finished recording

mixed media 1. use of different artistic media to create a single composition or work; 2. in advertising, use of different media (print, radio, television, Internet) in tandem for an ad campaign

mixing putting together different excerpts of audio, such as vocal commentary and music, to create a final piece for broadcasting

MMS [*see* **multimedia messaging service**]

mobile phone portable phone that operates by means of a series of locally based cellular radio networks

mobilization ability of the media to stir up people to take action

moblogging use of a mobile phone, or other handheld device, to post text in a WEBLOG

mode of address way that a media text "speaks" to its audience and, in so doing, helps to shape how it will be interpreted

modem [abbreviation of **modulator-demodulator**] device that enables computers to transmit and receive information over a telephone network. Modems can send and receive not only text information, but also sound, video, and other types of data.

modernism 1. early twentieth-century architectural style, also known as the Bauhaus School, emphasizing simplicity and conformity in design (as used in the building of early skyscrapers); 2. artistic trends that ran roughly from the 1920s to the 1970s and that generally emphasized formal elements rather than the naturalistic depiction of subjects

modernity type of society in which individuals are deemed to be fundamentally rational and therefore capable of determining their own

forms of social organization, without guidance from religious or political leaders. Societies that are modern, therefore, also tend to value freedom of speech and of association, democratic forms of government, knowledge, and diversity.

modulation system designed to increase the frequency of signals. The two main types of modulation are called amplitude modulation (AM) and frequency modulation (FM).

mogul an important or powerful owner of media

monochrome painting, drawing, or print in a single color or shades of a single color

monologue 1. dramatic speech made by a single speaker, such as a stage actor; 2. jokes or funny stories delivered by a comedian on stage

monopoly exclusive control of a commodity or service

monster movie movie in which the main character is a monster or in which monsters play a primary role. Many early monster movies were based on the "Frankenstein myth." *Frankenstein* was originally a horror novel written by the English author Mary Shelley in 1818, which tells the story of Victor Frankenstein, a scientist who tries to create a living being for the good of humanity but instead produces a monster.

montage 1. composite visual image made by bringing together different pictures or parts of pictures and superimposing them on each other, so that they form a blended whole while remaining distinct; 2. in cinema, rapid succession of scenes or images to create some effect (such as a dream sequence or a flashback)

moral panic 1. media-induced fear that an aspect of modern culture is leading people—especially children and youth—astray, into deviance, delinquency, or criminality; 2. sudden increase in public anxiety over a media product or event that is perceived as encouraging violence, sexism, or racism. The term was introduced by Stanley Cohen in his book *Folk Devils and Moral Panics* (1972).

mores traditional rules and customs of a group of people or a society about what is acceptable social behavior

Morley, David (1949–) well-known analyst of media audiences and critic of cultural imperialism. His best-known work is *Home Territories: Media, Mobility and Identity* (2000).

morpheme minimal form in language that has meaning. The word *impossible*, for instance, contains two morphemes: the prefix *im-*, which conveys the meaning "opposite of," and *possible*, also called the lexical morpheme (or morpheme with lexical meaning).

morphing in filmic language, changing something or someone into something or someone else in one continuous movement, achieved mainly by computer software. One of the first uses of morphing can be seen in the shape-changing Terminator character in *Terminator 2* (1991).

Morse code system for representing letters, numerals, and punctuation marks by a sequence of dots, dashes, and spaces transmitted as electrical pulses. The original system was invented by Samuel F.B. Morse in 1838 for his telegraph. The International Morse Code, a simpler version, was devised in 1851. The Morse code has been rendered obsolete by modern technologies.

motion picture [synonym for **movie** or **FILM**] a series of still photographs on film, projected in rapid succession onto a screen, giving the impression of continuous motion. The principal inventors of motion picture machines were THOMAS ALVA EDISON in the United States and the LUMIÈRE BROTHERS in France. Motion picture production was centered in France in the first two decades of the twentieth century. By 1920, movie studios expanded in the United States, reaching their pinnacle in the 1930s and 1940s, making the United States the center of filmmaking worldwide. The 1950s and 1960s brought a new internationalism to filmmaking. The same period also saw the rise of the independent filmmaker (the INDIE). Today, movies remain highly popular as forms of art and entertainment, and the American film industry (based in Hollywood), with its immense resources, continues to dominate the world film market.

Motion Picture Association of America [abbreviated as **MPAA**] American trade association founded in 1922, responsible for protecting the interests of the major Hollywood studios. It is also responsible for the movie rating system in use in the United States. Web site: www.mpaa.org

Motion Picture Experts Group Audio Layer 3 [abbreviated as **MP3**] format for compressing music (and other) files into very small computer files, while losing virtually no quality in the process. For example, sound data from a compact disc can be compressed to one-twelfth the original size without sacrificing sound quality. The MP3 format is very popular for transmitting music files over the Internet.

motivated shot camera shot that follows a particular action or sequence of actions that is prompted by an event in the action or sequence

motivational research investigation of the psychological reasons why individuals buy specific types of merchandise, why they respond to certain advertising appeals, why they watch particular kinds of television programs, or why they listen to certain radio stations

Motown [contraction of **Motor Town**, in reference to Detroit's automotive industry] recording company founded in Detroit in 1957 by songwriter Berry Gordy, Jr., becoming known nationwide shortly thereafter with the two hits *Shop Around* (1960) by the Miracles and *Please Mr. Postman* (1961) by the Marvelettes. The "Motown sound," which featured lyrical ballads sung to a catchy rhythmic accompaniment, was made famous by the Temptations, the Four Tops, the Supremes, Marvin Gaye, the Isley Brothers, Gladys Knight and the Pips, the Jackson 5, and Stevie Wonder. Gordy moved the company headquarters to Los Angeles in 1971, eventually selling the label to MCA in 1988. Motown is considered to be one of the most successful black-owned businesses and one of the most influential independent record companies in American pop music history.

mouse hand-controlled device for interacting with a digital computer that has a graphical user interface. It is called *mouse* because its shape is similar to that of the common rodent with the same name. The mouse can be moved to control the movement of a cursor on the computer screen. It can also be used to select text, activate programs, or move items around the screen.

mouseover feature on a Web page, such as a pop-up menu, that is activated when a user moves the cursor over a contact point on the page. This feature is designed to get the user to select it.

movie ratings system of classifying movies indicating for whom the movie is suitable, according to age

G	(General Audience): "All Ages Admitted"
PG	(Parental Guidance Suggested): "Some Material May Not Be Suitable for Children"
PG-13	(Parents Strongly Cautioned): "Some Material May Be Inappropriate for Children Under 13"
R	(Restricted): "Under 17 Requires Accompanying Parent or Adult Guardian"
NC-17:	"No One 17 and Under Admitted"

movie trailers brief films showing a few scenes from an upcoming movie or television program in order to advertise it

movies [*see* **motion picture**]

MP3 [*see* **Motion Picture Experts Group Audio Layer 3**]

MTV [abbreviation of **music television**] 24-hour cable music video channel that debuted in 1981 with *Video Killed the Radio Star*, by the Buggles. MTV quickly won a wide following among pop music fans worldwide, greatly influencing the pop music business. The network later expanded to include original programming such as the animated *Beavis and Butthead* show and the reality series *Real World*, separate international networks (MTV Europe, MTV Latin America, and MTV Russia), and the MTV Video Music Awards.

muckraking journalism that aims to uncover crime, corruption, or scandal

MUD [*see* **Multi User Dungeon**]

multi-actuality existence of many meanings, some of which may even be contradictory, attached to a given sign or symbol

multiculturalism 1. sociopolitical philosophy that promotes cultural diversity, supported by many educators in the United States who favor the teaching of different cultures for the purpose of understanding and appreciating them; 2. society that integrates other cultural systems within itself

multimedia computer system that allows the user to manipulate and use different types of media, such as text, sound, video, graphics, and animation. The most common multimedia system consists of a personal computer with a sound card, modem, digital speaker unit, CD-ROM, and portals for various devices. Commercial interactive multimedia systems include: cable television services with computer interfaces that allow viewers to interact with TV programs, high-speed interactive audiovisual systems, such as video game consoles, and virtual reality systems that create artificial sensory environments.

multimedia messaging service [abbreviated as **MMS**] system that allows for the transmission of audio, images, and animation in text messages

multimodality 1. use of several channels to access the same information; for example, accessing cinema listings through the press, by phone, and on the Internet; 2. the mixing of media forms; for example, the mixing of sound, image and graphics on television news programs or on Web sites

multiplex large cinema complex with many screens

multiplexing method of transmitting multiple signals simultaneously over a single wire or channel, in order to squeeze as much capacity into a network as possible

multistep flow theory theory asserting that media impacts are indirect and are mediated by group leaders. The theory maintains that people within different social classes have very different interpretations of media products, thus forming interpretive communities, which coincide with real communities such as families, unions, neighborhoods, and churches.

multitrack device or system capable of using different tracks in sound recording or reproduction

Multi User Dungeon [abbreviated as **MUD**] text-based game that can be played by multiple users across the Internet

Murdoch effect [after RUPERT MURDOCH] idea that journalism is becoming more and more obsessed with corporate gain

Murdoch, Rupert (1931–) Australian-born publisher who owns many media outlets in Australia, the United Kingdom, the United States, and other countries. His ownership of print businesses ranges from *The Times of London* to the *New York Post*. Murdoch is known especially for making financially struggling media operations profitable.

Murray, Janet (1946–) media analyst, whose book *Hamlet on the Holodeck: The Future of Narrative in Cyberspace* (1998), has become a reference point for discussing the metamorphosis of traditional genres as they are increasingly transferred to cyberspace

Murrow, Edward R. (1908–1965) prominent American broadcaster who foreshadowed EMBEDDED JOURNALISM when he broadcast eyewitness reports of World War II events such as the German occupation of Austria. In the 1950s he was an influential force for the free dissemination of information, producing a notable exposé of the tactics of Senator Joseph McCarthy that contributed to the demise of McCarthyism, the fanatical move-

ment investigating various government departments and questioning
witnesses about their suspected
communist affiliations. In 1954
Murrow used footage of McCarthy's
own press conferences on his CBS
See It Now documentary program to
expose the excesses of McCarthy's
anticommunist campaign. The Senate
subsequently reprimanded McCarthy.

music hall popular form of entertainment emerging in the late nineteenth
century that featured acts by singers,
comedians, dancers, and actors. Considered to cater primarily to vulgar
tastes, music halls evolved in the
early twentieth century into larger,
more respectable *variety theaters*,
which combined music, comedy acts,
and one-act plays.

music television [*see* **MTV**]

music video short film showcasing a particular song or artist. It is
claimed by many pop music analysts
that some artists, such as Madonna,
Michael Jackson, and the Euryth-
mics, owe much of their success to
the popularity of their videos.

musical theatrical production that
revolves around the music composed for it. Its roots can be traced to
eighteenth- and nineteenth-century
genres such as *opéra comique*. The
Black Crook (1866), considered to
be the first musical comedy, attracted
lovers of both opera and burlesque
shows. In the 1920s and 1930s composers such as Jerome Kern, George

Gershwin, Cole Porter, Richard
Rodgers, and Oscar Hammerstein
turned the musical into a form with
broad appeal. The genre flourished in
the 1950s with works by composers
such as Leonard Bernstein. In the late
1960s, musicals began diversifying,
incorporating elements from rock
music and other styles. Perhaps the
most famous of all contemporary
composers of the genre is Andrew
Lloyd Webber, whose musicals *Cats*
(1981), *The Phantom of the Opera*
(1986), and *Evita* (1996) continue to
be popular.

must-carry rules regulations established by the FCC (Federal Communications Commission) requiring
all cable operators to carry local
broadcasts on their systems, thereby
ensuring that local media outlets and
public television channels can benefit
from cable technology

MySpace online social networking
site founded in 2003 where personal
profiles can be posted. MySpace
is one of various Web sites where
people can post PROFILES and BLOGS,
leave messages, or connect with
friends. It also features an internal
search engine and e-mail system. It
is headquartered in Santa Monica,
California, but its parent company is
headquartered in New York City. As
of 2006, MySpace posted over 100
million profiles, with several hundred
thousand new members every day.
MySpace prohibits the posting of any
potentially dangerous information,
such as phone numbers and ad-

dresses. MySpace (and other online networking sites) now allows for the posting of other kinds of items, including profiles for companies and various artists (e.g., musicians, filmmakers), who upload songs, short films, and other work directly onto their profiles. Web site: www .MySpace.com

mystery ingredient technique advertising technique whereby a mystery ingredient in a drink, detergent, or other product is claimed to be the source behind the product's appeal or quality

myth 1. ancient story about gods, heroes, and supernatural events; 2. by extension, any story that aims to explain something in nonliteral or nonscientific ways

mythologie [French for **mythology**] as defined by ROLAND BARTHES, any modern-day spectacle or text that has mythic structure built into it. For example, superhero comics or movies are examples of *mythologies*, since they recast the mythic hero concept in modern form. For instance, Superman comes from another world, has a fatal weakness, brings about justice in human affairs, and so on, as did many ancient mythic heroes. The difference is that Superman's persona and story have been updated to reflect the modern imagination—Superman comes from another planet, the ancient hero from the heavens; Superman's weakness (or tragic flaw) is exposure to kryptonite (a substance from his original planet), while the ancient hero may have a weak heel (Achilles) or other flaw. The Superman story is not a real myth, serving the important cognitive functions that myths served in the ancient world; it is a recasting of myth to serve modern psychic needs.

mythology 1. group of MYTHS connected to each other in some way; 2. the study of myths. There are four main types of myths found throughout the world: *cosmogonic* myths aim to explain how the world came into being; *eschatological* myths foretell the end of the world; *birth and rebirth* myths indicate how life can be renewed or tell about the coming of an ideal world or savior; and *culture hero* myths tell about heroes who have changed the course of history.

mythos [in contrast to **lógos**] the form of thinking that generates MYTHS and many symbols to help explain the world. For example, the ancient Greeks symbolized the sun as the god Helios driving a flaming chariot across the sky. The Egyptians, on the other hand, represented the sun as a boat.

naming identifying a person (in relation to a kinship group or a particular society), a brand product, or some other thing to which people wish to refer in human terms by analogy (hurricanes, pets). In Anglo-American culture, given (or first) names can stand for such things as a month or object (*May, June, Ruby, Daisy*), pop culture icons (*Elvis, Marilyn*), or classical mythic personages (*Diana, Jason*), among many others. Traditionally, the names of ancestors or religious personages (*Mary, John*) are used everywhere in the world. Until the late Middle Ages, the given name was generally sufficient. Duplications, however, led to the coinage of *surnames* (literally, "names on top of names"), indicating such things as the individual's place of origin or parentage, personality, occupation, or some other recognizable trait. For example, a person living near a brook would have been called by that name *Brook*. Surnames such as *Woods, Moore, Church,* or *Hill* were also coined in this way. Surnames such as *Black, Short, Long,* etc., were coined instead to highlight traits perceived in individuals. Descendant surnames—for example, those created with *Mac-* or *Mc-* in Scottish or Irish surnames (*MacAdam*, "son or daughter of Adam") or *-son* in English surnames (*Johnson*, "son of John") were used to specify the family to which someone belonged. Surnames describing an occupation—*Smith, Farmer, Carpenter, Tailor, Weaver,* etc.—

were applied to the person who actually practiced the occupation, who may have belonged to a family with which the occupation was associated, or who was perceived as looking or behaving like someone practicing the occupation. Naming trends are remarkably stable in most societies because names link people to families and cultural traditions. However, in some modern cultures, fashion trends sometimes influence name-giving. Nevertheless, according to the U.S. Social Security Administration, one-fourth of the top twenty names given in 2004 were the same as those given in 1880.

nanotechnology technology permitting the manipulation of atoms and molecules to form larger structures. In the computer world, nanotechnology refers to any technology that allows for compression of data so that it can be stored and used by increasingly smaller devices.

Napster trade name for software that allows users to share files over the Internet. Napster is the first to have had legal challenges to its operations, with resulting legal measures being taken. Its name now is associated more with its legal battles than with its original technology.

narcotizing dysfunction according to one theory, the overloading of audiences with mediated information, which results in apathy

narrative any account (story, myth, tale, fable, etc.) that connects a sequence of events involving characters in certain situations that are usually resolved by the end. The narrative may be fact-based, as in a TV documentary, or fictional, as in a novel or movie. Narratives are constructed (normally) with four basic elements: the *plot*, which is what the narrative is all about; *characters*, the participants in the plot; the *setting*, which is where the plot takes place and the time frame within which it occurs; and the *narrator*, who is the teller of the story (a character of the narrative, the author, or some other person). Fictional narratives became popular worldwide after the Italian Giovanni Boccaccio wrote the *Decameron* (1351–1353), a collection of 100 fictional tales set against the background of the Black Death in Florence. The *Decameron* is the first true work of fiction in the modern sense of the word—the telling of stories simply for the sake of the telling.

narrative code recurring element within a narrative (prototypical characters such as heroes and villains, themes such as the journey into an unknown territory, and so on). The serious study of narrative codes was initiated by the Russian literary scholar VLADIMIR PROPP, who also argued persuasively in 1928 that ordinary discourse was built upon this very kind of code.

narrative paradigm theory that defines humans in terms of their tendency to tell stories and to understand the world in terms of narrative structures and forms

narratology formal study of NARRATIVES and NARRATIVE CODES

narrowcasting broadcasting directed at a limited target audience. In broadcasting theory, most audiences are divisible into segments defined by specific demographic and lifestyle characteristics. The contemporary specialty radio stations and TV channels, for example, are aimed at audiences with specific kinds of interests tied to age, gender, class, and other kinds of social variables.

National Broadcasting Company [abbreviated as **NBC**] major American commercial broadcasting company founded in 1926 by RCA Corporation, General Electric Company, and Westinghouse as the first company to operate a broadcast network. Directed by RCA's president David Sarnoff, it became wholly owned by RCA in 1930. In the 1990s NBC expanded its cable television programming, creating MSNBC (an alliance with Microsoft) and CNBC (an alliance with Dow Jones). Web site: www.nbc.com

national media media outlets and/or products that receive nationwide distribution and attention

national newspaper newspaper that achieves national popularity and is available in every part of a country.

The most well-known national newspaper in the United States is *The New York Times*, established in 1851.

National Public Radio [abbreviated as **NPR**] public (noncommercial) radio network established in 1967 in the United States by Congress to provide an alternative public radio system. Public radio stations are financed in much the same way as public television stations, through public and private donations and government support. NPR offers a wider variety of news, documentary, educational, and information programming than commercial radio stations. Web site: www.npr.org

naturalism 1. method of filmmaking whereby characters and locations are shot as they actually are, as opposed to creating artificial ones; 2. more generally, any form of representation that attempts to reproduce real-world features as accurately as possible

naturalistic illusion of television the impression that people receive from certain kinds of television programs that what they are watching is a representation of real life when, in fact, it is not

navigation activity of going from Web site to Web site on the Internet, either to search for something specific or else simply to find out what is on the Internet

NBC [*see* **National Broadcasting Company**]

NC-17 rating censorship classification in the United States indicating that a film cannot be seen by anyone under the age of 17 because of its adult-directed content (such as sexuality, excessive violence, foul language, nudity)

needle time agreed-upon maximum amount of time that a radio station can spend playing recorded music

needs theory in advertising, the theory that advertising should be based on linking a product to basic human needs and how it helps to fulfill them in some way. The most commonly identified needs are:

Achievement: the need to achieve meaningful objectives in life or to fulfill personal dreams

Popularity: the need to win the attention of others or to be accepted by peer groups

Dominance: the need to exert influence in relations or to get the upper hand in them

Diversion: the need to enjoy oneself and to attain pleasure in life

Understanding: the need to learn and instruct

Nurturing: the need to care for others and to be cared for by others

Sexuality: the need to express sexual feelings and urges

Security: the need to be free from harm and threat

Independence: the need to be self-reliant

Recognition: the need to be recognized or acclaimed in some way

Stimulation: the need to be excited or aroused

Novelty: the need to have new things

Affiliation: the need to win acceptance

Support: the need to receive emotional support

Consistency: the need to achieve order through consistency in lifestyle

negative in older photographic technology, type of film copy in which the tones are the opposite of those in the original

negotiated reading interpretation of a text that is a compromise reached between the maker's preferred reading of it and the reader's own reading

Negroponte, Nicholas (1943–) influential author on digital media and, especially, on how CONVERGENCE unfolds in cyberspace. His book *Being Digital* (1995) has been widely cited in the media and communications literature.

neologism 1. newly coined word or phrase that has not been generally accepted yet, such as *digiform* (a blend of *digital* and *form*); 2. use of a word with a new meaning, such

as the use of *so* as an emphatic form in expressions such as *That's so yesterday*

neomania [term coined by ROLAND BARTHES] the maniacal craving for new things, whether they are needed or not, prompted by consumerism and supportive media spectacles and advertising

neo-Marxist theory any media theory that espouses basic Marxist ideas, but coming after the mainstream form of Marxist criticism known as the FRANKFURT SCHOOL

neorealism Italian literary and cinematic movement that flourished after World War II, focusing on social realities as they are in actual everyday existence. Neorealist writers included Italo Calvino, Alberto Moravia, and Cesare Pavese. Neorealism in film embraced a documentary-like objectivity in style. The actors were often amateurs, and the action revolved around everyday situations. Two notable examples of neorealist films are Roberto Rossellini's *Open City* (1945) and Vittorio De Sica's *The Bicycle Thief* (1948).

Net [*see* **Internet**]

net audience total number of people reached by an advertising campaign. An individual is counted once in this method, regardless of whether she or he has seen the campaign more than once.

Net imperative the idea that it is crucial for organizations to use the Internet if they are to gain success in today's digital universe

netiquette informal set of rules regarding use of the Internet, including the type of language that is appropriate

netlingo [also called **netspeak**] forms of language used in chat rooms, text messages, social networking sites, and the like. Netlingo is marked by efficiency of structure, which manifests itself in such phenomena as abbreviations, acronyms, and the use of numbers, all of which are designed to make the delivery of linguistic messages rapid and highly economical. Some of these are listed below.

b4	=	before
bf/gf	=	boyfriend/girlfriend
f2f	=	face-to-face
gr8	=	great
h2cus	=	hope to see you soon
idk	=	I don't know
j4f	=	just for fun
lol	=	laughing out loud
cm	=	call me
2dA	=	today
wan2	=	want to
ruok	=	Are you OK?
2moro	=	tomorrow
g2g	=	gotta go

netphone phone that makes connections via the Internet

netspeak [*see* **netlingo**]

netsurfing [*see* **navigation**]

network 1. chain of radio or television stations linked technologically; 2. company that produces programming for such stations; 3. in computer science, system of computers interconnected to each other

network era period of television programming, from the early 1950s to the 1990s, when the big three networks (CBS, NBC, and ABC) were the dominant broadcasters, with little or no competition from other sources. The era went into decline with the advent of cable technology and Internet-based or Internet-connected broadcasting

Network News Transfer Protocol [abbreviated as **NNTP**] protocol for transferring newsgroup data across the Internet

network programming scheduling television programs over an entire network, in order to take into account time and regional differences

network society increasing tendency of society to use global computer networks for the purposes of communication, work, shopping, and most of the other things that previously were done in person in the so-called offline world

networking 1. building up an informal group of people to contact as a way to learn about job opportunities, especially by means of Internet communications; 2. inexpensive way of sending information quickly among computers connected together in a single room or building

new economy information-based (digital) economic systems, in contrast to the traditional industrial economic systems

new journalism type of journalism similar to GONZO JOURNALISM, in which the emotional content of a story is emphasized over its information value

new wave 1. group of individualistic French filmmakers who called for films to give more leeway to the director's own personal vision; 2. type of punk rock style popular in the mid- and late 1970s, which began partly as a backlash against the perceived superficial disco style; 3. style of science-fiction writing, which emerged in the 1960s, characterized by a pessimistic view of the world and revolving around antiheroes, rather than superheroes

newbie an inexperienced user of the Internet

Newcomb's ABX model of communication early (1953), but still often-cited, tripartite communication model consisting of the sender (A), the receiver (B), and the social situation in which the communication takes place (X)

news report of a current happening or happenings in a newspaper, on television, on radio, or on a Web

site. The early years of television offered little news coverage. In 1956 the NBC network introduced *The Huntley-Brinkley Report*, a half-hour national telecast presented in the early evening and featuring filmed reports of the day's events. The other networks soon followed with similar news programming formats. In media studies, news is now seen as a media genre, with as much entertainment value as any other genre.

news agency [also called **news service** or **wire service**] organization that compiles, writes, and distributes news to media outlets. The largest news agencies are United Press International, Associated Press, Reuters, and Agence France-Presse.

news anchor radio or television announcer who leads a news broadcast, usually by commenting and introducing reports from correspondents in several different cities, countries, or other areas

news blackout withholding of a particular news broadcast, for some specific social, political, or other kind of reason

news flash short news report that interrupts scheduled programming because it is deemed to be worthy of instant broadcasting to the viewing or listening audience

news magazine 1. print magazine published regularly, containing commentary on the news, investigative reporting features, and the like; 2. by extension, any radio, television, or online program formatted like a print news magazine. News magazines have gained wide popularity because they summarize and analyze the biggest news stories of the moment.

news peg aspect of a story that makes it newsworthy, important, or interesting

news server computer system that collects and distributes newsgroup postings

news service [*see* **news agency**]

news television channel that broadcasts only news and documentaries. The most widely known of these is CNN (The Cable News Network) founded by Ted Turner in 1980 to present 24-hour live news broadcasts, using satellites to transmit reports from news bureaus around the world.

news values criteria applied by journalists to evaluating which news stories are worthy of printing or broadcasting, and in which order of importance they should appear

newsbreak short news bulletin inserted in a radio or television program because it is deemed to be worthy of immediate attention

newscast broadcast of the news. Newscasting began on radio in the mid-1930s and increased significantly during World War II. The televi-

sion newscast began in 1948 with 15-minute programs that resembled movie newsreels.

newsgroup a news discussion group on the Internet. Newsgroups are organized into "interest categories" (for example, automobiles). A person starts a discussion by posting (uploading) an article and the follow-up replies form the discussion. Most newsgroups are connected via Usenet, a worldwide network that uses the NETWORK NEWS TRANSFER PROTOCOL.

newspaper print publication issued daily, weekly, or at regular times that provides news, features, information of interest to the public, and advertising. In 1690 Benjamin Harris of Boston founded *Publick Occurrences Both Forreign and Domestick*, the first newspaper in the American Colonies. The colonial government ordered it stopped after just one issue. In 1704 John Campbell put out *The Boston News-Letter*, the first regularly published newspaper in America. Newspapers developed rapidly in the 1800s, owing to wider literacy rates and advances in print technology. Newspaper publishing expanded greatly in the twentieth century. Today, newspapers undergo consolidation driven by media conglomerates or through the acquisition of smaller papers by larger ones. In 1980 *The Columbus Dispatch* became the first electronic newspaper in the United States. In addition to printing a regular paper edition, the

Dispatch started transmitting some of its content to computers in homes, businesses, and libraries. Today, most papers offer online versions.

newspeak imaginary form of speech in George Orwell's novel *1984* (1949) employed by people living in a bleak totalitarian society. In newspeak, words are twisted to mean the opposite of their real meaning so that they can be used ideologically by society's rulers. Language is simplified to impede original thinking and to make revolutionary thoughts impossible to express.

newsreader software that allows users to participate in newsgroups

newsreel news report shown on film in a movie theater, often before the main feature, popular from the 1920s to the 1950s

newsweekly newspaper or magazine that is published weekly. The most famous of these is *Time*, founded in 1923 by Henry R. Luce and Briton Hadden.

newsworthy stories that are believed to be interesting enough to be reported in the media

N-Gen [abbreviation of **Net Generation**] people who have grown up with the Internet from an early age

niche audience small target audience that is predisposed toward some particular type of broadcasting or product

niche marketing marketing to small, but potentially lucrative, specialized markets

nickelodeon type of movie theater popular around 1905, which opened mostly in commercial areas and in poorer neighborhoods. Because admission was only 5 cents, the nickelodeons attracted large audiences for movies, laying the foundations for the expansion of the fledgling movie industry.

Nielsen ratings national ratings of the popularity of television shows, developed by AC Nielsen in 1950. The method now samples television viewing in homes, by attaching a meter to television sets, which records the channels being watched and sends the data to a computer center for statistical analysis. Television networks use the ratings to set advertising rates for each program as well as to determine which programs to produce and which ones to cancel. Web site: www.nielsenmedia.com/ratings101.htm

nihilism philosophy rejecting any belief system claiming that life has a purpose. The term was first used to describe Christian heretics during the Middle Ages. It reemerged in Russia in the 1850s and 1860s in reference to young intellectuals who repudiated Christianity, considered Russian society backward, or advocated revolutionary change. The best-known fictional nihilist is Bazarov in Ivan Turgenev's 1862 novel *Ottsy i deti* (*Fathers and Sons*).

Nipkow, Paul (1860–1940) German inventor who, as early as 1884, had developed a scanning device that sent pictures over short distances. His system worked mechanically, rather than electronically, but is still considered to be a forerunner of television.

NNTP [*see* **Network News Transfer Protocol**]

noise in communication theory, anything that interferes with the transmission or reception of signals. In electronic transmissions, noise is static. By extension, in human communication, noise refers to any physical noise (sneezing, chatter, etc.) or to lapses of memory (psychological noise).

nominalism view of some medieval philosophers that reality is constructed by humans through their words and thus cannot exist apart from them. Nominalism was a reaction to realism, according to which reality has an independent existence prior to and apart from human knowledge of it. The most widely cited nominalist is the fourteenth-century English Scholastic philosopher William of Ockham, from whose name we derive the concept of *Ockham's* (or *Occam's*) *razor*, which asserts that the simplest of two or more theories is to be preferred and that it should explain what is unknown in terms of what is known.

nonverbal communication communication by means of facial expressions, gestures, postures, and other wordless signals. The term also includes indirect or implicit communication through grooming habits, hair and clothing styles, and such practices as tattooing and body piercing. Nonverbal communication plays an essential role in social interaction. The scientific study of nonverbal communication is called KINESICS, which was established as a separate field of inquiry and research by the twentieth-century American anthropologist Ray L. Birdwhistell, who recorded and analyzed body movements, facial expressions, gestures, and the like during social interaction. Birdwhistell claimed that it is possible to write a "kinesic grammar" in the same way that linguists wrote a verbal grammar by analyzing words and sentences. The main areas of nonverbal communication study are:

- eye contact (looking patterns)
- facial expressions
- posture, body orientation, sitting patterns
- gesture
- interpersonal zones (zones people maintain between each other)
- sensory signals
- hair and hairstyle
- clothing
- food
- spaces and buildings
- architecture and cities

Northcliffe revolution shift in the economic basis of newspaper publishing in the late nineteenth century when newspapers became dependent upon advertising revenues

nostalgia yearning for anything removed in space or time

nostalgia technique advertising technique that uses images from previous times when, purportedly, life was more serene, less dangerous, and idyllic

novel fictional prose narrative, longer than a NOVELLA. Literary critic Edmund Gosse traced the novel as far back as Aristides's sixth-century B.C.E. story about Miletus, called the *Milesiaka*. Unlike modern fiction, the story had many historically accurate elements, and thus often reads as history rather than as fiction. In eleventh century Japan, the Baroness Murasaki Shikibu wrote what many regard as the first fictional novel, *The Tale of Genji*. The modern concept of fiction starts with the FABLIAU in the medieval period, culminating in the fourteenth century with Giovanni Boccaccio's *Decameron* (1348–1353). Miguel de Cervantes's *Don Quixote de la Mancha* (Part I, 1605; Part II, 1615) is considered to be the first novel of true artistic merit, setting the stage for the novel as an important literary genre. Novels became dominant in the eighteenth and nineteenth centuries. They continue to be extremely popular, although they have been competing for dominance with movies throughout the twentieth and early twenty-first centuries. Many novels have formed the basis of movie scripts; today some movies are produced first and the novels written afterward. The movie is, essentially, a "visual novel," with the camera taking over the role of the narrator.

novella brief prose story, considered to be the precursor of the short story and the NOVEL. The first and still most widely read compilation of novellas is Giovanni Boccaccio's *Decameron* (1348–1353), consisting of 100 stories, told by a group of friends who had escaped the plague in Florence in order to entertain each another over a period of ten days.

NPR [*see* **National Public Radio**]

nudity the exposure of parts of the body that are considered unacceptable to expose in a public spectacle, performance, and the like. The criteria for such exposure will vary widely from place to place, and from age to age. The ancient Greek and Roman nude statues, Michelangelo's sculpture *David* (1501–1504), and Rodin's *The Thinker* (c. 1886) are considered works of art, rather than erotic or obscene representations; on the other hand, nude poses such as those found in contemporary magazines are interpreted in vastly different ways. In sum, nudity has meaning; it is perceived to have cultural (moral, aesthetic, etc.) value, rather than just biological meaning.

nursery rhyme poem written in catchy rhyme for children. An example is *London bridge is falling down*, derived probably from an old dance tune. Collections of nursery rhymes in print started appearing in the eighteenth century.

O&O's [full form: **owned and operated by networks**] television stations that are owned and operated by networks

object 1. in grammar, a noun or noun phrase that directly or indirectly receives the action of a verb, or follows a preposition; 2. in philosophy, anything that is knowable, as opposed to subject (any knower); 3. in semiotics, whatever a sign stands for

object language meanings and symbolic values attached to objects

objective journalism journalism that aims to present the news without opinion or bias

objective theory of art theory arguing that art is a projection of reality as seen by the artist. This contrasts with MIMETIC THEORY OF ART, which sees art as a mirror of reality.

obscenity any act, writing, depiction, or representation that is deemed to be deeply offensive or to violate community standards of morality and decency. The Supreme Court of the United States has ruled that materials are obscene if they appeal predominantly to a prurient interest in sexual conduct, depict or describe sexual conduct in a patently offensive way, and lack serious literary, artistic, political, or scientific value. Material deemed obscene under this definition is not protected by the free speech guarantee of the FIRST AMENDMENT.

obsolescence view that things should be constantly replaced by new things

OCR [*see* **optical character recognition**]

off the record comments made spontaneously and not intended to be published or broadcast

off-air events or dialogue taking place in a broadcasting studio but not put on the air

off-camera actions that are taking place out of the range of a movie or television camera

offline 1. a computer that is not connected to the Internet; 2. by extension, anything that exists outside of cyberspace (traditional media are now called *offline media*, in contrast to those media that are *online*)

offline newsreader software that allows users to read newsgroup articles without being online at the same time

off-network syndication process whereby older television programs that no longer run on prime time are made available to local stations, cable operators, online services, or foreign markets for reruns

Ogden, C.K. (1889–1957) British psychologist who is often cited in media studies for his works on meaning, especially the book he coauthored with I.A. Richards, titled *The Meaning of Meaning* (1923).

oligopoly situation whereby a media industry is monopolized by a small number of producers

omnibus radio or television program that combines all the episodes of a serial or soap opera that have already been broadcast

omnimax system of film projection that surrounds the audience in a semicircle, thus engaging a viewer's entire field of vision

on-camera actions taking place within the range of a movie or television camera

on demand any cable or satellite service that allows the customer to select the start time of a particular program (rather than viewing or listening to it at regularly scheduled times)

on the record any comment made that may be published or broadcast freely

online a computer that is connected to the Internet. Online services provide e-mail and access to the World Wide Web.

online advertising advertising that is created for viewing on Web sites

online auction consumer online service at which sellers present items for examination by Web users who bid against one another for the right to purchase them. The largest and most popular online auction site is eBay.

online database [also called **online resources**] database stored on a computer at a different location. Users gain access to these databases using a modem or other device that enables them to communicate with each other over a network. Databases can usually be downloaded.

online medium any medium (print, radio, television) that is delivered online instead of through more traditional transmission systems

online service provider [abbreviated as **OSP**] any provider of access to the Internet, such as America Online (AOL) and CompuServe

onomatopoeia use or creation of words imitating the sounds to which they refer: for example, *buzz*, *swoosh*, *drip*, *bang*

op art art style characterized by geometric shapes and luminous colors, often to create optical illusions

op ed article expressing a personal view, published opposite an editorial, that is, on the facing page to that on which the editorial appears

open source creed policy of making technology, information, or data freely available without charging any fees

open text [term coined by UMBERTO ECO] any text that is interpreted as having a limitless range of meanings. The open text requires the reader to have a certain erudition, whereas

Opera singer

cal styles of the late Renaissance. Jacopo Peri composed Camerata's first opera, *Dafne*, in 1597.

operating system software program designed to control the hardware of a computer so that users can employ it easily

opinion leader someone who influences the values, beliefs, and opinions of others in TWO-STEP FLOW THEORY, emphasizing the fact that a few people dictate lifestyle, fashion, and opinion, while most others are generally content to imitate and follow them

opinion piece article in which a journalist expresses an opinion on a topic, rather than simply reporting the facts

CLOSED TEXT does not. For instance, Samuel Beckett's *Waiting for Godot* (1952), which is an open text, requires readers who can make up their own minds as to what it means; on the other hand, a typical detective or crime scene story does not.

open-source software noncommercial software developed and shared freely on the Internet

opera theatrical play with all or most of its text, known as the *libretto*, set to music and choreographed in some way. Opera was created in Italy in the late sixteenth and early seventeenth centuries by a group of musicians who called themselves the *Camerata* (Italian for "salon"). The Camerata had two chief goals: to revive the ancient Greek melodrama and to develop an alternative to the rigid musi-

opinion poll survey designed to identify the attitudes, beliefs, opinions, or views of people. The target group may include millions of individuals. However, only a small number of them are actually polled (called a sample) because, if they have been properly chosen, their opinions are considered to usually reflect those of the entire group.

opposition feature of forms (words, texts, etc.) that keeps them differentiated and distinct. The two words *sip* and *zip* show a sound opposition that is sufficient to differentiate them for a speaker of English. The theory of opposition has been extended to include cultural ideas such as *good* vs. *evil*, *male* vs. *female*, etc., which are purported to reveal an unconscious mode of keeping things distinct and meaningful. Such oppositions are characteristically binary and hierarchical, involving a pair of concepts in which one member of the pair is assumed to be primary or fundamental, the other secondary or derivative. In DECONSTRUCTION, the idea is to displace the opposition by showing that neither concept is primary.

oppositional reading interpretation of a text that is in opposition to what the maker of the text had intended, which is known as the PREFERRED READING

optical character recognition [abbreviated as **OCR**] device that can recognize text characters and save them as a text document

optimization in advertising parlance, computer package that automatically devises a media schedule for an ad campaign

oral culture culture in which information and traditions are passed on from one generation to the next by storytellers. The forms of oral culture include poetry, folktales, and proverbs as well as magical spells, religious incantations, and stories of the past. The prevalence of radio, television, and newspapers in Western culture has led to the decline of oral traditions, though some survive, especially during childhood, when rhymes, stories, and songs are recounted orally.

orality use of the spoken word as the primary means to transmit information, in contrast to LITERACY

organizational communication system of communications set up among organizations (banks, government agencies, and the like) that is not (generally) open to the public

orientalism in cultural theory, the misrepresentation of non-Western cultures and peoples by the media. The term originated in the widely acclaimed book *Orientalism* (1978) by Palestinian-born American literary critic Edward Said, in which he examined Western stereotypes of the Islamic world, arguing that orientalist scholarship itself was based on Western ideological thinking.

Orkut online social networking site run by Google and founded in 2004 that allows people to communicate and form interest groups. Web site: www.orkut.com

orthography 1. any system of spelling; 2. the art and study of spelling

Oscar common name for an ACADEMY OF MOTION PICTURE ARTS AND SCIENCES award recognizing excellence in acting, directing, screenwriting, and other activities related to film production. The term is derived from the name given to the golden statuette that is handed out at the awards.

OSP [*see* **online service provider**]

The Oscar statue, 80th Annual Academy Awards, Hollywood, February 24, 2008

otherness [synonym of **alterity**] view emphasizing diversity in representational practices. This concept became widely known after MICHEL FOUCAULT's accusation in the 1980s that the "Other"—any person or group of different race, ethnicity, or sexual orientation—had been traditionally excluded from Western society's representational activities.

output hardware computer hardware that transfers information to the user, such as video displays and printers

outtake scene or sequence that is removed from the final edit of a movie or radio or television program

oxymoron figure of speech that combines contradictory ideas: for example, *deafening silence, pleasing pain*, etc.

P2P [*see* **peer-to-peer networking**]

package 1. audio text ready for broadcasting; 2. series of interview clips put together by an announcer or reporter

package unit system system of Hollywood film production, initiated in the 1950s, in which each movie is treated as a separate project with different actors and production team; it replaced the older studio system, allowing independent filmmakers easier access to the industry

packaging 1. creating a polished image for a media product through advertising; 2. designing the package, box, wrapping, or container of a product in order to enhance its look and appeal

Packard, Vance social critic, whose books *The Hidden Persuaders* (1957) and *The Waste Makers* (1960) brought to light the persuasive techniques used by advertisers to increase the use of products

packet unit of data sent over the Internet

Packet Internet Groper [abbreviated as **PING**] message that tests the connection between computers

Page, Larry (1973–) American cofounder of GOOGLE, along with Russian-born American SERGEY BRIN

page impression measure indicating how many times a Web page has been displayed to a visitor of a Web site

page reader device that converts written text to a form that a computer can process

page requests [also called **page views**] measure of the number of times a Web page has been visited daily, thus providing an indication of its popularity

pager small, portable electronic device that can receive and send messages through various wireless networks

pagination sequence of numbers given to pages in a document (such as a book)

painting 1. picture drawn or made using paint (or some other substance) on a two-dimensional surface; 2. art of creating pictures or drawings. Painting dates back to prehistoric images found on the walls of caves, such as those at Lascaux in France. Early societies controlled the subject matter of painting and determined its function (ritualistic, devotional, decorative). Painters were considered artisans rather than artists; eventually, in East Asia and Renaissance Europe, the "painter-as-artist" emerged as a distinct individual. In the early twentieth century painters began to experiment with

Petroglyphs on a rock in Canyonlands National Park, Utah (circa 1150 C.E.)

art in which formal qualities such as line, color, and form were explored rather than subject matter. In the late part of the century some critics forecast the "death of painting" in the face of new media such as video and computer art, yet artists continue to paint and fill the galleries with new works. Many of these use words and images, combining them in surprising ways, forcing the viewer to search for possible meanings and connections among the painting's visual elements.

palindrome a word, phrase, sentence, or numeral that reads the same in either direction (front to back, back to front): for example, *pop*; *race car*; *Madam I'm Adam*

PalmPilot a PERSONAL DIGITAL ASSISTANT (PDA) manufactured originally by Palm Computing in 1996. The first two generations of PDAs from Palm were called PalmPilots. The term quickly entered the vernacular as a general word for PDAs, regardless of the brand.

Palme d'Or highest honor awarded at the Cannes Film Festival, for best film of the year

pamphlet folded booklet that is often produced to promote a social cause or political issue. Pamphlets were widely used in sixteenth-century England, France, and Germany for religious or political causes. Foremost among the American writers of political pamphlets was Thomas Paine, whose 55-page pamphlet *Common Sense* (1776) became widely known for advocating independence. With more than 500,000 copies sold, the pamphlet is considered to be a factor in strengthening the early American colonists' resolve to gain autonomy from England. By the twentieth century, pamphlets came to be used more for information than for polemical reasons, retaining this function to the present day.

pan and scan technique for projecting widescreen movies on standard television screens

panel 1. brief text separated from the body of the main text by lines above and below, usually highlighting some aspect of the main text; 2. poster for advertising purposes; 3. group of individuals selected to perform a service, such as an investigation, or to discuss a topic

panopticism idea proposed by MICHEL FOUCAULT that surveillance methods are used by those in power to maintain control. The term comes from Jeremy Bentham's eighteenth-century design of prisons in which a large number of prisoners are kept under surveillance by a small number of guards located in a central viewing tower. Panopticism often refers to the modern-day use of video surveillance as an attempt to control human interaction.

panorama shot in film or television, a camera shot that provides a wide view of a scene or action sequence

pantomime 1. in ancient Rome, an actor who used gestures and body language rather than words; 2. any play or skit based on gestures and body language (without speech). Pantomime began in ancient theater, but was developed as part of spoken theater by the COMMEDIA DELL'ARTE, an improvised comedy style that was popular in sixteenth- and seventeenth-century Italy. Actors in silent motion pictures necessarily relied on pantomime.

paparazzi freelance photographers who pursue celebrities aggressively and persistently in order to take candid photos of them. The term comes from Federico Fellini's movie *La dolce vita* (1960), which includes a group of roving reporters who stalk famous people, seeking to get a sensational story about them. Fellini called one of the journalists *Paparazzo*.

Paper Tiger TV alternative media organization founded in 1981 and based in New York, devoted to promoting free access and distribution for independent producers. Web site: www.papertiger.org

paperback book with a soft flexible cover. Paperback books became popular in Europe and the United States during the 1800s, after the German publisher Tauchnitz began to issue paperback editions of classic literary works in 1841. By 1885, one-third of the books published in the United States were paperback, called

DIME NOVELS because they originally cost 10 cents.

papyrus paper-like material made from a pith of reeds, formed into a continuous strip and rolled around a stick, associated primarily with ancient Egyptian writing. Given the greater availability and affordability of papyrus, compared to the previous use of tablets, literacy came to be valued highly among common people.

parable 1. in ancient Greece, a literary illustration; 2. in the New Testament, a story used by Jesus to illustrate a spiritual truth

paradigm 1. set of assumptions, principles, or practices that are characteristic of a science or philosophical system; 2. in SEMIOTICS, feature or pattern that keeps signs distinct and differentiated. In pairs such as *cat-rat* and *sip-zip*, the first consonant is the paradigmatic feature that keeps the words distinct and differentiated.

paradox 1. statement or event that appears to be contradictory, but that somehow may actually be true; 2. any circular statement *(Which came first, the chicken or the egg?)*. Paradoxes constitute their own genre, having become famous for how they have provided insights into the nature of logic and mathematics. The most famous paradoxes are those of the fifth century B.C.E. Greek philosopher Zeno of Elea, who is the likely inventor of the paradox as a distinct form of language and logic. In Zeno's

time, deductive logic was seen as the ideal form of logic for gaining truth about the world. Zeno challenged this with a series of clever arguments, which came to be known as *paradoxes* (meaning literally, "conflicting with expectation"). In one of his paradoxes, Zeno argued cleverly that a runner would never be able to reach a race's finish line if deductive logic were used. He argued as follows. The runner must first reach *half* the distance to the finish line. Then (and logically) from the mid-position, the runner would face a new, but similar, task—he must cover *half of the remaining distance* between himself and the finish line. But after doing so, the runner would face a new, but again similar, task—he must once more cover half of the new remaining distance between himself and the finish line. Although the successive half-distances between himself and the finish line would become increasingly (indeed infinitesimally) small, Zeno concluded that the runner would come very close to the finish line, but would never cross it. Clearly, by experience we know that the runner will cross the finish line; but by logical argument, we have just shown that he can never do so— hence the term *paradox*.

paralanguage any aspect of language, such as tone of voice, that is used along with words

parallel broadcast broadcast that is transmitted by radio and/or television and/or the Internet at the same time

parallelism any statement made up of parts that parallel or mirror each other semantically: for example, *I am the president, the country's leader am I*

Paramount major Hollywood film studio founded in 1914. In 1966 Paramount was acquired by Gulf & Western, and the new company later changed its name to Paramount Communications. In 1994 it was acquired by Viacom, which in 2000 merged with CBS. Web site: www .paramount.com

paraphrase any rewording or summary of something, usually to explain it: for example, *going on a wild goose chase* can be paraphrased as *pursuing something foolish*

parasocial interaction 1. imaginary relationship that often develops between a viewer and an on-screen character; 2. social relationship at a distance. encouraged by the media

parchment ancient durable writing material made from the skins of sheep, goats, or calves. Parchment scrolls have survived from as far back as 1500 B.C.E.

parent brand [also called **master brand**] main brand in a brand family; for example, the Coca-Cola soft drink is the parent brand of all the other brands of soft drinks manufactured by the Coca-Cola Company

parody work making fun of someone or something (especially a famous

work) in an indirect fashion. Typically, a parody distorts the theme and characters of a work or style. Geoffrey Chaucer's "The Nun's Priest's Tale" (from *The Canterbury Tales*), for example, is a parody of the solemn language and style of ancient myth, since the clamor caused by Master Reynard the fox is suggestive of the fall of Troy. Sitcoms such as *Family Guy* and *The Simpsons* are examples of parodies of American society.

parole [*see also* **langue**] as defined by FERDINAND DE SAUSSURE, speech, or the use of language for purposes such as communication

participant observation in anthropology, research method whereby the researcher becomes a trusted member of the culture that she or he is studying, in order to observe the culture firsthand and thus to gain an inside perspective

partisan press press associated with a political party or ideology, generally showing a bias or allegiance to that party or ideology

passivity theory view that a typical audience accepts media representations passively and unreflectively

pastiche 1. media product that is created in imitation of another similar one; 2. text that is constructed with cluttered or mixed forms, associated primarily with POSTMODERNISM, which stresses collective or shared expression through a blend of borrowed styles

patent governmental grant to an inventor of the exclusive right to make, use, or sell an invention or media product. The first recorded patent for an industrial invention was granted in 1421 in Florence to the artist Filippo Brunelleschi. Generally, in the United States a patent term of twenty years is given from the date an application is filed.

pathetic fallacy the attribution of human feelings to inanimate things: for example, *the angry skies, a stubborn computer*, etc.

pathos a quality in a literary or artistic work or a media text that evokes sympathy or pity

patriarchy social system in which familial, social, economic, religious, and political authority is wielded by men. In FEMINIST THEORIES of media, the term is often used to refer to the ways in which some societies are structured to favor male domination over women. In this usage, patriarchy implies that the men control the material and symbolic resources of a society and that these are often used to oppress women. Explanations for the emergence of this form of oppression vary from evolutionary theories, in which males are said to be the more "aggressive" and thus "dominant" of the two sexes because of evolutionary processes that have conditioned males to be this way, to cultural theories, in which males are said to be conditioned by the culture in which they are reared.

pattern advertising campaign that is designed to have a broad appeal

pay services [*see* **pay-per-view**]

pay-for-play interactive game Web site that charges a fee for usage

pay-per-view service provided by cable and satellite operators that allows viewers to select and purchase movies or special programming on a per-feature basis

Payne Fund Studies series of studies of controversial media effects, conducted between 1929 and 1933, published subsequently in eight volumes, that purported to show a link between movies and such social aberrations as crime and violence

payola characterization of the bribes that were given to popular radio DJs, especially during the 1950s, who were in a position to influence public tastes, by record companies or artists. The term is used today more generally to refer to any type of bribery designed to promote artists and works in some medium.

PBS [*see* **public broadcasting service**]

PC [*see* **personal computer**]

PDA [*see* **personal digital assistant**]

peer-to-peer networking [abbreviated as **P2P**] system that interconnects users of the Internet to each other. The P2P architecture allows individual users to share files among themselves without recourse to a central server.

Peirce, Charles Sanders (1839–1914) American philosopher who, along with FERDINAND DE SAUSSURE, is considered a founder of modern-day SEMIOTICS. Peirce characterized semiotics as the "doctrine" of signs, meaning a "system of principles." Contrary to Saussure, Peirce saw the relation between signs and sign users not as an arbitrary one, but rather as an interpretive one; essentially, every time a sign (such as a word) is used, it is subject to variant interpretations according to context and other external factors. Peirce is also known as a founder of philosophical pragmatism, which maintains that the value of a theory lies mainly in its applications.

penetrated market market in which more of a company's products are sold, compared to all potential markets

penetration strategy in advertising, a plan for promoting a company's products in a particular part of the potential market

pen name [also called **pseudonym**] fictitious name used by an author instead of his or her real name. During the 1800s, some women writers adopted masculine pen names because of sexual discrimination. The British novelist Mary Ann Evans, for example, concealed her femininity with the pen name George Eliot. Two famous pen names are Lewis Carroll, adopted by the English writer and mathematician Charles Dodgson; and Mark Twain, adopted by the American author Samuel Clemens.

People meter device invented by the AC NIELSEN Media Research Company that is installed in a remote control unit to electronically record the selection of television channels. The device is thus used to determine television viewing behavior.

perception discernment of objects or qualities of objects by means of the senses. According to classic psychological theory, most percepts (= units of perception) result from the association of sensory cues with past experience.

performance 1. formal exhibition or presentation before an audience of a play, a musical program, and the like; 2. representation and communication of a text, put on display for an audience; 3. in linguistics, the actual use of language in concrete situations

performative in discourse theory and pragmatic linguistics a word or phrase that indicates the performance of something, or at least the will to do something. When someone says "I am cutting grass," that person is performing what the utterance says he is doing. The term comes from John Austin's 1962 book, *How to Do Things with Words.*

performing rights permission to perform a piece of music to which the performer does not hold copyright

periodical publication that is issued at regular intervals, including newspapers, magazines, journals, and the like

persona 1. character in a work, especially in theater parlance; 2. in psychoanalysis, the role one plays in social contexts, as separate from the inner self. In ancient Greece, the word *persona* signified a "mask" worn by an actor on stage. Subsequently, it came to have the meaning of "the character of the mask-wearer." This meaning can still be found in the theater term *dramatis personae*, or "cast of characters." Eventually, the word came to be refashioned as *person* in English, with its present meaning, perhaps indicating the historical importance of the theater as a medium of portraying human character.

personal computer [abbreviated as **PC**] microcomputer so named because it is smaller than a mainframe computer. Early mainframes and their peripheral devices often took up the floor space of a house, making them impractical for personal use. The PC, which was developed in the early 1970s, fits on an individual user's desk.

Typical PDA

personal digital assistant [abbreviated as **PDA**] handheld or pocket-sized computer, offering a wide range of features, including calculation, time-keeping, computer games, access to the Internet, e-mail service, radio, video, etc.

personification portrayal or characterization of inanimate objects, animals, or ideas as if they were people or possessed human characteristics: for example, *My computer is sick today*

perspective technique of representing images (of people, objects) as they would appear to visual perception in reality. Although there is evidence that the ancient Greeks already knew how to create an illusion of depth or length in two-dimensional surface drawings, the Italian Renais-

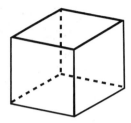

Cube

sance artist Filippo Brunelleschi rediscovered and then entrenched this technique in painting. For example, the figure above is perceived as a three-dimensional box, rather than a two-dimensional drawing, because of the principles of perspective, which trick the eye into seeing depth.

persuasion techniques in advertising, techniques designed to persuade consumers to buy or endorse a product. These include the following:

- Repetition is the technique whereby the content of radio and television commercials is reiterated in the print media (newspapers, magazines, posters, displays) in order to capture the attention of a large segment of potential customers.
- The something-for-nothing lure is designed to grab the attention of potential consumers: *Buy one and get a second one free*; *Send for free sample*; *Trial offer at half price*; *Finish this sentence and win $1,000,000 in cash, an automobile, or a trip to Florida for two*; *No money down*; etc.
- Humorously contrived ads and commercials convey friendliness and thus help to portray a product as agreeable.

- Endorsements of products by celebrities make them appear reliable.
- Appeals to parents induce parents to believe that giving their children certain products will secure for them a better life and future.
- Implicit appeals that are designed to convince parents that they should get their children some product.
- Scare copy techniques are designed to promote such goods and services as insurance, fire alarms, cosmetics, and vitamin capsules by evoking the fear of poverty, sickness, loss of social standing, and/or impending disaster.

PG rating [full form: **parental guidance**] film classification indicating that a movie may be seen by anyone, but that parents should exercise discretion regarding its suitability for their children

PG-13 rating [full form: **parental guidance–under thirteen**] film classification indicating that a movie may be seen by anyone, but that parents should exercise discretion regarding its suitability for their own children if they are under the age of 13

phallocentrism in FEMINIST THEORY, the idea that the male perspective is the dominant one in a patriarchal society, such as traditional Western society, and thus is expressed in representations and media

phatic function as defined by RO-MAN JAKOBSON, the social purpose of certain forms of discourse, formulaic forms of speech that are used for social contact rather than for the communication of ideas: for example, *Hey, how are you? What's up?*

phenomenology twentieth-century movement in philosophy and the arts emphasizing the role of sensory stimulation and the emotions. The founder was the German philosopher Edmund Husserl. German philosopher MARTIN HEIDEGGER claimed that phenomenology was particularly useful for explaining the structure of everyday experience.

phish in NETLINGO, to trick someone into providing personal details by sending an e-mail that presents itself fraudulently as emanating from a bank or Internet provider

phone-in radio or television program that receives phone calls from audience members, who are encouraged to ask the host or guest questions, make comments, or take part in a discussion

phoneme sound unit in language that signals differences in meaning. For example, the /p/ can replace other consonants, such as /w/ and /b/, to make English words—*pin* vs. *win* vs. *bin.* It is thus a phoneme in that language, because it has the ability to signal differences in the meaning of these words.

phonetics study and classification of speech sounds. Modern phonetics began with Alexander Melville Bell, whose book *Visible Speech* (1867) in-

troduced a system of precise notation for writing down speech sounds.

phonograph [also called **record player**] device for reproducing sounds. A phonograph record produces sound when a stylus is placed on its rotating surface. Its invention is generally credited to THOMAS ALVA EDISON. Before radio and motion pictures, the phonograph reigned for several decades as the great modern innovation in pop culture and entertainment.

phonology study of the sounds in a language and how they are used in the formation of words and other structures

photo opportunity occasion when celebrities, politicians, or other public figures pose for photographers, usually to get exposure or for some form of publicity

photocopy copy of a document or image, printed directly on paper by the action of light in a machine built for this purpose

photodigital memory computer memory system that employs a laser to transfer data to a piece of film, which can be read again many times

photograph image recorded by a camera and reproduced on a photosensitive surface

photographic truth former belief that photographs do not lie. With the advent of digital technology this belief is no longer held, given that images can now be easily and readily manipulated.

photography art, craft, or science of taking and developing PHOTO-GRAPHS. Photography originated in the early nineteenth century when the combined discoveries of Frenchmen Joseph Nicéphore Niépce and Louis Jacques Mandé Daguerre led to the invention of the first commercially successful photographic process, called the daguerreotype (1839). In the 1860s the Englishman Henry Peach Robinson pioneered a method of creating one print from several different negatives. At the turn of the twenty-first century, photographers started using digital technology, expanding the uses of photography considerably and to a large extent replacing previous photographic technologies.

photojournalism news reporting in which photography plays a more important role than the accompanying text

photomontage art of combining different photographic images to compose a single image

picaresque novel novel revolving around the episodic adventures of a rogue or adventurer who is portrayed as drifting from place to place in order to survive. The genre originated in Spain with Mateo Alemán's *Guzmán de Alfarache* (1599) being an early

example. The growth and popularity of the realistic novel led to its decline.

pictography use of pictures or visual symbols for writing purposes. Pictographs are drawn to stand for an object or idea directly. The "smiley" (☺), for example, is a modern-day pictograph. A pictograph that stands for an idea rather than something concrete is called an IDEOGRAM (such as the Nike "swoosh" logo, representing speed).

pictorial newspaper or magazine that has many visual images, often more than it has written text

picture library photography store, device, or Web site from which photographs may be borrowed or reproduced for use in books, magazines, or other print materials

picture messaging sending images and photographs from one mobile phone to another

pilot radio or television program made as an experiment or trial so as to glean the audience's reaction to it as the first episode in a potential new series

pilot study preliminary study intended to identify the suitability of conducting a full study

PING [*see* **Packet Internet Groper**]

piracy unauthorized duplication, distribution, or broadcasting of copyrighted material for profit

pirate radio radio station that broadcasts illegally without a license, often attracting large numbers of listeners

plain-folks pitch advertising strategy whereby a product is associated with common people using it for practical purposes

planned obsolescence claim by some social critics that certain manufacturers design their products to last a short time so that customers will be forced to buy them over and over

planted news propaganda disguised as news

plasma screen flat display screen for computers and television sets, which gives clearer images than other forms of screen technology

Plato (c. 428–347 B.C.E.) ancient Greek philosopher who coined the term *philosophy* ("love of knowledge"). His Doctrine of Forms, by which he proposed that objects resemble the perfect forms with which all humans are born, is the basis (or stimulus) of several modern-day ideas, including that of the ARCHETYPE. His writings include the *Republic*, the *Apology* (which portrays Socrates' self-defense of the charges against him), *Phaedo* (which portrays the death of Socrates and in which he discusses the Doctrine of Forms), and the *Symposium*.

play story acted out on a stage (or some other place or through another medium); a dramatization

play theory of mass communication idea that the mass media do not produce harmful effects because people use them, by and large, for entertainment, rather than for information

playlist list of musical recordings that are scheduled to be aired by a radio station

pleasure principle [*see also* **id**] desire for the fulfillment of natural urges, such as sexual ones, regardless of social or moral sanctions. Its operation is unconscious in adults, playing an especially important role in modes of expression that have a nonrational motivation, such as the making of art.

plot 1. events that take place in a narrative; 2. main action in a story

plug-in tiny add-on program to a browser that allows a user to play animations, videos, or sound files

pluralism 1. notion that all cultural and value systems are equal and should be allowed to coexist in the same social situation or system; 2. view that the media should reflect social diversity

POD [abbreviation of **Print on Demand**]

podcasting activity of providing immediate audio and/or video files over the Internet to subscribers, for playback on mobile devices and/or personal computers

Sunday Afternoon on the Island of La Grande Jatte (1886) by Georges Seurat

poem piece of writing, usually in verse form, that is more songlike, using more emotionally suggestive language than ordinary speech or prose. The oldest surviving Greek poems, and still the most referenced ones in all kinds of texts, are the great epics the *Iliad* and the *Odyssey*, which are attributed to Homer and were probably written during the eighth century B.C.E. They were composed from excerpts of Greek oral poetry, such as folktales and songs. After Homer's time, people recited the two works, often from memory, before audiences at festivals.

point of presence [abbreviated as POP] phone number that a computer dials via the modem

pointillism painting style in which color "points" are used to cover a ground (background and/or foreground), appearing to blend together when viewed from a distance, producing a glowing effect. The works of Georges Seurat and his followers in late nineteenth-century France best exemplify this style.

political advertising advertising used for political purposes, such as political campaigning

political correctness language or conduct that deliberately avoids giving offense, especially regarding sensitive topics such as gender, religion, and race

Andy Warhol's silkscreen painting
Orange Marilyn (1964)

polysemy 1. multiple meanings that some words have; for example, the word *play* means "drama" and "to take part in a game"; 2. by extension, the different ways in which media texts are interpreted by different audiences

POP [*see* **point of presence**]

pop art [full form: **popular art**], art movement surfacing in the late 1940s that emphasized the representation and/or incorporation of the objects of mass culture. The movement was initially a reaction against abstract expressionism, with brand products, comic strips, and the like forming the subject matter of the artists in the movement. Perhaps the best-known pop artist was Andy Warhol, who produced paintings and silk-screen prints of commonplace objects and celebrities.

pop culture [full form: **popular culture**] culture that can be defined as the "culture of the marketplace," and thus produced by the people, rather than commissioned and sponsored by an aristocrat, institution, or the like (as in the past). Pop culture is thus subject to the same economic laws connected to the making and consumption of material goods. Pop culture includes television programs, advertising, comic books, popular music (rock 'n' roll, hip-hop), fashion, sports, shopping, etc. It rejects both the supremacy of the "high culture" of the past and the pretensions of avant-garde intellectual trends of the present. It is highly appealing for this very reason. It bestows on common people the assurance that "culture" is mass consumption, not just for an elite class of cognoscenti. It is thus populist, popular, and public. The spread of pop culture as a kind of mainstream culture has been brought about by developments in technology. The rise of music as a mass art, for instance, was made possible by the advent of recording and radio broadcasting technologies at the start of the twentieth century. Records and radio made music available to large audiences, converting it from an art for the elite to a commodity for one and all. The spread and appeal of pop culture throughout the globe today is due to the advent of satellite technology and the Internet.

pop language term coined by writer Leslie Savan in her 2005 book titled *Slam Dunks and No-Brainers: Lan-*

guage in Your Life, the Media, Business, Politics, and, Like, Whatever, referring to language used in media but picked up by the population at large: *That is so last year; I hate it when that happens; Don't go there; Get a life;* and so on. Savan compares Disney's 1953 cartoon *Peter Pan* with the 2002 sequel *Return to Never Land.* The former was free of packaged phrases and slang. The sequel, on the other hand, is scripted on the basis of pop language, including such phrases as: *In your dreams, Hook; Put a cork in it; Tell me about it; You've got that right;* and *Don't even think about it.*

pop music [full form: **popular music**] music intended to be appreciated by ordinary people, usually intended to provide entertainment and pleasure, and including such genres as jazz, swing, rhythm and blues, rock, and rap. Pop music surfaced at the start of the twentieth century, spreading in the 1920s with the rise of jazz music. In 1923 the Broadway musical *Running Wild* helped turn the Charleston into what most historians of pop culture consider to be the first dance craze. By the late 1920s, the cheapness and availability of mass-produced records entrenched pop music as mainstream music. In the 1950s rock music came onto the scene as mainstream pop music. Many styles have emerged since, from punk and disco to rap and metal.

pop star individual in media who has become an icon in his or her field,

becoming a symbol of a trend or lifestyle

populism political philosophy that champions the common person, combining elements of the political left and right, opposing large business and financial interests, but also frequently showing an open hostility to established labor organizations

pop-under ad Internet ad that appears in a separate browser window

pop-up ad advertisement that is activated, popping up on the screen, when a user visits a particular Web site

pornography depiction of erotic behavior intended to cause sexual excitement, primarily in movies. The word originally signified any work depicting the life of prostitutes. The development of photography and motion pictures in the nineteenth and twentieth centuries contributed greatly to the proliferation of pornography, as has the advent of the Internet in the late twentieth century. During the twentieth century, restrictions on pornography were relaxed throughout much of Europe and North America, though regulations remained strict in Asia, the Middle East, and Africa. Child pornography is universally prohibited. According to some media analysts, pornography is central to understanding pop culture. When the pornographic movie *Deep Throat* premiered in 1972, it was perceived not just as a new form of blatant sexual depiction, but was also described by some critics as a serious threat to the political and social order. Pornography continues to be a form of social criticism against authoritarianism, albeit much less so today since it has become virtually mainstream. Some media analysts distinguish between the erotic and the pornographic. The former term is used to describe the sexual activities that have been represented in the art of most cultures since antiquity. In Greek pottery and Indian temples, for example, sex in its different forms appears as just one feature among many. It is only in modern secular cultures that a distinction has come to be made between the two supposedly different kinds of sexual representation.

portal entry point to the Internet, such as a search engine

portrait 1. painting, photograph, or drawing of a person, focusing on the face, extended to mean the depiction of someone's personality in some way; 2. by extension, any penetrating depiction of someone or something. Portraits can be traced as far back as 3100 B.C.E. in Egypt. They serve various social functions, ranging from the exaltation of rulers and important cultural figures to sketches of common people.

positioning advertising products in appropriate market segments through appropriate media. For example, advertising for women's

perfume is positioned in magazines dealing with women's issues or in fashion magazines; men's deodorants, on the other hand, are typically positioned in corresponding magazines for men.

positive appeal advertising intended to demonstrate why a product is attractive or important to possess

positivism philosophical system that confines itself to empirical facts, emphasizing the achievements of science

post 1. to send a message to a newsgroup or bulletin board on Internet; 2. to update a database; 3. to show text online at a Web site

Postal Act of 1879 legislation that allowed magazines to be mailed at low cost, leading to the growth of the magazine industry

post-broadcast media the shift that has occurred in the way that media texts are delivered, due to the advent of the Internet and digital technologies:

Broadcast	*Post-broadcast*
public	private
passive	active
analogue	digital
one-to-many	many-to-many
mass	interactive
television	computer
standardized	customized

postcolonialism the period after a colonizing country has departed from the area it once controlled

poster appealing print announcement or advertisement that is displayed publicly to promote a product, event, or idea. Posters were popular in the nineteenth century, following the invention of lithography, which allowed color to be used in the making of posters. Henri de Toulouse-Lautrec was noted for his poster art, which was often used to advertise cabaret shows. The early twentieth century gave rise to advertising posters for every conceivable product; the poster remains a primary advertising tool to this day.

post-feminism approach to culture and media that still holds to basic feminist criticism, expanding the original paradigm in order to reevaluate some of the original assumptions of feminism, especially the role of sexual representations of women in the media. Post-feminism emerged as a backlash to Eurocentric and elitist strands of feminism, and especially ideas such as those put forward by radical anti-male feminists such as Andrea Dworkin, arguing that it is a delicate balance to differentiate between sexual explicitness and sexual exploitation and sexism. Perhaps inspired by artists such as Madonna in the 1980s, post-feminism celebrates previously taboo areas among feminists such as sexual attractiveness and fashion.

post-Fordism [in contrast to **Fordism**] trend of moving away from traditional industries toward service and technology-based work involving digital media

post-humanism secular philosophy that aims to reassign humanity to its place among natural species, bringing it down from its privileged position. According to this claim, humans have no inherent right to destroy nature or set themselves above it. Post-humanism has also been enlisted to suggest that human bodies can be ameliorated through technological intervention such as genetic engineering.

posting message sent to a newsgroup

Postman, Neil (1931–2003) well-known critic of media technologies, entertainments, and their effects on people and cultures. Among his best-known works are *Amusing Ourselves to Death* (1985) and *The End of Education* (1995).

postmodernism movement in philosophy and art rejecting traditional narrative and aesthetic structures. The term was coined by architects in the early 1970s to designate a building style that was adopted at the time to contrast with modernist Bauhaus style (characterized by boxlike skyscrapers and tall apartment buildings). Postmodern architects emphasized eclecticism and eccentricity in design, putting, for example, a triangular roof structure on skyscrapers. The term caught on more broadly, becoming the moniker for a more general trend in art and philosophy.

postmodernity generally a synonym for POSTMODERNISM, but sometimes used to refer to the state of the world, rather than to the artistic or philosophical aspects of the postmodern movement

post-production final stage in the making of a recording, film, or television program, involving editing, dubbing, and other special effects

poststructuralism movement in SEMIOTICS that challenges basic structuralist theories, such as that of BINARY OPPOSITION, initiated by the psychoanalyst JACQUES LACAN and the philosopher JACQUES DERRIDA. In structuralism, signs are implicitly assumed to be the bearers of meanings, independently of their users; in poststructuralism, signs bear no meaning, apart from the meanings we give them in specific situations.

post-testing evaluation of an advertising campaign in order to determine its effectiveness

PR [*see* **public relations**]

pragmatics study of how language is used in social contexts. Pragmatics deals with who says what to whom in specific situations. For example, saying good-bye can unfold with the expression *Good-bye* or with the expression *I'm outta here*. The former is used in formal situations and the latter is typical of the language used among friends.

pragmatism philosophical movement developed by CHARLES S. PEIRCE and William James, claiming that the validity of anything (an idea, a theory, etc.) lies in its practical uses or effects

precision journalism type of journalism that attempts to make news reporting a scientific enterprise with rigorous methods such as surveys and questionnaires

preferred reading interpretation of a media text that is the one intended by its maker or that is shaped by the ideology of the society in which it is made

prejudice unfair opinion formed by an individual or group, who may twist or even ignore facts that conflict with that opinion

pre-production work to be done before the filming or recording stage of a text or program, such as script reading and budgeting

prequel story set at a time before the action of an existing work, especially one that has achieved success

press 1. those involved in journalism; 2. company that publishes books. The term was originally applied to print journalism, specifically newspaper journalism, but in the late twentieth century it started being applied to electronic forms of journalism as well.

press conference meeting where the press and other media reporters are invited to hear announcements of an important nature

press gallery location in a courtroom or legislature where the press can sit and take notes or record the ongoing proceedings

press kit package of background material for a product or campaign distributed to the press by an agency or publicity department

press release announcement, usually in a print form, providing facts to the media so that they can be reported or broadcast

pressure group group of people who work together in order to make their common concerns known to the media or government in the hope of influencing them

prestige advertising advertising in high-quality magazines or media programs, with the aim of enhancing the company's reputation

pre-testing the testing of an advertisement or ad campaign before it is launched

preview text (poster, short film, etc.) describing or showcasing an upcoming media event (a movie, TV program, etc.)

primacy effect theory notion that the information most likely to be remembered is the one that occurs first in a text, film, or program

primary text media text created before it is transmitted or made known

prime time period in a radio or television schedule when the potential audience is the largest, generally weekday evenings from around 7 P.M. to 10 P.M.

priming process of organizing news items in order of their perceived importance

print 1. medium of communication utilizing written text, rather than visual or audio images; 2. edition of a book, newspaper, or magazine, made at a specific time; 3. photograph produced from a negative or by a digital process. The invention of the PRINTING PRESS is widely thought to be the origin point of mass communications. Some historians suggest that print was instrumental in bringing about all the major shifts in science, religion, politics, and the modes of thought that are associated with modern societies.

Print on Demand [abbreviated as POD] printing technology by which books and other print materials are printed only after they have been requested. Such technology has been made possible because of the advent of digital printing. POD is used, for instance, by presses to reprint older titles for which there is a moderate demand.

printing press machine used for printing materials from movable metallic characters, perfected by Johannes Gutenberg during the mid-1400s

privacy 1. right to be let alone, to be free from surveillance by the state, official institutions, or one's fellow citizens; 2. right to control the disclosure of personal information

privatization process of transferring ownership of a media outlet or institution from the public sector to the private one

process model theoretical model of communication in which the meaning of a message is assumed to be the one intended by the sender, with no input on the part of the receiver

producer member of a film team, a television program, or radio show responsible for general supervision and financing

product character fictional person or cartoon animal used in advertisements over a long period. The character becomes highly familiar to people and thus provides enduring identification with a company's products. Well-known product characters include Tony the Tiger, Betty Crocker, Mr. Clean, and Ronald McDonald.

product placement marketing strategy whereby a brand product is featured in a prominent venue or event, such as a film or television program. This strategy goes back to the 1950s when TV programs such as *Texaco Theater*, *General Electric Theater*, and *Kraft Theater* became associated exclusively with one sponsor continuing a previous radio tradition. In 1982 the extraterrestrial creature in Stephen Spielberg's *E.T.* was seen snacking on *Reese's Pieces*—increasing sales for the product enormously. That event started a trend in Hollywood. In 1983 Tom Cruise donned a pair of Wayfarers (Rayburn sunglasses) in *Risky Business*, and sales for that product shot up. The placement of brands in the scripts of TV programs and movies is now so common that it goes largely unnoticed. Its main objective is to amalgamate brand identity with pop culture.

production work of putting together a media text (a film, a television program)

profile in NETLINGO, the pages that users of a Web site set up to share information, including photos, residence address, interests in music, movies, TV, books, etc. A typical profile has the name of the user, sometimes written with mismatched letters (for example, JohNnY), a list of personal details (sex, age, marital status, zodiac sign), interests (music, sports), and commentaries.

program 1. any radio or television text or spectacle; 2. set of commands that allow users to operate a computer

program director person responsible for the selection and scheduling of programs for broadcasting or podcasting

progressive rock rock music style that emerged in the late 1960s, emphasizing creative freedom, often drawing on blues and jazz styles in combination

projection television television system in which an amplified picture is projected onto a screen

promo advertisement for another program or movie

propaganda materials, strategies, etc. (overt or covert), used to spread particular ideologies or opinions in order to convince or persuade people of their validity

propaganda model media and mass communication model, associated primarily with NOAM CHOMSKY, which claims that those who control the funding and ownership of the media determine how the media select and present their news and events, making the media nothing more than a propaganda arm of governments and business institutions

Propp, Vladimir (1895–1970) Russian literary critic who developed a list of basic character roles and plot settings that, he claimed, were present in all kinds of stories, including the hero (or anti-hero), the villain, the object of the quest, the hero's helper or companion, etc.

props small objects on a movie or television set that are used as part of a scene or a sequence

prose ordinary language (as opposed to poetry); for example, novels, essays, reviews, critiques, and the like are all written in prose; on the other hand, cards (such as those given on Valentine's Day) are typically written in poetic style

prosody 1. poetic versification; 2. tones, pitches, and stress patterns that accompany the pronunciation of words, phrases, and sentences

protocol software that controls connections between computers on the Internet

prototype theory psychological theory claiming that the concept that most people generate in their minds when a word is used is the most common, basic, or prototypical exemplar of a category. For example, when the word *cat* is used, people typically generate an image of the common cat. They do not normally think of a *cat* as a *feline*, as is a *lion* or a *tiger*. If asked what kind of cat, people might refer to it as a *Siamese* cat, a *Persian* cat, and the like. The word *feline* reflects a *superordinate* concept (a concept with a general classificatory function); *cat* a *basic* or *prototypical* concept; and *Siamese* a *subordinate* concept.

proverb traditional saying that expresses an intrinsic truth or else gives practical advice: for example, *Don't count your chickens before they're hatched* (= exercise caution). Every culture has proverbs; they are part of what anthropologists call folk wisdom.

proxemics study of the kind of zones that people maintain while interacting, introduced into anthropology by Edward T. Hall, who measured such zones, finding that they varied from culture to culture (allowing for predictable statistical variation). In North American culture, for instance, Hall found that a zone of 6 inches was perceived as an intimate one; while one from 1.5 to 4 feet was experienced as a safe zone. A stranger intruding upon the limits set by such boundaries causes discomfort and anxiety. If the safe distance is breached by an acquaintance, on the other hand, it would be felt to signal a sexual or aggressive advance.

pseudoevent a staged event for the media, planned for the sole purpose of playing to huge audiences

pseudonym [*see* **pen name**]

psychedelic hallucinogenic drug that distorts perception. The term was used in various phrases in the counterculture era of the 1960s: for example, *psychedelic rock, psyche-*

delic poetry, etc. The term is from Aldous Huxley's book on mescaline, *The Doors of Perception* (1954).

psychoanalysis psychological method, developed by SIGMUND FREUD, based in part on the assumption that unconscious instinctual drives (the libido) are primary motivators of behavior. Freud introduced the techniques of free association and dream interpretation to explore unconscious drives and anxieties. Freud's tripartite model of personality—including the ID, the EGO, and the SUPEREGO—has been used by various media and advertising analysts to explain how we relate to texts unconsciously.

psychographics study of the psychological profiles of different people for advertising and marketing purposes. Psychographics differs from DEMOGRAPHICS, which studies lifestyle patterns and other social characteristics of subjects.

Public Broadcasting Act of 1967 U.S. legislative act that established the Corporation for Public Broadcasting, which oversees the Public Broadcasting Service (PBS) and National Public Radio (NPR)

Public Broadcasting Service [abbreviated as **PBS**] nonprofit organization that oversees public radio and television programming in the United States, made possible by the Public Broadcasting Act of 1967. PBS stations operate on contributions from viewers, corporate gifts, foundation grants, and support from the Corporation for Public Broadcasting. Similar services exist in other countries. Web site: www.pbs.org

public domain realm of works that are free from copyright or patent and that can be used or released without the payment of royalties

public relations [abbreviated as PR] activities and techniques used by organizations and individuals to establish favorable attitudes and responses by the general public or special groups

public service announcement announcement carried free by a media outlet promoting a program or project (usually sponsored by a government or educational institution) that is deemed to be of interest to the general public

publicity any favorable information about something or someone in order to stimulate public interest or to raise awareness

publisher company that produces books, journals, or other print materials

publishing trade, profession, or activity of producing material in print or electronic form for distribution to the public

puff piece 1. an article that gives uncritical support for a person or cause;

2. in advertising, an ad that borders on exaggeration

Pulitzer Prize set of prizes awarded by Columbia University for outstanding public service and achievement in American journalism, letters, and music, named after editor and journalist Joseph Pulitzer

pulp fiction magazines and novels (originally produced on cheap paper) that deal with popular and titillating themes, such as crime, sex, and horror

pun play on the different senses of the same word or else on the senses or sounds of different words: for example, *Dee Light is a delight*; *The analyst is called Anna List*

punk rock aggressive style of rock music starting in the mid-1970s, developed from counterculture rock of artists such as the Velvet Underground and Iggy (Pop) and the Stooges and represented by American rockers such as Patti Smith and the Ramones. The style soon took root in London—where distinctly "punk" fashions, including spiked hair and ripped clothing, were adopted by punk bands such as the Sex Pistols and the Clash. The fashion items introduced into pop culture by the punk movement include: chains, dog collars, army boots, and "Mohawk" hairdos.

Q & A [full form: **questions and answers**] style of radio or television reporting in which an announcer asks a correspondent questions about a story

quadraphonic four-channel (four-speaker) sound system

qualified privilege legal right allowing reporters and journalists to report judicial or legislative proceedings even though statements made in the proceedings may be libelous

qualitative research method of media and advertising research that is based on observational techniques such as in-depth interviews and focus groups

quantitative research method of media and advertising research that emphasizes the measurement of trends and their statistical implications

queer theory in culture studies, idea that sexuality cannot be defined rigidly, and that non-heterosexual forms of representation (in the media) are as legitimate as heterosexual ones

quest in a NARRATIVE, the journey that a protagonist undertakes in order to achieve or find something important

questionnaire method of conducting research on media and advertising based on the use of specifically designed questions. These can be of two general types: closed and open. The former asks respondents to select their answers from various choices; the latter asks them to give their opinions in their own words.

quiz show [also called **game show**] radio or television show designed to test the knowledge, luck, or skill of contestants or experts. Two of the most popular quiz shows on American television are the *Wheel of Fortune* and *Jeopardy.*

quiz show scandals the fraudulent practices by quiz shows of the mid-1950s, when some producers began feeding answers to contestants who had been chosen to win. Government investigations led to a demise of the big-money quiz shows. These regained popularity only in the 1970s.

quota restriction on the amount of time a particular media product may be given airtime

quotation piece of writing or oral speech used, for example, in a book and enlisted for some purpose (to support an idea, to embellish a presentation)

R rating film classification in the United States indicating that a movie cannot be viewed by anyone under the age of 17 unless accompanied by a parent or guardian

racism any action or practice based on the erroneous belief that some group(s) of humans is (are) superior or inferior to others

radical reading one of three supposed readings or interpretations applied to a media text (the other two being DOMINANT and SUB-ORDINATE), in which the audience rejects the meanings, values, and viewpoints built into the text by its makers

radio transmission of sounds converted into electromagnetic waves directly through space to a receiving device, which converts them back into sounds

Radio Act of 1912 first radio legislation passed by the U.S. Congress, which addressed the problem of amateur radio operators jamming the airwaves by regulating the licensing of transmitters

Radio Act of 1927 radio legislation passed by the U.S. Congress creating a Federal Radio Commission, stating that radio operators could own their channels if they operated them to serve the public interest, defining the broadcast band, and standardizing frequency designations

radio broadcasting broadcasting through radio technology. Evidence of a plan for radio broadcasting to the general public is found in a 1916 memorandum written by David Sarnoff, an employee of American Marconi, which would eventually become the Radio Corporation of America (RCA). Sarnoff recommended that radio be made into a "household utility." The memo was given little if any consideration at first. After World War I ended in 1918, however, several companies took up Sarnoff's idea for the mass marketing of home radio receivers very seriously. In an effort to boost radio sales, the Westinghouse Electric Corporation of Pittsburgh established what many historians consider to be the first commercially owned radio station to offer a schedule of programming to the general public. It was called KDKA, after it received its license from the Department of Commerce (which held regulatory power following the end of the war) in October 1920. KDKA aired mainly entertainment programs, including recorded music, using a phonograph placed within the range of a microphone. The station did not charge user fees, nor did it carry advertisements. Westinghouse used KDKA simply as an enticement for people to purchase home radio receivers. Radio broadcasting reached the pinnacle of its popularity and influence during World War II, when American commentator EDWARD R. MURROW changed the nature of news reporting permanently with his eyewitness descriptions of street scenes during the German bombing raids of London, delivered from the rooftop of the CBS news bureau there. U.S. president Franklin D. Roosevelt was among the first politicians to understand the power of radio as a propaganda tool. He used the radio to bypass the press and directly address the American people with his so-called fireside chats during the Great Depression. Roosevelt clearly understood that the emotional power of the voice would be much more persuasive than would any logical argument he might put into print. The chats continue to this day as part and parcel of the American presidency.

Radio Corporation of America [abbreviated as **RCA**] company established during World War I to pool radio patents, giving the United States control over the new mass medium of radio broadcasting. Web site: www.rca.com

radio frequency spectrum portion of the electromagnetic spectrum that is used for all radio, wireless communication, and television channels

radio genres programming genres associated with radio broadcasting, either currently or in the past. At first, radio simply adapted various genres of traditional stage drama, transforming them into radio dramas, action serials, situation comedies, and so-called soap operas. It looked

to vaudeville to garner and adapt material for its comedy-variety programming. And it modeled its news coverage on the format of daily newspapers—announcers would, in fact, often simply read articles from the local newspaper over the air. Because of its capacity to reach large numbers of people, from the 1920s to the early 1950s radio broadcasting evolved into society's primary medium of information, arts appreciation, and entertainment. Only after the advent of television in the late 1940s did radio's hegemony in this domain begin to erode, as its audiences split into smaller, distinct segments. Today, radio is primarily a medium for specialized purposes (for example, automobile and office use). People listen to it in their cars as they drive from location to location, or in their offices (or other places) as they do something else. Aware of this, radio stations typically present traffic information in a regular interspersed fashion throughout their broadcasts, or else present uninterrupted stretches of music during certain periods of the working day. Radio stations are, typically, specialized according to music genre (classical music station, country music station) or service (all day news station, religious station, etc.).

Radway, Janice (1949–) leader of POST-FEMINIST thought, who has studied women's representational and social issues and the power of women-centered texts. Her most influential work is *Reading the*

Romance: Women, Patriarchy, and Popular Literature (1991).

ragtime popular music of the late nineteenth and early twentieth centuries characterized by syncopated rhythms—the term, in fact, probably derives from "ragged time," alluding to its basis in syncopation. The most celebrated ragtime composer of the early period was Scott Joplin. Ragtime is considered an important influence on the development of pop music.

random probability testing technique of carrying out a survey on a representative test group, without any restrictions as to type of person surveyed

random sample sample taken from any given population, in which each person maintains equal chances of being selected

rap musical style in which lyrics are rapped (chanted) to rhythmic musical accompaniment, associated in its origin with African American youth. The first rap records were made in the late 1970s by small, independent record companies. Although rapper groups such as Sugarhill Gang had national hits during that period, the musical style did not enter the pop culture mainstream until 1986, when rappers Run-D.M.C. and the hard-rock band Aerosmith collaborated on the song *Walk This Way*, creating a broader audience for rap. The terms *rap* and HIP-HOP are often

used interchangeably. But the former, which derives from Sugarhill Gang's *Rapper's Delight* (1979), refers to the musical style itself, whereas the latter refers to the attendant lifestyle that those who listen to rap tend to adopt. Rap's lyric themes can be broadly categorized under three headings: those that are blatantly sexual, those that chronicle and often embrace the so-called gangsta lifestyle of youths who live in inner cities, and those that address contemporary political and philosophical issues related to the black experience and its history. By the mid-1990s, rap developed into a more eclectic musical form, as rap artists borrowed from folk music, jazz, and other music styles. Consequently, it became more melodious and traditional in its use of instrumentation.

rapport talk style of speech aimed at establishing harmony among individuals

rating point one percentage of all TV households who are viewing a particular station at a given time, or one percentage of all listeners who are listening to a particular radio station at a given time

ratings estimated size of a radio or TV audience for a program, broadcast, series, etc. Ratings are used to help broadcasters determine the popularity of a radio or TV program and to allow sponsors to determine how many people they are reaching with their advertising. This system has no use on broadcasting Web sites, where visitors to the sites can simply be tracked and recorded.

rational appeal technique of designing advertising to appeal to customers by using logical arguments that demonstrate how the product might fulfill some need

rationalism philosophy stressing the role of reason in obtaining knowledge. Rationalism has its roots in ancient Greek philosophy, especially in the works of ARISTOTLE, but it has come to be associated with seventeenth-century French philosopher and mathematician René Descartes, who expressed the essence of his view with the widely known expression *Cogito ergo sum* ("I think, therefore I am").

rave venue for electronic dance music, also called *techno*, that first appeared in the United States in the 1980s. Raves took place primarily in the form of all-night dance parties, often involving use of the hallucinogenic drug ecstasy.

RCA [*see* **Radio Corporation of America**]

reach estimated number of individuals who are tuned into a radio station or a television program

reader person decoding or interpreting a text. Traditional literary analysis has focused on how a reader tries to figure out what the

author of a work intended. In recent critical approaches, however, the meaning of a work is described as a system of meanings to which a reader responds, according to his or her personal experiences and the particular context (social, historical, psychological) in which the reading occurs.

reader response theory [*see* **reception theory**]

reading in media studies, a wide range of processes such as reception, interpretation, and understanding of texts

Read-Only Memory (abbreviated as **ROM**) form of computer memory that remains, keeping its content even when the power supply is cut off; the content cannot be altered once it is manufactured.

realism 1. view positing that universals in human cognition and/ or culture exist and can be identified with logical analysis; 2. view that objects exist independently of human perception and identification; 3. in media theory, the degree to which a text accurately reflects things as they really are, and not as we wish them to be. In literature it refers to works that depict everyday life. Realist writers include French writers Gustave Flaubert and Guy de Maupassant, Russian author Anton Chekhov, English novelist George Eliot, and American writers Mark Twain and Henry James.

reality television [also called **reality show**] genre of television programming that presents purportedly unscripted situations, featuring ordinary people instead of professional actors. Reality television covers a wide range of programming, from QUIZ SHOWS to those showing a group of people trying to survive (in a particular situation, such as on a faraway island) and those in which people compete for a prize by having to go through a difficult trial or test. The television show *Candid Camera* was one of the first reality shows on television, debuting in 1948. An actor pulled pranks on ordinary people and the "candid camera" showed their reactions. Another early prototype was the 1973 PBS series *An American Family*, which dealt with a modern family going through a divorce. Reality television as it is currently understood can be traced directly to several television shows that began in the late 1980s, such as: ABC's *Cops*, which started in 1989, showing police officers on real duty apprehending real criminals; MTV's *The Real World*, which began in 1992, putting strangers together for an extended period of time and recording the situations that ensued; and *Temptation Island* (2001), which achieved notoriety by placing several couples on an island surrounded by unmarried people in order to test the couples' commitment to each other. Today there are reality shows in all kinds of genres, from talk shows, such as *The Jerry Springer Show*, to shows in which people compete for a job.

real-time 1. any event that is transmitted or broadcast as it is occurring; 2. any film, program, etc., whose plot lasts the same period of time that it would take if it occurred in the real world; an example is the TV series *24*

recall test [*see* **recognition test**]

receiver 1. person or device capable of receiving particular kinds of signals; 2. entity or device to which/whom a message is directed

reception theory any media theory attempting to explain how audiences interpret texts. Reception theory was at its most influential during the 1970s and early 1980s, especially through the work of STUART HALL, one of its main proponents. The approach focuses on the kinds of "negotiation" or "opposition" strategies employed by the audience. Reception research has found that audience readings of texts are based on cultural background and life experiences. In essence, the meaning of a text is not present within the text itself, but is created in the dynamic between the text and its reader.

recital 1. repeating or reading something out loud; 2. musical or dance performance

recognition test [also called **recall test**] research tool designed to check how well someone can recall an advertisement, with or without prompting

record 1. an account or history; 2. disc, cylinder, or other device that contains sounds that can be played with the appropriate equipment

recording permanent copy of music on a disc, CD, DVD, or other device

reductionism view that complex structures or concepts are reducible to simple physical or psychological principles

redundancy any feature that counteracts NOISE. In language, for example, redundancy can be seen in the high predictability of certain words in particular utterances and the repetition of elements.

reference 1. note directing a reader's attention to a source of information; 2. source of information quoted in a text; 3. process of pointing out or identifying something. Reference is to be distinguished from *sense*. For example, the words *rabbit* and *hare* make reference to the same kind of animal. But the sense of each term is different—*hare* is the more appropriate term for describing the mammal if it is larger, has longer ears and legs, and does not burrow; *rabbit* is the animal that people would normally think of as a "pet."

reference work dictionary, encyclopedia, atlas, or other written or electronic work containing specialized information

referent the thing or idea that a word or a symbol stands for

referential code CODE guiding the interpretation of references found in a narrative, especially scientific and specialized ones

referential framework narrative technique of portraying a story as representing real life, by relating it to the lives and experiences of audiences

referential function as defined by ROMAN JAKOBSON, any utterance that is designed, simply, to refer to something real: "Main Street is two blocks away." This utterance has the specific referential function of indicating where a street can be found. It conveys, in other words, information about some real phenomenon.

reflection theory view that language mirrors the things it represents in some way (through imitation of its sound properties, through allusion to its appearance, etc.)

reflexivity way in which modern societies constantly examine their own cultural practices critically, resulting in their alteration

reformer in advertising jargon, person who wants products that will improve the quality of his or her life, rather than products that appeal to a sense of lifestyle

reggae type of popular music combining elements of calypso, rock, and soul. Reggae originated in the mid-1960s in Jamaica, as a means of expressing social discontent. It was popularized by the movie *The Harder They Come* (1972), starring the singer Jimmy Cliff, and by Bob Marley, its greatest and best-known exponent.

register type of language that fits into a particular social situation: *Would you be so kind as to tell me where you live?* (= high/formal register); *Hey, where do you live?* (= low/informal register)

regulation activity of controlling what occurs in media

reification 1. rendering an idea real by expressing or representing it in some way; 2. in Marxist theory, the tendency of people to associate with the commodities they produce

reinforcement effect theory that exposure to specific kinds of acts in the media, especially violent ones, may reinforce tendencies in some people (toward violence) that they may already have

relativism 1. theory that culture shapes an individual's worldview; 2. philosophical view that there is no moral system that applies to all people

remake new version of an old film or program

reminder advertising technique designed to make consumers recall an advertisement they have already viewed

remote control device that operates a system from a distance. Remote controlled systems include television sets, garage door openers, robots, and spacecraft. The first machines operated by remote control were motorboats. The German navy developed them during World War I (1914–1918). Automatic garage door openers were introduced in the late 1940s and TV remote controls in the mid-1950s. Today, using applications on the World Wide Web, people can control such devices as robots and cameras remotely.

repertoire list of works that a company, an actor, a musician, and the like can perform at any time

repetition and difference combination of expected and unexpected elements in a media text that are designed to create interest in audiences

repetition in advertising technique consisting of the use of different media to repeat the same message, adapting it to the properties of the different media

replay an event or occurrence recorded (on tape, video) and played again (as in a sports program) to highlight the event (such as a goal that was scored)

replicability view in the social sciences that research findings based on the testing of sample populations are valid if they can be obtained again by different researchers at different times

report account of news presented by a journalist in print, broadcast, or Internet form

reportage 1. use of a medium (print, broadcast, Internet) to present the news; 2. corpus of news; 3. a style of reporting news

reporter someone who presents the news in print, broadcast, or Internet form

report-talk speech style in which the exchange of information and content of a message are emphasized over any emotional factor

repositioning marketing strategy of changing a product's image either by shifting its POSITIONING (the target audience to whom advertisements of the product are aimed), by changing its design, or by changing the style of advertising used to promote it

representation way in which someone or something is portrayed or depicted in media. For example, in news reporting, a specific crime event can be represented either as a common everyday occurrence or else as something much more sinister, such as a symptom of society's loose moral standards. Representations generally possess an underlying view. For example, some television sitcoms depict (or have depicted) the family as an ideal social structure for resolving emotional problems (as was evident in the 1950s American sitcom *Father Knows Best*), while

others depict it as a dysfunctional one (as was evident in *All in the Family* in the 1970s and *Married with Children* in the 1990s).

representation and reality view that the ways in which media represent events, situations, and people are construed to either mirror or construct reality. Research has shown that events that are showcased on TV or on Internet are felt as being more significant and historically meaningful to society than those that are not. Events such as the John Kennedy and Lee Harvey Oswald assassinations, the Vietnam War, the Watergate hearings, the Rodney King beating, the O.J. Simpson trial, the death of Lady Diana, and the 9/11 attack are perceived as portentous and prophetic historical events through the filter of media coverage. The horrific images of the Vietnam War that were transmitted into people's homes daily in the late 1960s and early 1970s are considered to have brought about an end to the war by mobilizing social protest. Significantly, an MTV flag was hoisted by East German youths over the Berlin Wall as they tore it down in 1989. The images of the two planes smashing into the World Trade Center buildings on September 11, 2001, brought about an international reaction, whose consequences are still being felt.

rerelease music recording, movie, or other media product that has been released again to the public in order to gain a new audience

rerun repeat broadcast of recorded entertainment, especially a television series

resistive reading act of reading a media text by consciously opposing its apparent meaning or function

resolution optical quality of images on a screen (television, computer) or photograph

resonance positive reaction that a viewer has to a television broadcast or other media event because it corresponds closely to his or her experiences or expectations, thus reinforcing them

response function measure of the effect that a particular amount of advertising has on a person

response mechanism method of showing people's responses to Internet advertising by measuring the way that people respond to it through such means as direct clicking and "faxback" sheets

responsive chord theory concept put forward by sound archivist Anthony Schwartz, which holds that media activates ideas that are already present in people, Media do not transport information to audiences. Rather, they strike a responsive chord with information that people already possess.

restricted codes discourse patterns that are thought to be characteristic of less-educated working-class individuals, involving the use of a smaller vocabulary, simpler grammar, and the like

retention preservation of brand loyalty by means of appropriate ad campaigns and marketing strategies

reterritorialization any media strategy of reclaiming cultural "territory" by representing cultural meanings and artifacts in new ways

retrospective article or program that looks back at an earlier occurrence, such as a news event or a musical trend

Reuters trade name for a London news agency, founded in 1851 by German journalist Paul Reuter, that provides international news. Web site: www.reuters.com

review critical assessment of a movie, television series, book, or other media product in a newspaper, in a magazine, on a radio or television program, or on a blog

rhetoric 1. effective speaking or writing; 2. discipline studying how language is used effectively in various domains (from poetry to advertising). Rhetorical analysis explains how figures of speech create powerful meanings. The use of rhetorical language is particularly evident in advertising.

rhetoric of the image in media theory, the way in which images are used in advertising and filmmaking so as to persuade the viewer to accept a message or to reinforce it

rhetorical question a question asked for effect, in order to emphasize something, rather than to obtain an answer

rhyme feature of verse in which words that have corresponding sounds and word stress are used, particularly in various linguistic genres (especially poetry), especially at the ends of lines: for example, *some* and *come*; *win* and *sin*

rhythm regular recurrence of similar beats in language forms (such as poetry) and music, in alternation with each other and combined into some pattern

rhythm and blues style of music developed by African American blues musicians, after they left the rural South and moved to Chicago and other northern cities in the late 1940s. There, they developed a style of music combining elements of both blues and jazz.

rich e-mail e-mail that has a voice message attached to it

Richards, I.A. (1893–1979) English literary critic who emphasized the role of METAPHOR in literature and ordinary language. In *The Philosophy of Rhetoric* (1936), he provided a still widely used terminology for describing metaphor—the *tenor* (what the

metaphor is about), the *vehicle* (what is used to characterize the tenor), and the *ground* (the meaning of the metaphor). For instance, in *My grandson is a sly fox: My grandson* is the tenor, *fox* the vehicle, and the *ground* is something like "My grandson is a shrewd, crafty person."

riddle linguistic puzzle playing on word meanings. The oldest riddle known is the so-called Riddle of the Sphinx: *What is it that has four feet in the morning, two at noon, and three at night?* The answer is *human beings*, who crawl on four limbs as infants (in the morning of life), then walk upright (at the noon hour of life), and finally walk with the aid of a cane in old age (at the twilight of life). As this riddle shows, there is a play on the metaphorical meanings of the words standing for the times of day.

right of reply the right of an individual or group represented in the media to answer back if dissatisfied with the representation

risk society any group or community that is preoccupied with the risks posed by modernization

ritual any meaningful activity intended to symbolize an event; for example, the use of ritual dances to exorcise spirits. By extension, the term is now used to refer to any symbolic activity that is performed recurrently or systematically—for example, ritual media interaction such as ritual TV watching, ritual Web navigating, etc.

road blocking [*see* **repetition in advertising**]

road movie film genre that depicts the adventures of an individual and/or group who leave their residence and travel from place to place, often to escape from their current lives

roadshow live open-air radio or television broadcast that travels from place to place and usually centers on a theme (for example, life across the American Midwest, life in the city)

rock [abbreviation of **rock and roll** or **rock 'n' roll**] musical style that arose in the mid-1950s, becoming a dominant form of popular music until the 1990s. The first rock songs reflect a blend of the blues, gospel, doo wop, boogie woogie, and honky tonk. They were recorded and released by small, independent record companies and promoted by controversial radio disc jockeys such as Alan Freed, who helped spread the term *rock and roll*, first used by the Boswell Sisters in 1934 in their song titled *Rock and Roll*, although their term referred to the back-and-forth movement of a rocking chair, not to the meanings developed later. By the time Elvis Presley recorded *Good Rockin' Tonight* in 1954 (a remake of Wynonie Harris's 1948 rendition of the song), rock had established itself as a new trend in pop culture. After Bill Haley and the Comets recorded *Rock Around the*

Elvis Presley (1935–1977) during his second appearance on the *Ed Sullivan Show,* October 28, 1956

Clock in 1955, the music genre was appropriated by the teenagers of the era. Throughout the 1960s, 1970s, 1980s, and 1990s, rock developed various genres, from disco and punk to grunge and techno. Rock musicians and bands that have became icons include Elvis Presley, Jerry Lee Lewis, Little Richard, the Beatles, the Rolling Stones, Madonna, and Nirvana, among many others. In 1995 the Rock and Roll Hall of Fame opened in Cleveland, Ohio. Also in the 1990s, several major television documentaries were produced on the history of rock and roll, and historical box-set recordings were reissued featuring rock artists from the past.

rockabilly musical style emerging in the 1950s in Memphis, Tennessee, which combined elements of country music with ROCK AND ROLL and RHYTHM AND BLUES. Elvis Presley, Carl Perkins, Jerry Lee Lewis, and

Johnny Cash began their careers as rockabilly performers. Some country performers of the 1990s, including the Mavericks and Mark Collie, revived the rockabilly style.

rockumentary filmed or televised documentary about rock music or a rock musician or band

role character or part played by an actor or performer in a movie, television series, etc.

role fulfillment [also called **role reversal**] in a narrative, the way in which characters subvert the expectations that people attach to the traditional roles they typically play, such as a hero playing the role of villain, and the effect this role reversal has on audiences

ROM (abbreviation of **Read-Only Memory**)

romance 1. originally, a medieval narrative (in verse or prose), written in a Romance language (a language derived from Latin), revolving around the amorous exploits of knights and other chivalric personages; 2. by extension, any media text (novel, movie) revolving around love and romance. In *Reading the Romance* (1991), JANICE RADWAY argues that romances are popular among women because they provide an escape from domestic life.

romantic comedy humorous comedy genre involving a love story that usually ends happily

Romanticism literary, artistic, musical, and philosophical movement that began in Europe in the eighteenth century and lasted until the end of the nineteenth century. Romanticism emphasized subjective and emotional art forms, as well as exotic, occult, and monstrous themes. In literature, the Romantic hero was often a rebel or outlaw. Romantic composers, such as Frédéric Chopin and Robert Schumann, wrote highly emotional works that broke with existing traditions. In the visual arts, Romantic painters depicted faraway exotic subjects and dramatic scenes of nature, suggesting a mysterious, otherworldly quality that went beyond nature itself.

rotary press press that prints on paper passing between a supporting cylinder and a cylinder that contains the printing plates. It is used mainly today in high-speed, Web-fed operations in which the press takes paper from a roll.

rough cut 1. first stage of editing a movie or program in which all parts are put in order; 2. preliminary version of a movie, with only basic editing performed on it

royalties 1. fees paid for the right to play commercially produced music on radio; 2. money payable to a writer or artist, according to copyright for sales of his or her material (book, recording, etc.)

rule of thirds technique of dividing a scene or frame into three sections (horizontally and vertically), in order to create a balanced composition

run of network banner advertising that runs across a network of Web sites

run of site banner advertising that runs on a specific Web site

run of station television advertising to which no particular time slot has been assigned

run of week advertising space bought at the basic rate, but not assigned to any specific media outlet

run on text that continues on the next line or column

running head heading printed on every page, or every other page, of a book, indicating its title or a chapter or section title .

running story news story that is followed in a series of articles over different editions of the same newspaper or program

Russian formalism school of SEMIOTICS and literary criticism, prominent from 1916 to around 1930, which stressed the role of figurative language in all kinds of representations and discourses, not just poetry

safe harbor broadcast times, usually from 10 P.M. to 6 A.M., when children are not likely to be a listening or viewing audience and thus when adult programming can be safely aired

saga 1. narrative genre dealing with prominent figures and events of the heroic age in Norway and Iceland, that is, during the late twelfth and thirteenth centuries; 2. by extension, any narrative about heroic figures or events

Said, Edward (1935–2003) important commentator on the cultural politics of the Middle East and the originator of the theory of ORIENTALISM, which claims that Western representations of Middle Eastern peoples and cultures have been constructed in accordance with Western views and are thus often inaccurate or misleading

sales house company that sells advertising space in the media

sales literature leaflets, brochures, and other printed information about a product that can be used by salespeople to promote it

salience meanings in a text that are relevant to specific audiences, but not to others. For example, the *Star Trek* series of television series and movies has great salience for "trekkies" (fans) but not necessarily for others.

salutation displays cues, such as gestures and facial expressions, which betray if someone is inclined or not to enter into a conversation

sample 1. representative group of people chosen for research; 2. music snippets taken from an existing recording and used as a part of a new recording. Early rap is the best-known pop music genre to use samples from prerecorded material.

sample survey statistical survey targeting a specific group of individuals, aiming to collect information on particular subjects, such as buying habits and program preferences

Sapir-Whorf Linguistic Relativity Hypothesis [also called **Whorfian Hypothesis**] theory, associated primarily with linguists Edward Sapir and BENJAMIN LEE WHORF, which maintains that the categories of a specific language tend to condition the ways in which its speakers think

sarcasm mocking or satirical language: for example, *How slim you look these days!* (uttered to someone who has put on weight)

satellite [full form: **communications satellite**] earth-orbiting system capable of receiving a signal and relaying it back to the ground. Satellites have played a significant role in the development and use of communications technologies since the 1970s

satellite dish dish-shaped aerial capable of receiving broadcast signals via satellite

satellite footprint surface area covered by a satellite signal

satellite phone wireless phone that connects callers via satellite

satellite radio radio stations, such as SIRIUS and XM, that broadcast via satellite and usually operate on a pay-per-service basis

satellite television television broadcasting received via satellite that offers a large number of channels to its subscribers. Millions of homes in many countries receive signals from DIRECT BROADCAST BY SATELLITE (DBS). Most DBS programming is provided by the same services that supply programs to cable television.

satire literary, dramatic, or cinematic work that ridicules someone or something, for example, the TV sitcom *The Simpsons* is considered a satire of American culture.

saturation advertising strategy of flooding the various media outlets (print, television, etc.) with the same ads or ad campaign so as to garner a broad audience

Saussure, Ferdinand de (1857–1913) Swiss founder of modern linguistics and semiotics, born in Geneva. As a student he wrote *Mémoire*

sur le système primitif des voyelles dans les langues indo-européennes (*Memoir on the Original Vowel System in the Indo-European Languages*, 1879), on the vowel system of Proto-Indo-European. Although he never published another book, after his death, two of his assistants compiled notes from his lectures into the seminal work *Cours de linguistique générale* (1916; *Course in General Linguistics*). The book became the basis for both semiotic and linguistic theories and methods.

scenario 1. plot summary of a dramatic or literary work; 2. actual screenplay for a movie

scene 1. subdivision of a play, a movie, or other work; 2. particular situation in a play, a movie, or other work (for example, a love scene); 3. motion picture or television episode or sequence; 4. main picture or view in a painting

scenery set or decorations providing the background for a play, movie, or other work

scenography art of making and/or using SCENERY

schedule order of programs on a broadcasting system (channel, station) for a day, week, month, or year, devised in such a way as to reach target audiences

schedule evaluation assessment of how a particular media plan or strategy has performed with respect to its target audience

schema 1. any diagram that represents something in outline form; 2. pattern representing something in its essential features

Schramm, Wilbur (1907–1987) leading researcher on the effects of mass communications on people and society. His most famous work is *Process and Effects of Mass Communication* (as editor, with Donald F. Roberts, 1954). Schramm's model of communication expanded on the BULL'S-EYE MODEL. Schramm broke down the communication process into four major components: a source (S) of the communication; a message (M); a channel (C) for transmitting it from one place to another; and a receiver (R) at whom the message is aimed. It is also known as the Source-Message-Channel-Receiver (SMCR) model. Schramm also refined the notions of *feedback* and *noise*, viewing the former as any mechanism between the source and the receiver that regulates the flow of the communication, and the latter as any distortion or errors that are introduced in an exchange. Schramm completed his model a little later with two other components: the *encoder*, which converts the message into a form that can be transmitted through an appropriate channel; and a *decoder*, which reverses the encoding process so that the message can be received successfully. The SMCR has been used extensively in media

studies because of its simplicity and applicability to all types of media.

sci-fi [*see* **science fiction**]

science fiction [abbreviated as **sci-fi**] literary and cinematic genre in which the science of the future is portrayed as having impacts of various kinds (psychological, social) on human beings. The predecessors of the genre are Lucian of Samosata's *True History* (160 C.E.), in which he describes an imaginary trip to the moon; *Utopia* (1516), by Thomas More, which depicts a futuristic world; and *Micromegas* (1752) by French satirist Voltaire, in which he tells of visitors from other planets. As we understand the genre today, however, science fiction originates with the novel *Frankenstein* (1818) by Mary Shelley. The first writer to specialize in the new genre was Jules Verne. His hugely popular works include *Journey to the Center of the Earth* (1864) and *Around the World in Eighty Days* (1873). H.G. Wells followed Verne with *Time Machine* (1895), *The Island of Dr. Moreau* (1896), and *The War of the Worlds* (1898). Mass-distribution magazines, called PULP FICTION, also published many science fiction stories, including those of Edgar Rice Burroughs, beginning in the 1890s. (The first pulp fiction magazine is thought to be Frank Munsey's revamped Argosy Magazine of 1896.) In the twentieth century the popularity of science fiction grew with the publication of *Brave New*

World by Aldous Huxley in 1932 and *1984* by George Orwell in 1949. In the 1950s and 1960s a New Wave subgenre emerged, which focused on the loss of human values in a world of increasing technology. New Wave science fiction writers include Robert Heinlein, Isaac Asimov, Ray Bradbury, Philip K. Dick, and Ursula K. Le Guin. In the 1980s another subgenre, called CYBERPUNK, began to focus on the dangers of computer technologies; an example is *Neuromancer* (1984) by William Gibson. Numerous science fiction television shows have become part of pop culture lore, including *The Twilight Zone*, *Lost in Space*, *Star Trek*, and *The X-Files*, among others.

scoop story appearing initially in only one newspaper, on only one radio or television news program, or on only one blog. A scoop is, essentially, a story published by one media outlet ahead of the competition.

scopophilia (from a Greek word meaning "pleasure of looking") in Freudian psychology, the desire in people to see the unseeable. In FEMINIST THEORY it refers to the male gaze as it seeks pleasure in looking at women on the screen.

score music composed expressly for a movie, play, or other work

scrambler electronic device that garbles telecommunications or broadcast signals, so that they can only be unscrambled by a special device

screen 1. flat surface on which images are projected; 2. general term for the film industry, known more specifically as the *silver screen*

screen test audition for a film or television role in which various actors are asked to play the role briefly in order to assess which one is best suited for it

screen violence general fear that exposure of children to violence on the screen (movie, television, video game, Internet) will produce a negative effect. But research has rarely found any correlation between exposure to screen violence and negative effects such as a propensity to commit violent acts. MEDIA EFFECTS MODELS, on the other hand, have always sustained a correlation between the two. But such models have been criticized for:

- focusing on the mass media rather than on the perpetrators of violence themselves
- viewing children as passive malleable creatures, incapable of making distinctions between fantasy and reality
- being motivated by political conservative ideologies
- defining their study focus inadequately, often selecting media samples in order to verify biases in the models themselves
- portraying mass audiences as intellectually inferior and thus incapable of making up their own minds

screenplay script and shooting directions for a movie

screenwriter [also called **scriptwriter**] person who writes the SCREENPLAY for a movie

screwball comedy genre of comedy, originating in the cinema of the 1930s, featuring the humorous adventures of appealing characters and showcasing a world of sophisticated glamour and audacity

scribes persons in the medieval era, mainly monks and nuns, who copied manuscripts so that they could be distributed. Scribes made important contributions to the development of the modern book, separating words with spaces, using capital and small letters, and establishing a system of punctuation to make reading easier.

script written text of a play, screenplay, or broadcast, used in production or performance

script doctor writer who is asked to improve a script written by someone else, to make it conform to production expectations

script theory language theory positing that conversations are often structured in a scriptlike manner, unfolding in terms of so-called vocabulary frames that are adapted by speakers to fit a situation

sculpture a three-dimensional work of art, often executed by modeling a substance (clay, stone, etc.) into a figure. Sculpture has been found in virtually every culture throughout history. Early sculpture was primarily representational, but in the twentieth century sculpture became largely abstract or conceptual in nature, often incorporating found objects and nontraditional materials. For example, Judy Chicago's *Dinner Party* (1974–1979) integrates traditional women's crafts such as weaving and embroidery with ceramics on a large triangular table, paying tribute to the key role of women in social history.

search directory Web site that organizes links to information sources alphabetically and thematically

search engine computer system that allows users to enter key words or queries in order to locate sites on the World Wide Web. Search engines consist of three components: a program (or programs), called a spider, crawler, or bot, which "crawls" through the Internet gathering information; a database, which stores the gathered information; and a search tool, which users employ to search through the database by typing in keywords describing the information desired.

season package or set of episodes of a television program, scripted to form a coherent sequence

secondary viewing act of watching television while doing something else, such as reading or doing housework

second-generation digital wireless technology, as opposed to earlier technology

secretive statement technique advertising technique designed to create the effect that a secret is being communicated, thus capturing people's attention by stimulating curiosity: *Don't tell your friends about . . .* ; *Do you know what she's wearing?*

Section 315 section of the Communications Act of 1934 that stipulates the "equal time" rule in election campaigns, whereby the broadcast media must make equal air time available to all qualified candidates; if one candidate is accorded free air time, opposing candidates must be accorded equivalent free air time

secularism philosophy that is based on indifference to, or rejection of, religion or religious ideas. One of the most famous of all early secularists was the Florentine politician Niccolò Machiavelli, who argued in favor of separating the political sphere of society from religion. His ideas were pursued further by English philosopher Thomas Hobbes.

secure server Internet server that allows for encryption and is therefore appropriate for e-commerce

secure Web site Web site that encrypts messages to prevent the unauthorized retrieval of information that was utilized or exchanged between previous visitors and the Web site

segmentation 1. the division of television schedules in terms of genre or channel; 2. division of audiences according to demographics for advertising purposes

seditious libel act of defaming a public official or other individual in print

selective attention tendency to avoid messages, texts, and representations that conflict with our beliefs and values

selective exposure tendency of audiences to view media products that correspond to their preexisting beliefs and values

selective perception refers to the initial reading of a media text and what the audience or individual gets from the information

selective retention tendency of people to select from media texts only those meanings that reinforce their preexisting beliefs and values. Anti-pornography individuals who watch a TV debate on freedom of expression have been shown to take away from the debate only the views that are consistent with their particular beliefs; libertarian individuals, on the other hand, tend to take away from it a sense of triumph by virtue of the fact that the debate occurred in the first place (thus legitimizing the topic). This view suggests that media may have limited impacts on most individuals, and that the communities in which they are reared have more of an influence on their worldview than do the media.

self-censorship act on the part of journalists to censor themselves because they are under pressure not to raise sensitive questions from either governments or the institutions that employ them

self-regulation practice of some industries to set up their own regulatory agencies

semantic code one of five codes (the others being ACTION, ENIGMA, REFERENTIAL, SYMBOLIC) used in the interpretation of texts, whereby the interpreter focuses on the meanings conveyed by "human voice" and the semantic features of the text itself

semantic differential technique developed by C.E. Osgood, G.J. Suci, and P.H. Tannenbaum in *The Measurement of Meaning* (1957) for assessing the social and/or emotional meanings associated with certain words or concepts. The technique consists of posing questions about things or concepts—*Is it good or bad? Weak or strong?*—to subjects, who respond by using seven-point scales. The answers are then analyzed statistically. Research has shown that people's assessments form culture-specific patterns. In other words, meanings are constrained by culture; for example, *noise* turns out to be a highly an-

noying thing for the Japanese, who rate it typically at the ends of the scales, whereas it is a fairly neutral concept for Americans, who rate it typically in the mid-range of the scales.

semantics study of meaning in language in all its dimensions, including word meaning, phrase meaning, sentence meaning, utterance meaning, etc.

semiology [term coined by FERDINAND DE SAUSSURE] the study of SIGNS. Although still used, SEMIOTICS has become the more common term.

semiosphere sphere of life governed by SIGNS and their meanings, including words, texts, and codes (sign systems) that humans have created to understand the world

semiotic power ability of an audience to assign meanings to media representations, even if these were not intended

semiotics the study of SIGNS and their uses in human life. Semiotics has become an important part of media analysis, used especially to decode the meanings of ads, programs, and the like. The first definition of sign as a physical symptom came from Hippocrates.

sender person or device who/which initiates and transmits a message

sensationalism lurid, superficial coverage of news, events, celebrities, or public figures in any medium

sense [in contrast to REFERENCE] any accrued meaning that a word or text takes on in cultural context. The REFERENT is the object named, whereas the sense is a mode of understanding it. So, the word *cat* has a mammal referent, but it has various senses attached to it that have accrued over time (a pet, an animal with superstitious effects if its color is black, and so on).

sense ratio according to MARSHALL MCLUHAN, the degree to which each of the physical senses are used in communication and in understanding. The sense ratios are equally calibrated at birth, but depending on culture, one or the other will become dominant. In an oral culture, the auditory sense ratio dominates; in an alphabetic one, the visual sense ratio dominates. Sense ratios are not preclusive. The raising or lowering of the ratios depends on the type of information being processed.

sensitization as used in media studies, way or ways in which media coverage can influence audiences to react to the events covered (sympathetically, empathically, etc.). An example of a television program designed to sensitize audiences is one that deals with social issues such as poverty or abuse, presenting them in a way that emphasizes "human suffering."

sensorium as defined by MARSHALL MCLUHAN, the environment in which the senses are stimulated. In media studies, it refers to the total sensory experience that is evoked by a text.

sequel film, series, or novel that continues a story started in a previous film, series, or novel

sequelitis [colloquial] the tendency of some authors and/or filmmakers to write or produce a story in anticipation of producing sequels

sequence section of a movie showing a single incident or set of related incidents

serial 1. novel, popular in the 1830s and 1840s, that was divided into a number of consecutive episodes that were published in installments; 2. movie presented in a series of episodes over several days, weeks, or months. The first widely popular serial movie, called *The Perils of Pauline* (1914), was followed by The *Hazards of Helen*, which ran for 119 episodes from 1914 to 1917. A serial episode typically had a "cliff-hanger" ending, enticing viewers to anticipate its resolution in the subsequent episode. Serials remained popular with movie audiences, especially children, well into the 1940s. A revival of the serial concept can be found in the 1981 movie *Raiders of the Lost Ark* and its sequels.

series popular form of broadcast drama unfolding in episodes; for example, TV police dramas, private-eye series, Westerns, science-fiction series, and series that follow the exploits of lawyers, doctors, or families

server storage system that controls network services available on other computers. On the World Wide Web, for example, a server is a computer that uses the HTTP protocol to send Web pages to someone's computer when the user requests them. Essentially, servers are host centers run by universities, corporations, government agencies, and other organizations, all of which are connected to the Internet.

service area geographical area over which a broadcasting station can transmit signals

service provider company that provides people with access to the Internet, usually charging a regular fee. Service providers may also offer browsers, e-mail accounts, and a personal Web page.

set location (along with appropriate scenery) where a film or television show is being shot

set designer person responsible for designing scenery and props for a movie set, television program, or stage production

set top box [abbreviated as **STB**, also called **converter**] device that provides an interface between a television set and incoming signals

from cable providers, satellites, or the Internet. An STB can be a separate device from the television set or can be built into it.

sets in use [abbreviated as **SIUs**] number of television sets that are tuned into a particular broadcast during a specific period of time

setting place and conditions in which a narrative, play, or poem takes place

seventy-eights [also called **78 rpm records**] previous record type made of shellac that played sound on a turntable at 78 revolutions per minute (rpm). Seventy-eights were the only kinds of records produced until the 1950s, when technological advances made the production of other types possible.

sex symbol any celebrity who is known primarily for his or her sexuality and attractive appearance

sexism 1. practice of some media products of emphasizing purported sexual differences in a stereotypical fashion; 2. generally, any unequal treatment of the sexes

sexploitation [blend of **sex** and **exploitation**] deliberate use of sexual material or themes to make a product, such as an advertisement or a movie, commercially successful

Shannon, Claude (1916–2001) American engineer who was a pioneer in communications, information science, and artificial intelligence (a branch of computer science that aims to design computer systems capable of processing information in a manner that resembles human cognition). During the 1950s and 1960s, Shannon developed early computers that played chess against human opponents.

Shannon and Weaver's model of communication one of the first models of communication (1949) put forward by CLAUDE SHANNON and Warren Weaver, also known as the BULL'S-EYE MODEL. The model depicts information transfer between two humans as a process dependent on probability factors, that is, on the degree to which a message is to be expected or not in a given situation. The model also introduced several key terms into the general study of communication: *channel, noise, redundancy,* and *feedback.* The *channel* is the physical system carrying the transmitted signal. *Noise* refers to an interfering element (physical or psychological) in the channel that distorts or partially effaces a message. *Redundancy* features are built into communication systems for counteracting noise. These allow for a message to be decoded even if noise is present. Finally, *feedback* refers to the fact that senders have the capacity to monitor the messages they transmit and to modify them to enhance their decodability.

share [*see* **share-of-audience**]

share-of-audience [abbreviated as **share**] percentage of people who are tuned to a particular program at a given time; for example, the number of people watching television between the hours of 8:00 P.M. to 11:00 P.M.

shareware software that can be downloaded from the Internet and used free of charge for a trial period

sheet music print publication of musical compositions. The publication of nonreligious music in the United States started in the 1790s in New York, Boston, Philadelphia, and Baltimore, where the major music publishers were located. These publishers produced sheet music, mostly for solo voice with piano accompaniment, of popular melodies. Many historians trace the origins of pop culture to the rise of the sheet music industry, because it was among the first industries to make music available to large audiences.

shield law legislation that protects a journalist from having to reveal his or her sources of information for a story. In the United States, shield laws are enacted at the state level; more than 30 states have passed some form of such legislation.

shock jock any disc jockey or radio host who uses vulgar language or expresses extreme views, in order to provoke, offend, or shock listeners

shock site Web site designed to shock or offend viewers

shooting actual filming of a movie; may also refer to television programs and to still photography

shopping channel television channel offering items for sale, usually with several presenters who demonstrate and talk about them. Products can be purchased by dialing a phone number or visiting a Web site shown on the screen.

short film running for a short period of time, usually 30 minutes or less

short message service [abbreviated as **SMS**] communications protocol for TEXT MESSAGES, sent in real time among computer or cellular phone users

short ordering network practice of ordering only a couple of episodes of a new television series

short story short prose fiction. Early short stories include such diverse works as tales told in ancient Egypt, the fables of the Greek slave Aesop (sixth century B.C.E.), the stories of Ovid (43 B.C.E.–17 C.E.) and Lucius Apuleius (second century C.E.), the Indian *Panchatantra* (fourth century C.E.), and many others. Such narratives became popular in Europe after Giovanni Boccaccio published the *Decameron* (1348–1353). The modern short story traces its roots to nineteenth-century writers such as Edgar Allan Poe and Anton Chekhov.

short subject [*see* **short**]

shortfall signal gesture or facial expression that conveys insincerity or suggests some hidden emotion

short-wave radio radio that transmits waves that have lengths shorter than those of waves used in amplitude modulation (AM) transmissions. Short waves carry frequency modulation (FM) radio broadcasts and television signals.

shoshkeles [also called **floating ads**] online advertising technique in which animated objects, such as a car, are projected across the screen

shot 1. actual piece of film; 2. single photographic exposure; 3. single sequence of a movie or television program captured by a camera without interruption

show public performance of a media text (a play, a musical, a movie, a concert)

show business the entertainment world, including movies, radio, television, and records

show reel compilation of a movie director's work, usually intended to bring out his or her particular skills

showtime time when a performance or show is scheduled to take place

sidebar short accompanying piece for a larger story, often with a human interest angle, usually separated from the main text in some way

sign anything that stands for something other than itself in some capacity, such as a word standing for an object, or a visual sign such as the cross standing for Christianity. The physical structure of a sign is called the *signifier* or *representamen*; the "something other than itself" for which it stands is known as its *referent, signified*, or *object*. Its overall meaning is called *signification* or *interpretation*.

signal emission or movement that naturally or conventionally triggers a reaction on the part of a receiver

signature in electronic communication, a piece of text that is pasted automatically onto an e-mail or newsgroup posting

signature tune [also called **theme song**] musical theme used to introduce a television program, radio show, or serial

significant symbolizer sign that is used in communal settings; for example, clapping the hands, along with other audience members, to indicate praise

signification 1. overall meaning or use of a SIGN; 2. actual concept that is evoked when a sign and a REFERENT are linked

signified what a sign refers to. The signified of the visual V-sign can be:

the letter V, the sign for victory, the symbol for peace, and so on.

signifier physical structure of a sign. For example, the sounds *t-r-e-e* are not perceived to be random physical sounds, but sounds that are structured to refer to something in particular. In FERDINAND DE SAUSSURE's original theory, the connection between the signifier and the SIGNIFIED, once established, is binary—that is, one implies the other. For example, the word *tree* is a word signifier in English because it has a recognizable phonetic structure that generates a mental concept of something else (an arboreal plant):

Today, the signifier is interpreted more broadly as any recurrent verbal or nonverbal structure that produces a mental image of something other than itself.

silence not speaking, which conveys something in communicative settings

silent film early film made without sound. In most large theaters, silent films were accompanied by music, recorded or played separately, often prepared specifically for the film. Most silent films had subtitles. The 1927 film *The Jazz Singer* brought about the end of the silent film era. Although the movie was silent for much of its length, the American entertainer Al Jolson sang and spoke in four of its scenes. The film was not the first talking motion picture, but it was the first to succeed at the box office.

silver screen movies or the cinema industry in general

simile comparing ideas using the words *like* or *as*: for example, *She smells like a rose*; *He is as strong as an ox*

simulacrum theory [adopted from JEAN BAUDRILLARD] view claiming that the media simulate reality and in so doing impart the sense that they are indistinguishable from reality. In effect, audiences end up not being able to distinguish between reality and media simulations (called *simulacra*).

simulation 1. process by which a sign represents something by resemblance or imitation: for example, the word *drop* simulates the audio properties perceived when something falls to the ground; 2. creation of electronic representations of objects or ideas that respond to changing factors on a computer

simulcast simultaneous broadcast of a program by radio and television, or by any of these together with an Internet site

Sirius Satellite Radio satellite pay-per-service radio system operating in the United States and Canada, providing music, sports, news, entertainment, and other types of programming. Sirius was previously known as CD Radio, changing its name in 1999. It is distinguished from most other radio systems by the fact that it hires or involves celebrities in its programming, making it highly attractive to listeners. Web site: www .sirius.com

sitcom [*see* **situation comedy**]

situated audience view that audiences tend to perceive media representations in terms of their own everyday situations

situation analysis gathering and evaluation of information to identify the target group and strategic direction of an advertising campaign

situation comedy [abbreviated as **sitcom**] genre based on social situations with which audiences can easily identify, broadcast on a recurring basis. The sitcom has proven to be the most durable and popular of American broadcasting genres. It uses stock characters and recurring situations to explore life in the home, the workplace, and other common locations in a funny, often satirical way. *I Love Lucy* (1951–1957), which starred Lucille Ball, was the first hit sitcom. The longest-running sitcom is *The Simpsons*, an animated series created by Matt Groening, an American cartoonist. It originated in 1987 as a short feature on the weekly Tracey

Ullman television show, premiering as a continuing series in 1990.

SIUs [*see* **sets in use**]

sketch comedy comedic skit with a VAUDEVILLE structure, that is, with segments consisting of singing, acrobatic acts, and other types of performance

skin flick colloquial name for pornographic movie

skit 1. short comic sketch; 2. comic work that satirizes something or someone

skyscraper in NETLINGO, online billboard placed down the side of a Web page

slander any untrue or misleading statement that damages someone's reputation

slang 1. any language used by certain groups (such as adolescents) for purposes of group identity; 2. informal speech in general. In the twentieth century, the mass media have been instrumental in spreading slang broadly. The Internet has recently brought a great deal of slang created and used by computer users into common usage: *snail mail* (letters delivered by the postal service), *hacker* (an expert computer programmer often involved in illegal activities), *flaming* (a hostile response from a user), and *spamming* (unsolicited messages).

slapstick comedy revolving around crude practical jokes. The word is traced to a slapping device used in vaudeville shows, made of two flat pieces of wood fastened at one end, and used for slapping onstage.

sleeper effect response to a message contained in a media text that is not immediately apparent, but which surfaces later

slogan catchy expression used in advertising and publicity: for example, *I'm lovin' it!* (McDonald's slogan); *You're in good hands with Allstate!* Slogans help create a favorable image of a company, a brand product, a politician, or a cause.

slow motion method of filming scenes or sequences so that they appear slower than normal on the screen, for a desired effect

smart card small plastic card that has a built-in microprocessor to store and process data and records

SMCR model [abbreviation of Source-Message-Channel-Receiver model; *see* **Schramm, Wilbur**]

SMS [*see* **short message service**]

snail mail in NETLINGO, mail sent through the postal service, as distinct from e-mail

sneak preview public screening of a film before its general release

snob-appeal technique advertising technique that aims to convince consumers that using a product will elevate their social status

soap opera serial drama genre, aimed originally at a female radio audience. Soap operas began in the early 1930s as 15-minute radio episodes and continued on television from the early 1950s as 30-minute and later hour-long episodes. The genre was named *soap opera* because the original sponsors were detergent companies. Soap operas typically revolve around romance, infidelity, loyalty, and intrigue.

social cognitive theory view that people learn through observation. The theory has been used to support MEDIA EFFECTS MODELS.

social constructivism [also called **social constructionism**] 1. belief that identity is not inherent in an individual or group but, rather, is a result of cultural, political, and historical forces; 2. view that cultures construct realities through signs and symbols and thus that people come to view the world through them

social controls ideas, beliefs, values, and mores that people pick up from the societies in which they are reared and that condition how they behave and communicate

social learning theory a theory that attempts to explain how people learn through experience and through the experience of others living in their own social context. The theory has been applied to explain the ways in which people read media texts.

social responsibility model view that journalists should monitor what they are reporting to make sure that it is ethical, fair, principled, and just, so that people can make wise decisions regarding social and political issues

socialism political philosophy in which private property and income are deemed to be subject to social control. The term was first used to describe the doctrines of Charles Fourier and other Romantic social theorists who saw spiritual and physical benefits emanating from socialist communities. Marxists see socialism as a transitional stage between capitalism and communism.

sociometrics study of social relations and power structures among the members of small groups

Socrates (c. 470–399 B.C.E.) Greek philosopher who believed that knowledge is gained primarily through oral discussion. He emphasized reason in the quest for knowledge.

Socratic irony feigning ignorance of something in order to make a point more forcefully

soft-core any representation that is sexually suggestive or provocative, but not explicit

soft news news reported in an informal, often chatty, style

soft sell method of advertising products and services that uses subtle forms of persuasion, rather than blatant ones

software detailed instructions used to operate a computer for a specific purpose. The term was coined around 1960 to differentiate the programs that run on the computer from the equipment, or hardware, that makes up the machine. Most early software was developed to meet a specific need. Often, it was included with a computer manufacturer's hardware. Later, it was sold separately. Software is divided into a number of categories: operating or system software, which allows the computer to operate commands; application software, which allows people to use computers in specific ways; network software, which links computers to the Internet; and language software, which provides the tools for writing programs.

soliloquy monologue presenting a series of reflections. Soliloquy allows stage characters to confide in the audience.

something-for-nothing lure advertising technique that offers a potential buyer a "something-for-nothing" deal: for example, *Buy one and get the second one free! Finish this sentence and win a trip to the Caribbean for two!*

soul music style of popular music emerging in the 1960s, sung and performed primarily by African American musicians such as James Brown, Ray Charles, Sam Cooke, and Aretha Franklin, having its roots in gospel and rhythm and blues

sound bite short extract from an interview or a speech used to support a statement or viewpoint in a broadcast or a print publication

sound card expansion card that can convert analog sound (as from a microphone or audio tape) to digital form, or convert digitized audio signals (as from an audio file) to analog signals that can be played on a computer's speakers

sound effects imitations of natural and other kinds of sounds to accompany the action and to suggest realism in a movie, play, or program

sound image any sound that is perceived or interpreted in the same way as a picture

soundtrack 1. narrow band recorded on the side of the film image; 2. general term for the dialogue, music and sound effects in a film or video

source person, organization, book, or document that a journalist uses for information or evidence

spaghetti Western film genre in the style of Hollywood Westerns, but actually filmed in Italy during the

1960s and 1970s. The most famous of all spaghetti Western directors was Sergio Leone, who won a wide audience with *A Fistful of Dollars* (1964), the first Italian-made spaghetti Western, starring Clint Eastwood, who also acted in Leone's equally popular *For a Few Dollars More* (1965) and *The Good, the Bad, and the Ugly* (1966). These films initially received poor critical reviews, but Leone was eventually recognized for his sense of historical accuracy and his realistic use of scenery.

spam unsolicited e-mails sent to a large number of electronic addresses

special television program that is not part of the normal schedule

special effects artificial effects introduced into a movie or television show. The earliest special effects were created with special camera lenses. The growing use of computer animation and imagery has made it possible to create elaborate and highly realistic effects. Some animated movies are now made solely with computer animation, which has moved special effects artistry to a new level.

spectacle any performance that has enormous appeal because of its "extravaganza" style. The term was used originally to describe the lavish productions of circus performances. Typically, a spectacle unfolded as the band played, the ringmaster sang, and performers in elaborate costumes and animals paraded in front of the audience. The circus spectacle generally ended with a long mount, in which some elephants rested their front legs on the backs of the elephants directly in front of them.

speech the use of language in face-to-face conversations, in writing, etc. By extension, it is used in media studies to refer to any special kind of language (*newspaper speech*, *Web speech*, etc.).

speech act utterance intended to bring about an actual physical act or desire for some action; for example, *Stop! Go!*

speech therapy [also called **speech-language pathology**] the science of speech disorders. Speech therapists work with people whose speech interferes with communication, calls attention to itself, and frustrates both speaker and listener.

speech-recognition technology hardware and software that enable a computer to recognize spoken words and convert them into commands, thus eliminating the need to input information manually

spin the presentation of news or ideas according to a particular point of view (usually political)

spin doctor person working in public relations whose job is to put a SPIN on an item of news in order to protect someone's public image or reputation (usually that of a politician)

spiral of silence theory developed by Elizabeth Noelle-Neumann, which holds that people who have views that they think are not widely held (whether true or not) tend to acquiesce, while those who believe that their views are widespread tend to express them strongly, leading to a spiral in which some views are expressed and others are not

splash page Web page that is displayed to visitors before they reach the home page

split run 1. printing of the same issue of a newspaper or magazine at separate times so that different ads may be included in the different printings, allowing the effects of the ads to be assessed and compared; 2. special versions of a given print publication with different content to suit specific demographic and regional groups

spoiler print publication (newspaper or magazine) that is released at the same time as a rival publication in order to divert interest from it

sponsor company that pays for radio or television programming by purchasing advertising time

sportscast radio or television broadcast of a sports event or of news related to sports

spot announcements commercial or public service announcements that are placed on television or radio programs

spread story or advertisement in a print publication or on a Web page that occupies more than a column or page

spy genre literary and cinematic genre that deals with espionage, mystery, or intrigue revolving around an intelligence agent or spy, who is the hero of the narrative. The best-known are the James Bond movies, originally cinematic adaptations of novels by British writer Ian Fleming, including *Dr. No* (1962), *From Russia with Love* (1963), *Goldfinger* (1964), *Thunderball* (1965), and *Casino Royale* (1967), all featuring James Bond, the high-living secret agent 007, one of the most successful characters of twentieth-century cinema.

spyware software that can secretly gain access to a computer user's hard drive through an Internet connection, capable of extracting information from the hard drive without the user's knowledge

stage 1. the theater or plays in general; 2. actual appearance of a play as created by lighting, scenery, costumes, and sound effects

stand-in any actor replacing another actor in a film or program, usually when the action is dangerous and the stand-in is trained specifically to participate in it

star [synonym for **celebrity**] person who is in the public eye because of his or her achievements in cinema, sports, or some other field

star system publicity strategy developed by Hollywood in its heyday, emphasizing movie stars, rather than the movies themselves, as a way to attract audiences to movie theaters. A movie starring John Wayne, for example, would be promoted in such a way to attract the many fans of the star, rather than to focus attention on the movie itself.

station [full form: **radio station**] place from which a radio broadcast originates. There are two main types of radio stations: commercial and public. The former are owned by private companies, making profits from advertisements; the latter are funded by the government. Some countries also have nonprofit stations, operated mainly by educational institutions. Although the term *station* is often applied to the place where television broadcasting originates, the more accurate term in this case is STUDIO.

station break interruption of a radio or television program, often to provide information on the program itself or on the sponsor of the program

status conferral gaining social status simply by being portrayed in the media

STB [*see* **set top box**]

stereo [full form: **stereophonic**] any electronic audio playback system that is capable of reproducing high-quality sound that comes from various directions (usually through speakers)

stereoscopy process of making photographs appear to have three dimensions, using a special camera with two lenses set a small distance apart

stereotype biased assessment of a person, group, or idea. The term is applied typically to describe the expectations that people have of others according to their age, gender, physical appearance, ethnic group, race, or occupation. Stereotypes are oversimplified assessments applied as generalizations, constituting a form of biased prejudgment.

still static photograph, usually of actors or scenes in a motion picture for publicity or documentary purposes

stimulation model a model of media violence, which claims that exposure to media violence can increase aggressive behavior in viewers

stimulus-response model a model describing the relation between an advertisement and the particular type of audience reaction it tends to receive. The model is based on the school of psychology called *behaviorism*, which dominated the field from 1913 to around 1970. The stimulus-response model investigated complex forms of behavior by measuring and analyzing the responses of human subjects to various stimuli.

story 1. fictional narrative shorter than a novel; 2. general term used to describe any news report or documentary program

storyboard 1. blueprint for a film sequence or TV commercial, which is drawn to portray copy, dialogue, and action, with caption notes regarding filming, audio components, and script; 2. in advertising, roughly drawn version of a proposed advertisement

strategic marketing method that assesses a specific market and then provides input on how to design advertising for that market

stream of consciousness literary device in which the reader is exposed to the thoughts and feelings of a character as they unfold. The term was coined by William James in his book *The Principles of Psychology* (1890). Notable exponents of this genre are James Joyce, William Faulkner, and Virginia Woolf.

streaming in NETLINGO, broadcasting material (audio, video) via Internet in real time. Streaming is made possible by browsers with "player" software, which allows a user to play audio or video files as they are being downloaded.

stripping the showing of programs five days a week that are either reruns or programs made for syndication

structuralism mode of inquiry based on the notion that signs and texts beget their meanings through OPPOSITIONS. For example, *left* is understood in opposition to *right*, *night* to *day*, and so on. Structuralism originated with

FERDINAND DE SAUSSURE. Both linguistics and semiotics are sometimes called structuralist sciences.

studio 1. place from which a television broadcast originates; 2. commercial film production company

studio system the Hollywood studios that dominated film production from the 1930s to the 1950s, an era when independent filmmakers had few opportunities to break into the movie market. The studios controlled all those who worked for them by contract, including actors and directors.

stunt double person who takes the place of a screen actor in scenes that involve danger or require special physical skills

style 1. patterned variation in language, according to its social functions; 2. the specialized use of language in works of literature; 3. type of clothing that is in fashion; 4. particular mode of representing or performing something (adventure style, jazz style, Hitchcock style, Seinfeld style)

subbrand secondary brand that builds on the associations of a MASTER BRAND

subconscious [alternative of **unconscious**] in psychology, mental processes that occur without people being aware of them. These were first studied scientifically by the French neurologist Jean Martin Charcot in the 1800s by means of hypnosis. Soon after, doctors realized that many mentally ill people, such as those with hysteria, were influenced by unconscious thoughts and feelings. It was, however, SIGMUND FREUD who developed the first theory of the unconscious, which claimed, essentially, that unconscious thoughts seek expression in various forms and modes, such as in dreams and routine conversations.

subculture any variation within a specific form of culture, developed by a group in order to set itself apart from the larger society. Subcultures may develop in ethnic groups, occupational groups, age groups (especially adolescents), and other groups within a larger culture. Subcultures differentiate themselves typically through language (slang), clothing, musical preferences, and the like, providing members with a sense of being a single collectivity.

subject 1. topic or main theme of a work; 2. what a sentence or proposition is about

subliminal advertising technique based on hiding a meaning or form in an ad. The theory is that the unconscious mind will pick up the image, which will create a need for the product. However, no evidence has ever emerged to show the effectiveness of such advertising.

subordinate reading one of three supposed readings or interpretations

applied to a media text (the other two being DOMINANT and RADICAL), whereby the audience accepts, by and large, the meanings, values, and worldview built into the text by its makers

subplot plot that is subordinate to the main plot of a work; for example, the subplot can be introduced to hide the resolution (in a mystery story), to provide comic relief (in a tragedy), or to shed light on the actions or personality of a character

subscription money paid to a media outlet (newspaper, magazine, Web site, satellite television service) to receive its media products on a regular basis

subtext text (and its message) implicit within the main text; for example, a mythic story embedded into an ad by means of suggestive images (snake figures, dark tones, etc.)

subtitle 1. dialogue appearing between the scenes of a silent motion picture; 2. dialogue appearing as a translation at the bottom of the screen in a motion picture or television show in a foreign language

succeeder in advertising parlance, person who wants products that will enhance his or her quality of life or social position

suggestion in advertising, process by which someone's views are influenced by the message or SUBTEXT in an ad

Sundance Film Festival annual motion picture festival of independent filmmaking, founded in 1976, giving awards in various categories, from best film to best sound effects. Web site: www.festival.sundance.org

superego in psychoanalysis, one of the three basic constituents of human character, the others being the EGO and the ID. The superego controls behavior and develops through parental and social conditioning.

superhero fictional character who has the characteristics of the ancient mythic heroes. For example, the comic book figure of Superman, who was introduced in 1938 by *Action Comics*, and published separately a little later in *Superman Comic Books*, represents a fictional superhero, who, like the ancient heroes, is indestructible, morally upright, and devoted to saving humanity from itself. Moreover, like some mythic heroes, he has a "tragic flaw": exposure to "kryptonite," a substance that is found on the planet where he was born, renders him devoid of his awesome powers. In mythology and legend, a hero is an individual, often of divine ancestry, who is endowed with great courage and strength, celebrated for his or her bold exploits, and sent by the gods to Earth to play a crucial role in human affairs. Heroes are character roles that embody lofty human ideals for all to admire—truth, honesty, justice, fairness, moral strength, and so on. Modern-day audiences feel this intuitively, as did the ancient Greek audiences who watched stage performances of Aeschylus's *Prometheus Bound, Prometheus Unbound*, and *Prometheus the Fire-Bringer.* Rather than being sent by the gods from the spiritual world to help humanity (something that would hardly be appropriate in a secular society), Superman came to Earth instead from a planet in another galaxy; he leads a "double life," as superhero and as Clarke Kent, a "mild-mannered" reporter for a daily newspaper; he is adored by Lois Lane, a reporter for the same newspaper who suspects (from time to time) that Clark Kent may be Superman.

superstation local independent television station whose signals are distributed nationally via satellite to cable and other television systems

superstitial animated ad that pops up between Web page views on the Internet

support advertising promotion designed to back up a campaign (political, social)

surfing to go on the Internet in search of various Web sites, for information, recreation, or some other motive

Surrealism twentieth-century movement in literature and the arts founded by André Breton in Paris in 1924, revolving around dream images and other fantastic imagery. Members of the movement include Max Ernst, René Magritte, and Salvador Dalí.

surround sound [also called **ambisonics**] recording and playback system that uses three or more channels or speakers in order to create the effect of sound surrounding the listener

surveillance society view that people today can be easily tracked down and spied upon because of sophisticated satellite and other technologies

survey study that measures attitudes, beliefs, and views by asking people directly about them. Surveys are used often in audience studies because they provide valuable information that can be assessed to identify trends, among other things.

suspension of disbelief acceptance of unlikely situations in a plot so that the story can be enjoyed

swashbuckler story about a swordsman or adventurer: for example, *The Three Musketeers* (1844) by Alexandre Dumas, père

sweeps survey of television ratings used to determine advertising prices

symbol something that stands for something else in a conventional way. A flag, for example, stands for a country. White is a symbol of mourning for Chinese people, while black is the color of mourning in Western societies. Almost anything can be a symbol. For example, the alphabet character A can stand for the best (such as a grade in school) or the musical scale or key that has A as its keynote.

symbolic code one of the five codes used in the construction of media texts, based on the interpretation of texts with high symbolic content and how they generate meaning through the use of symbols. The other codes are called ACTION, ENIGMA, REFERENTIAL, and SEMANTIC.

synchrony use, meaning, and/or function of signs, codes, and texts at a specific point in time (usually the present)

syndicated program television or radio program that is distributed in more than one market by an organization other than a network

synecdoche rhetorical technique whereby a part is used to represent the whole, or vice versa: for example, *Scotch tape* for *adhesives*; the *White House* for the *American government*

synergy strategy of actively forging linkages between related areas of entertainment. For example, mergers, such as that of Time Warner with AOL, allow for content developed in one medium, say television, to be reused and recycled in other media (movies, Internet).

synesthesia fusion of sensory reactions to words and texts created by juxtaposition: for example, *hot pink* (= feeling + sight); *smooth melody* (= touch + hearing)

syntagm pattern resulting from a combination of elements; for example, in word construction, the order of sounds is subject to rules of combination (*pfing* is not a legitimate word in English because *pf* cannot be used at the beginning of words)

syntax 1. organization of words to form sentences; 2. study of how words are combined to create larger structures

tabloid small format newspaper that is roughly half the size of a standard newspaper, usually containing sensational coverage of crime, scandal, gossip, violence, or news about celebrities. Tabloids also typically include lurid photographs, cartoons, and other graphic features.

tabloid TV television news program that is styled after newspaper TABLOIDS

tachistoscope testing in advertising research, the measurement of a person's recognition and perception of various elements within an ad by using the different lighting and exposure techniques of a tachistoscope, a device that projects an image at a fraction of a second

tag 1. piece of data that can be used to facilitate retrieval of text; 2. the HTML codes that create hypertext

tag question a word or phrase added to the end of a sentence or utterance that is intended to seek confirmation, agreement, or some similar response, rather than information: for example, *You like this a lot, don't you? This is a good movie, isn't it?*

tagline 1. slogan or phrase that conveys the most important attribute or benefit that an advertiser wishes to convey about a product (for example, Taco Bell's *Think outside the bun!*); 2. short phrase attached to the title of a movie that makes a commentary or captures attention

take 1. in filmic language, repetition of the same shot because the previous one was not satisfactory; 2. single session in which a piece of music is recorded in a recording studio

talk show genre of radio or television program in which people discuss aspects of their lives or current issues with a host. Late-night talk shows emphasize entertainment; others may focus on politics, controversial social issues, or sensational topics. Some talk shows allow listeners or viewers to take part in the program by telephoning the station to ask questions or give their opinions.

talkie movie with a soundtrack. The term was coined in 1927 to characterize the new technology that allowed soundtracks to be integrated with pictures in films.

talking head shot of a person on television that focuses on his or her head and shoulders as he or she is seen talking

tango sensual ballroom dance style originating in Argentina, made popular in the United States by Vernon and Irene Castle, a famous ballroom dancing team. By 1915 it was being danced throughout Europe, becoming a craze after Rudolph Valentino and his partner featured the tango in the motion picture *Four Horsemen of the Apocalypse* (1921). The dance form communicates passion through alternate long slow steps and short quick ones, with sudden turns and sexually suggestive poses.

tap dance a style of dance using precise rhythmical foot movements and audible foot tapping. The form is derived from the traditional jigs and reels of Ireland and Scotland. It was a popular staple of nineteenth-century minstrel shows. By 1925 the dance had become popular in variety shows and early musicals.

tape plastic thin layer used for recording and playing back sound. Tape recording was, until recently, widely used by the recording industry and in radio and television broadcasting. Though it still has many uses, it is being replaced by DVD and other technologies.

target audience group at whom a specific media product or advertising strategy is directed. Advertisers gather data on people (through discussions, interviews, etc.) to find out all they can about them—for example, age, class, gender, lifestyle preferences—and then use the information to determine the best way to advertise to them.

target market group of individuals who are the intended audience of an advertiser's message and prospective purchasers of its products or services

t-commerce business conducted by means of interactive television technology

TCP/IP [*see* **Transmission Control Protocol/Internet Protocol**]

teaser 1. preview of a broadcast or publication intended to elicit interest; 2. advertisement that gives little information about a product, thus making consumers curious to know more

technical director member of a film or television crew responsible for overseeing technical operations, such as camera equipment and sound equipment

Technicolor process for making motion pictures in color, developed in the early 1900s, resulting in color reproduction of high quality. The first full-length film made in Technicolor was *The Gulf Between*, appearing in theaters in 1917. Many Technicolor films were made in the 1930s and 1940s. Today, Technicolor has largely been replaced by simpler and less expensive color film processes.

techno music [also called **electronica**] dance music that first appeared in the 1980s and became globally popular in the 1990s, using synthesizer melodies with rapid electronic rhythms. Techno was adopted by the ravers, young people who organized all-night dance parties that often featured the hallucinogenic drug ecstasy.

technological determinism idea that technology shapes the course of human evolution. Many historians of science argue that technology has not only become an essential condition of advanced, industrial civilization, but also that the rate of techno-logical change has developed its own momentum. Innovations appear at a rate that increases geometrically, unhindered by geographical limits or social systems. These innovations tend to transform traditional cultural systems, frequently with unexpected social consequences. Some social critics therefore define technology as both a creative and a destructive process.

technophobia fear of technology. Technophobia is usually associated with fear of rapid innovations in science, such as genetic engineering, Internet technology, and the like.

telecast short for "television broad-cast"

telecommunications general term for all electronic communications and transmission at a distance, over cables, wireless radio relay systems, or via satellite links. Modern tele-communication systems can transmit large volumes of information over long distances.

Telecommunications Act of 1996 legislative act that opened up the United States telecommunications industry to competition, leading at the same time to a wave of media consolidation. The act also requires broadcasters to add captions to an increasing number of programs. Under the act, all programs must be captioned in English by 2008 and in Spanish by 2012.

telecommuting work performed at home by means of telecommu-nication networks, rather than at a conventional place of work such as an office

teleculture concept suggesting that television is a dominant influence in society, helping both mirror and shape cultural institutions, replac-ing books, families, and educators as primary influences in cultural transmission

teledemocracy view that democracy will spread because of telecommu-nications, which help disseminate information freely across the globe, thus encouraging large groups of people to make up their own minds about issues and thus develop a sense of democracy

teledrama drama filmed expressly for television audiences

telefilm film made expressly for television audiences

telegenic the quality of appearing attractive on television

telegram printed message sent by TELEGRAPHY

telegraphy electrical system that can send and receive electrical signals over long-distance wires. The first commercial telegraph systems were developed in Great Britain in the early nineteenth century. In the 1840s the American inventor Samuel F.B. Morse developed a code that came to be adopted internationally. The code—known as the MORSE CODE—utilized "on" and "off" signals to represent individual letters of the alphabet. The telegrapher at one end of the line would tap on an electrical key, and the telegrapher at the other end would decode the tapping as it came in, write down the message, and send it to the recipient by messenger. Telegraph cable was laid under the Atlantic Ocean in 1858, and regular transatlantic service began in 1866. It was the first interconnected global communications system. Telegraphy was gradually replaced by telex systems in the early twentieth century. These gradually eliminated the need to use a code. Users could type in a message, and the identical message would appear at the recipient's end, carried over telegraph and telephone lines to telex machines anywhere in the world. As early as the 1930s these lines were also used to transmit pictures, an event that introduced Wirephoto service in international communications. Today, telegraphy has been largely abandoned, being replaced by e-mail and other digital technologies.

telemarketing use of the telephone as a medium to sell, promote, or solicit goods and services

telematics technology that allows for the exchange of computer data through a telephone line

telenovela melodramatic genre of SOAP OPERA popular in South America

telephone device designed for simultaneous transmission and reception of the human voice. In 1876 the Scottish-born American inventor ALEXANDER GRAHAM BELL patented the first telephone. Bell believed his invention would be used to transmit musical concerts, lectures, and sermons. But after founding his own company, he quickly discovered that the appeal of the phone lay much more in allowing ordinary people to talk to each other. So, in 1878 the Bell Telephone Company established the first telephone exchange—a switchboard connecting any member of a group of subscribers to any other member. By 1894, roughly 260,000 Bell telephones were in use in the United States, about one for every 250 people. By the 1960s the telephone had become an essential service. Near the end of the twentieth century, the telephone was used to provide access to the Internet by means of devices called modems (modulator-demodulators). Advances in electronics have introduced a number of "smart" features in telephone manufacturing, such as automatic redialing, caller identification, call waiting, and call forwarding.

teleplay play written expressly for television audiences

teletext service providing television viewers with written text containing news stories, stock market listings, and other kinds of information

telethon lengthy television program produced to collect money for a charity or cause

teletype instrument that was used for much of the twentieth century to transmit and receive printed messages via telephone cables or radio relay systems. Today teletype has given way to e-mail and fax communications.

televangelism evangelism carried out primarily via television, featuring a charismatic preacher, a large audience, and emotional sermons, often accompanied by healing events

television [abbreviated as **TV**] broadcasting by means of electronically transmitted visual signals. In 1884 engineer PAUL NIPKOW built a scanning disc that created television images. In 1926 John Logie Baird, perfected Nipkow's device, and in 1931 Vladimir Zworykin built the prototype of the TV camera. The first home television set was put on display in Schenectady, New York, in 1928, by Ernst F.W. Alexanderson. By the late 1930s, television service had begun in several Western countries. The Radio Corporation of America (RCA) showcased television sets at the 1939 New York World's Fair. Right after World War II, network broadcasting started in the United States. Television programs opened up Web sites in the 1990s to complement their mode of delivering programming.

television culture view that since the 1950s, the history of television has become the history of Western society. TV has showcased racial protests, riots, and other significant social events, thus influencing social change. Some critics claim that without television, there would have been no civil rights legislation, no Vietnam War protests, and diminished or different public reactions to politics after Watergate. Moreover, many TV programs have been pivotal in bringing about a change in social mindset and mirroring changes in mores. For example, in 1977 the miniseries *Roots* was the first to deal forcefully with the enduring problem of racism; in 1968 *Star Trek* featured the first interracial kiss in an episode titled *Plato's Stepchildren*; in 1991 the first scene of women kissing each other was aired on an episode of *L.A. Law*. With the advent of satellite technologies, television has also become a source of influence across the globe.

test market smaller market that is thought to be representative of a larger one and on which an advertising strategy is tried out in order to determine its effectiveness, before introducing it to the larger market

test screening showing of a provisional version of a movie to assess an audience's reaction to it

testimonial technique advertising method that incorporates statements from famous people or satisfied customers, who endorse a product. Under U.S. government regulations, endorsers must use the advertised product if they claim they do so.

text anything constructed to express, represent, or communicate something—speeches, poems, television programs, scientific theories, musical compositions. Work on texts in recent years has produced a convenient typology. A *paratext*, for example, is defined as the physical and conventional characteristics associated with certain kinds of texts; paratextual features include such things as titles, headings, footnotes, dust jackets, and so on; an *architext* is the prototype from which other texts are derived (for example, the *Iliad* is the architext on which many stories are based); a *metatext* is a text that makes an explicit or implicit critical commentary on another text; a *hypotext* is a text based on another text that it alters in some way; a *hypertext* is a text within a main text that is linked to it in some way.

text message short written message sent from one mobile phone or device to another

text theory any theory aiming to explain how we create and interpret texts. The twentieth-century American philosopher SUSANNE LANGER claimed that there were two ways in which we read texts, *discursively*
and *presentationally*. Discursive texts have "detachment," which simply means that their constituent elements can be considered separately—for example, one can focus on a digit in a number or on a single word in a novel, detaching it from its location in the text, without impairing the overall understanding of the text. In contrast, the elements in presentational texts cannot be detached from them without impairing the overall meaning—for example, one cannot detach a note or phrase from a melody without destroying the sense of the melody. The relation between the structure of a text and its interpretation has become a primary area of research within media studies. Especially interesting is the "location" of a text's meaning. Does it lie in the intentions of the makers of texts? And, consequently, is successful interpretation of the text on the part of the reader a straightforward matter of trying to determine the maker's intentions? Or does the meaning of the text reside instead in the reader, regardless of the maker's intentions? Both the nature of the text itself and the author's intentions constrain the range of interpretations. When a given interpretation goes beyond this range, people tend to evaluate it as erroneous, extreme, far-fetched, or implausible.

textuality style and pattern of techniques used to create texts

theater 1. building or outdoor area for dramatic performances or other forms of entertainment; 2. dramatic or comedic literature performed by actors for an audience. Scholars trace the origin of theater to ancient ceremonial practices. In ancient Greece the first dramas revolved around myth and legend. The actors wore masks, a practice that also had a ritualistic source. Comedy was developed in ancient Greece alongside tragedy for criticizing and satirizing both individuals and society in general. After the fall of the Roman Empire in 476 C.E., the Christian church discouraged comedy for more than 500 years, promoting instead a liturgical form of theater based on biblical stories. By the fifteenth century, the latter had evolved into the *morality play*, performed by professional actors, which dealt with religious themes. Interest in comedic theater was revived by the movement known as the COMMEDIA DELL'ARTE. *Commedia* actors developed comic routines, called *iazzi*, which they could execute on demand, especially when it was felt that a sudden laugh was needed. For instance, a performer might pretend to trip and tumble into a pail of water during the exit sequence. Many of the routines and ideas of the *commedia* live on in contemporary forms such as vaudeville, burlesque, and even television sitcoms. By the mid-sixteenth century, a new, dynamic secular theater had developed. The most important concept in its design was *verisimilitude*—the appearance of truth. Characters were common individuals. The plays had a single plot, which took place within a 24-hour period, and occurred only in one locale. In the Romantic nineteenth century, theater took another turn, concentrating on a search for the spiritual nature of humankind. One of the best examples of Romantic drama is *Faust* (Part I, 1808; Part II, 1832), by the German playwright Johann Wolfgang von Goethe. Based on the classic legend of a man who sells his soul to the devil, the play depicts humankind's attempt to master knowledge and power. As plays attracted larger and larger audiences, playwrights became more and more involved in writing about everyday life, focusing on psychological realism and social problems. This new realistic trend in theater led to the notion of the *director* as the one who interprets the text, determines acting style, suggests scenery and costumes, and gives the production its overall quality—a tradition that continues on to this day. By the first decades of the twentieth century, a reaction against realism erupted in the world of theater. Paralleling contemporaneous radical visual art and musical movements, a movement known as *absurdist* theater emerged. The emphasis of this new form of theater was on the absurdity of the human condition. The subtext in all absurdist drama is that of humanity as lost in an unknown and unknowable world, where all human actions are senseless. Absurdism reached its peak in the 1950s, but continues to influence drama to this day.

theater testing in advertising, a method used to test viewer responses to an ad in a theater-like setting

third generation latest version of telecommunications devices or systems (such as mobile phones)

third person effect personal belief that one is not influenced by media messages, but that others are

thirty-threes [full form: **33 1/3 rpm record**, also called LP for **long playing record**] vinyl record popular in the 1950s through 1970s that allowed recorded sound to run for many more minutes than SEVENTY-EIGHTS

three-dimensional [abbreviated as **3-D**] any medium or text (such as a movie or a computer game) that creates the illusion of experiencing it in three-dimensional space

thriller genre of novel or movie designed to hold audience interest by the use of intrigue, adventure, and/or suspense

tie-in product that accompanies and helps publicize a major film release, such as, for example, a novel based on the movie script

time-lapse photography technique of shooting something so that, when projected, a slow action (such as the opening of a flower bud) can be shown in a sped-up fashion

Tin Pan Alley name given to West 28th Street between Broadway and Sixth Avenue in Manhattan where, from the 1880s to the 1950s, most popular music was composed, often by anonymous composers working for low wages. Tin Pan Alley songs were important elements in the sheet-music and popular-recording industries of the day, as well as in radio, vaudeville, and film. Tin Pan Alley is most closely associated with popular ballads, show tunes, and love songs. Notable Tin Pan Alley composers include Irving Berlin, Hoagy Carmichael, Dorothy Fields, Johnny Mercer, Cole Porter, Richard Rodgers, and Jerome Kern.

title 1. name given to a book, movie, or program, usually by its author; 2. heading, including credits, that appears at the beginning and/or end of a film or television program

title role main part or leading role in a film, play, or television program

title track song in a multi-song recording whose name is used as the title of the recording

TiVo digital box attached to a television set allowing viewers to control incoming broadcasts. The device automatically records broadcasts according to the viewer's preferences and also allows viewers to control programs in the same manner that they can control videotapes (pause, rewind).

Tomlinson, John (1949–) well-known critic of globalization and the evolution of media in new technological forms. Among his best-known works are *Media and Modernity*

(1995) and *Globalization and Culture* (1999).

tonality 1. organization of music around a TONE; 2. in painting, the relationship and effect of the colors and/or shades of light and dark

tone 1. in music, sound made by the vibration of a musical instrument or of the human voice; 2. in language, variation in the pitch of the voice while speaking, usually signaling a meaning difference; for example, in Mandarin Chinese the word *man* may mean either "trick" or "slow," depending on its pitch; 3. in painting, any variation in color or shades of light and dark

Top 10 the best 10 in any pop culture sector: "top 10 records," "top 10 singers," etc.

Top 40 radio format that plays the most popular single recordings—the top 40 on record sales charts. This was a dominant radio format from the 1950s to the 1970s, uniting musical tastes across audiences, promoting mainly ROCK AND ROLL. By the 1980s, audiences became highly fragmented, leading to a reduction in the importance of Top 40 radio in the promotion of recordings.

Toronto International Film Festival prestigious film festival, founded in 1976, held annually in Toronto in September. Many consider it to be second only to the CANNES FILM FESTIVAL in importance.

total audience package advertising strategy of scheduling advertisements across time segments on radio and television, so as to reach a wide range of listeners or viewers

totemism belief in an animal, plant, or natural object as the emblem of a clan or family, often revered as its founder, ancestor, or guardian

touch mode of communication with the hands. In most cultures, a basic form of greeting involves handshaking, which may have started as a way to show that neither person was holding a weapon. Other forms include patting someone on the arm, shoulder, or back to indicate agreement or to compliment; linking arms to indicate companionship; putting one's arm around the shoulder to indicate friendship or intimacy; holding hands with family members or a lover to express intimacy; hugging to convey happiness at seeing a friend or a family member; and so on.

touchscreen a computer screen that responds to touch so that it can be operated without a keyboard or mouse

town meeting on television, a program in which people from a region or walk of life debate a certain issue moderated by a host

track [*see* **soundtrack**]

tracking study type of research study that follows the same group of subjects over an extended period of time

trade advertising promotions that are directed at dealers and professionals through appropriate trade publications and media

trademark legally protected sign (name, design, picture, sound) that distinguishes the products of one company from those of another. Most trademarks appear on the product, on its container, or in advertisements for it.

traditional transmission passing on information by means of language from one generation to another

traffic in NETLINGO, number of visitors to a Web site

tragedy [*see* **theater**] traditional THEATER genre, dating to ancient Greece, typically with an unhappy or disastrous ending brought on by fate or a flaw in the main character

tragicomedy genre combining elements of tragedy and comedy. The third-century B.C.E. Roman playwright Plautus coined the word to denote a play in which gods and mortals or masters and slaves reversed their traditional roles. Today, the term suggests a text in which laughter is seen as the only response left to characters faced with an empty or problematic life.

trailer [also called **preview**] brief film showing snatches from an upcoming motion picture so as to entice people to see the movie

transaction journalism in cyberadvertising, the direct linkage of editorial content to sales

transactional analysis study of the motives behind the discourse used during interpersonal communication

transborder data flow transmission of information across national borders so that it can be received, stored, or used outside the originating jurisdiction

transcription recording of a broadcast or other event to be shown or reviewed at a later time

transformational appeal advertising technique designed to link the product to meaningful emotional experiences (love, understanding, etc.)

transgressivity in FEMINIST THEORY, defiance of social norms. This notion has been used to explain the power of such forms of representation as PORNOGRAPHY and cross-dressing.

transient advertisement promotion that is placed in specific locales, such as in movie theaters before the feature is shown

transistor small device that can amplify, control, and generate electrical signals, invented by Bell Labs in 1947, displacing the vacuum tube. Single transistors were superseded in the 1960s by integrated circuits. Today, transistors have different functions in every type of electronic equipment.

transmission sending messages to a receiver

Transmission Control Protocol/ Internet Protocol [abbreviated as TCP/IP] set of rules that define how computers on the Internet (and on other computer networks) transmit and exchange information

transmissional perspective view that media transmit information for the purpose of controlling cultural and social trends

transparency realistic mode of constructing media representations, making their construction undetectable to readers or viewers

trial by media term used figuratively in reference to the belief that media coverage often provides and/or influences judgments about a public figure by creating a widespread perception of guilt regardless of any verdict in an actual trial.

tribalism 1. early form of human group life marked by individual allegiance to and identification with a tribe; 2. in the contemporary era, loyalty shown by individuals to specific groups (*teen tribalism, gang tribalism*)

trope figure of speech. Since the 1980s the term METAPHOR has been used increasingly in place of trope.

tune 1. a melody; 2. a catchy popular song

tunesmith composer of popular songs

turnover number of times something is sold during a particular period

turntable [also called **record player** or **phonograph**] instrument that rotates a phonograph record; a stylus is placed on the record and sound is reproduced through loudspeakers. Turntables were largely replaced by cassette tape recorders and compact disc systems in the 1980s.

TV [*see* **television**]

TV newsmagazine television news program format, pioneered by CBS's *60 Minutes* in the 1960s, that features interviews and investigative reporting, with a general focus on controversial issues

Twentieth Century Fox major Hollywood film studio founded in 1935, known especially for its blockbuster films, including the *Star Wars* anthology of films. Web site: www.foxmovies.com

two-step flow theory model of the mass media claiming that media products are shaped and modified by interactions with social groups, especially opinion leaders. The theory asserts that media impacts are indirect and are mediated by opinion leaders and thus that audiences tend to view media products as interpretive communities. The name of the theory derives from the fact that its primary proponents, PAUL LAZARSFELD and

ELIHU KATZ, viewed the reception of a mass media message as a two-step flow, in contrast to the HYPODERMIC NEEDLE theory, which saw it as a one-step flow that reaches an audience directly. In two-step flow theory, the first step is through an opinion leader(s) of a group, who takes in media content, interprets it, and then passes it on to group members, who have less frequent contact with the media.

typification schemes in cultural theory, meanings that people assign typically to certain texts, which, in turn, are incorporated by media and advertising to bring about a PRE-FERRED READING

typography art, practice, or process of printing with type. Typography originated after the invention of movable type in the mid-fifteenth century.

UHF [*see* **ultrahigh frequency**]

ultrahigh frequency [abbreviated as **UHF**] type of short radio wave widely used in television broadcasting. UHF waves also are used in aircraft and ship navigation, in emergency communications systems, and cellular telephone networks.

umbrella advertising promotion of an organization rather than of a single product

unbalanced flow the unequal flow of news reportage between countries

uncensored any publication, movie, or program that has been released or broadcast without prior censorship

unconscious [*see* **subconscious**]

uncut [*see* **uncensored**]

underground a movement or group that has separated itself from the prevailing social environment, often exerting a subversive or transgressive influence on that environment

underground press any publishing organization that is anti-establishment and thus likely to attract controversy and/or censorship. The term surfaced in the 1960s.

uniform resource locator [abbreviated as **URL**] Internet address of a resource or service. The address

contains three elements: the type of protocol used to access the file (for example, HTTP for a Web page), the domain name of the server where the file resides, and, optionally, the pathname to the file (description of the file's location). For example, the URL www .utoronto.ca/libraries instructs the browser to use the HTTP protocol, go to the www.utoronto.ca Web server, and access the file named libraries.

United Press International [abbreviated as **UPI**] international news agency founded in 1907, providing news in English, Spanish, and Arabic. Web site: www.upi.com

Universal Copyright Convention agreement among the member states of UNESCO, first adopted in 1952, revised in 1971, "to provide for the adequate and effective protection of the rights of authors and other copyright proprietors in literary, scientific and artistic works, including writings, musical, dramatic and cinematographic works, and paintings, engravings and sculpture." Web site: www.unesco.org/culture/laws/ copyright

Universal Pictures major Hollywood film studio, founded in 1912, producing blockbuster movies such as *Spartacus* (1960) and *E.T.* (1982)

unmetered Internet service that is available at a flat rate, rather than by connection time

UPI [*see* **United Press International**]

uploading [opposite of **downloading**] copying files from a computer to another on the Internet

urban legend story often thought to be factual by those who circulate it, generally through the Internet, but which turns out to be not exactly as recounted. It may be entirely untrue or, in some cases, partly true. Often, the events it describes may be explained in different ways. A story may be started by someone in a chatroom, through e-mails, based on events that the originator had actually witnessed. When it starts to circulate and is retold by different people, the story gathers momentum and a logic of its own, becoming an urban legend.

urban music pop music genres that appeal to an urban audience, including rhythm and blues and hip-hop. Urban is one of radio's more popular formats.

URL [*see* **uniform resource locator**]

Ur-text original text that becomes a template for subsequent texts

usage-based segmentation in advertising, classification of consumers according to how much they consume a certain product

Usenet [abbreviation of **Users Network**; also called **network news**] internationally distributed BULLETIN BOARD system on the Internet. Usenet predates the World Wide Web, constituting the original discussion forum covering thousands of topics.

uses and gratifications theory view, associated primarily with ELIHU KATZ in the 1970s, that audiences use the mass media for their own purposes, especially to fulfill needs such as gaining information or being entertained. According to this theory, the audience views the media in a self-confirmatory way. Thus, certain items in a representation are selected either because they provide entertainment or because they satisfy some need. The theory maintains that media do not do things to people but rather that people do things with media.

utterance word or words (written or spoken) used in a specific social communicative situation

validity effect theory that people tend to accept an idea, statement, or opinion as valid or true if it is repeated enough times in the media

VALS [*see* **values and lifestyles research**]

value 1. as defined by FERDINAND DE SAUSSURE, what something means in practical terms; for example, the value of a letter such as A assigned to an essay in university is perceived as different from that of a B; 2. in cultural theory, any assumption that something is important and crucial; 3. in the visual arts, the degree of lightness or darkness of a hue or shade

values and lifestyles research [abbreviated as **VALS**] advertising research method based on grouping consumers according to their values and lifestyles. VALS measures psychological factors, such as how consumers feel about products and how they represent lifestyle aspirations.

Van Dijk, Jan [*see* **Dijk, Jan A.G.M. van**]

vanity press a publisher that prints books for authors who pay all or most of the costs of publication and distribution

variety show live or televised show made up of various kinds of performances: musical, comedic, acrobatic, magical

vaudeville principal form of popular entertainment in North America before the advent of cinema in the late nineteenth and early twentieth centuries. Vaudeville was also called burlesque, variety, or music hall. It consisted of a series of unrelated acts (singer, juggler, magician, dancer, dog act) presented in a theater (the vaudeville house or venue) to a paying audience. With the advent of film, radio, and television, vaudeville effectively died as a form of entertainment, although its main features were incorporated into the Hollywood musical and the radio or television variety show.

V-chip electronic chip in a television set that allows parents to block out programming with sexual and violent content. It is often assumed that the V stands for "violence," when in fact it stands for "viewer choice."

VCR [*see* **video cassette recorder**]

vehicle specific channel or publication for carrying an advertising message to a target audience. For example, in the medium of magazines, a vehicle would be *Time* magazine.

Venice Film Festival annual film festival, founded in 1932, held in Venice every year in late August–early September; one of three major European film festivals (the other two are the Cannes and Berlin festivals). Web site: www.labiennale.org/en/cinema

verbal communication exchange of information by means of language. Among the various models of verbal communication, the model devised by the linguist and semiotician RO- MAN JAKOBSON is one of the most widely used in media and communication studies. Jakobson posited six constituents undergirding all instances of verbal communication: an *addresser* who initiates a communication; a *message* that she or he recognizes must refer to something other than itself; an *addressee* who is the intended receiver of the message; a *context* that permits the addressee to recognize that the message is referring to something other than itself; a mode of *contact* by which a message is delivered (the physical channel) and the primary social and psychological connections that exist or are established between the addresser and addressee; and a *code* providing the signs and structural patterns for constructing and deciphering messages. Jakobson then pointed out that each of these constituents determines a different communicative function: *emotive* is the influence of the addresser's emotions, attitudes, and social status in the making of the message; *conative* is the effect— physical, psychological, social—that the message has or is expected to have on the addressee; *referential* is a message constructed to convey information unambiguously; *poetic* is a message constructed to deliver meanings effectively, like poetry; *phatic* is a message designed to establish social contact; *metalingual* is a message designed to refer to the code being used.

vernacular everyday form of language, in contrast to official, religious, or bureaucratic forms

vertical integration acquisition of the different sectors involved in the production of media; for example, vertical integration occurs when a single newspaper company acquires the printing company that produces its newspapers or the agency that distributes them

very high frequency [abbreviated as **VHF**] electromagnetic waves that the Federal Communications Commission has assigned to television and frequency modulation (FM) radio stations and to amateur radio operators

VHF [*see* **very high frequency**]

VHS most common type of videotape used in home video recorders, being replaced by DVD and other advanced technologies

vicarious reinforcement in cultural theory, the view that the observation of something in the media operates as if it were actual reinforcement. This framework is used to explain why an individual does not expect actual rewards or punishments from observing something, but anticipates them to happen.

video 1. general term for anything recorded on a visual device (a videotape, a DVD); 2. a videotape, DVD, or other image-carrying device

video blog BLOG that uses video material as its primary means of communication

video cassette flat rectangular plastic box that contains videotape

video cassette recorder [abbreviated as **VCR**] device that records and plays images and sound back on a TV set. The first commercial VCRs were marketed by Sony Corporation in 1969. The first commercially successful VCR for home use was the Sony Betamax, launched in 1975. It was joined in the marketplace by the incompatible VHS format, launched by JVC in 1976, which grew to dominate the market. The heyday of the VCR was the 1980s. Its market share has dwindled in the face of competition from digital recorders and the DVD player.

video clip short video sequence, generally created to promote something such as a new song

video conference conference in which participants are located in different places but are linked by audio and video technology

video feed recorded video sent from one location to another

video frequency frequency used to carry television broadcast signals

video game [also called **electronic game**] game played by an electronic device and displayed on a television screen or other monitor. Most video games are controlled by a tiny computer. Video games deal with a range of subjects, such as war, space, adventure, horror, mystery, sports, playing cards, backgammon, chess, and so on. Some are educational, helping players learn to spell or count. Overall, video games are now seen to constitute texts within the larger pop culture environment.

video insert prerecorded film footage played at an appropriate point in a TV show

video jockey person who plays videos, especially music videos, on television

video nasty a video containing explicitly violent or pornographic material

video news release [abbreviated as **VNR**] video segments released to accompany a news story

video on demand [abbreviated as **VOD**] PAY-PER-VIEW cable service, allowing viewers to instantly order programming to be delivered digitally to their television sets

video vérité use of video to create documentaries of people and events

videodisc general term for a disc that contains both video and audio. It can be played on a machine attached to a conventional television receiver. The most common type of videodisc today is the DVD.

videography making of movies or television programs with video cameras

videophile someone who enjoys watching video texts and making video recordings

videophone device that can transmit and receive audio and video, composed of a camera, receiver, and screen

videotape magnetic tape on which audio and video can be recorded and played back

videotext [also written as **videotex**] obsolete type of delivery of textual information via telephone networks. Videotext was used mainly by libraries to offer various services in homes.

viewer person who watches television

viewfinder 1. device on a camera showing the area that will be included in the photograph; 2. miniature television screen with a magnifying lens mounted on a video camera, which allows the user to select a scene to record by viewing it through the eyepiece on the lens

viewing act of watching television and the psychological processes this entails

viewscreen screen on a digital camera showing the image that has just been recorded

vignette 1. brief scene from a movie; 2. in the visual arts, a drawing without a border that gradually fades at the edges

villain [opposite of **hero**] in a narrative, a character who represents the "bad" person whom the hero has to defeat

viral advertising promotion that attempts to capture consumers' attention by encouraging them to "pass it on" (like a virus) to others

viral marketing technique whereby communicative networks are used to spread messages, such as affiliate programs, co-branding, e-mails, word-of-mouth techniques, and so on

virtual community group of people who interact on the Internet, for example in chatrooms, because they share interests or business

virtual reality [abbreviated as **VR**] technology that lets people engage in three-dimensional (3-D) environments created by computers. VR devices enable users to manipulate virtual objects as if they were real. The user wears a head-mounted display (HMD) with screens for each eye.

virus computer program designed to copy itself into other programs, with the intention of altering or damaging them. The corrupted programs may continue to operate according to their intended functions while also executing the virus's instructions, thus further propagating it. The virus may transfer itself to other computers through storage devices, computer networks, and online systems. Antivirus software is used to detect and remove viruses from a computer, but it must be updated frequently for protection against new viruses.

visual culture culture that gets a large part of its information through visual electronic media such as television and the Internet

vlog BLOG that incorporates a large amount of visual material

VNR [*see* **video news release**]

VOA [*see* **Voice of America**]

vocable word constructed with no apparent meaning: for example, *krunt, jint*

VOD [*see* **video on demand**]

voice 1. sound made by human vocal cords; 2. characterization of the right to express oneself as an individual or as part of a group: for example, women's voices, the voices of African Americans, etc.

Voice of America [abbreviated as **VOA**] U.S. government-funded broadcasting system, launched in 1942, that provides radio, television, and Internet services, especially news, in over 40 languages. Web site: www.voanews.com

voicemail oral message left on a phone's answering machine or recording system

voiceover technique of using the voice of an unseen speaker in films

Voice-over-Internet-Protocol [abbreviated as **VoIP**] technology that allows voice messages to be sent via the Internet

voice-pitch analysis advertising technique in which a subject's voice is analyzed during his or her responses, in order to assess the subject's emotional reaction to an ad

VoIP [*see* **Voice-over-Internet-Protocol**]

volumetrics study of the influence of the relation between the overall number of people exposed to an advertising campaign and the number of those who buy the product

vortal Web portal that enables e-commerce transactions among various businesses

vox pop the replies given to a reporter's questions by people on the street

voyeurism obtaining gratification from secretly viewing sexual acts. As a cinematic technique, it has been used effectively in movies such as *Eyes Wide Shut* (1999).

VR [*see* **virtual reality**]

W3 [*see* **World Wide Web**]

W3C consortium of experts in various areas seeking to guide the development of the World Wide Web

walk-on actor who has a small part in a play, movie, or program

walkie-talkie two-way radio enabling voice communication over short distances. Unlike many other two-way communication devices, a walkie-talkie cannot transmit and receive signals at the same time.

walled garden in NETLINGO, a controlled-access area that attempts to keep users within its confines; for example, AOL is a walled garden in that it attempts to provide users with everything they may need within its own services

WAN [*see* **wide area network**]

want ad classified advertisement in a newspaper, magazine, or Web site requesting or offering something for acquisition

WAP [*see* **Wireless Application Protocol**]

war film cinematic genre dealing with war, usually featuring a military hero; for example, the series of *Rambo* movies

War of the Worlds radio broadcast 1938 radio adaptation of H.G. Wells's novel about interplanetary invasion, delivered in the style of an actual news broadcast, causing many to believe that the reports were real

Warhol, Andy (1928–1987) American pop artist who is considered one of the initiators of the postmodern era in the visual arts. Many of his works depict commonplace objects, such as soup cans, and include photographs of celebrities. In 1994 the Andy Warhol Museum was established in Pittsburgh.

Warner Brothers major Hollywood film studio, founded in 1918, responsible for producing such highly popular features as the Looney Tunes cartoon series and the Superman and Harry Potter films

watchdog individual or organization on the lookout for unacceptable or offensive practices by the media

weather forecast radio or television broadcast of weather conditions

web [*see* **World Wide Web**]

Web browser computer program allowing users to gain access to pages on the World Wide Web

Web hosting business providing server space for storage on a Web site

Web marketing online marketing

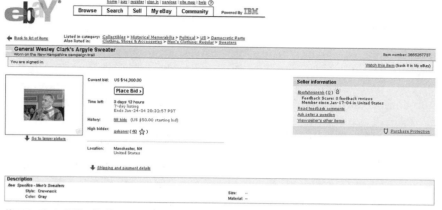

Typical Web page

Web page a computer file displayed as a "page" on a computer screen, accessible through the World Wide Web by means of a WEB BROWSER. Web pages are multimedial, containing some or all of text, graphics, files, sound, video, and hyperlinks. The first Web page, created by TIM BERNERS-LEE, went online in 1991.

Web phone service allows users to make phone calls over the Internet with other software users

Web portal WEB PAGE on a particular topic that provides links to other Web pages

Web radio radio programming delivered to homes equipped with a special receiver via the Internet

Web site [also written as **website**] interconnected set of WEB PAGES

Web TV [full form: **web television**] high-definition television programming delivered to homes via the Internet

Webby annual international award made by the International Academy of Digital Arts for an outstanding Web site

webcam digital camera connected to the Internet, capable of transmitting images live

webcast 1. video filmed with a webcam that can be viewed on the Internet or downloaded from the Internet; 2. any broadcast on the World Wide Web

webcrawler computer program that allows users to search through Web pages for documents containing a specific word, phrase, or sequence of symbols

web-enabled any mobile phone or handheld device capable of accessing the World Wide Web

webform electronic document similar to a printed form that is used to collect information from a visitor to a Web site

webhead frequent visitor of the World Wide Web

webisode episode, trailer, television program, or music video on a Web site

weblish form of English used online, characterized by abbreviated words, lack of appropriate punctuation, and various ungrammatical forms

weblog [*see* **blog**]

webmaster person responsible for creating, organizing, and updating a Web site

webzine [full form: **web magazine**] magazine that publishes on the World Wide Web

Wedom and Theydom characterization of the tendency of some media of representing the world in terms of "us" and "them" in order to make a news report more forceful and attention-grabbing

weekly newspaper or magazine published once a week

Western literary and cinematic genre set in the American West, during 1850–1900, involving cowboys, featuring lawlessness and gun violence. Owen Wister's *The Virginian* (1902) is regarded as the founding novel of the genre, whose popularity peaked in the middle decades of the twentieth century, declining thereafter. Movie versions of the Western played an important role in establishing a plot formula—the conflict between outlaws and the defenders of law and order. One of the first important movies, *The Great Train Robbery* (1903), was a Western. From the 1920s through the 1950s, hundreds of Westerns made celebrities of cowboy actors Gene Autry, Tom Mix, Roy Rogers, Gary Cooper, and John Wayne. In the 1990s some films portrayed cowboys in less heroic terms, as in Clint Eastwood's *Unforgiven* (1992); the film *Dances with Wolves* (1990) revisited the role of Native Americans (called "Indians" in previous Westerns) in the history of the West, restoring dignity to that role. Network television contributed to the popularity of Westerns in the 1950s and 1960s with long-running series such as *Gunsmoke* (1955–1975), *Maverick* (1957–1962), *Have Gun Will Travel* (1957–1963), *Wagon Train* (1957–1965), and *Bonanza* (1959–1973).

Western culture general designation of the cultures originating with people of European origin. The term is often used in opposition to ORIENTALISM, often understood as "any culture" other than the Western one on an "east-west" geographic plane. It is opposed to "southern cultures" on a "north-south" geographic plane. These are, however, artificial dichotomies, since they assume homogeneity in culture and inevitable opposition among cultures.

Westerstähl and Johansson's model of news factors model devised by Jorgen Westerstähl and Folke Johansson in 1994, which claims that proximity to the ideological mindset of the country reporting a news item and the perceived importance of that country in an international context are keys to how it is perceived in other countries

whistleblower person who divulges information to the media about a secret event, a scandal, or an issue that is of interest to the public

white noise radio noise spread over a wide range of frequencies

Whorf, Benjamin Lee (1897–1941) American linguist who kindled widespread interest in the view that language affects worldview

wide area network [abbreviated as WAN] computer network covering a broad geographical region or area, the largest being the Internet

widescreen 1. type of movie projection whereby the picture shown is wider than it is tall; 2. a television set whose screen is larger than traditional screens

Wiener, Norbert (1894–1964) mathematician who pioneered cybernetics. His ideas contributed to the building of modern-day computers.

Wi-Fi [*see* **wireless fidelity**]

wiki name given to a WEB SITE that allows the visitors themselves to edit and change its content, sometimes without the need for registration. The first software to be called a wiki was WikiWikiWeb, so named by its maker Ward Cunningham, a computer programmer who took it from the name of a Hawaiian airport shuttle.

Wikipedia the most popular of the Internet WIKIS, Wikipedia is a multilingual online free encyclopedia launched on March 1, 2002. The name is a blend of the words *wiki* and *encyclopedia.* It is written collaboratively by volunteers. Most of its articles can be edited by almost anyone with access to the Web site, and for this reason there is controversy over Wikipedia's accuracy, being perceived as susceptible to vandalism and trendiness. Web site: www .wikipedia,org

Williams, Raymond (1921–1988) British media critic who drew attention to the various forms of culture involved in a mediated society. He distinguished between residual, dominant and emerging cultural forms: residual forms are those that have historical significance and thus are still around; dominant forms are those that have current salience; and emerging forms are those that are fomenting and that will soon become dominant.

WIPO [*see* **World Intellectual Property Organization**]

wire service news story sent by computer from a national or international news agency

Wireless Application Protocol [abbreviated as **WAP**] protocol for transmitting data between mobile phones and other such devices

wireless fidelity [abbreviated as **Wi-Fi**] marketing term for wireless networking technologies based on the Institute of Electrical and Electronics Engineers (IEEE) 802.11b and 802.11a specifications. Wi-Fi networks are used to wirelessly connect computers to each other, or to connect computers to the Internet or other networks, including Ethernet networks.

wireless Internet capacity to access the Internet without having to connect to a phone line

wireless local area network [abbreviated as **WLAN**] local area network that allows laptops with appropriate technology to connect with other computers without the need for cables

WLAN [*see* **wireless local area network**]

women's liberation movement social movement seeking equal rights for women, dating back to the ENLIGHTENMENT. The first important expression of the movement was Mary Wollstonecraft's *A Vindication of the Rights of Woman* (1792). American women gained the right to vote in 1919, but their participation in the larger social system outside the home remained limited. Landmarks in the rise of modern feminism include Simone de Beauvoir's *The Second Sex* (1949), Betty Friedan's *The Feminine Mystique* (1963), and the founding of the National Organization for Women (1966). Efforts in the 1970s to pass the Equal Rights Amendment failed, but its aims had been largely achieved by other means by the end of the twentieth century.

word magic belief that words evoke magical events or can cause things to happen by simply uttering them. Word magic is a common theme in literature. A well-known example is the "Open Sesame" phrase used by Ali Baba in the *Arabian Nights* to open the door of a cave. Another is *abracadabra*, which is made from the letters in an inverted pyramid design of an amulet that was popular several centuries ago. Each letter was supposed to vanish until only the A remained. As the letters disappeared, so did the problems of its wearer.

word painting technique used in the radio broadcast industry that uses highly descriptive words during dramatizations to evoke images in reading material as an attempt to place the listener into the scene

World Intellectual Property Organization [abbreviated as **WIPO**] specialized agency of the United Nations, established in 1970, which administers and develops policy on intellectual property. Web site: www .wipo.org.

World Wide Web [abbreviated as **W3** or **WWW**] system of computer files linked together on the Internet, created in 1989 by TIM BERNERS-LEE and his colleagues at CERN (Conseil Européen pour la Recherche Nucléaire), a nuclear physics laboratory near Geneva in Switzerland. The Web provides access to a vast array of documents that are connected to each other by means of HYPERTEXT or HYPERLINKS. Users may access any page by typing in the appropriate address on a search engine.

worm in Internet parlance, self-replicating computer program capable of sending copies of itself without any user intervention. Unlike a VIRUS, it does not need to attach itself to an existing program. Worms harm the network, whereas viruses corrupt files on a targeted computer. The name derives from a science fiction novel, *The Shockwave Rider* (1975), by John Brunner. John F. Shoch and John A. Hupp used the term in a technical paper they published in 1982.

writing 1. speech executed on some surface with symbols and signs; 2. literature in general.

WWW [*see* **World Wide Web**]

xerography copy-making process that is the basis of the most widely used document-copying machines, or photocopiers. Xerography was invented in the 1930s by American physicist Chester F. Carlson and was developed in the 1940s and 1950s by the Haloid Corporation, later renamed Xerox. The first commercially successful xerographic copier was introduced in 1959.

XM satellite radio founded in 1992 as American Mobile Radio Corpo-ration, a satellite service in the United States and Canada providing pay-for-service radio programming, with music, news, sports, talk, entertainment, and weather channels. Most of the channels are available via the Internet. XM also offers music downloads. Web site: www.xmradio.com

X-rated previous movie classification, replaced by NC-17, indicating that a film should not be viewed by anyone under the age of 17 because of its adult content

Yahoo! American Internet service providing a full range of Web services, founded by Jerry Yang and David Filo in 1994. It was originally called "Jerry's Guide to the World Wide Web," but was renamed "Yahoo!" The term was derived from Jonathan Swift's *Gulliver's Travels*, where it was defined as someone "rude, unsophisticated, uncouth." Web site: www .yahoo.com

yellow journalism use of lurid and sensationalized reporting to attract readers and increase circulation. The term was coined in the 1890s to describe the rivalry between two New York papers, the *World* and the *Journal*. Some of the techniques used by the two newspapers have actually become permanent features of journalistic presentation, including banner headlines, colored comics, and numerous illustrations.

youth culture various forms of music, clothing, language, and general lifestyle that are adopted by young people. These forms have become powerful forces in modern-day urban society where a dividing line between youth and adult forms of culture are no longer clear-cut. Indeed, trends in the adolescent world quickly become the cultural norm, dictating look, taste in music, and fashion for many. Before the 1950s, there were few media outlets aiming their products (movies, radio programs) at young audiences. By the mid-1950s, however, the courtship of such audiences by the media and various entertainment industries (especially the music and movie ones) began in earnest. Songs and movies became progressively juvenilized in content. By the 1960s, youth culture came to constitute a true community in the ethnographic sense, a self-contained system within the larger societal framework.

zapping 1. flicking between television channels with a remote control; 2. in postmodern theory, the view that by offering so much programming today, television has led to zero consciousness, the art of watching nothing

zeugma figure of speech in which a single word, especially a verb or an adjective, is applied to two or more nouns, even though its sense is actually appropriate to only one of them, or to both in different ways: for example, *The room was not light, but his fingers were*

zine [abbreviation of **magazine**] self-published magazine, especially on the Internet, released at irregular intervals and, generally, with characteristic content

Zipf's Law [also called **Principle of Least Effort**] principle defined in the 1930s by the Harvard linguist George Kingsley Zipf, who found that many phenomena in language could be explained as the result of an inborn tendency in the human species to make the most of its communicative resources with the least expenditure of effort (physical, cognitive, and social). This tendency was independent of individual and culture. It explains, Zipf claimed, why speakers minimize articulatory effort by shortening the length of words and utterances. At the same time, people want to be able to interpret the meaning of words and utterances unambiguously and with least effort. Zipf demonstrated that there exists an intrinsic interdependence between the length of a specific word (in number of sounds or letters) and its rank order in the language (its position in order of its frequency of occurrence in texts of all kinds). The higher the rank order of a word (the more frequent it is in actual usage), the more it tends to be "shorter" (made up with fewer phonemes). For example, articles *(a, the)*, conjunctions *(and, or)*, and other function words *(to, it)*, which have a high rank order in English (and in any other language for that matter), are typically monosyllabic, consisting of one to three phonemes. What is even more intriguing is that this "miniaturization" force does not stop at the level of function words, as Zipf and others subsequently found. It can be seen to manifest itself, above all else, in the tendency for phrases that come into popular use to become abbreviated *(FYO, UNESCO, Hi, Bye, ad, photo, Mr., Mrs., Dr., 24/7, etc.)* or changed into acronyms *(aka, VCR, DNA, laser, GNP, IQ, VIP, etc.).* It can also be seen in the creation of tables, technical and scientific notation systems, indexes, footnotes, bibliographic traditions, and so on and so forth. In effect, the general version of Zipf's Law proclaims that the more frequent or necessary a form for communicative purposes, the more likely it is to be rendered "compressed" or "economical" in physical structure. And the reason for this seems to be an inherent tendency in the human species to expend the least effort possible in representation and communication.

zone culturally specific space that people keep between themselves when interacting

zombie in Internet parlance, any WORM transmitted from one infected computer to another. Networks of such computers are often referred to as *botnets* and are very commonly used by spammers for sending junk e-mail or to cloak their Web site's address. A botnet's originator can control zombie programs remotely. These have become a significant part of the Internet.

zooming filmic technique of making something appear larger or closer to the camera than it is

zoosemiotics study of communication in animals

Zworykin, Vladimir (1889–1982) Russian-born American electronic engineer who invented the iconoscope (a TV transmission tube) in 1923 and the kinescope (a TV receiver) in 1924, which together constituted the first true TV system

CHRONOLOGY

The following timelines include selected events that indicate only some of the major "signposts" in the development of the major media.

BOOKS AND MAGAZINES

2400 B.C.E.	Papyrus made from plant reeds found along the Nile River is used for writing.
350 C.E.	The codex is produced by the Romans with parchment pages bound together.
600	Illuminated manuscripts featuring decorative designs on each page are created by scribes (primarily monks and nuns).
700	Arab traders introduce paper to the West.
1000	Movable clay typesetting invented in China.
1234	Movable metal typesetting invented in Korea.
1453	Johannes Gutenberg turns a wine press into a printing press that uses movable type for the mass production of books.
1455	The Gutenberg Bible is one of the first books published with the new print technology.
1602	The first lending library, the Bodlian is established.
1640	The first book published in the American colonies, *The Bay Psalm Book*, is printed in Boston.
1731	One of the first magazines, *The Gentleman's Magazine*, is published in England.
1732	*Poor Richard's Almanack* by Benjamin Franklin is published.
1741	Colonial magazines appear in Boston and Philadelphia.
1751	The first encyclopedia is produced by French scholars.

1790	First U.S. copyright law passed. Publishing houses start proliferating.
1821	The *Saturday Evening Post* is launched, becoming the first magazine to appeal directly to women.
1830	Sarah Josepha Hales becomes the first editor of *Godey's Lady's Book*, creating the first modern women's magazine.
1846	The rotary press is invented in the United States. *Harper's Weekly* begins publication.
1860s	The dime novel (pulp fiction) becomes a mass culture device.
1879	The Postal Act of 1879 lowers the postal rate for magazines, allowing magazine distribution to thrive.
1880s	Linotype and offset lithography lower the cost of book production.
1900	Magazine muckraking reporting becomes highly popular.
1909	The Copyright Act of 1909 is passed.
1922	*Reader's Digest* is launched.
1923	*Time* magazine, founded by Henry Luce, starts publication.
1936	*Life* magazine starts publication.
1939	Robert de Graaf introduces Pocket Books, America's first paperbacks.
1953	*TV Guide* is launched, indicating that various media were starting to converge.
1954	*Sports Illustrated* begins publication.
1960s	Computer-based composition (typesetting) begins.
1967	Rock and roll gets its own magazine with the launching of *Rolling Stone*.
1969	The *Saturday Evening Post* succumbs to specialized competition.
1971	Borders opens its first store in Ann Arbor. Chain bookstores and superstores start springing up across America shortly thereafter.
1974	*People* magazine starts publication.
1980s	Desktop publishing gets under way.
1995	Amazon.com is established, but it will only turn its first profit in 2002.
1998	The Digital Millennium Copyright Term Extension Act is passed.
2000s	Microsoft and Adobe start making online books (e-books) available. E-zines, e-toons, and other magazine genres also start proliferating in online versions.

NEWSPAPERS

| 1600s | Corantos, the first newssheets, are published in northern Europe. |
| 1640s | Diurnals, the first daily newspapers, are published in England. |

1644	English poet John Milton calls for freedom of speech in his pamphlet titled *Areopagitica*.
1690	Boston printer Benjamin Harris publishes the first American newspaper, *Publick Occurrences, Both Foreign and Domestick*.
1721	The *New England Courant* begins publication.
1735	Freedom of the press is defended as a legitimate mode of expression after a jury rules in favor printer Peter John Zenger, who had criticized the government in print and who had been charged with libel.
1776	American Declaration of Independence disseminated throughout the nation by newspapers.
1783	The first daily, the *Pennsylvania Evening Post and Daily Advertiser*, published in America.
1789	Freedom of the press is enshrined in the American Constitution by enactment of the First Amendment.
1790	The Copyright Act is passed.
1798–1800	The Alien and Sedition Acts attempt to curtail press criticism of the government.
1827	The first African American newspaper, *Freedom's Journal*, makes its appearance.
1828	The first Native American newspaper, *The Cherokee*, makes its debut.
1833	The penny press era is ushered in after the *New York Sun* is published, costing only one cent and thus starting the trend of making newspapers affordable.
1848	Six newspapers form the Associated Press, relaying news stories around the country via telegraphy.
1860	*New York Morning* reaches a circulation of 80,000, highlighting the fact that newspapers have become an integral part of mass communications.
1878	Joseph Pulitzer starts the new journalism movement. The movement had great appeal with afternoon editions, and featuring entertainment, crime and scandal, and devoted more space to advertising and illustrations.
1883	Pulitzer buys the *New York World*, ushering in the era of yellow journalism.
1895	William Randolph Hearst enters newspaper publishing with sensationalistic techniques, further promoting yellow journalism.
1896	Adolph Ochs buys the *New York Times*, making achievement of the goals of responsible journalism its primary objective.
1914	First Spanish-language paper in the United States, *El Diario–La Prensa*, is founded in New York.

1917	The Pulitzer Prize is established at Columbia University, rewarding achievement in journalism and other areas.
1920s	Newspaper chains spring up, marking a decline in the number of daily metropolitan newspapers.
1930–1934	Hundreds of syndicated columns start up between 1930 and 1934.
1955	The *Village Voice* is launched as the first underground newspaper in Greenwich Village.
1972	Watergate scandal stimulates a new era of investigative journalism.
1980	Ohio's *Columbus Dispatch* is the first newspaper to go online.
1982	*USA Today* is launched, the first paper modeled after television.
1998	The *Dallas Morning News* is the first newspaper to break a major story on its Web site instead of its front page. Increasing use of the Internet leads to the development of blogs, discussion groups, and the like, which take on many functions of traditional newspapers.
2000s	By 2003, thousands of newspapers offer some kind of online news service.

ADVERTISING

1625	The first true ad appears in an English newspaper.
1735	Benjamin Franklin sells ad space in the *Pennsylvania Gazette*.
1792	The first propaganda ministry is established in France.
1804	The first classified ads in Colonial America run in the *Boston News-Letter*, featuring land deals and ship cargoes.
1830s	The penny press becomes the first advertising-supported media outlet.
1841	The first ad agency is established in Boston by Volney Palmer to represent newspaper publishers.
1860s	Advertising is incorporated into magazines.
1869	The first true modern ad agency working for advertisers and companies is established by N.W. Ayer in Philadelphia.
1871	P.T. Barnum establishes his Greatest Show on earth, creating a wave of publicity stunts, posters, etc., which bring the advertising age into being.
1880s	Brands (products with names) appear.
1887	*Ladies Home Journal* is designed to be a medium for consumer advertising.
1914	The Federal Trade Commission is established to help monitor advertising practices.

1920s   Newspapers and magazines start depending heavily on advertising revenues for their survival.

1922   Newspaper columnist Walter Lippmann publishes a controversial book, *Public Opinion*, in which he illustrates how slogans and other such devices shape public perception. The first radio commercial is aired.

1942   The systematic study of propaganda and advertising effects is begun by the U.S. military.

1950s–1960s 30-second and 60-second TV commercials become routine.

1957   Vance Packard's *The Hidden Persuaders* is published, warning people of the dangers of persuasive advertising.

1971   Tobacco ads are banned from television.

1984   Apple's Macintosh commercial at halftime of the Super Bowl changes the nature of advertising.

mid-1980s Brand placement and a general partnership between advertising and pop culture solidifies.

1994   Internet banner advertising begins.

1995   The Internet advertising agency DoubleClick is founded.

1998   Tobacco ads are banned from billboards.

2000s   The Internet and the World Wide Web become increasingly attractive as sites for advertising. New forms of advertising, such as pop-ups, appear online.

RADIO AND SOUND RECORDING

1877   The wax cylinder phonograph is invented by Thomas Edison, which allows for sound to be recorded and played back.

1887–1888 Emile Berliner develops the gramophone, which can play the music on mass-produced discs.

1896   Guglielmo Marconi develops the first radio transmitter.

1906–1907 Lee De Forest invents the vacuum tube, called the Audion tube, improving radio reception, and Reginald Fessenden makes the first radio broadcast from the Metropolitan Opera House in New York City.

1910   Congress passes the Wireless Ship Act requiring ships to be equipped with wireless radio.

1912   Congress passes the Radio Act, constituting the first piece of government regulation for licensing radio transmitters.

1916   David Sarnoff, the commercial manager of American Marconi, writes his famous "Radio Box Memo," in which he proposes to his boss to make radio a "household utility."

1916–1920 Frank Conrad founds KDKA in Pittsburgh as the first

	experimental radio station in 1916. The station's broadcast of the 1920 presidential election results on November 2, 1920, is generally considered the beginning of professional broadcasting.
1922	The first uses of radio for commercial purposes begin with the airing of the first advertisements by AT&T on station WEAF. This causes an uproar, as people challenge the right of the public airwaves to be used for commercial messages.
1926	The first radio broadcasting network, NBC, is created by RCA. AT&T abandons radio broadcasting.
1927	Congress's new Radio Act creates the Federal Radio Commission.
1933	FM radio is developed.
1934	Congress passes the Federal Communications Act, creating the Federal Communications Commission (FCC) and allowing commercial interests to control the airwaves. AM stations are allocated.
1938	Mercury Theater of the Air broadcasts *War of the Worlds*, demonstrating how quickly a mass medium can cause public panic.
1941	Chain broadcasting rules are developed.
1948	Radio starts to lose audiences to television. Magnetic audiotape is developed by 3M. Wynonie Harris records *Good Rockin' Tonight*, the first true rock and roll song.
1948	33 1/3 records are introduced by Columbia Records and 45-rpm records are introduced by RCA Victor. The DJ radio era takes off.
1949	*Red Hot 'n Blue* becomes one of the first radio rock and roll shows.
1955	Top 40 radio becomes the most popular type of radio format, indicating that radio is becoming more and more a marketing arm of the recording industry. Rock and roll enters the scene in the mid-1950s, dominating pop music radio and the recording industry until the early 1990s.
1956	Stereo recordings are introduced.
1962	Cassette tapes are introduced.
1960s	Rock music is linked with social protest, spearheading the counterculture movement.
1967	The Beatles release *Sgt. Pepper's Lonely Hearts Club Band*, the first true concept album.
1970s	FM radio stations gain popularity, transforming radio into a more specialized medium.
1971	National Public Radio starts broadcasting with *All Things Considered*.

1979	Sony engineer Akio Morita invents the portable Walkman.

1979 Sony engineer Akio Morita invents the portable Walkman.
1979–1980 Rap emerges out of hip-hop clubs in New York City.
1981 Music Television (MTV) is born, becoming a new arm of the recording industry.
1982 Compact discs are introduced. Rock fragments into many genres, from disco to punk, grunge, and techno. Rap and hip-hop start dominating pop music recordings until the early 2000s.
1987 WFAN is launched as the first all-sports radio station.
1990s Talk radio becomes popular. Old and new musical genres, from country to gospel and opera, become popular with target audiences, creating niche recording and radio markets.
1996 Congress passes the Telecommunications Act of 1996, allowing for consolidation in radio ownership across the United States.
1997 DVDs make their debut, offering more storage space than CDs and making music videos popular.
1998 Music download sites proliferate on the Internet.
2000 MP3 technology shakes up the music industry, as Internet users share music files on Napster. Napster is eventually ordered to stop unauthorized file sharing.
2000s Satellite and Web-based radio programs emerge in 2002. File-sharing, online radio programs, etc., become highly popular. Rap and hip-hop remain popular, but lose their market domination.
2001 Peer-to-peer Internet services make music file sharing popular.
2003 Apple Computer's iTunes music store makes its debut, making it possible to buy music on the Internet.

FILM AND VIDEO

1877 Eadweard Muybridge captures motion on film for the first time.
1888 Thomas Edison develops the first motion picture camera.
1889 Hannibal Goodwin develops film technology that allows movies to be created.
1894 Thomas Edison opens up the first kinetoscope parlors with coin-operated projectors.
1895 The Lumière brothers show the first short films in Paris.
1896 Thomas Edison invents the Vitascope, which is capable of large-screen projection.
1903 Edwin S. Porter's *The Great Train Robbery*, an early Western, gains popularity, indicating that the era of cinema is just around the corner. The movie is the first violent film story.
1907 Storefront movie parlors, called nickelodeons, with a five-cent admission, begin to flourish.

1910s   Silent films become popular. The first movie celebrities emerge in the late 1910s and early 1920s.

1914   Movie palaces start opening up in New York City.

1915   The first racist film, D.W. Griffith's *Birth of a Nation*, is also the first true feature film, gaining commercial success.

1920s   The Big Five studios (Paramount, MGM, Warner Brothers, 20th Century Fox, RKO) and the Little Three studios (Columbia, Universal, United Artists) are established in the late 1920s.

1922   The American movie industry institutes voluntary censorship.

1927   Soundtrack technology turns silent films into talkies. The first talkie is *The Jazz Singer* (1927) starring Al Jolson.

1930s   The era of the "golden age" of cinema.

1946   Cinema becomes a major influence in society, as over 90 million attend movies weekly.

1947   The House Un-American Activities Committee starts holding hearings on communism in Hollywood.

1957   In *Roth v. United States*, the Supreme Court sets community standards as the criteria for defining obscenity.

1968   Motion Picture Association of America (MPAA) movie ratings introduced.

1976   VCRs are introduced, creating a new movie rental and purchase industry.

1977   *Star Wars* initiates a new era of big-budget blockbusters.

1990s   Independent films become popular and successful, becoming also a source for identifying new talent.

1995   The first megaplex movie theater is built in Dallas, leading to a wave of megaplexes. *Toy Story* is the first completely computer-generated movie, starting a new trend in movie production.

1997   DVDs come onto the scene in 1997, displacing videotapes.

2000s   Movies integrate with the Internet, where trailers are shown and even full features can be seen.

TELEVISION

Late 1800s   The invention of the cathode ray tube makes television technology possible.

1884   Paul Nipkow patents the electrical telescope in Germany, which becomes the basis for TV technology.

1927   Philo T. Farnsworth (barely 21 years of age) transmits the first TV picture electronically. Farnsworth applies for a TV patent.

1935   Farnsworth conducts the first public demonstration of television in Philadelphia.

1936	First television service debuts in Britain.

1936 First television service debuts in Britain.

1939 NBC starts regular television broadcasts from New York City.

1941 The FCC sets standards for television broadcasting.

1948 Milton Berle and Ed Sullivan go on the air with the first TV variety shows, ushering in the "golden age" of television. The first community antenna television (CATV) is established.

1950 The AC Nielsen Market Research Company starts tracking TV audience behaviors. The first swear words are heard on the *Arthur Godfrey Show.*

1950s Television becomes a dominant medium, with previous radio genres and radio personalities moving to TV. Sitcoms like *I Love Lucy* (starting in 1951), the *Today* and *Tonight Shows* (1952), and later *The Beverly Hillbillies* (1964) establish the standards for TV broadcasting, bringing out the entertainment function of television to the viewing public.

1954 Color television technology is introduced, but does not become a marketable technology until the 1970s. The U.S. Senate begins hearings on the purported effects of television violence on juvenile delinquency.

1960 The first satellite system, called Telstar, is established. The Kennedy-Nixon presidential debates reveal the power of television to influence public opinion, as Kennedy, the underdog, appeals to viewers as a young, handsome, dynamic candidate.

1961 A second round of Senate hearings begins on television violence. The first exposure of a navel occurs on the *Dr. Kildare* series.

1966 Prime time programs are broadcast in color.

1967 Congress creates the Corporation for Public Broadcasting, leading to the establishment of public television.

1968 *60 Minutes* starts broadcasting, showing the power of television to influence public opinion. The National Commission on the Causes of Violence concludes that TV violence encourages violent behavior. The first interracial kiss is seen on a *Star Trek* episode.

1971 *All in the Family* changes the character of sitcoms, introducing controversial social issues into the content of prime time programming.

1972 FCC makes cable available to cities. The U.S. Surgeon General releases a research report on the relation between television and social behavior.

1975 HBO (Home Box Office) begins broadcasting via satellite. VCRs are introduced. Under FCC pressure, broadcasters adopt a

	"family hour" format to provide wholesome early evening family programming.
1976	Cable comes onto the scene, with Ted Turner's WTBS in Atlanta, which uplinks to satellite technology, becoming the first true "superstation."
1977	The eight-part miniseries *Roots* sets new standards for television broadcasting with its probe of the African American experience. The miniseries also shows the first bare female breasts on television.
1980s	The popularity of programs such as *M*A*S*H* (1983) and the *Cosby Show* (1985) prompt some media critics to define this decade as the "era of the sitcom."
1980	CNN premieres as a 24-hour cable news network, owned originally by Ted Turner, revolutionizing newscasting and television formats.
1981	Cable also brings MTV onto the scene in 1981.
1987	Rupert Murdoch's Fox television makes its debut.
mid-1980s–1990s	New channels and networks open up, such as UPN (United Paramount Network) and WB (Warner Brothers). Specialty cable channels emerge, from A&E and Discovery to the Movie Channel and the Disney Channel. Programs such as *The X-Files* and other such series become staples of prime time, as they co-opt themes in pop culture so as to appeal to a large audience. Quiz shows such as *The Wheel of Fortune*, *Jeopardy*, and *Who Wants to Be a Millionaire* rate highly as well.
1990	The Children's Television Act mandates children's programming.
1991	The first homosexual kiss on American television is seen on an episode of *L.A. Law.*
1994	The direct broadcast satellite (DBS) industry debuts.
1996	The Telecommunications Act abolishes most TV ownership restrictions.
1997	Parental advisories are mandated for TV programs.
1998	The V-chip is introduced. HDTV broadcastings start.
2000s	Narrowcasting becomes a reality, with all the specialty channels available along with network programming: TBS, Spike, ESPN, Discovery Channel, Weather Channel, A&E, TLC, USA Network, etc. Television and the Internet merge to create a co-broadcasting system, whereby television channels and Internet Web sites deliver the same or complementary content. Sitcoms such as *Everybody Loves Raymond* (2000) and *Will & Grace* (2000) continue to be popular.

| 2002 | The FCC rules to end antenna-based broadcasting by 2009, transforming the TV medium gradually into a digital one. |
| 2003 | VOD (video on demand) is introduced. |

THE INTERNET, WORLD WIDE WEB, AND DATA TRANSMISSION

1822	Charles Babbage develops a computer prototype.
1830s	The introduction of telegraphy constitutes a data network forerunner.
1866	Transoceanic telegraph service begins.
1876	The telephone is introduced.
1915	The first transcontinental phone call is made.
1939	John Vincent Atanasoff of Iowa State University is credited with designing the first modern computer.
1945	ENIAC, the first general-purpose computer, is invented by J. Presper Eckert and John Mauchly, mainly for military purposes.
1951	Eckert and Mauchly introduce UNIVAC as the first civilian computer.
1962	The first communications satellite, the first digital phone networks, and the first pagers are introduced.
1964	The first local area network (LAN) is put into service to support nuclear weapons research.
1965	A highly usable computer language, BASIC, is developed.
1969	Arpanet is the first communication network established by the U.S. Department of Defense.
1971	Microprocessors are developed, leading shortly thereafter to PC technology.
1972	The first video game, Pong, is introduced. Urban cable is allowed to proliferate. E-mail is developed for communications on Arpanet.
1975	The first personal computer, Altair, is introduced.
1977	First fiber optic network is created.
1978	Cellular phone service begins. Nicholas Negroponte of MIT introduces the term *convergence* to describe the intersection of media.
1980s	Fiber-optic cable is developed in the 1980s, making it possible to transmit digital messages. Hypertext is developed in the mid-1980s, leading eventually to the creation of the World Wide Web.
1982	The National Science Foundation sponsors a high-speed communications network, leading to the establishment of the Internet.
1983	Arpanet starts using Transmission Control Protocol/Internet Protocol (TCP/IP), essentially launching the Internet.

1984	Apple Macintosh is the first PC with graphics.
1989	Tim Berners-Lee develops concepts and techniques that a few years later are converted into the World Wide Web. A new company called AOL (America Online) is formed, later becoming the first successful Internet service provider.
1990	The first Internet search engine, Archie, is developed.
1991	The Internet opens to commercial uses, HTML is developed, and the World Wide Web is finally launched by Berners-Lee.
1993	The first point-and-click Web browser, Mosaic, is introduced.
1994	The first Internet cafés open. Jeff Bezos launches Amazon.com.
1995	Digital cellular phones are introduced to the market. The first online auction house, eBay, is launched.
1996	The Telecommunications Act and the Communications Decency Act are passed. Google is launched.
2000	Cookies technology allows for information profiles to be created, enabling data-mining practices to burgeon.
2001	Instant messaging services appear.
2002	Broadband technology is developed by South Korea.
mid– late 2000s	The Internet converges with previous media (radio, television, etc.) to produce online versions of previous broadcasting. It also becomes a source of new forms of communication, with Web sites such as MySpace and YouTube.

BIBLIOGRAPHY

GENERAL WORKS

Baran, Stanley J. *Introduction to Mass Communication, Media Literacy, and Culture.* New York: McGraw-Hill, 2004.

Berger, Arthur A. *Manufacturing Desire: Media, Popular Culture, and Everyday Life.* New Brunswick, NJ: Transaction, 1996.

————. *Making Sense of Media: Key Texts in Media and Cultural Studies.* Oxford: Blackwell, 2005.

Biagi, Shirley. *Media/Impact: An Introduction to Mass Media.* Belmont, CA: Wadsworth/ Thomson Learning, 2001.

Branston, Gill, and Roy Stafford. *The Media Student's Book.* London: Routledge, 1999.

Briggs, Asa, and Peter Burke. *A Social History of the Media.* London: Polity, 2002.

Briggs, Asa, and Paul Cobley, eds. *The Media: An Introduction.* Essex: Addison Wesley Longman, 1998.

Campbell, Richard, Christopher R. Martin, and Bettina G. Fabos. *Media & Culture: An Introduction to Mass Communication.* Boston: Bedford/St. Martin's, 2005.

Carey, James W. *Communication as Culture: Essays on Media and Society.* Boston: Unwin Hyman, 1989.

Danesi, Marcel. *Understanding Media Semiotics.* London: Arnold, 2002.

Dizard, Wilson P. *Old Media, New Media.* New York: Longman, 1997.

Genosko, Gary. *McLuhan and Baudrillard.* London: Routledge, 1999.

Hanson, Ralph E. *Mass Communication: Living in a Media World.* New York: McGraw-Hill, 2005.

Newbold, Chris, Oliver Boyd-Barrett, and Hilde Van Den Bulck, eds. *The Media Book.* London: Arnold, 2002.

O'Sullivan, Tim, Brian Dutton, and Philip Rayner. *Studying the Media.* London: Arnold, 2003.

Straubhaar, Joseph, and Robert LaRose. *Media Now: Communications Media in the Information Age.* Belmont, CA: Wadsworth/Thomson Learning, 2002.

MEDIA EFFECTS

Berger, Arthur A. *Media and Communication Research Methods*. London: Sage, 2000.
Gunter, B. *Media Research Methods*. London: Sage, 2000.
Liebert, Robert M., and Joyce N. Sprafkin. *The Early Window: Effects of Television on Children and Youth*. New York: Pergamon, 1988.
McQuail, Denis. *Mass Communication Theory: An Introduction*. London: Sage, 2000.
Staiger, Janet. *Media Reception Studies*. New York: New York University Press, 2005.
Van Zoonen, Liesbet. *Feminist Media Studies*. London: Sage, 1994.

Print (Books, Newspapers, Magazines)

Eisenstein, Elizabeth L. *The Printing Press as an Agent of Change: Communications and Cultural Transformations in Early-Modern Europe*. Cambridge: Cambridge University Press, 1979.
Epstein, Jason. *Book Business: Publishing Past, Present, and Future*. New York: Norton, 2001.
GoughYates, Anna. *Understanding Women's Magazines*. London: Routledge, 2003.
Harris, Michael, and Tom O'Malley. *Studies in Newspaper and Periodical History*. Westport, CT: Greenwood Press, 1997.
Innis, Harold A. *Empire and Communication*. Toronto: University of Toronto Press, 1972.
Janello, Amy, and Brennon Jones. *The American Magazine*. New York: Abrams, 1991.
Winship, Janice. *Inside Women's Magazines*. London: Pandora, 1987.
Wright, Bradford W. *Comic Book Nation*. Baltimore: Johns Hopkins University Press, 2000.

Radio, Sound Recordings, Television

Abercrombie, Nicholas. *Television and Society*. Cambridge: Polity Press, 1996.
Dovey, Jon. *Freakshow: First Person Media and Factual Television*. London: Pluto, 2000.
Fiske, John. *Television Culture*. London: Methuen, 1987.
Holland, Patricia. *The Television Handbook*. London: Routledge, 2000.
Kubey, Robert, and Mihaly Csikszentmihalyi. *Television and the Quality of Life*. Hillsdale, NJ: Lawrence Erlbaum, 1990.
McQueen, David. *Television: A Media Student's Guide*. London: Arnold, 1998.
Miller, Mark Crispin. *Boxed In: The Culture of TV*. Evanston, IL: Northwestern University Press, 1988.
Neer, Richard. *FM: The Rise and Fall of Rock Radio*. New York: Villard, 2001.
Newcomb, H. *Television: The Critical View*. New York: Oxford University Press, 2000.

Film and Video

Abrams, Nathan, Ian Bell, and Jan Udris. *Studying Film*. London: Arnold, 2001.
Balio, Tino. *The American Film Industry*. Madison: University of Wisconsin Press, 1979.

Ellis, John. *Visible Fictions: Cinema, Television, Video.* London: Routledge, 1992.
Sklar, Robert. *Movie-Made America: A Cultural History of American Movies.* New York: Vintage, 1994.

Internet and the World Wide Web

Hafner, Katie, and Matthew Lyon. *Where Wizards Stay Up Late: The Origins of the Internet.* New York: Simon & Schuster, 1996.
Herman, Andrew, and Thomas Swiss, eds. *The World Wide Web and Contemporary Cultural Theory.* London: Routledge, 2000.
Slevin, James. *The Internet and Society.* London: Polity, 2000.
Van Dijk, Jan. *The Network Society.* London: Sage, 1999.
Wise, Richard. *Multimedia: A Critical Introduction.* London: Routledge, 2000.

Advertising

Berger, Arthur A. *Ads, Fads, and Consumer Culture: Advertising's Impact on American Character and Society.* Lanham, MD: Rowman & Littlefield, 2000.
Danesi, Marcel. *Brands.* London: Routledge, 2006.
Goldman, Robert, and Stephen Papson. *Sign Wars: The Cluttered Landscape of Advertising.* New York: Guilford, 1996.
Key, Wilson B. *Subliminal Seduction.* New York: Signet, 1972.
————. *The Age of Manipulation.* New York: Holt, 1989.
Kilbourne, Jean. *Can't Buy My Love: How Advertising Changes the Way I Feel.* New York: Simon & Schuster, 1999.
Leiss, William, Stephen Kline, Sut Jhally, and Jackie Botterill. *Social Communication in Advertising: Consumption in the Mediated Marketplace.* London: Routledge, 2005.
Twitchell, James B. *Twenty Ads That Shook the World.* New York: Crown, 2000.
Williamson, Judith. *Consuming Passions.* London: Marion Boyars, 1985.

RESOURCES ON THE WORLD WIDE WEB

General

Action Coalition for Media Education: www.acmecoalition.org
Broadcasting & Cable News: www.broadcastingcable.com
Corporation for Public Broadcasting: www.cpb.org
Images (Journal of Media Criticism): www.imagesjournal.com
Media Education Foundation: www.mediaed.org
Media History Project: www.mediahistory.umn.edu
National Public Radio: www.npr.org
Paper Tiger TV: www.papertiger.org
Public Radio Information: www.pri.org
Web Journal of Mass Communication Research: www.scripps.ohiou.edu/wjmcc/

Advertising

Ad Council: www.adcouncil.org
Ad Forum: www.adforum.com
Adbusters: www.adbusters.org
Advertising Age: www.adage.com/datacenter.cms
Advertising World: www.advertising.utexas.edu/world
Adweek: www.adweek.com
American Association of Advertising Agencies: www.aaaa.org
Cannes International Advertising Festival: www.canneslions.com
Clio Awards: www.clioawards.com

Cultural Aspects

Alt Culture: www.altculture.com
Critical Communication Theory: www.theory.org.uk

Marshall McLuhan Studies: www.mcluhan.utoronto.ca
Pop Culture: www.popcultures.com
Urban Dictionary: www.urbandictionary.com

Film and Video

Academy of Motion Picture Arts and Sciences: www.oscars.org
Cannes Film Festival: www.festival-cannes.fr
DreamWorks SKG: www.dreamworks.com
Hollywood Movies: www.hollywood.com
Internet Movie Database: www.us.imdb.com
Metro-Goldwyn-Mayer: www.mgm.com
Motion Picture Association of America: www.mpaa.org
Movieweb: www.movieweb.com
New Line Cinema: www.newline.com
Sony Pictures: www.sonypictures.com
Sundance Film Festival: www.sundance.org
Toronto International Film Festival: www.e.bell.ca/filmfest
Touchstone Pictures: http://touchstone.movies.go.com
20th Century Fox: www.foxmovies.com
Universal Studios: www.universalstudios.com
Walt Disney Pictures: http://disney.go.com/disneypictures
Warner Bros.: www.warnerbros.com

Internet and the World Wide Web

Center for Democracy and Technology: www.cdt.org
Internet2: www.internet2.edu
Internet History: www.isoc/internet/history.org
Internet Information: www.netvalley.com
Internet News: www.zdnet.com
Internet Society: www.isoc.org/internet/
Netlore: www.urbanlegends.about.com

Media Law, Watchdogs, Regulatory Agencies, and Media Expression

Center for Media and Democracy: www.prwatch.org
Electronic Frontier Foundation: www.eff.org
Federal Communications Commission: www.fcc.gov
Freedom Forum: www.freedomforum.org
Mediawatch: www.mediawatch.org
World Intellectual Property Organization: www.wipo.int
World Press Freedom Committee: www.wpfc.org

Print Media, Press Organizations, and News Agencies

All Headline News: www.allheadlinenews.com
Associated Press: www.ap.org
Bookwire: www.bookwire.com
E-Reads: www.ereads.com
Gutenberg Bible: www.gutenberg.de/english/bibel.htm
International Federation of Journalists: www.ifj.org
Magazine Publishers of America: www.magazine.org
New York Times: www.nytimes.com
Newseum: www.newseum.org
Online Newspaper: www.onlinenewspapers.com
Project Gutenberg: www.gutenberg.net
Reporters Sans Frontières: www.rsg.org
Reuters: www.reuters.com
United Press International: www.upi.com
USA Today: www.usatoday.com
Washington Post: www.washingtonpost.com
World Association of Newspapers: www.wan-press.org

Radio and Sound Recordings

All Music Guide: www.allmusic.com
Billboard Magazine: www.billboard.com
Freenet: www.freenetproject.org
Internet Radio: www.radio-locator.com
Radio History: www.radiohistory.org
Recording Industry Association of America: www.riaa.com
Rock and Roll Hall of Fame: www.rockhall.com
Web Radio: www.radio-directory.com

Television

ABC: www.abc.com
CBS: www.cbs.com
Classic Television: www.classic-tv.com
CNN: www.cnn.com
Fox: www.fox.com
MTV: www.mtv.com
NBC: www.nbc.com
TiVo: www.tivo.com
Ultimate TV: www.ultimatetv.com

ABOUT THE AUTHOR

Marcel Danesi is Professor of Semiotics and Anthropology at the University of Toronto. He has published extensively in the fields of media and popular culture. Among his recent publications are *Brands* (2006), *Popular Culture: Introductory Perspectives* (2007), and *The Quest for Meaning: A Guide to Semiotic Theory and Practice* (2007). He is currently the editor-in-chief of *Semiotica*. He is also a Fellow of the Royal Society of Canada.